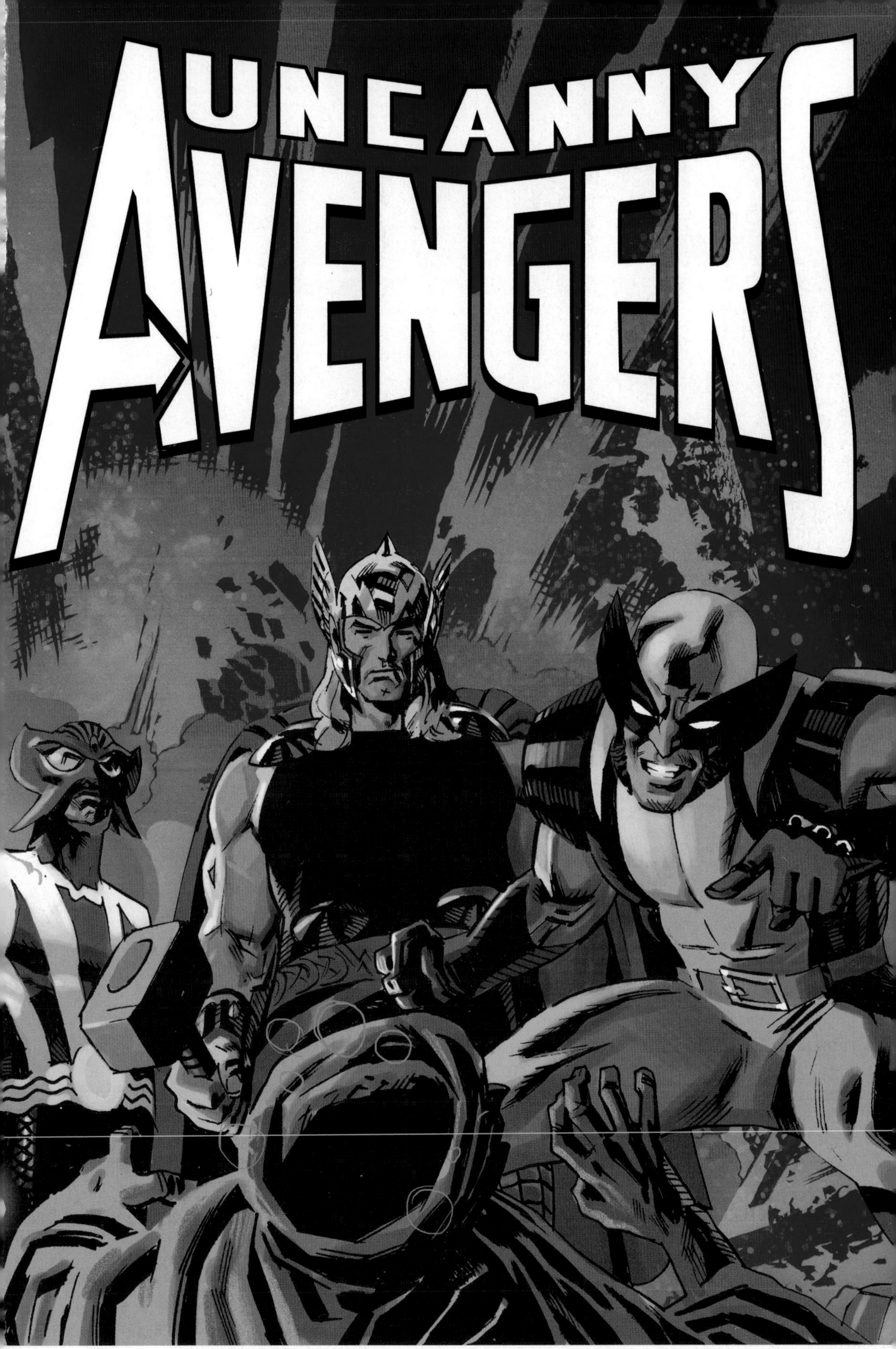
UNCANNY
AVENGERS

THE APOCALYPSE TWINS

BхT 3/14   24.99

PREVIOUSLY

Following the death of Professor Charles Xavier, founder and leader of the X-Men, a reignited mutant race emerged into a world that has never hated or feared them more. Hoping to set an example for the world to follow, Captain America approached longtime X-Man Havok to lead a team of Avengers that will demonstrate mutants and humans can work side by side. But the newly formed Avengers unity squad is immediately put to the test when the Red Skull incites anti-mutant hysteria in New York City. To make matters worse, during a press conference held in the aftermath of the attack, Rogue accidentally kills the villainous Grim Reaper using power borrowed from his brother, Wonder Man.

Meanwhile, a longtime Avengers adversary, the time-traversing villain known as Kang the Conqueror, is carrying out a mission of his own — a mission that spans centuries...

UNCANNY AVENGERS VOL. 2: THE APOCALYPSE TWINS. Contains material originally published in magazine form as UNCANNY AVENGERS #6-11 and #8AU. First printing 2013. ISBN# 978-0-7851-6845-4. Published by MARVEL WORLDWIDE, INC., a subsidiary of MARVEL ENTERTAINMENT, LLC. OFFICE OF PUBLICATION: 135 West 50th Street, New York, NY 10020. Copyright © 2013 Marvel Characters, Inc. All rights reserved. All characters featured in this issue and the distinctive names and likenesses thereof, and all related indicia are trademarks of Marvel Characters, Inc. No similarity between any of the names, characters, persons, and/or institutions in this magazine with those of any living or dead person or institution is intended, and any such similarity which may exist is purely coincidental. **Printed in the U.S.A.** ALAN FINE, EVP - Office of the President, Marvel Worldwide, Inc. and EVP & CMO Marvel Characters B.V.; DAN BUCKLEY, Publisher & President - Print, Animation & Digital Divisions; JOE QUESADA, Chief Creative Officer; TOM BREVOORT, SVP of Publishing; DAVID BOGART, SVP of Operations & Procurement, Publishing; C.B. CEBULSKI, SVP of Creator & Content Development; DAVID GABRIEL, SVP of Print & Digital Publishing Sales; JIM O'KEEFE, VP of Operations & Logistics; DAN CARR, Executive Director of Publishing Technology; SUSAN CRESPI, Editorial Operations Manager; ALEX MORALES, Publishing Operations Manager; STAN LEE, Chairman Emeritus. For information regarding advertising in Marvel Comics or on Marvel.com, please contact Niza Disla, Director of Marvel Partnerships, at ndisla@marvel.com. For Marvel subscription inquiries, please call 800-217-9158. **Manufactured between 8/23/2013 and 10/7/2013 by R.R. DONNELLEY, INC., SALEM, VA, USA.**

10 9 8 7 6 5 4 3 2 1

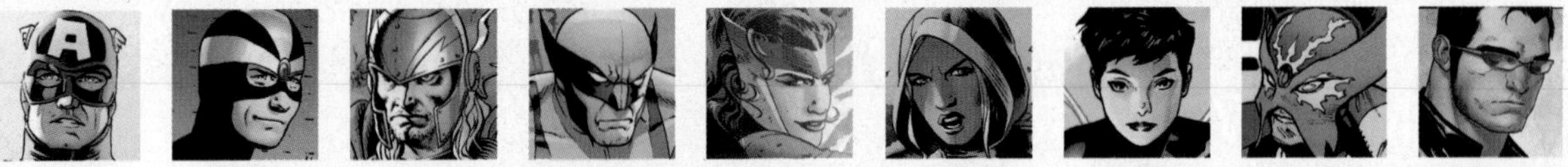

CAPTAIN AMERICA | HAVOK | THOR | WOLVERINE | SCARLET WITCH | ROGUE | WASP | SUNFIRE | WONDER MAN

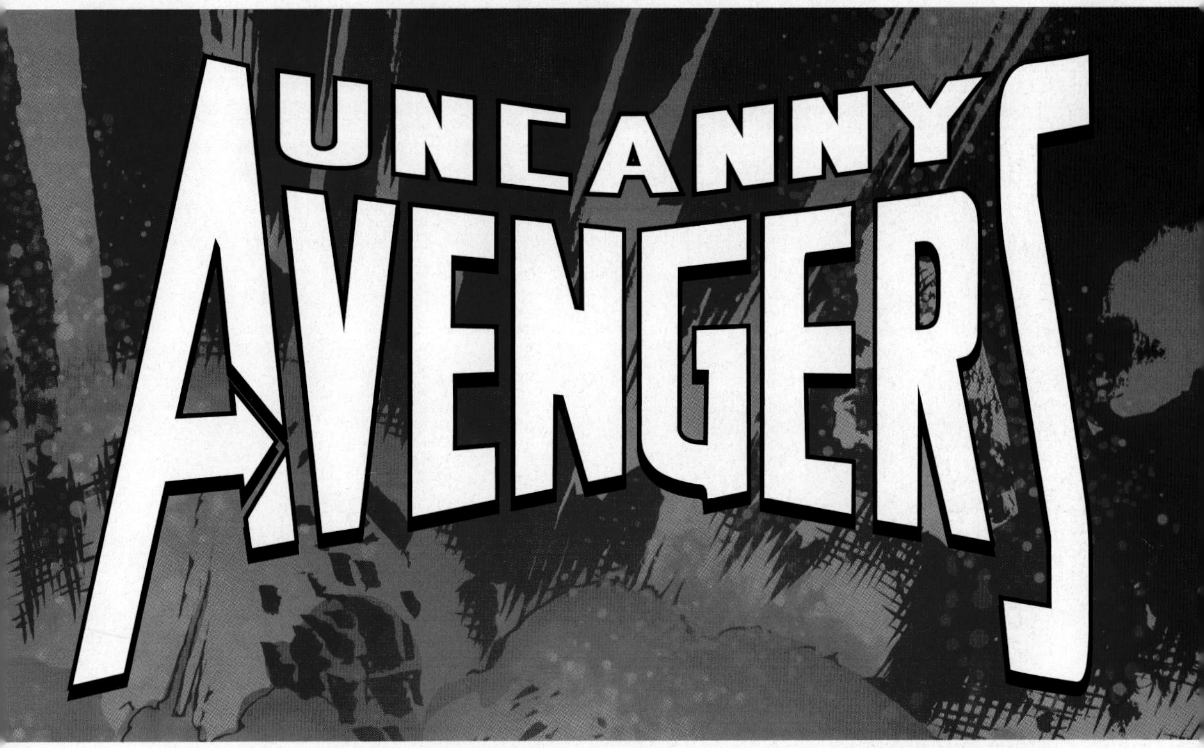
UNCANNY
AVENGERS

THE APOCALYPSE TWINS

WRITER
RICK REMENDER

ARTIST
DANIEL ACUÑA

LETTERER
VC'S CHRIS ELIOPOULOS

COVER ART
JOHN CASSADAY & LAURA MARTIN

UNCANNY AVENGERS #8AU

WRITERS
RICK REMENDER & GERRY DUGGAN

ARTIST
ADAM KUBERT

COLOR ARTIST
FRANK MARTIN

LETTERER
VC'S CORY PETIT

COVER ART
JIM CHEUNG, MARK MORALES & JUSTIN PONSOR

EDITORS
TOM BREVOORT WITH DANIEL KETCHUM

COLLECTION EDITOR: JENNIFER GRÜNWALD
ASSISTANT EDITORS: ALEX STARBUCK & NELSON RIBEIRO
EDITOR, SPECIAL PROJECTS: MARK D. BEAZLEY
SENIOR EDITOR, SPECIAL PROJECTS: JEFF YOUNGQUIST
SVP OF PRINT & DIGITAL PUBLISHING SALES: DAVID GABRIEL

EDITOR IN CHIEF: AXEL ALONSO
CHIEF CREATIVE OFFICER: JOE QUESADA
PUBLISHER: DAN BUCKLEY
EXECUTIVE PRODUCER: ALAN FINE

UNCANNY AVENGERS #6

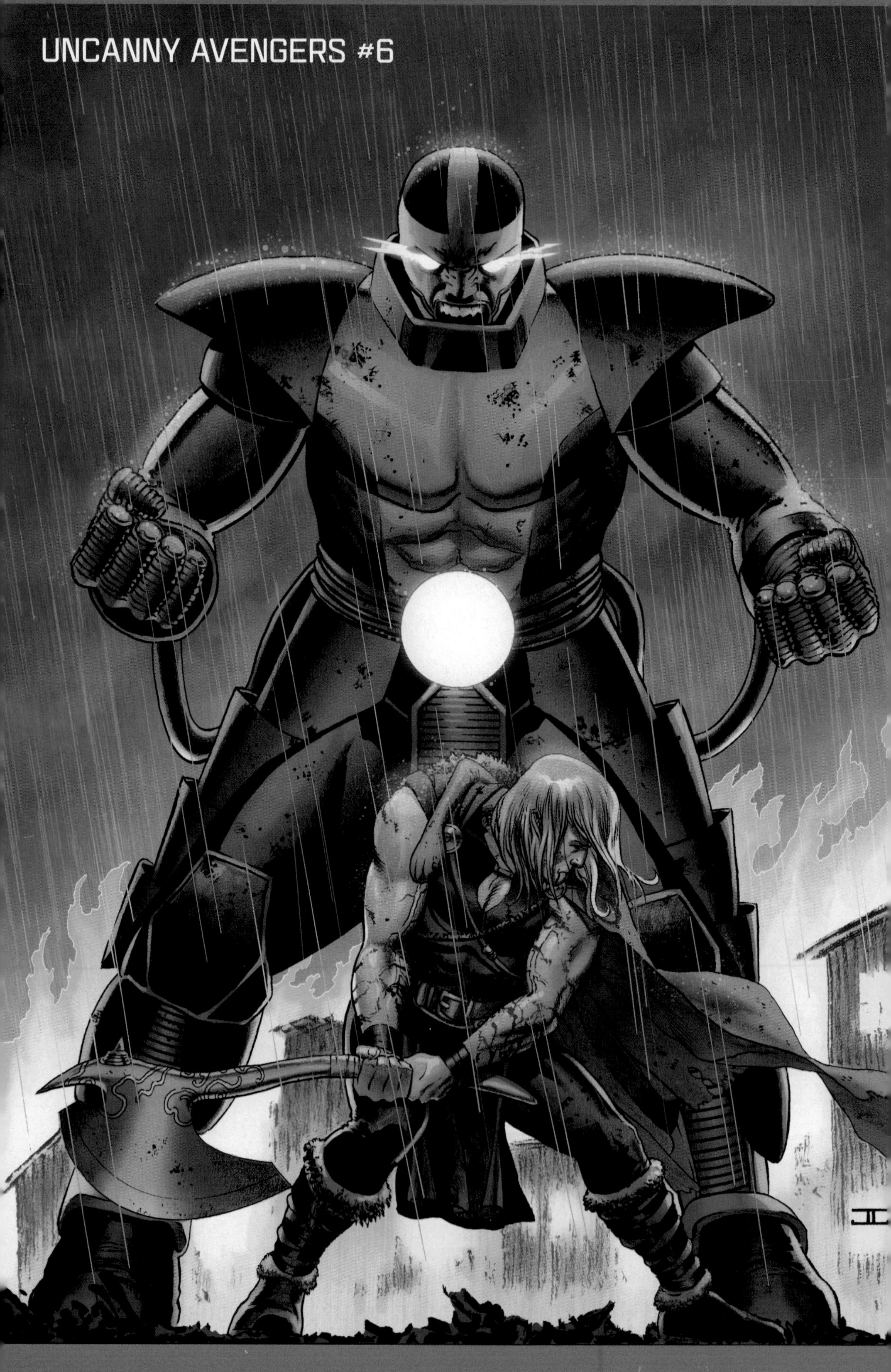

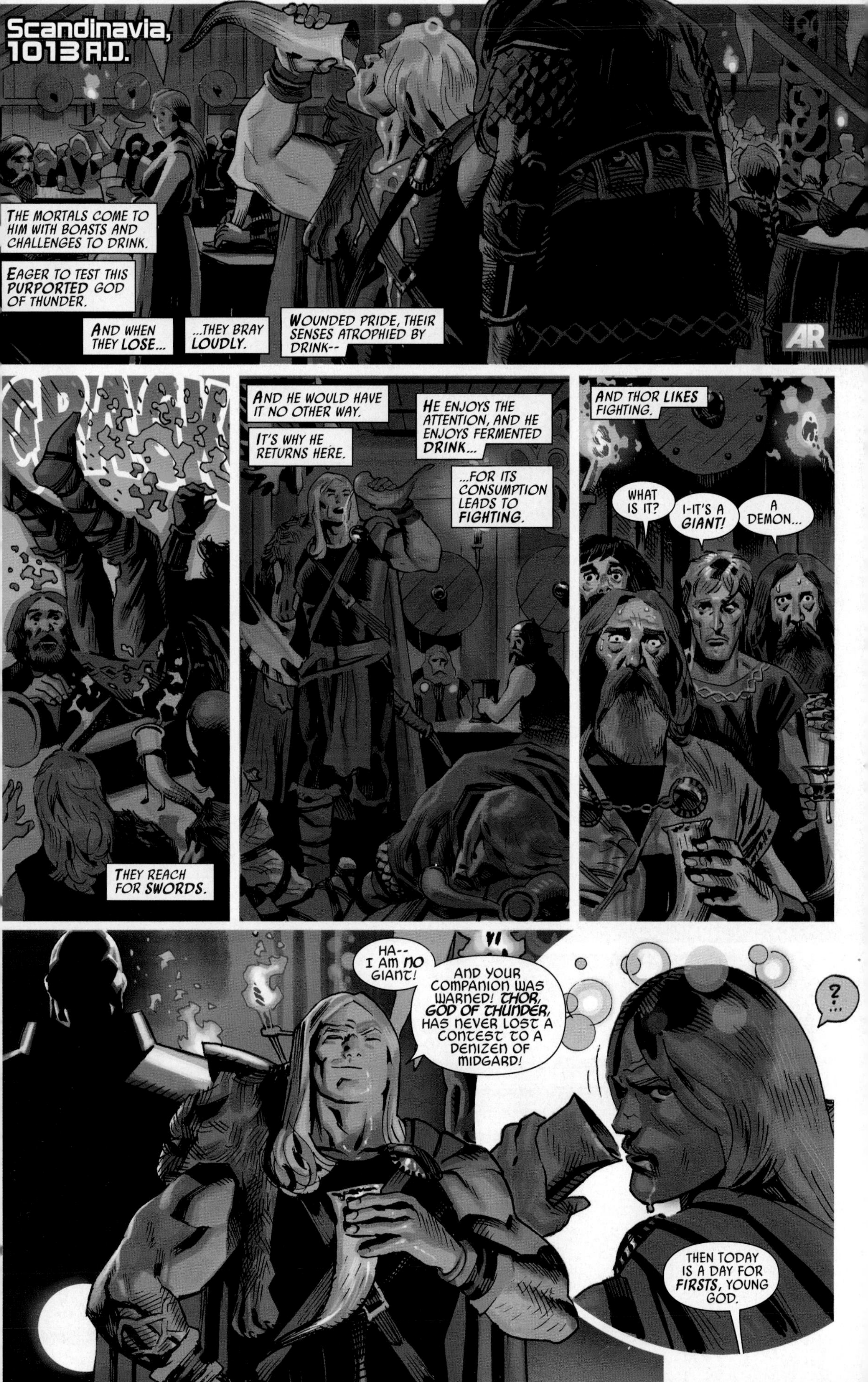
Scandinavia, 1013 A.D.
THE MORTALS COME TO HIM WITH BOASTS AND CHALLENGES TO DRINK.
EAGER TO TEST THIS PURPORTED GOD OF THUNDER.
AND WHEN THEY LOSE...
...THEY BRAY LOUDLY.
WOUNDED PRIDE, THEIR SENSES ATROPHIED BY DRINK--
THEY REACH FOR SWORDS.
AND HE WOULD HAVE IT NO OTHER WAY.
IT'S WHY HE RETURNS HERE.
HE ENJOYS THE ATTENTION, AND HE ENJOYS FERMENTED DRINK...
...FOR ITS CONSUMPTION LEADS TO FIGHTING.
AND THOR LIKES FIGHTING.
WHAT IS IT?
I-IT'S A GIANT!
A DEMON...
HA-- I AM NO GIANT!
AND YOUR COMPANION WAS WARNED! THOR, GOD OF THUNDER, HAS NEVER LOST A CONTEST TO A DENIZEN OF MIDGARD!
?...
THEN TODAY IS A DAY FOR FIRSTS, YOUNG GOD.

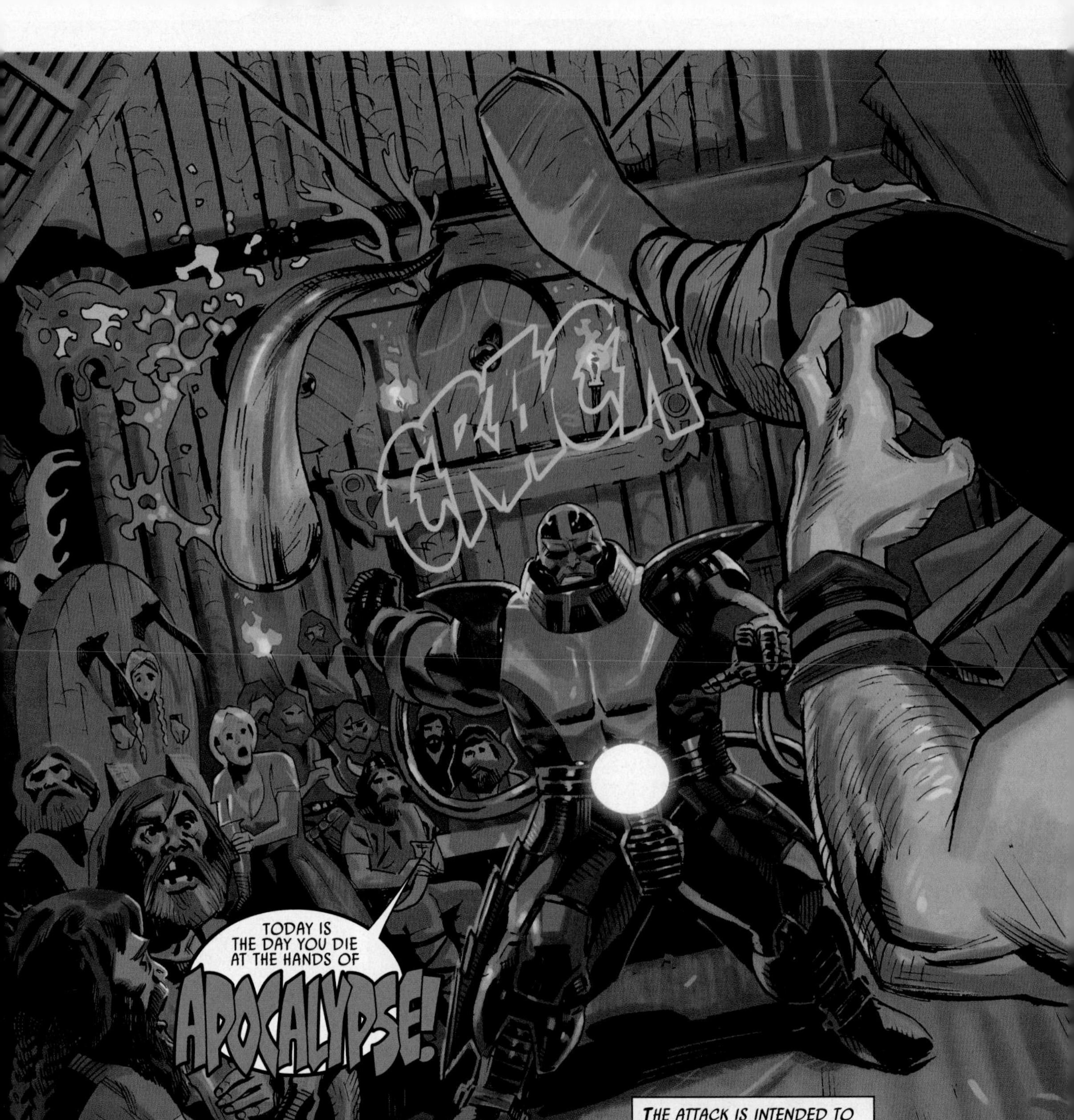
CRACK
TODAY IS THE DAY YOU DIE AT THE HANDS OF APOCALYPSE!
THE ATTACK IS INTENDED TO REMOVE SKULL FROM SPINE.

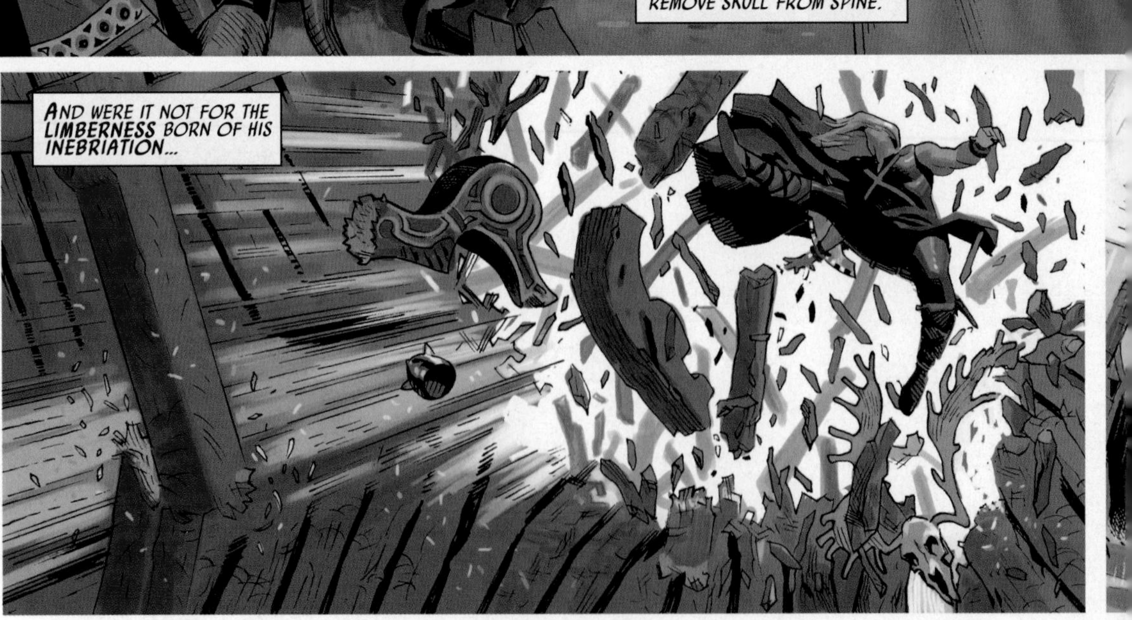
AND WERE IT NOT FOR THE LIMBERNESS BORN OF HIS INEBRIATION...

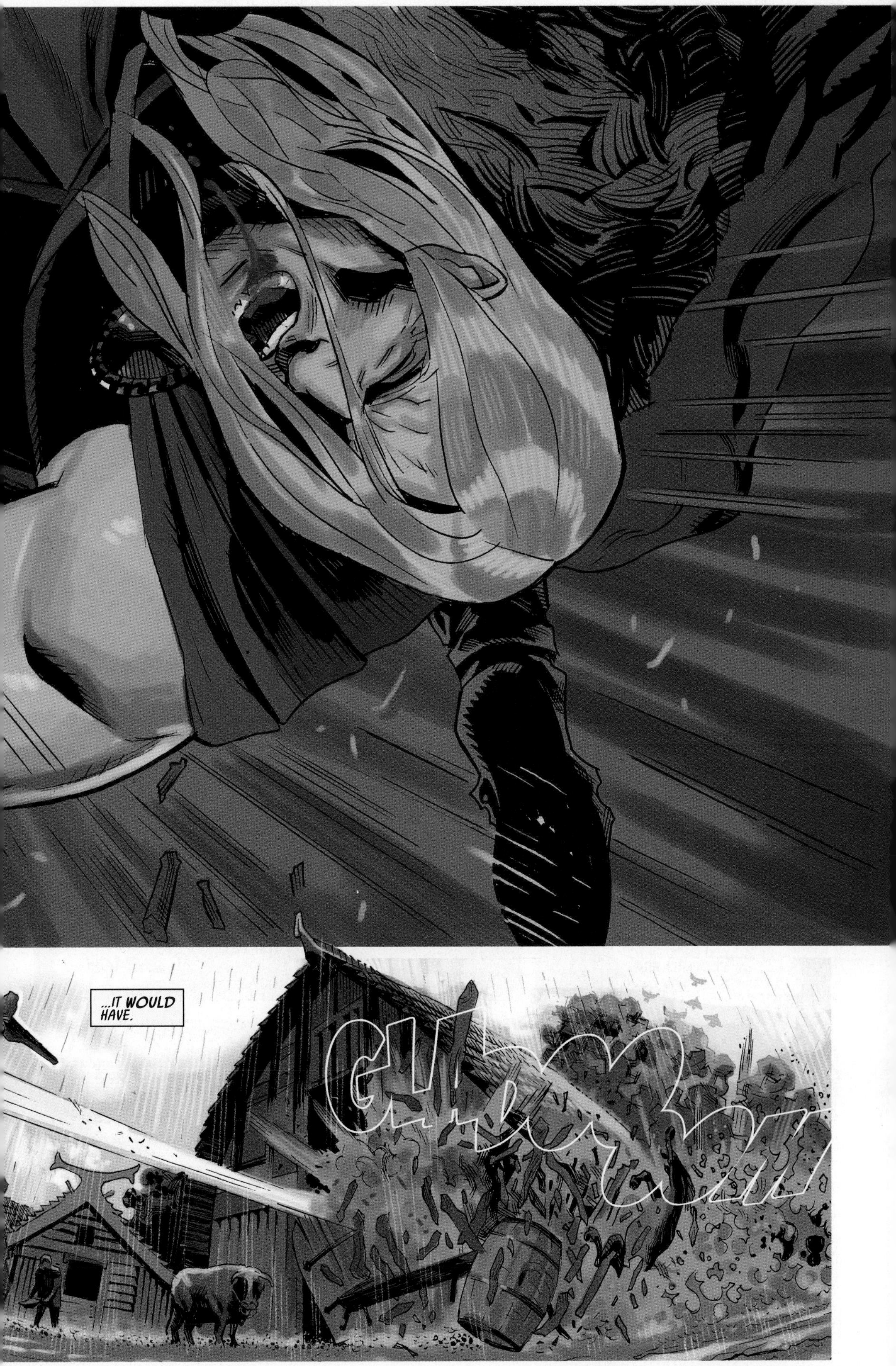
...IT WOULD HAVE.

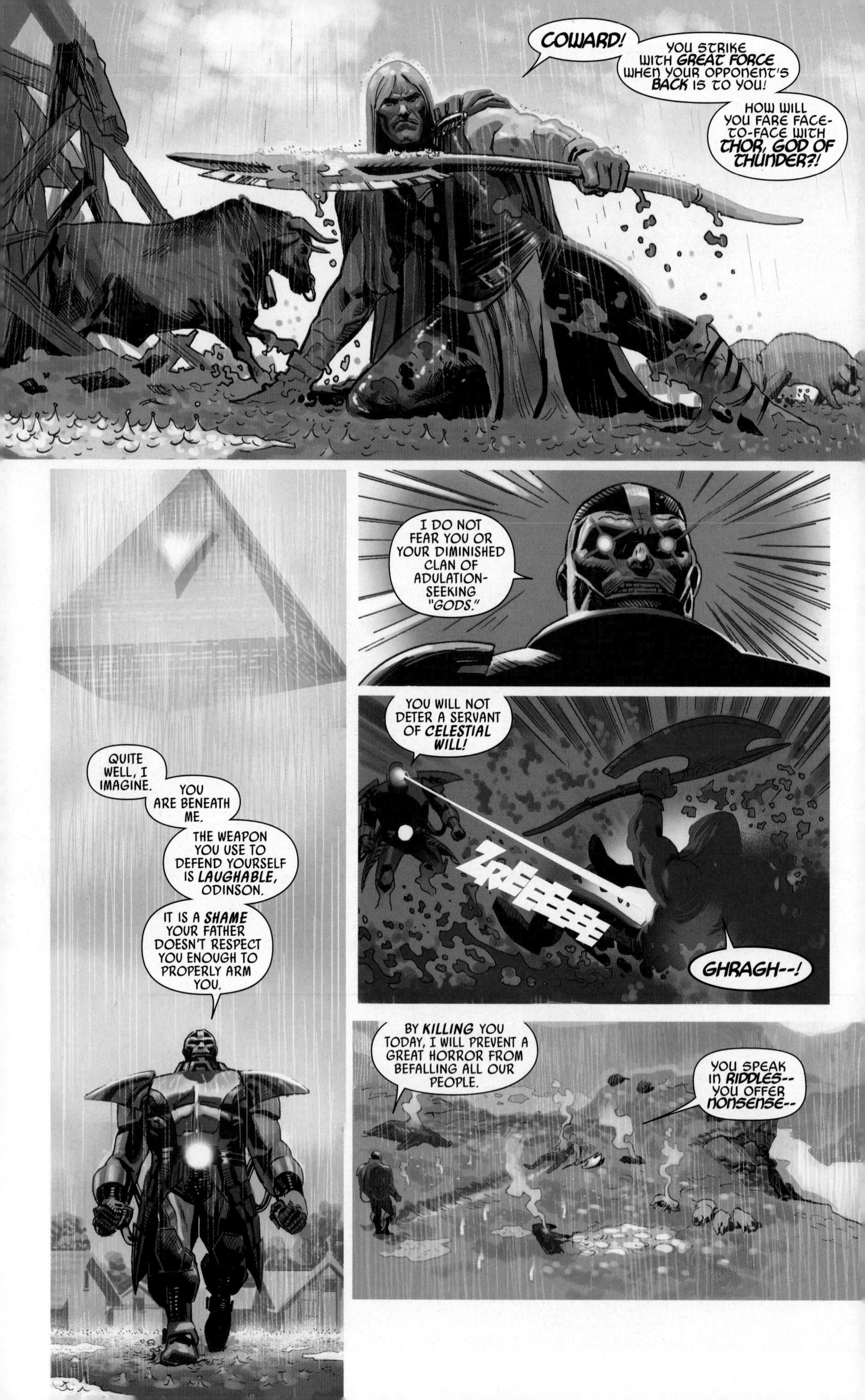
COWARD!
YOU STRIKE WITH GREAT FORCE WHEN YOUR OPPONENT'S BACK IS TO YOU!
HOW WILL YOU FARE FACE-TO-FACE WITH THOR, GOD OF THUNDER?!
QUITE WELL, I IMAGINE.
YOU ARE BENEATH ME.
THE WEAPON YOU USE TO DEFEND YOURSELF IS LAUGHABLE, ODINSON.
IT IS A SHAME YOUR FATHER DOESN'T RESPECT YOU ENOUGH TO PROPERLY ARM YOU.
I DO NOT FEAR YOU OR YOUR DIMINISHED CLAN OF ADULATION-SEEKING "GODS."
YOU WILL NOT DETER A SERVANT OF CELESTIAL WILL!
ZREEEEEE
GHRAGH--!
BY KILLING YOU TODAY, I WILL PREVENT A GREAT HORROR FROM BEFALLING ALL OUR PEOPLE.
YOU SPEAK IN RIDDLES-- YOU OFFER NONSENSE--

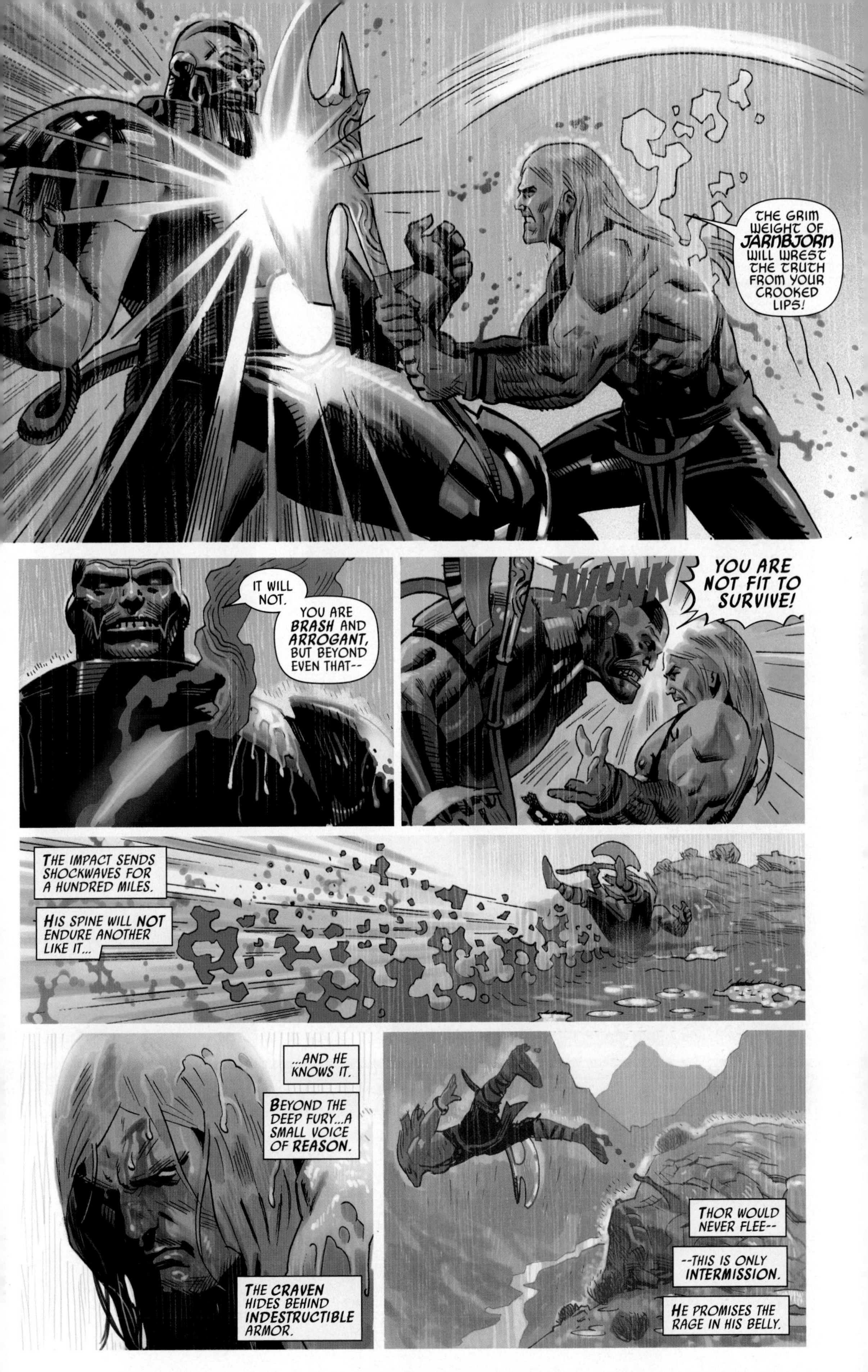
THE GRIM WEIGHT OF JARNBJORN WILL WREST THE TRUTH FROM YOUR CROOKED LIPS!
IT WILL NOT.
YOU ARE BRASH AND ARROGANT, BUT BEYOND EVEN THAT--
TWUNK
YOU ARE NOT FIT TO SURVIVE!
THE IMPACT SENDS SHOCKWAVES FOR A HUNDRED MILES.
HIS SPINE WILL NOT ENDURE ANOTHER LIKE IT...
...AND HE KNOWS IT.
BEYOND THE DEEP FURY...A SMALL VOICE OF REASON.
THE CRAVEN HIDES BEHIND INDESTRUCTIBLE ARMOR.
THOR WOULD NEVER FLEE--
--THIS IS ONLY INTERMISSION.
HE PROMISES THE RAGE IN HIS BELLY.

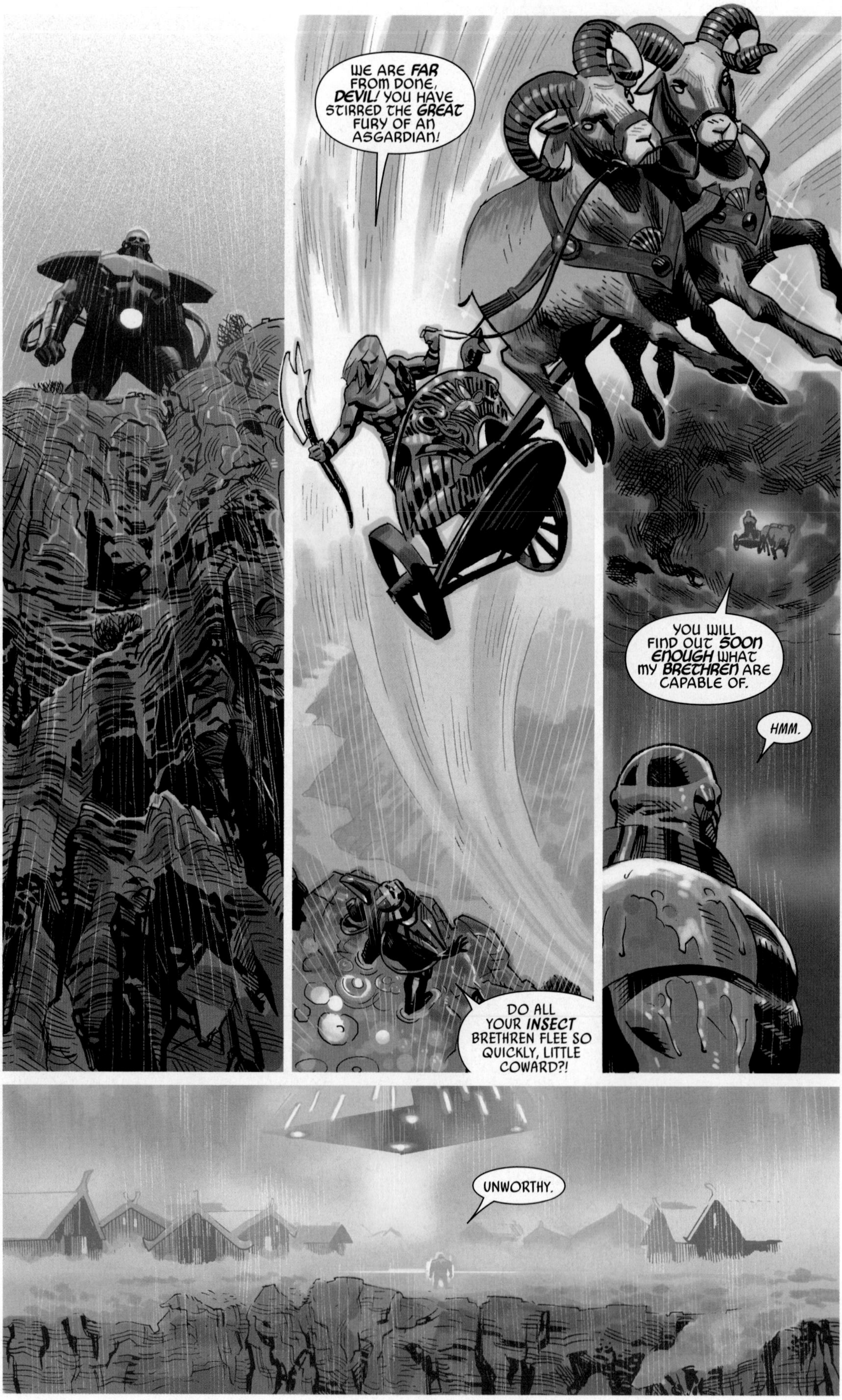
WE ARE FAR FROM DONE, DEVIL! YOU HAVE STIRRED THE GREAT FURY OF AN ASGARDIAN!
DO ALL YOUR INSECT BRETHREN FLEE SO QUICKLY, LITTLE COWARD?!
YOU WILL FIND OUT SOON ENOUGH WHAT MY BRETHREN ARE CAPABLE OF.
HMM.
UNWORTHY.

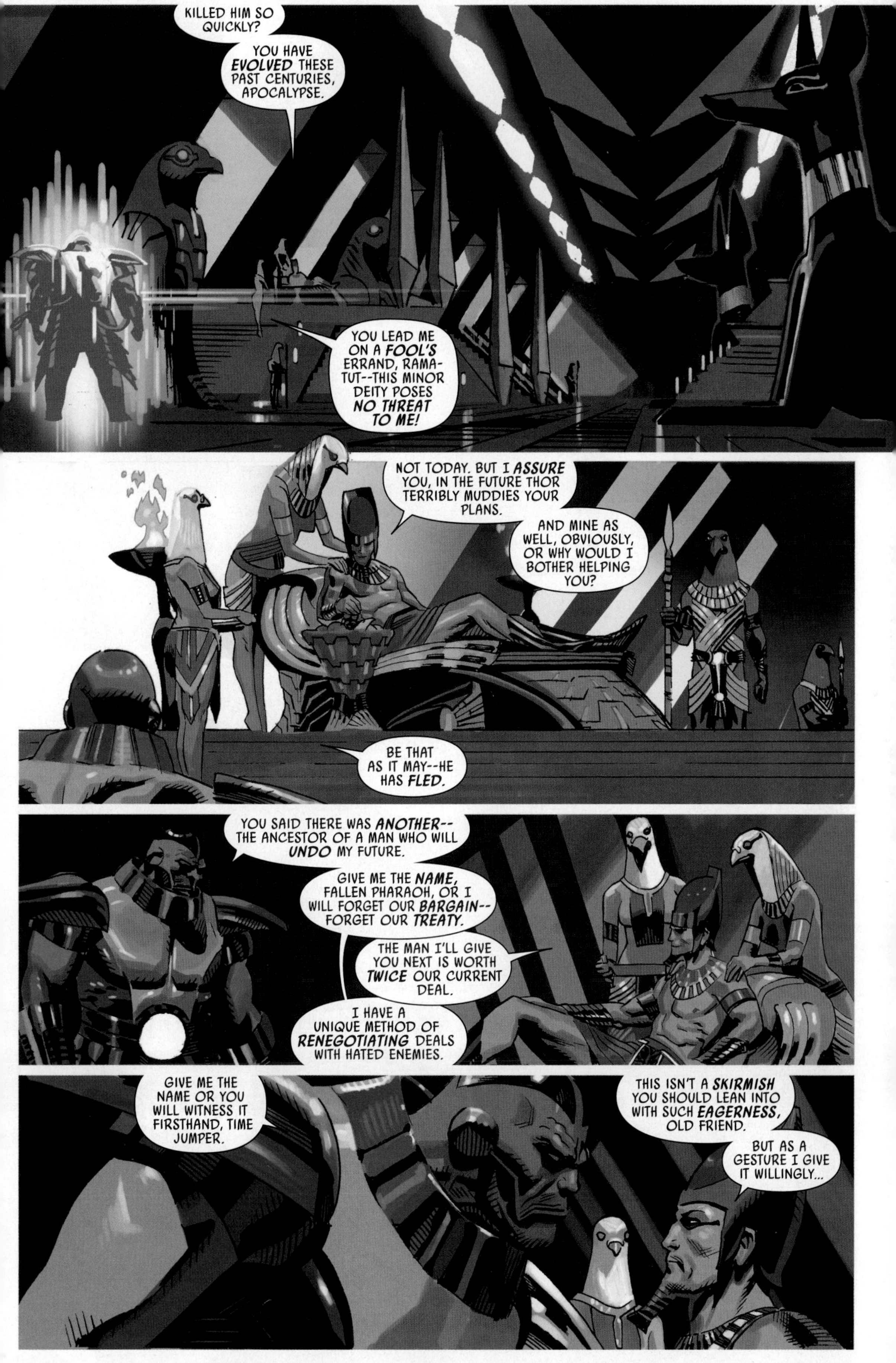
KILLED HIM SO QUICKLY?
YOU HAVE EVOLVED THESE PAST CENTURIES, APOCALYPSE.
YOU LEAD ME ON A FOOL'S ERRAND, RAMA-TUT--THIS MINOR DEITY POSES NO THREAT TO ME!
NOT TODAY. BUT I ASSURE YOU, IN THE FUTURE THOR TERRIBLY MUDDIES YOUR PLANS.
AND MINE AS WELL, OBVIOUSLY, OR WHY WOULD I BOTHER HELPING YOU?
BE THAT AS IT MAY--HE HAS FLED.
YOU SAID THERE WAS ANOTHER-- THE ANCESTOR OF A MAN WHO WILL UNDO MY FUTURE.
GIVE ME THE NAME, FALLEN PHARAOH, OR I WILL FORGET OUR BARGAIN-- FORGET OUR TREATY.
THE MAN I'LL GIVE YOU NEXT IS WORTH TWICE OUR CURRENT DEAL.
I HAVE A UNIQUE METHOD OF RENEGOTIATING DEALS WITH HATED ENEMIES.
GIVE ME THE NAME OR YOU WILL WITNESS IT FIRSTHAND, TIME JUMPER.
THIS ISN'T A SKIRMISH YOU SHOULD LEAN INTO WITH SUCH EAGERNESS, OLD FRIEND.
BUT AS A GESTURE I GIVE IT WILLINGLY...

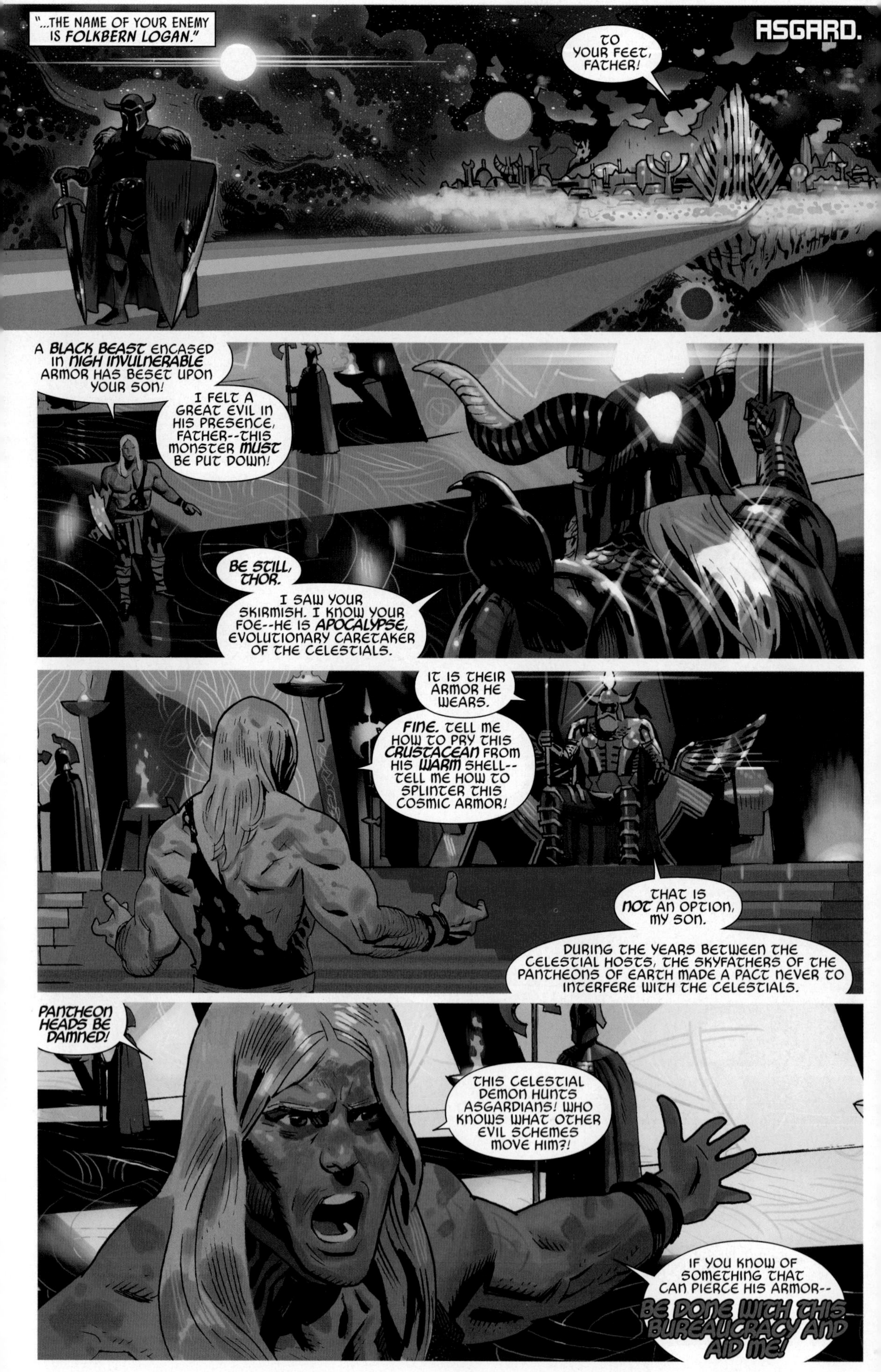
"...THE NAME OF YOUR ENEMY IS FOLKBERN LOGAN."
ASGARD.
TO YOUR FEET, FATHER!
A BLACK BEAST ENCASED IN NIGH INVULNERABLE ARMOR HAS BESET UPON YOUR SON!
I FELT A GREAT EVIL IN HIS PRESENCE, FATHER--THIS MONSTER MUST BE PUT DOWN!
BE STILL, THOR.
I SAW YOUR SKIRMISH. I KNOW YOUR FOE--HE IS APOCALYPSE, EVOLUTIONARY CARETAKER OF THE CELESTIALS.
IT IS THEIR ARMOR HE WEARS.
FINE. TELL ME HOW TO PRY THIS CRUSTACEAN FROM HIS WARM SHELL--TELL ME HOW TO SPLINTER THIS COSMIC ARMOR!
THAT IS NOT AN OPTION, MY SON.
DURING THE YEARS BETWEEN THE CELESTIAL HOSTS, THE SKYFATHERS OF THE PANTHEONS OF EARTH MADE A PACT NEVER TO INTERFERE WITH THE CELESTIALS.
PANTHEON HEADS BE DAMNED!
THIS CELESTIAL DEMON HUNTS ASGARDIANS! WHO KNOWS WHAT OTHER EVIL SCHEMES MOVE HIM?!
IF YOU KNOW OF SOMETHING THAT CAN PIERCE HIS ARMOR--
BE DONE WITH THIS BUREAUCRACY AND AID ME!

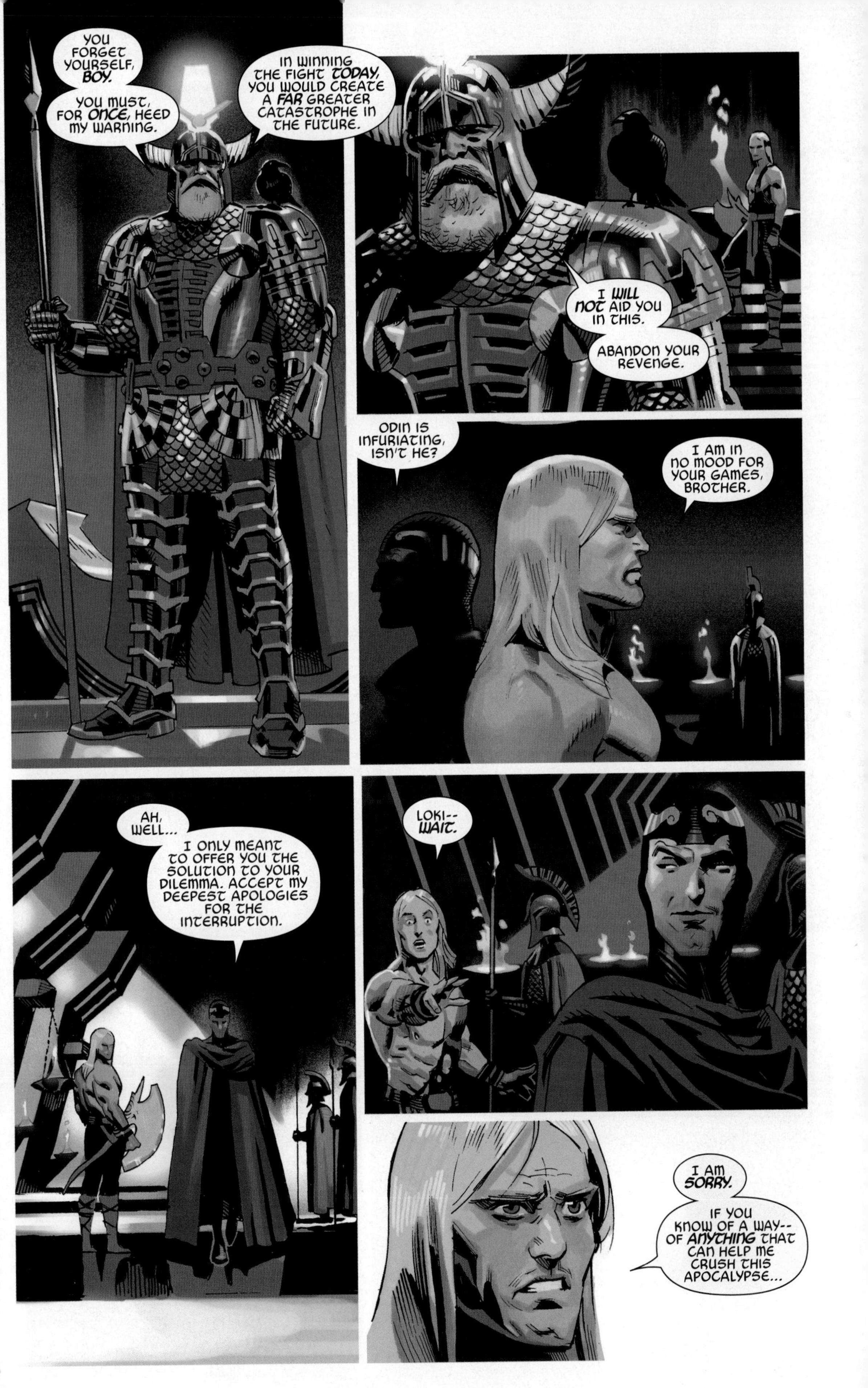
YOU FORGET YOURSELF, BOY.
YOU MUST, FOR ONCE, HEED MY WARNING.
IN WINNING THE FIGHT TODAY, YOU WOULD CREATE A FAR GREATER CATASTROPHE IN THE FUTURE.
I WILL NOT AID YOU IN THIS.
ABANDON YOUR REVENGE.
ODIN IS INFURIATING, ISN'T HE?
I AM IN NO MOOD FOR YOUR GAMES, BROTHER.
AH, WELL...
I ONLY MEANT TO OFFER YOU THE SOLUTION TO YOUR DILEMMA. ACCEPT MY DEEPEST APOLOGIES FOR THE INTERRUPTION.
LOKI-- WAIT.
I AM SORRY.
IF YOU KNOW OF A WAY-- OF ANYTHING THAT CAN HELP ME CRUSH THIS APOCALYPSE...

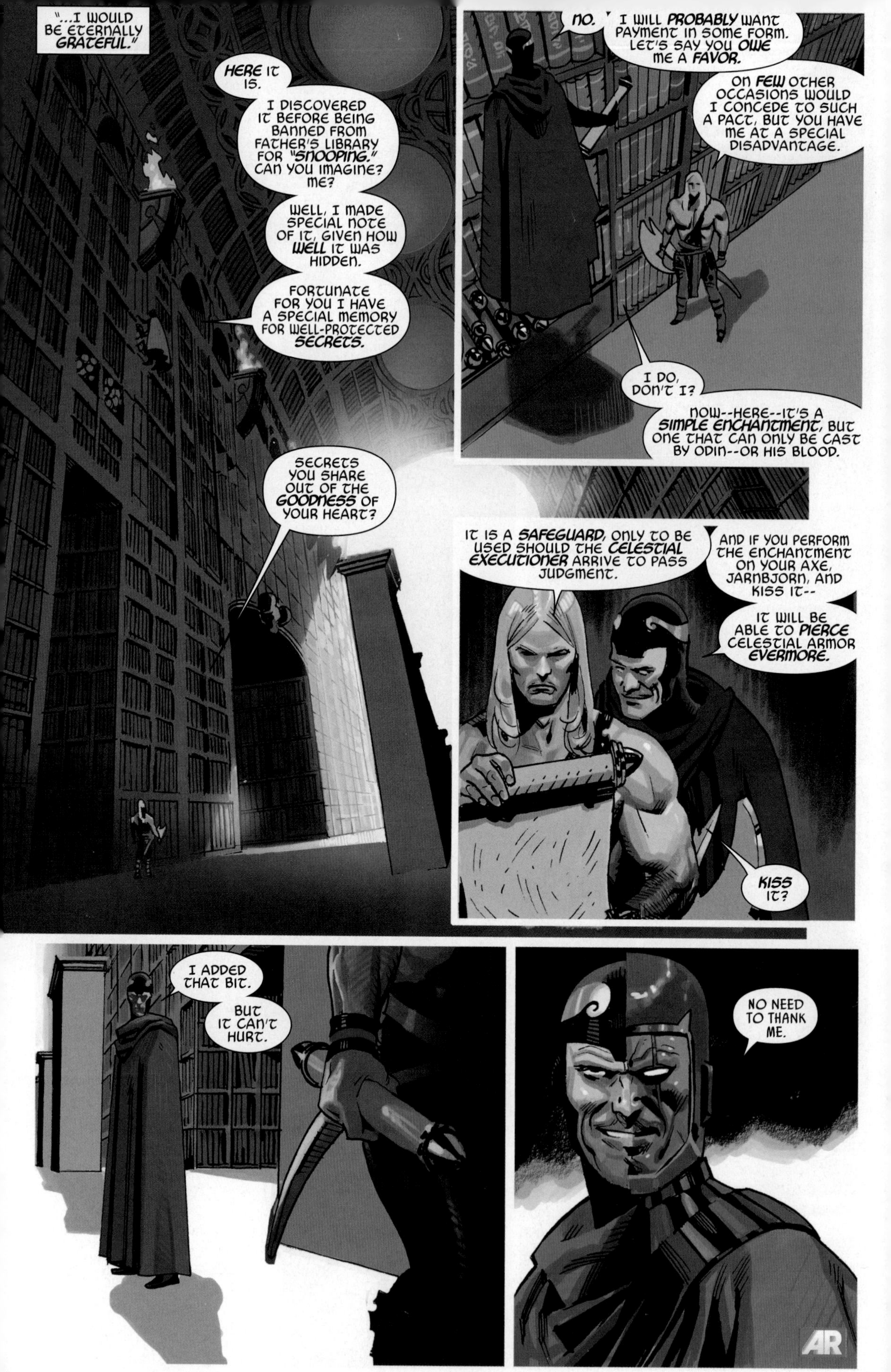
"...I WOULD BE ETERNALLY GRATEFUL."
HERE IT IS.
I DISCOVERED IT BEFORE BEING BANNED FROM FATHER'S LIBRARY FOR "SNOOPING." CAN YOU IMAGINE? ME?
WELL, I MADE SPECIAL NOTE OF IT, GIVEN HOW WELL IT WAS HIDDEN.
FORTUNATE FOR YOU I HAVE A SPECIAL MEMORY FOR WELL-PROTECTED SECRETS.
SECRETS YOU SHARE OUT OF THE GOODNESS OF YOUR HEART?
NO.
I WILL PROBABLY WANT PAYMENT IN SOME FORM. LET'S SAY YOU OWE ME A FAVOR.
ON FEW OTHER OCCASIONS WOULD I CONCEDE TO SUCH A PACT, BUT YOU HAVE ME AT A SPECIAL DISADVANTAGE.
I DO, DON'T I?
NOW--HERE--IT'S A SIMPLE ENCHANTMENT, BUT ONE THAT CAN ONLY BE CAST BY ODIN--OR HIS BLOOD.
IT IS A SAFEGUARD, ONLY TO BE USED SHOULD THE CELESTIAL EXECUTIONER ARRIVE TO PASS JUDGMENT.
AND IF YOU PERFORM THE ENCHANTMENT ON YOUR AXE, JARNBJORN, AND KISS IT--
IT WILL BE ABLE TO PIERCE CELESTIAL ARMOR EVERMORE.
KISS IT?
I ADDED THAT BIT.
BUT IT CAN'T HURT.
NO NEED TO THANK ME.
AR

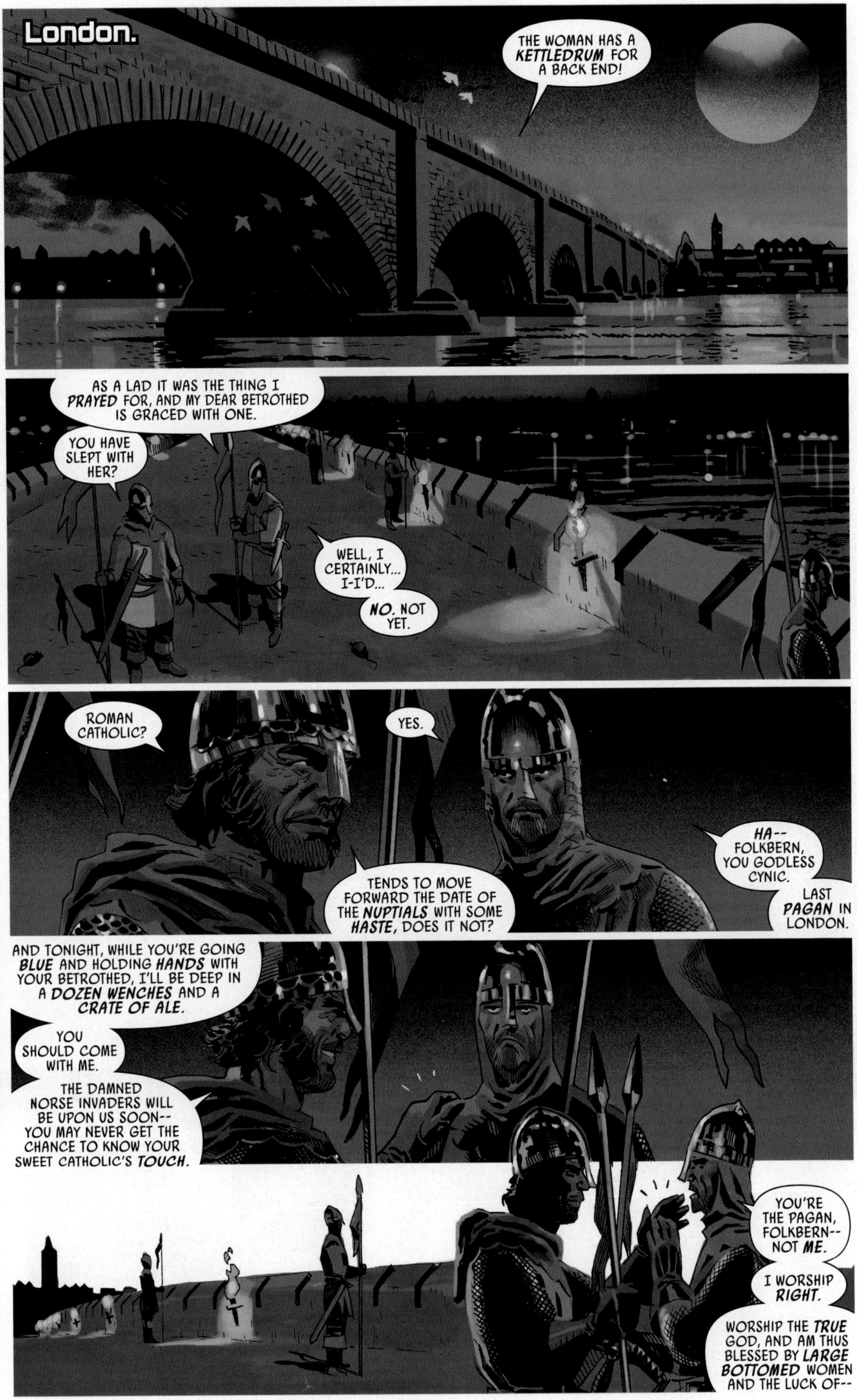
London.
THE WOMAN HAS A KETTLEDRUM FOR A BACK END!
AS A LAD IT WAS THE THING I PRAYED FOR, AND MY DEAR BETROTHED IS GRACED WITH ONE.
YOU HAVE SLEPT WITH HER?
WELL, I CERTAINLY... I-I'D...
NO. NOT YET.
ROMAN CATHOLIC?
YES.
TENDS TO MOVE FORWARD THE DATE OF THE NUPTIALS WITH SOME HASTE, DOES IT NOT?
HA-- FOLKBERN, YOU GODLESS CYNIC.
LAST PAGAN IN LONDON.
AND TONIGHT, WHILE YOU'RE GOING BLUE AND HOLDING HANDS WITH YOUR BETROTHED, I'LL BE DEEP IN A DOZEN WENCHES AND A CRATE OF ALE.
YOU SHOULD COME WITH ME.
THE DAMNED NORSE INVADERS WILL BE UPON US SOON-- YOU MAY NEVER GET THE CHANCE TO KNOW YOUR SWEET CATHOLIC'S TOUCH.
YOU'RE THE PAGAN, FOLKBERN-- NOT ME.
I WORSHIP RIGHT.
WORSHIP THE TRUE GOD, AND AM THUS BLESSED BY LARGE BOTTOMED WOMEN AND THE LUCK OF--

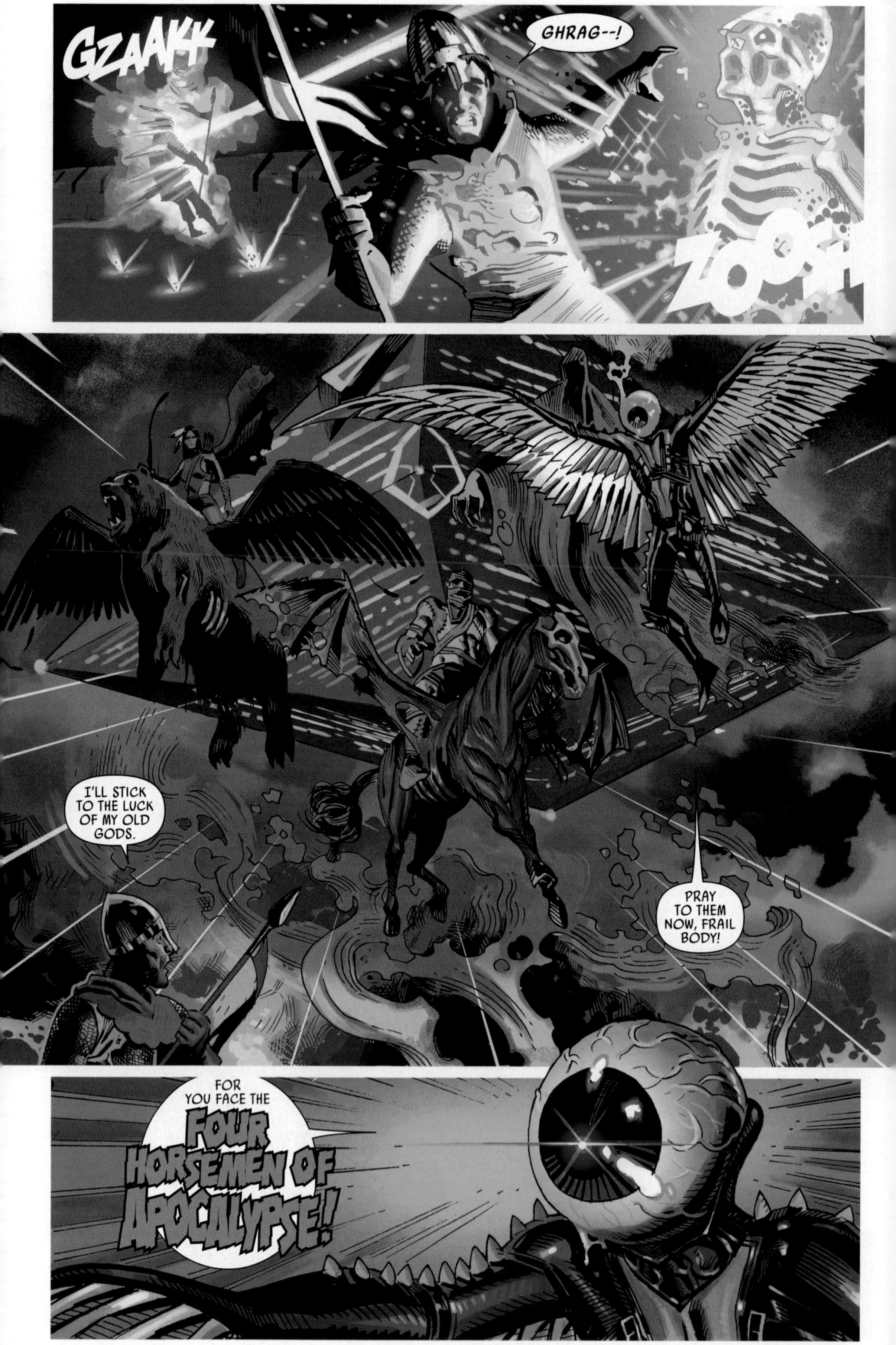
GZAAKK
GHRAG--!
ZOOSH
I'LL STICK TO THE LUCK OF MY OLD GODS.
PRAY TO THEM NOW, FRAIL BODY!
FOR YOU FACE THE FOUR HORSEMEN OF APOCALYPSE!

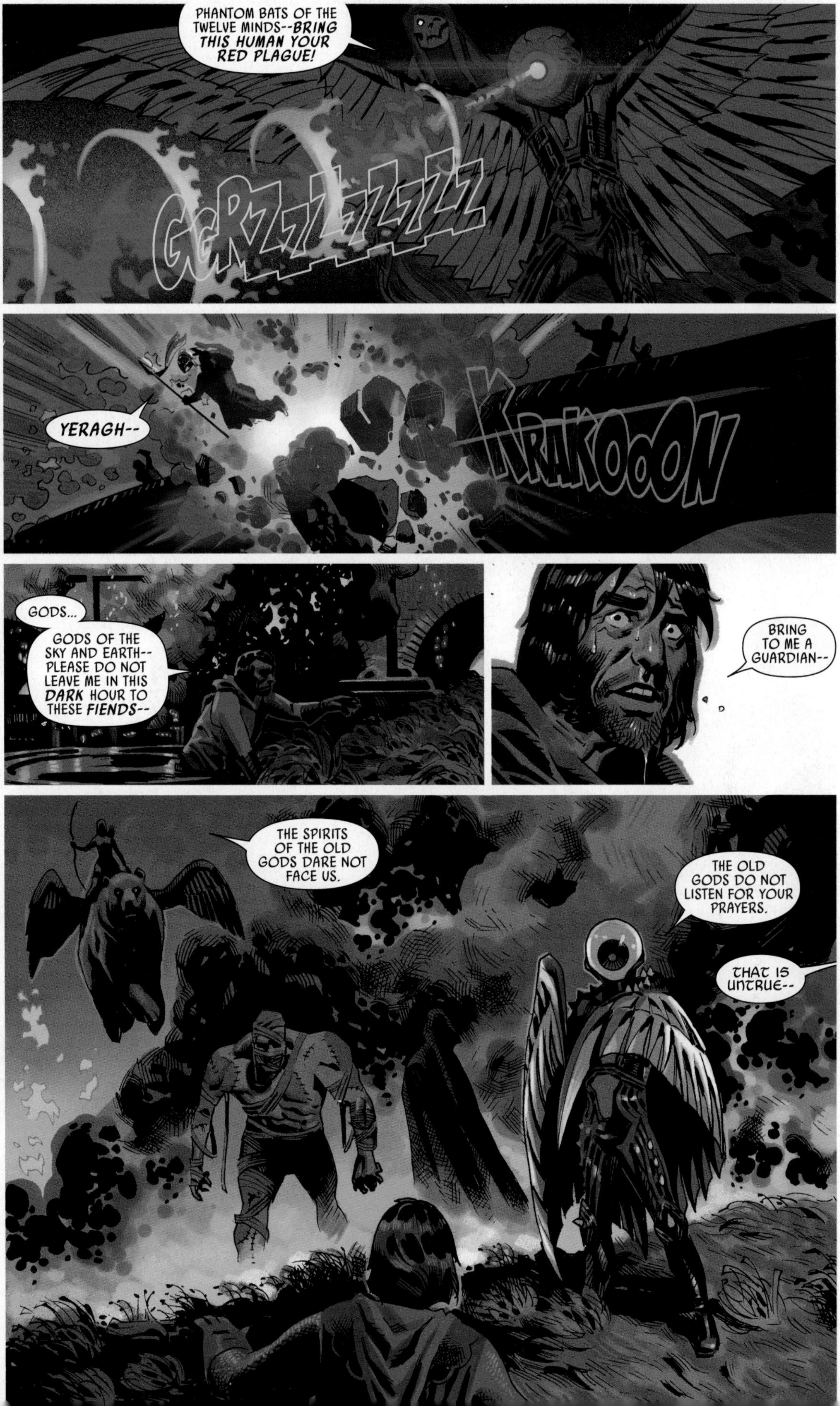
PHANTOM BATS OF THE TWELVE MINDS--BRING THIS HUMAN YOUR RED PLAGUE!
GGRZZZZZZZZ
YERAGH--
KRAKOOON
GODS...
GODS OF THE SKY AND EARTH--PLEASE DO NOT LEAVE ME IN THIS DARK HOUR TO THESE FIENDS--
BRING TO ME A GUARDIAN--
THE SPIRITS OF THE OLD GODS DARE NOT FACE US.
THE OLD GODS DO NOT LISTEN FOR YOUR PRAYERS.
THAT IS UNTRUE--

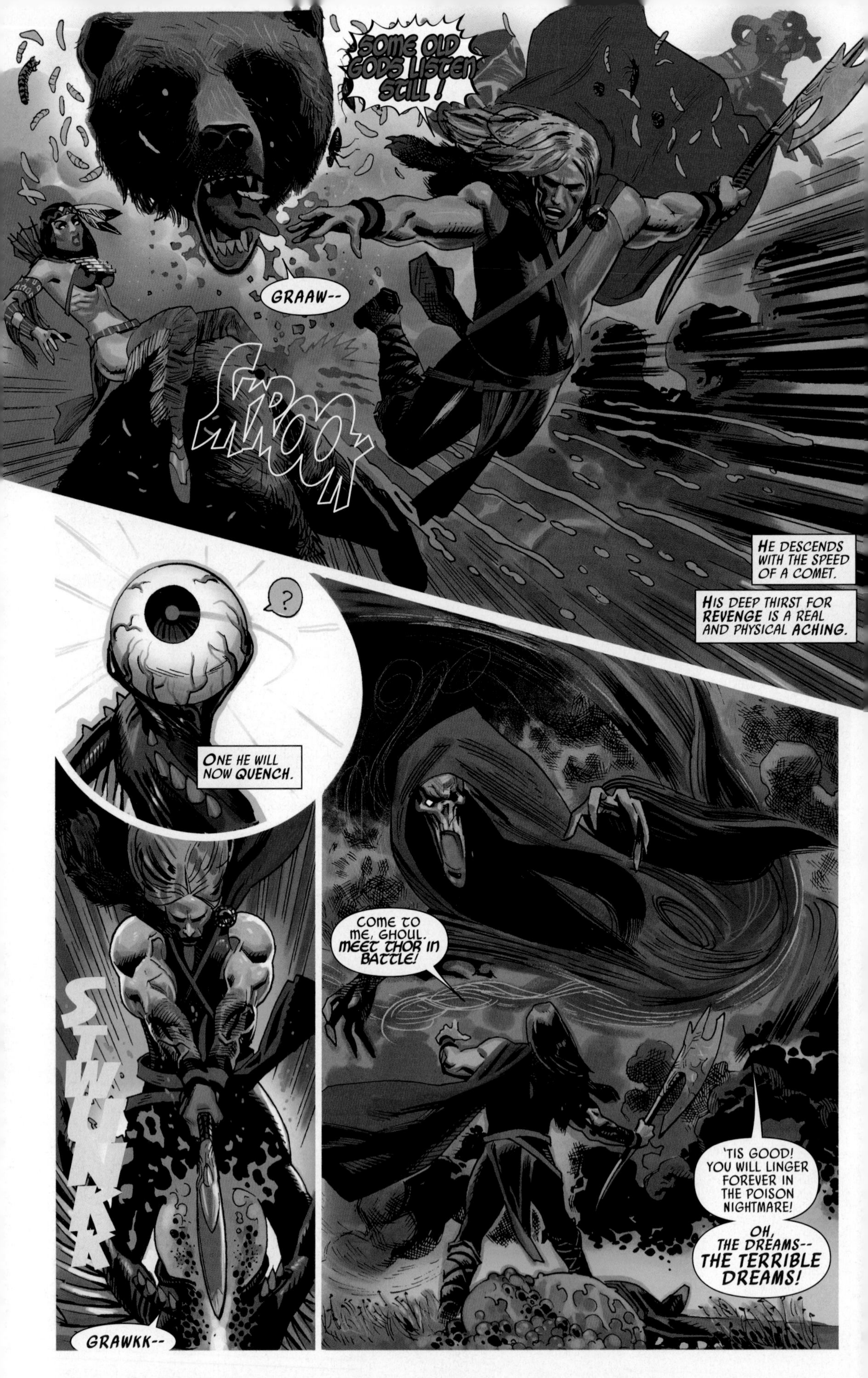
SOME OLD GODS LISTEN STILL!
GRAAW--
SPROOK
HE DESCENDS WITH THE SPEED OF A COMET.
HIS DEEP THIRST FOR REVENGE IS A REAL AND PHYSICAL ACHING.
?
ONE HE WILL NOW QUENCH.
STHUNKK
GRAWKK--
COME TO ME, GHOUL. MEET THOR IN BATTLE!
'TIS GOOD! YOU WILL LINGER FOREVER IN THE POISON NIGHTMARE!
OH, THE DREAMS-- THE TERRIBLE DREAMS!

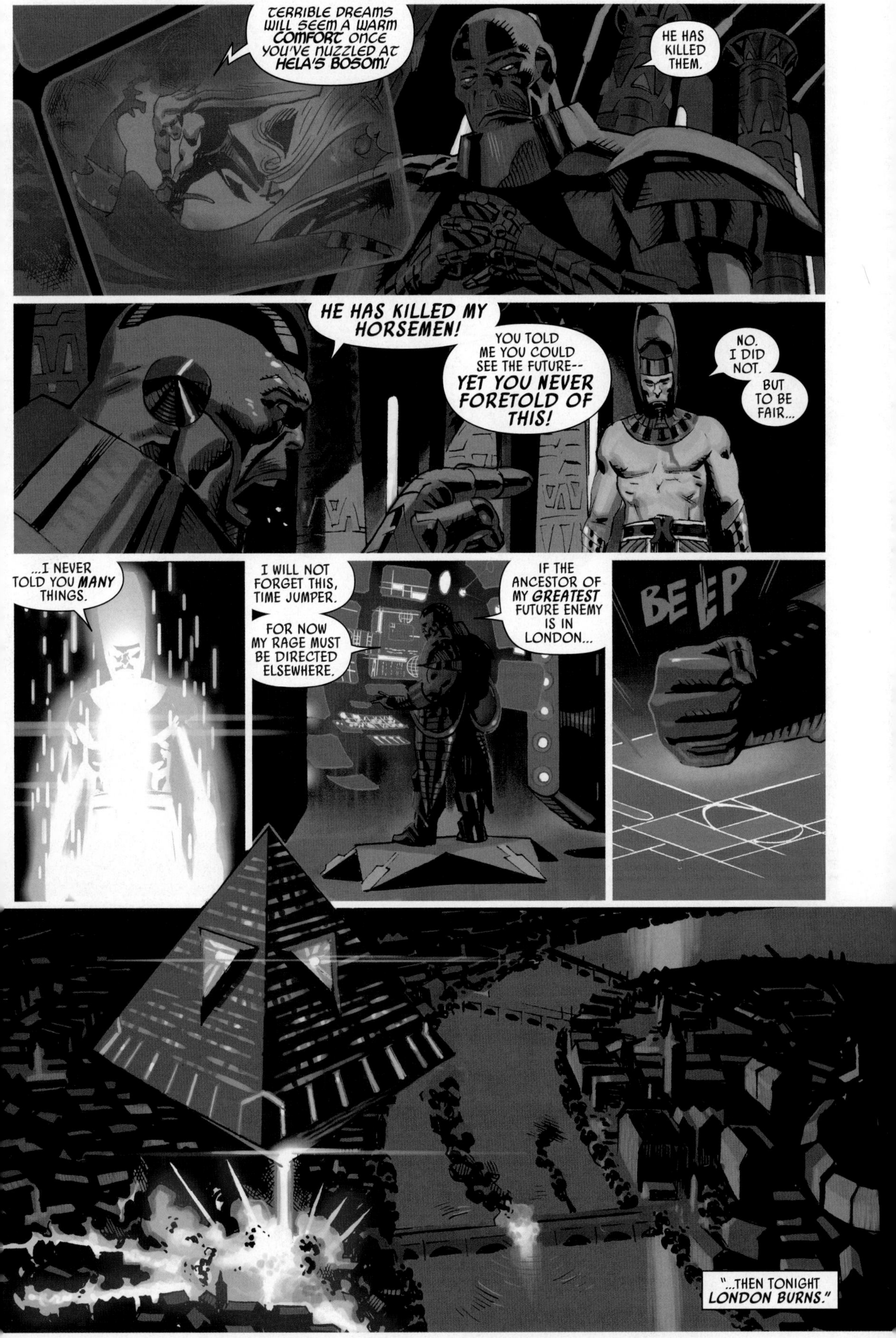
TERRIBLE DREAMS WILL SEEM A WARM COMFORT ONCE YOU'VE NUZZLED AT HELA'S BOSOM!
HE HAS KILLED THEM.
HE HAS KILLED MY HORSEMEN!
YOU TOLD ME YOU COULD SEE THE FUTURE-- YET YOU NEVER FORETOLD OF THIS!
NO. I DID NOT.
BUT TO BE FAIR...
...I NEVER TOLD YOU MANY THINGS.
I WILL NOT FORGET THIS, TIME JUMPER.
FOR NOW MY RAGE MUST BE DIRECTED ELSEWHERE.
IF THE ANCESTOR OF MY GREATEST FUTURE ENEMY IS IN LONDON...
BEEP
"...THEN TONIGHT LONDON BURNS."

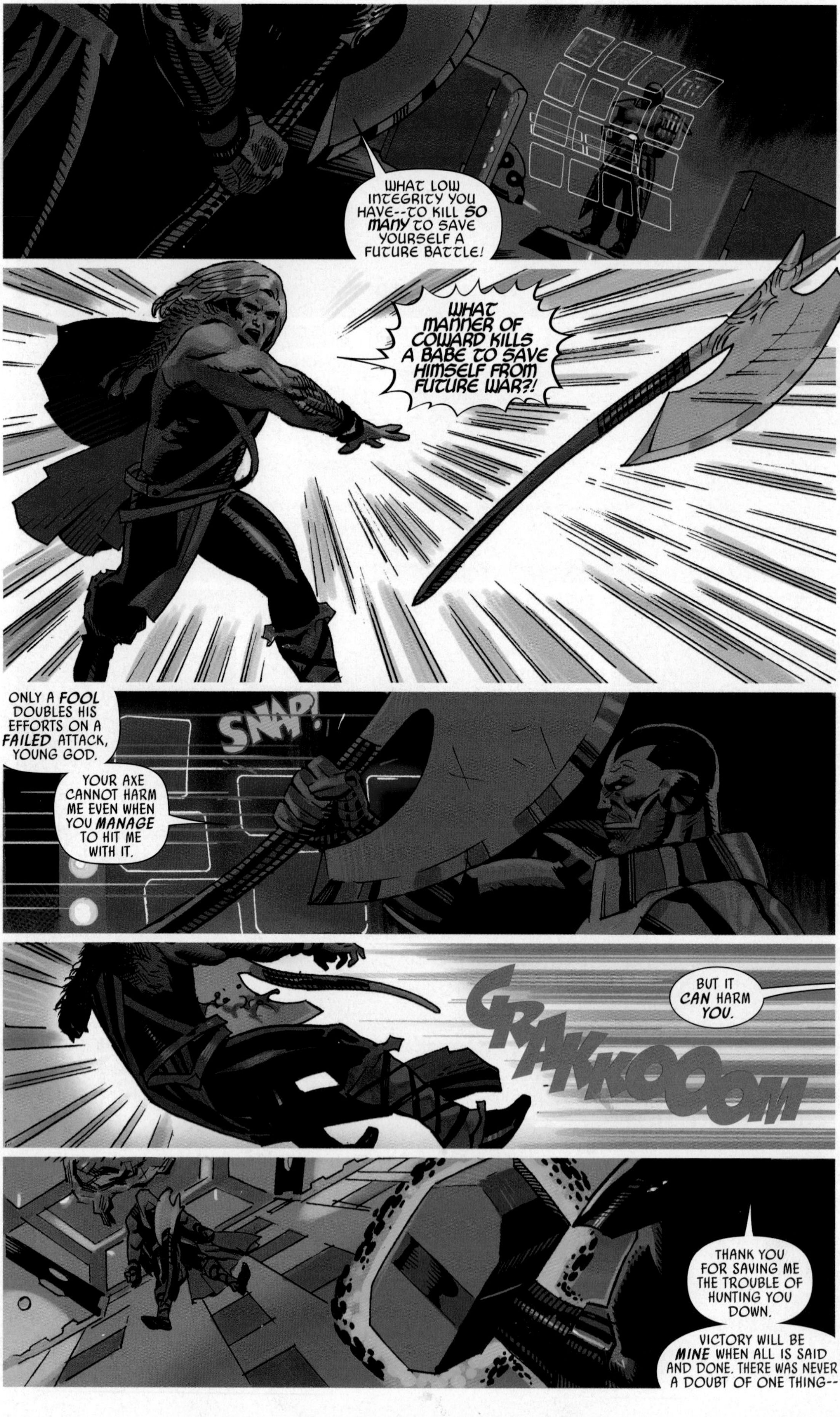
WHAT LOW INTEGRITY YOU HAVE--TO KILL SO MANY TO SAVE YOURSELF A FUTURE BATTLE!
WHAT MANNER OF COWARD KILLS A BABE TO SAVE HIMSELF FROM FUTURE WAR?!
ONLY A FOOL DOUBLES HIS EFFORTS ON A FAILED ATTACK, YOUNG GOD.
SNAP!
YOUR AXE CANNOT HARM ME EVEN WHEN YOU MANAGE TO HIT ME WITH IT.
CRAKKOOOOM
BUT IT CAN HARM YOU.
THANK YOU FOR SAVING ME THE TROUBLE OF HUNTING YOU DOWN.
VICTORY WILL BE MINE WHEN ALL IS SAID AND DONE. THERE WAS NEVER A DOUBT OF ONE THING--

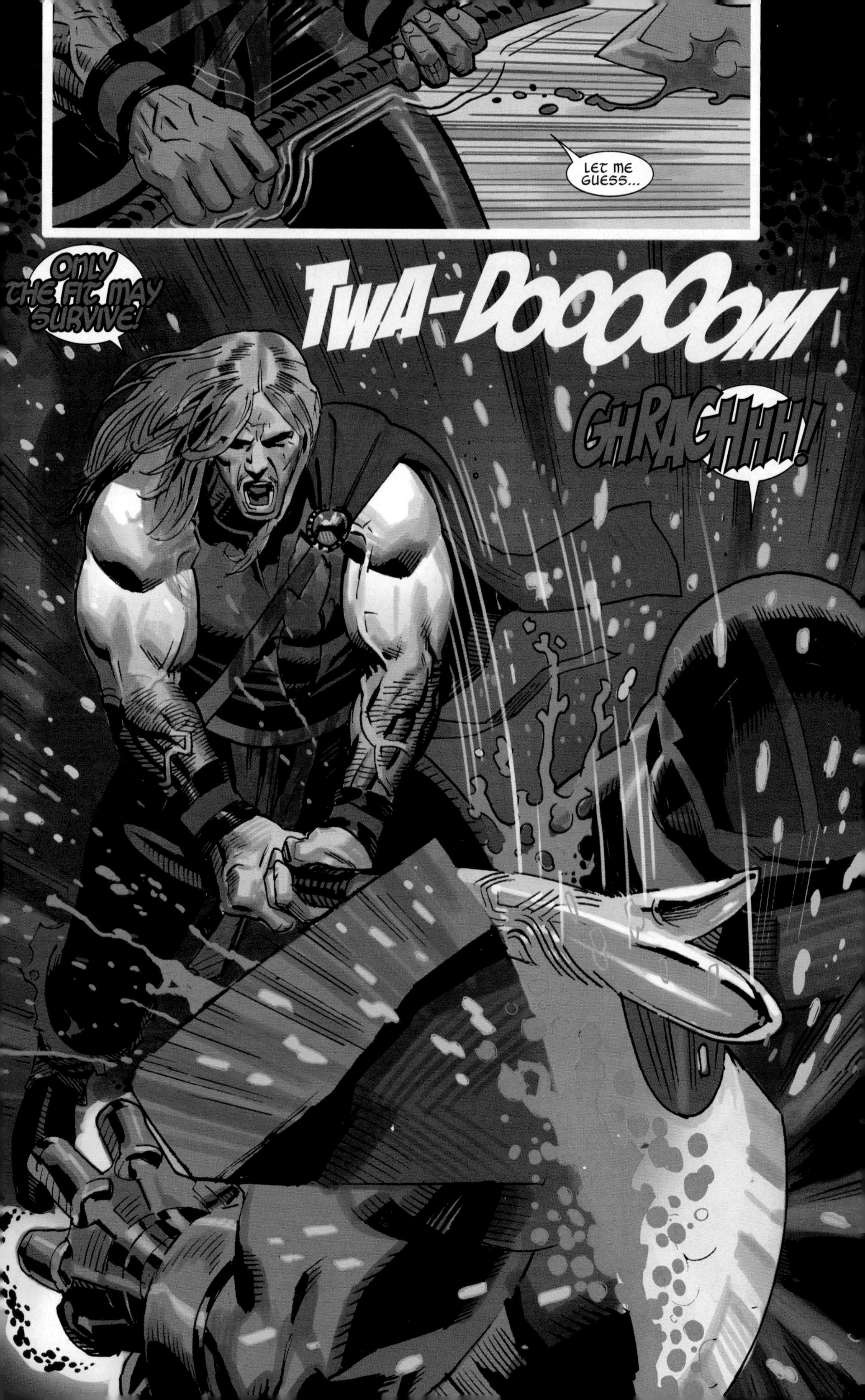
LET ME GUESS...
ONLY THE FIT MAY SURVIVE!
TWA-DOOOOOOM
GHRAGHHH!

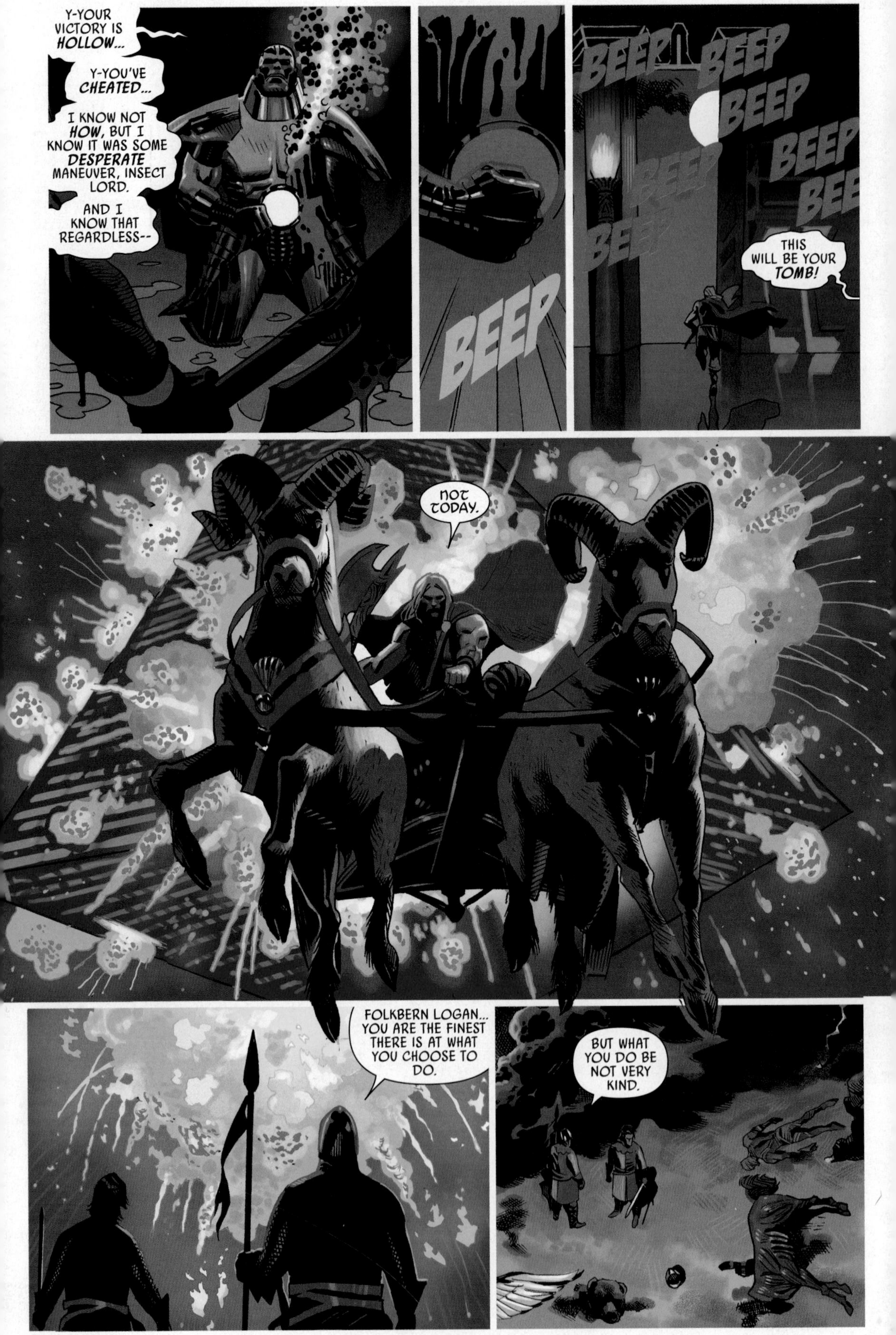
Y-YOUR VICTORY IS HOLLOW...
Y-YOU'VE CHEATED...
I KNOW NOT HOW, BUT I KNOW IT WAS SOME DESPERATE MANEUVER, INSECT LORD.
AND I KNOW THAT REGARDLESS--
BEEP
BEEP BEEP BEEP BEEP BEE BEEP BEEP
THIS WILL BE YOUR TOMB!
NOT TODAY.
FOLKBERN LOGAN... YOU ARE THE FINEST THERE IS AT WHAT YOU CHOOSE TO DO.
BUT WHAT YOU DO BE NOT VERY KIND.

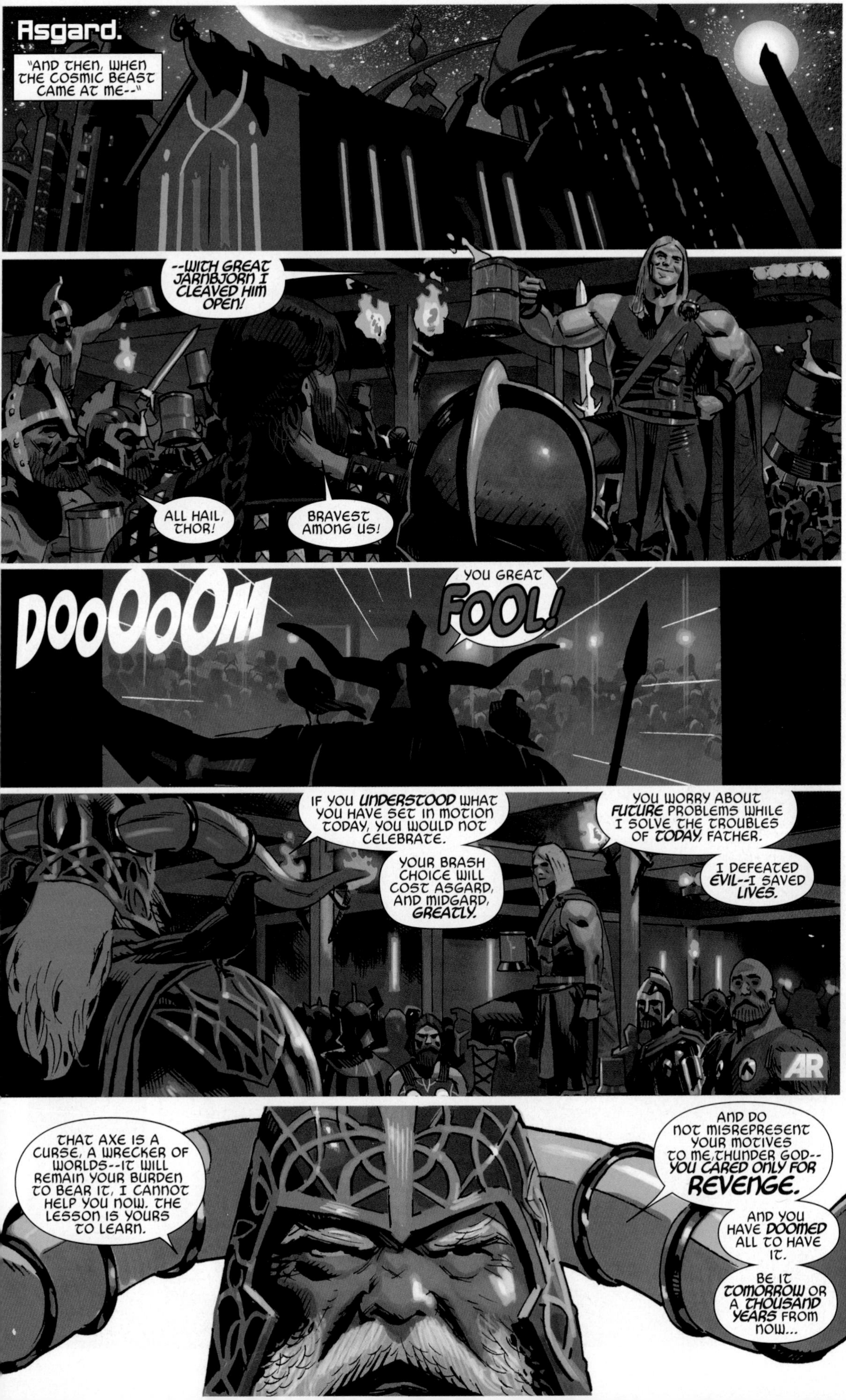
Asgard.
"AND THEN, WHEN THE COSMIC BEAST CAME AT ME--"
--WITH GREAT JARNBJORN I CLEAVED HIM OPEN!
ALL HAIL, THOR!
BRAVEST AMONG US!
DOOOOOM
YOU GREAT FOOL!
IF YOU UNDERSTOOD WHAT YOU HAVE SET IN MOTION TODAY, YOU WOULD NOT CELEBRATE.
YOUR BRASH CHOICE WILL COST ASGARD, AND MIDGARD, GREATLY.
YOU WORRY ABOUT FUTURE PROBLEMS WHILE I SOLVE THE TROUBLES OF TODAY, FATHER.
I DEFEATED EVIL--I SAVED LIVES.
AR
THAT AXE IS A CURSE, A WRECKER OF WORLDS--IT WILL REMAIN YOUR BURDEN TO BEAR IT, I CANNOT HELP YOU NOW. THE LESSON IS YOURS TO LEARN.
AND DO NOT MISREPRESENT YOUR MOTIVES TO ME,THUNDER GOD--YOU CARED ONLY FOR REVENGE.
AND YOU HAVE DOOMED ALL TO HAVE IT.
BE IT TOMORROW OR A THOUSAND YEARS FROM NOW...

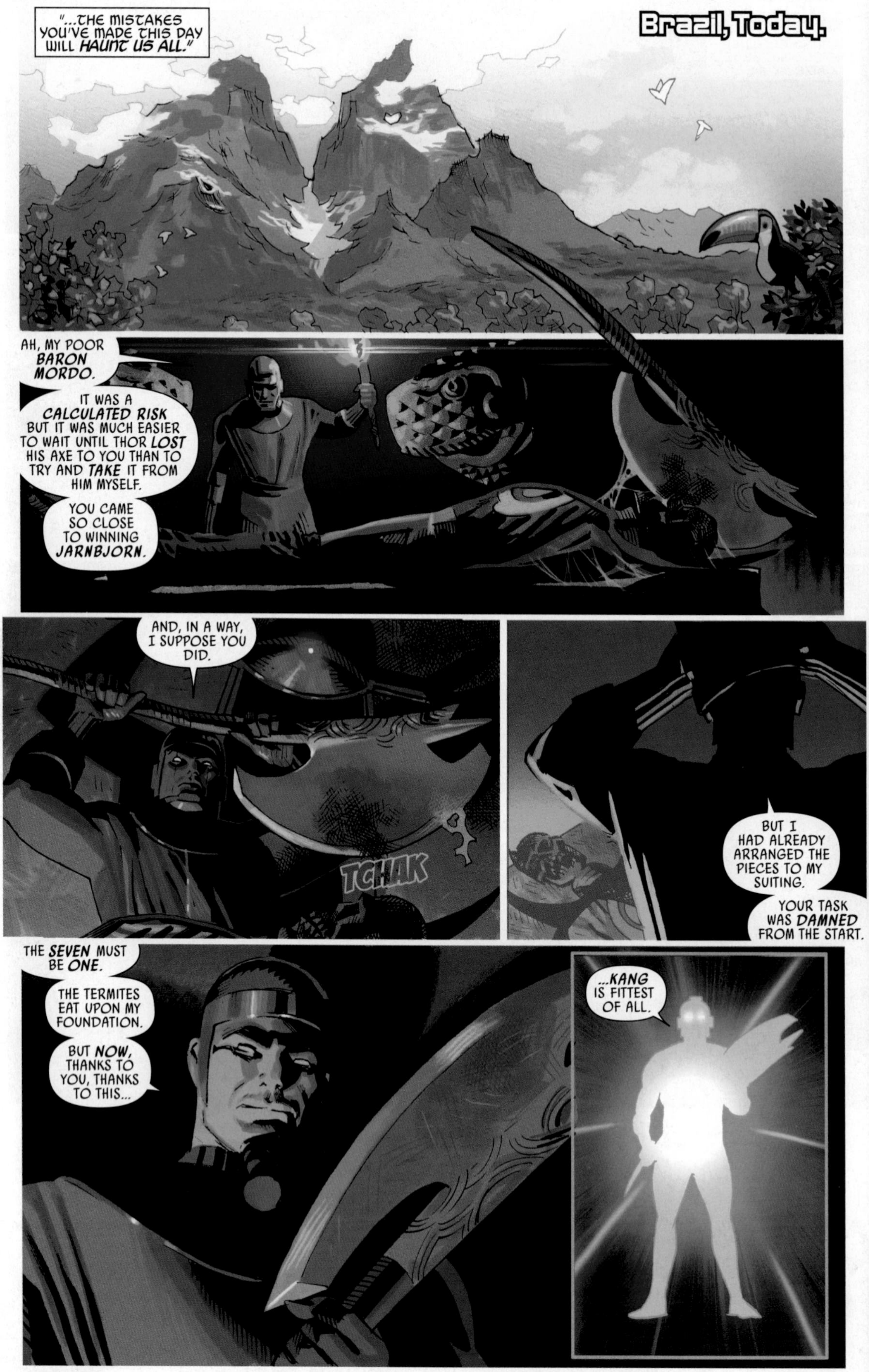
"...THE MISTAKES YOU'VE MADE THIS DAY WILL HAUNT US ALL."
Brazil, Today.
AH, MY POOR BARON MORDO.
IT WAS A CALCULATED RISK BUT IT WAS MUCH EASIER TO WAIT UNTIL THOR LOST HIS AXE TO YOU THAN TO TRY AND TAKE IT FROM HIM MYSELF.
YOU CAME SO CLOSE TO WINNING JARNBJORN.
AND, IN A WAY, I SUPPOSE YOU DID.
TCHAK
BUT I HAD ALREADY ARRANGED THE PIECES TO MY SUITING.
YOUR TASK WAS DAMNED FROM THE START.
THE SEVEN MUST BE ONE.
THE TERMITES EAT UPON MY FOUNDATION.
BUT NOW, THANKS TO YOU, THANKS TO THIS...
...KANG IS FITTEST OF ALL.

UNCANNY AVENGERS #8AU

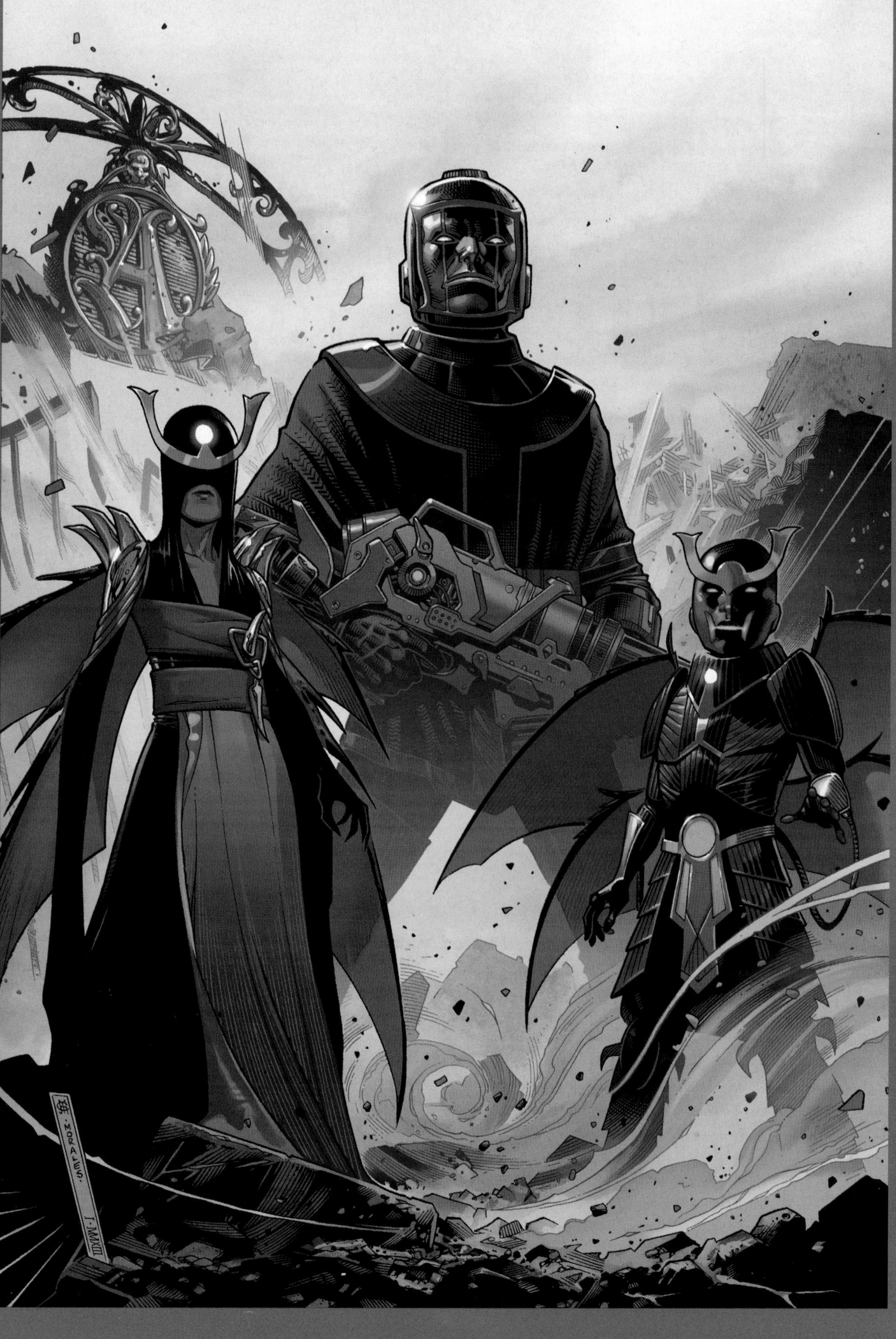

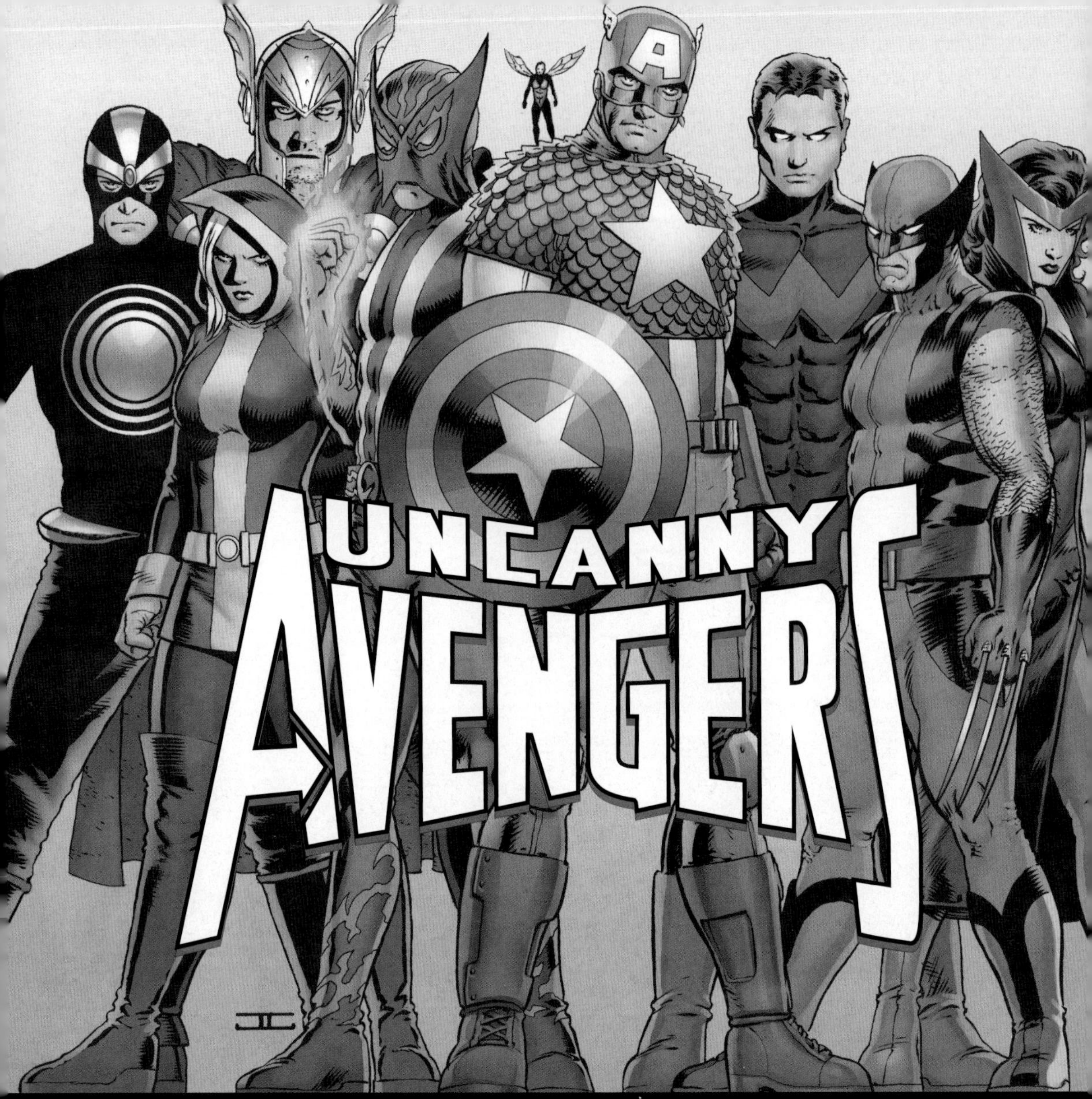
UNCANNY
AVENGERS

PREVIOUSLY IN UNCANNY AVENGERS...

LONGTIME AVENGERS ADVERSARY KANG THE CONQUEROR IS ON A MISSION, ONE SPANNING CENTURIES. WITH A PENCHANT FOR SCHEMING AND THE ABILITY TO TRAVEL THROUGH TIME, KANG HAS TAKEN POSSESSION OF JARNBORN, THE ENCHANTED AXE POSSESSED BY THOR IN HIS YOUTH, AND ALSO THE APOCALYPSE TWINS — CHILDREN OF THE CORRUPTED X-MAN ARCHANGEL. NOW KANG CONTINUES HIS QUEST OF MOLDING THE TIMESTREAM TO HIS LIKING, STARTING WITH THE ABDUCTED TWINS...

PREVIOUSLY IN AGE OF ULTRON...

YEARS AGO, FOUNDING AVENGER HENRY PYM INVENTED THE ARTIFICIAL INTELLIGENCE KNOWN AS ULTRON. UPON ACHIEVING SENTIENCE, ULTRON DEDICATED HIS EXISTENCE TO DESTROYING HUMANITY...AND EVENTUALLY SUCCEEDED. DETERMINED TO STOP ULTRON BY ANY MEANS, WOLVERINE USED A TIME TRAVEL DEVICE TO JOURNEY TO THE PAST, WHERE HE KILLED PYM BEFORE HE COULD CREATE THE MACHINE. BUT UPON RETURNING TO THE PRESENT, WOLVERINE HAS DISCOVERED THAT HIS ACTIONS HAD UNEXPECTED CONSEQUENCES AND COMPLETELY ALTERED THE UNIVERSE...

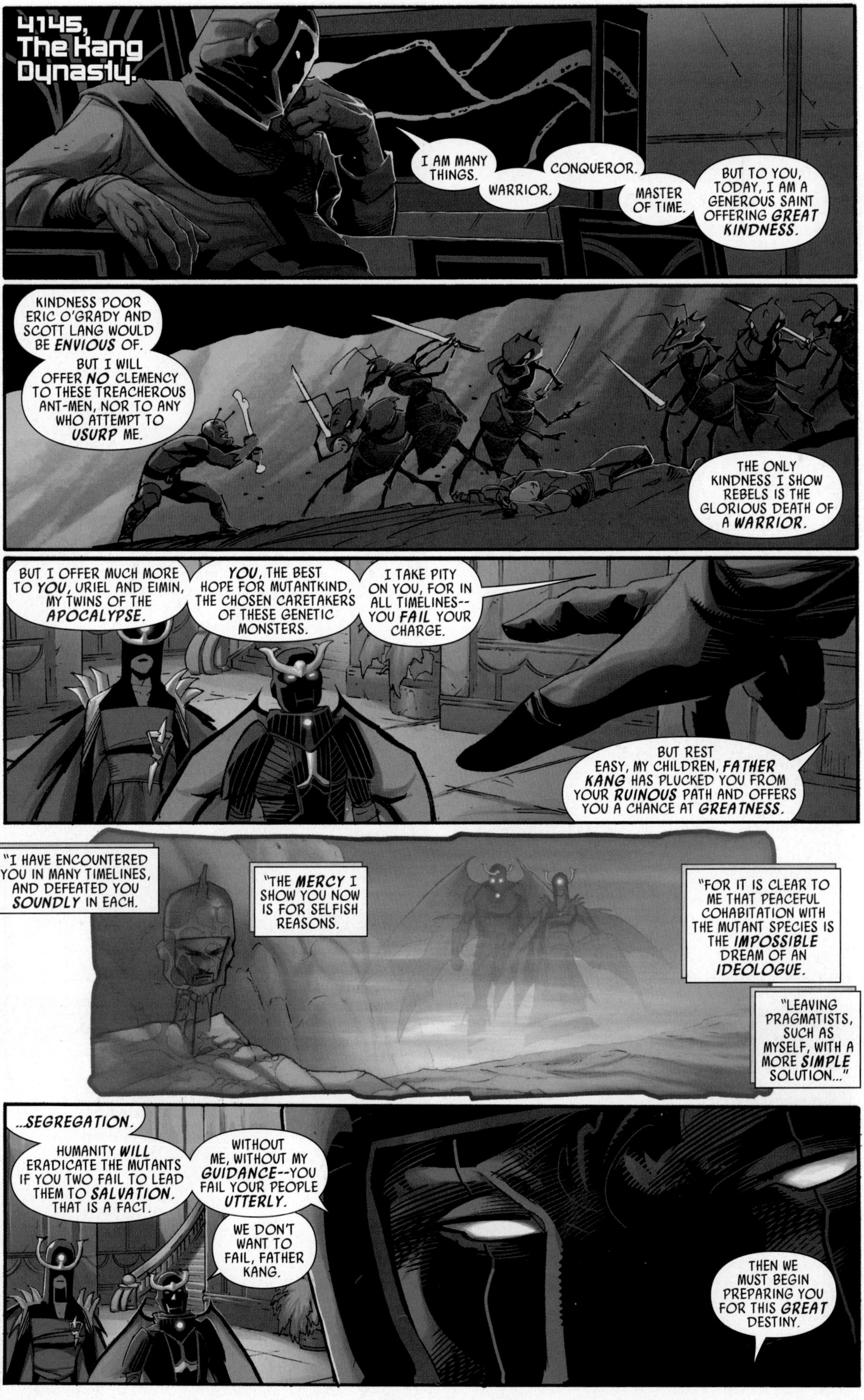
4145, The Kang Dynasty.
I AM MANY THINGS.
WARRIOR.
CONQUEROR.
MASTER OF TIME.
BUT TO YOU, TODAY, I AM A GENEROUS SAINT OFFERING GREAT KINDNESS.
KINDNESS POOR ERIC O'GRADY AND SCOTT LANG WOULD BE ENVIOUS OF.
BUT I WILL OFFER NO CLEMENCY TO THESE TREACHEROUS ANT-MEN, NOR TO ANY WHO ATTEMPT TO USURP ME.
THE ONLY KINDNESS I SHOW REBELS IS THE GLORIOUS DEATH OF A WARRIOR.
BUT I OFFER MUCH MORE TO YOU, URIEL AND EIMIN, MY TWINS OF THE APOCALYPSE.
YOU, THE BEST HOPE FOR MUTANTKIND, THE CHOSEN CARETAKERS OF THESE GENETIC MONSTERS.
I TAKE PITY ON YOU, FOR IN ALL TIMELINES-- YOU FAIL YOUR CHARGE.
BUT REST EASY, MY CHILDREN, FATHER KANG HAS PLUCKED YOU FROM YOUR RUINOUS PATH AND OFFERS YOU A CHANCE AT GREATNESS.
"I HAVE ENCOUNTERED YOU IN MANY TIMELINES, AND DEFEATED YOU SOUNDLY IN EACH.
"THE MERCY I SHOW YOU NOW IS FOR SELFISH REASONS.
"FOR IT IS CLEAR TO ME THAT PEACEFUL COHABITATION WITH THE MUTANT SPECIES IS THE IMPOSSIBLE DREAM OF AN IDEOLOGUE.
"LEAVING PRAGMATISTS, SUCH AS MYSELF, WITH A MORE SIMPLE SOLUTION..."
...SEGREGATION.
HUMANITY WILL ERADICATE THE MUTANTS IF YOU TWO FAIL TO LEAD THEM TO SALVATION. THAT IS A FACT.
WITHOUT ME, WITHOUT MY GUIDANCE--YOU FAIL YOUR PEOPLE UTTERLY.
WE DON'T WANT TO FAIL, FATHER KANG.
THEN WE MUST BEGIN PREPARING YOU FOR THIS GREAT DESTINY.

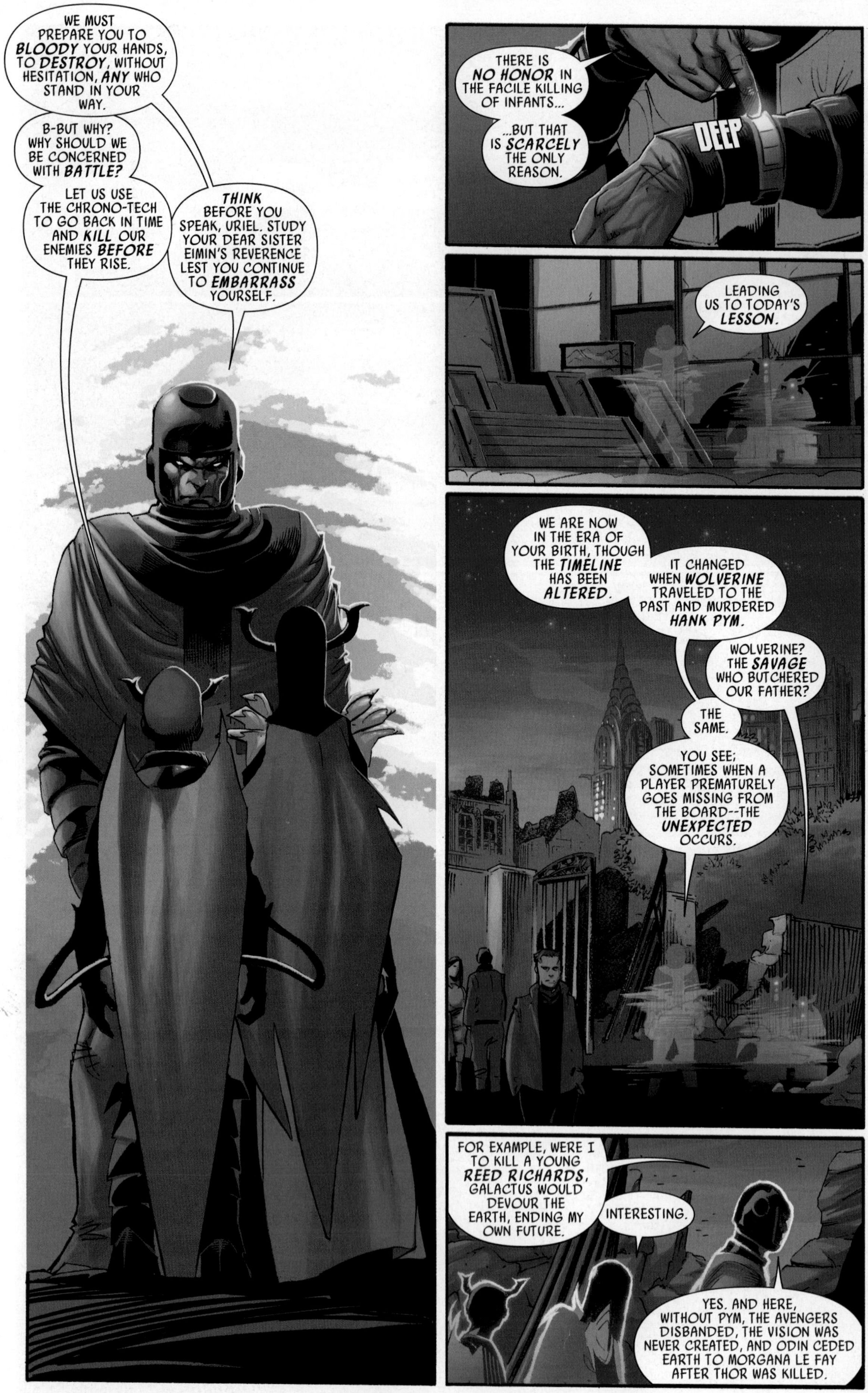
WE MUST PREPARE YOU TO BLOODY YOUR HANDS, TO DESTROY, WITHOUT HESITATION, ANY WHO STAND IN YOUR WAY.
B-BUT WHY? WHY SHOULD WE BE CONCERNED WITH BATTLE?
LET US USE THE CHRONO-TECH TO GO BACK IN TIME AND KILL OUR ENEMIES BEFORE THEY RISE.
THINK BEFORE YOU SPEAK, URIEL. STUDY YOUR DEAR SISTER EIMIN'S REVERENCE LEST YOU CONTINUE TO EMBARRASS YOURSELF.
THERE IS NO HONOR IN THE FACILE KILLING OF INFANTS...
...BUT THAT IS SCARCELY THE ONLY REASON.
DEEP
LEADING US TO TODAY'S LESSON.
WE ARE NOW IN THE ERA OF YOUR BIRTH, THOUGH THE TIMELINE HAS BEEN ALTERED.
IT CHANGED WHEN WOLVERINE TRAVELED TO THE PAST AND MURDERED HANK PYM.
WOLVERINE? THE SAVAGE WHO BUTCHERED OUR FATHER?
THE SAME.
YOU SEE; SOMETIMES WHEN A PLAYER PREMATURELY GOES MISSING FROM THE BOARD--THE UNEXPECTED OCCURS.
FOR EXAMPLE, WERE I TO KILL A YOUNG REED RICHARDS, GALACTUS WOULD DEVOUR THE EARTH, ENDING MY OWN FUTURE.
INTERESTING.
YES. AND HERE, WITHOUT PYM, THE AVENGERS DISBANDED, THE VISION WAS NEVER CREATED, AND ODIN CEDED EARTH TO MORGANA LE FAY AFTER THOR WAS KILLED.

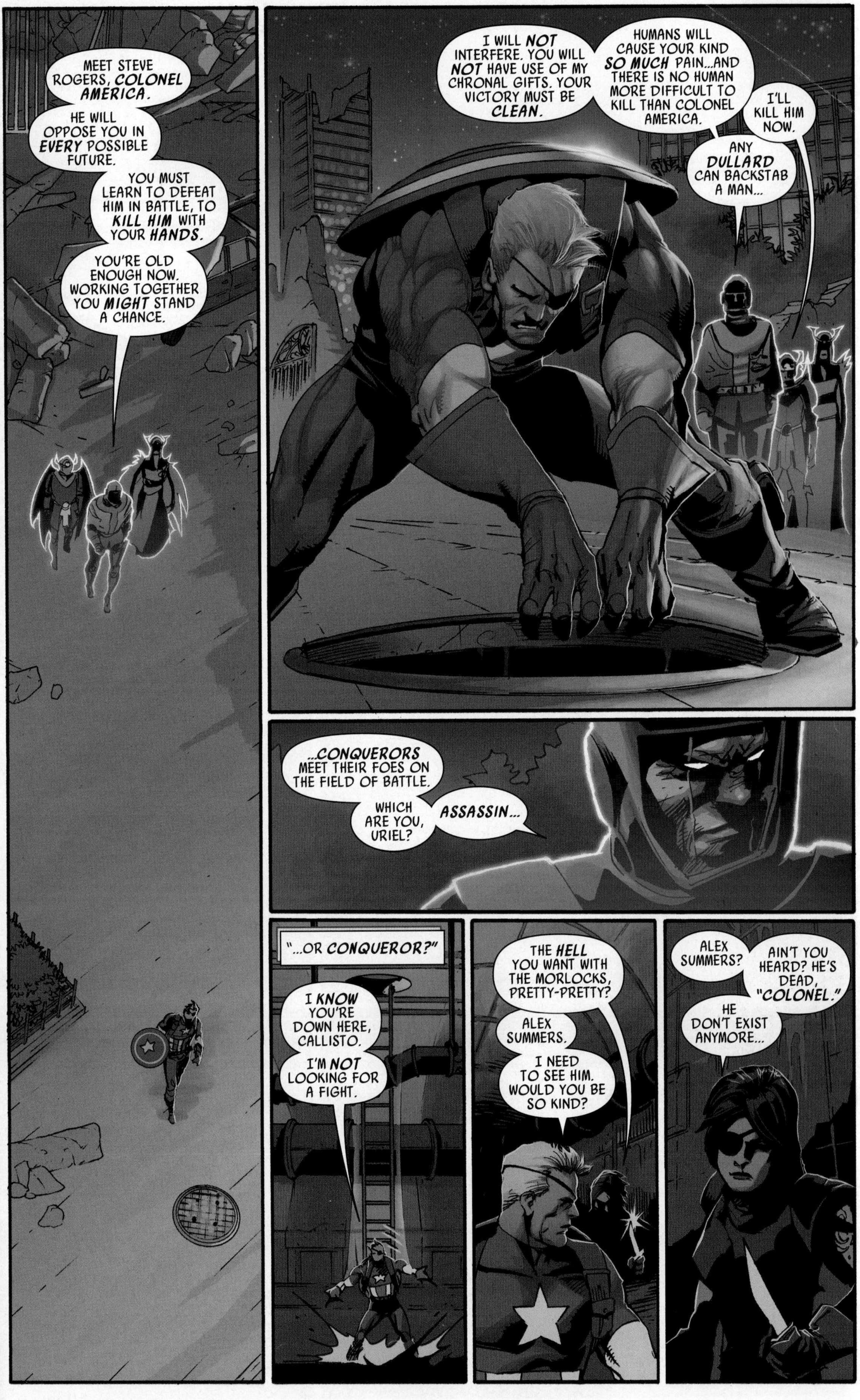

MEET STEVE ROGERS, COLONEL AMERICA.
HE WILL OPPOSE YOU IN EVERY POSSIBLE FUTURE.
YOU MUST LEARN TO DEFEAT HIM IN BATTLE, TO KILL HIM WITH YOUR HANDS.
YOU'RE OLD ENOUGH NOW. WORKING TOGETHER YOU MIGHT STAND A CHANCE.
I WILL NOT INTERFERE. YOU WILL NOT HAVE USE OF MY CHRONAL GIFTS. YOUR VICTORY MUST BE CLEAN.
HUMANS WILL CAUSE YOUR KIND SO MUCH PAIN...AND THERE IS NO HUMAN MORE DIFFICULT TO KILL THAN COLONEL AMERICA.
I'LL KILL HIM NOW.
ANY DULLARD CAN BACKSTAB A MAN...
...CONQUERORS MEET THEIR FOES ON THE FIELD OF BATTLE.
WHICH ARE YOU, URIEL?
ASSASSIN...
"...OR CONQUEROR?"
I KNOW YOU'RE DOWN HERE, CALLISTO.
I'M NOT LOOKING FOR A FIGHT.
THE HELL YOU WANT WITH THE MORLOCKS, PRETTY-PRETTY?
ALEX SUMMERS.
I NEED TO SEE HIM. WOULD YOU BE SO KIND?
ALEX SUMMERS?
AIN'T YOU HEARD? HE'S DEAD, "COLONEL."
HE DON'T EXIST ANYMORE...

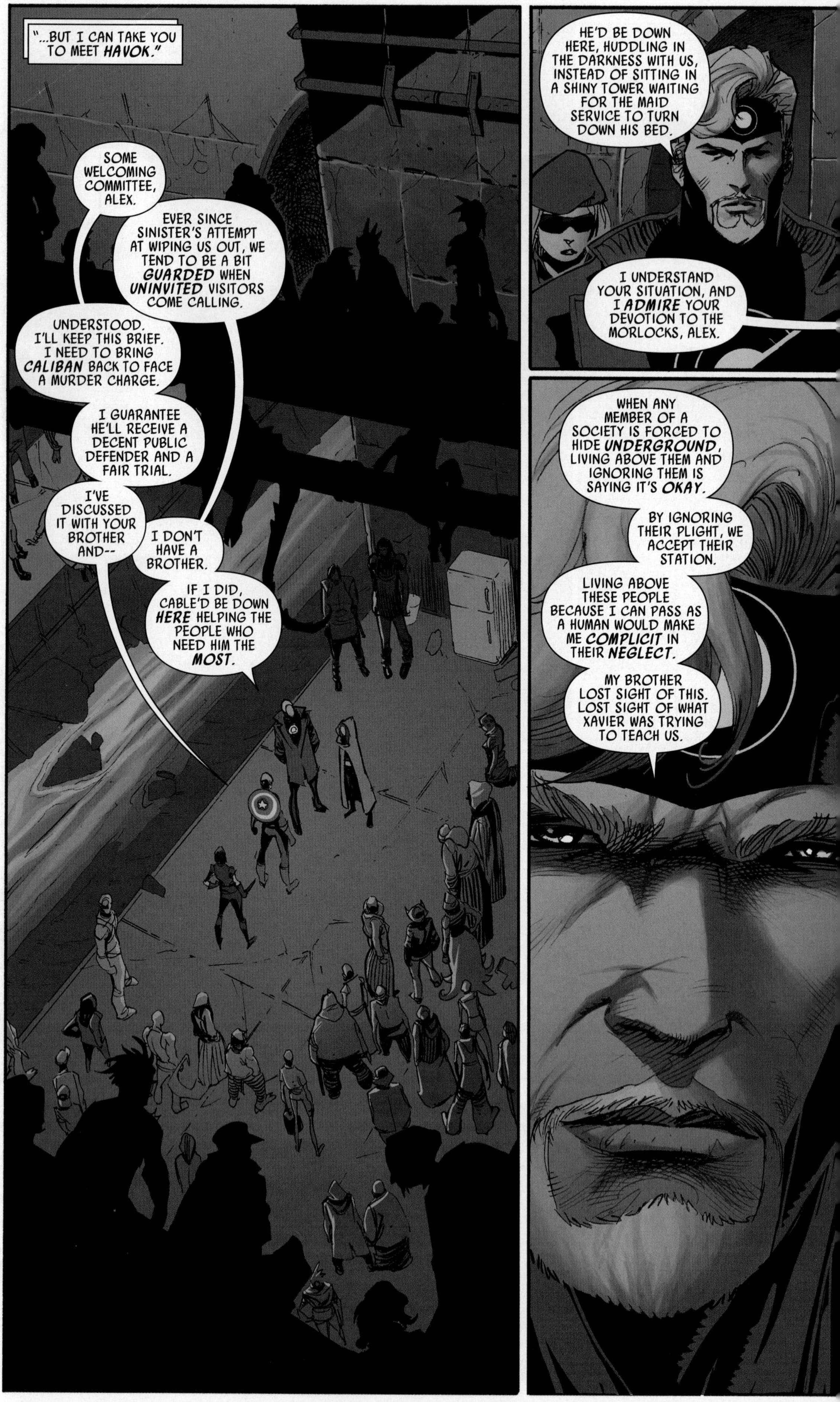
"...BUT I CAN TAKE YOU TO MEET HAVOK."
SOME WELCOMING COMMITTEE, ALEX.
EVER SINCE SINISTER'S ATTEMPT AT WIPING US OUT, WE TEND TO BE A BIT GUARDED WHEN UNINVITED VISITORS COME CALLING.
UNDERSTOOD. I'LL KEEP THIS BRIEF. I NEED TO BRING CALIBAN BACK TO FACE A MURDER CHARGE.
I GUARANTEE HE'LL RECEIVE A DECENT PUBLIC DEFENDER AND A FAIR TRIAL.
I'VE DISCUSSED IT WITH YOUR BROTHER AND--
I DON'T HAVE A BROTHER.
IF I DID, CABLE'D BE DOWN HERE HELPING THE PEOPLE WHO NEED HIM THE MOST.
HE'D BE DOWN HERE, HUDDLING IN THE DARKNESS WITH US, INSTEAD OF SITTING IN A SHINY TOWER WAITING FOR THE MAID SERVICE TO TURN DOWN HIS BED.
I UNDERSTAND YOUR SITUATION, AND I ADMIRE YOUR DEVOTION TO THE MORLOCKS, ALEX.
WHEN ANY MEMBER OF A SOCIETY IS FORCED TO HIDE UNDERGROUND, LIVING ABOVE THEM AND IGNORING THEM IS SAYING IT'S OKAY.
BY IGNORING THEIR PLIGHT, WE ACCEPT THEIR STATION.
LIVING ABOVE THESE PEOPLE BECAUSE I CAN PASS AS A HUMAN WOULD MAKE ME COMPLICIT IN THEIR NEGLECT.
MY BROTHER LOST SIGHT OF THIS. LOST SIGHT OF WHAT XAVIER WAS TRYING TO TEACH US.

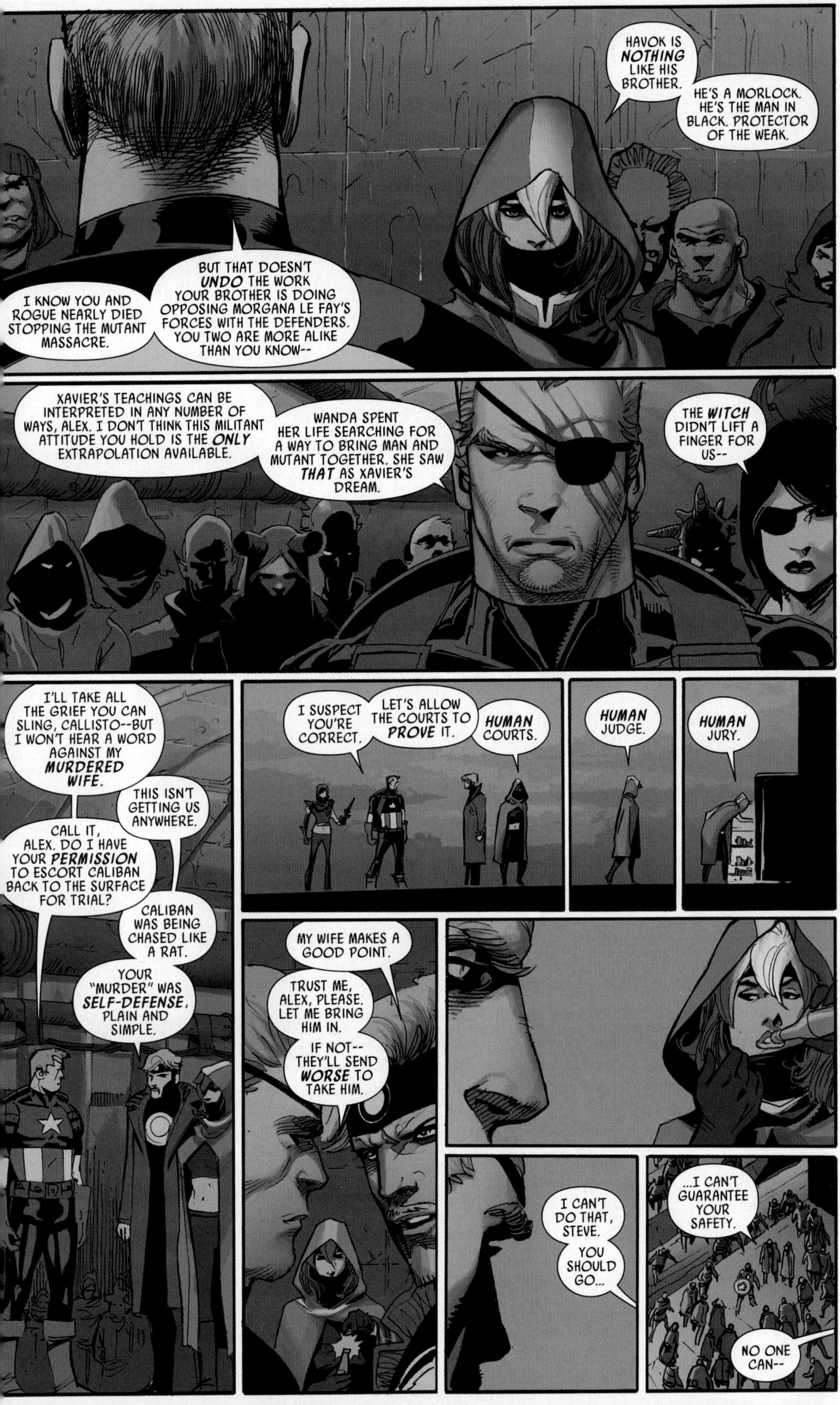
HAVOK IS NOTHING LIKE HIS BROTHER.
HE'S A MORLOCK. HE'S THE MAN IN BLACK. PROTECTOR OF THE WEAK.
I KNOW YOU AND ROGUE NEARLY DIED STOPPING THE MUTANT MASSACRE.
BUT THAT DOESN'T UNDO THE WORK YOUR BROTHER IS DOING OPPOSING MORGANA LE FAY'S FORCES WITH THE DEFENDERS. YOU TWO ARE MORE ALIKE THAN YOU KNOW--
XAVIER'S TEACHINGS CAN BE INTERPRETED IN ANY NUMBER OF WAYS, ALEX. I DON'T THINK THIS MILITANT ATTITUDE YOU HOLD IS THE ONLY EXTRAPOLATION AVAILABLE.
WANDA SPENT HER LIFE SEARCHING FOR A WAY TO BRING MAN AND MUTANT TOGETHER. SHE SAW THAT AS XAVIER'S DREAM.
THE WITCH DIDN'T LIFT A FINGER FOR US--
I'LL TAKE ALL THE GRIEF YOU CAN SLING, CALLISTO--BUT I WON'T HEAR A WORD AGAINST MY MURDERED WIFE.
THIS ISN'T GETTING US ANYWHERE.
CALL IT, ALEX. DO I HAVE YOUR PERMISSION TO ESCORT CALIBAN BACK TO THE SURFACE FOR TRIAL?
CALIBAN WAS BEING CHASED LIKE A RAT.
YOUR "MURDER" WAS SELF-DEFENSE, PLAIN AND SIMPLE.
I SUSPECT YOU'RE CORRECT.
LET'S ALLOW THE COURTS TO PROVE IT.
HUMAN COURTS.
HUMAN JUDGE.
HUMAN JURY.
MY WIFE MAKES A GOOD POINT.
TRUST ME, ALEX, PLEASE. LET ME BRING HIM IN.
IF NOT-- THEY'LL SEND WORSE TO TAKE HIM.
I CAN'T DO THAT, STEVE.
YOU SHOULD GO...
...I CAN'T GUARANTEE YOUR SAFETY.
NO ONE CAN--

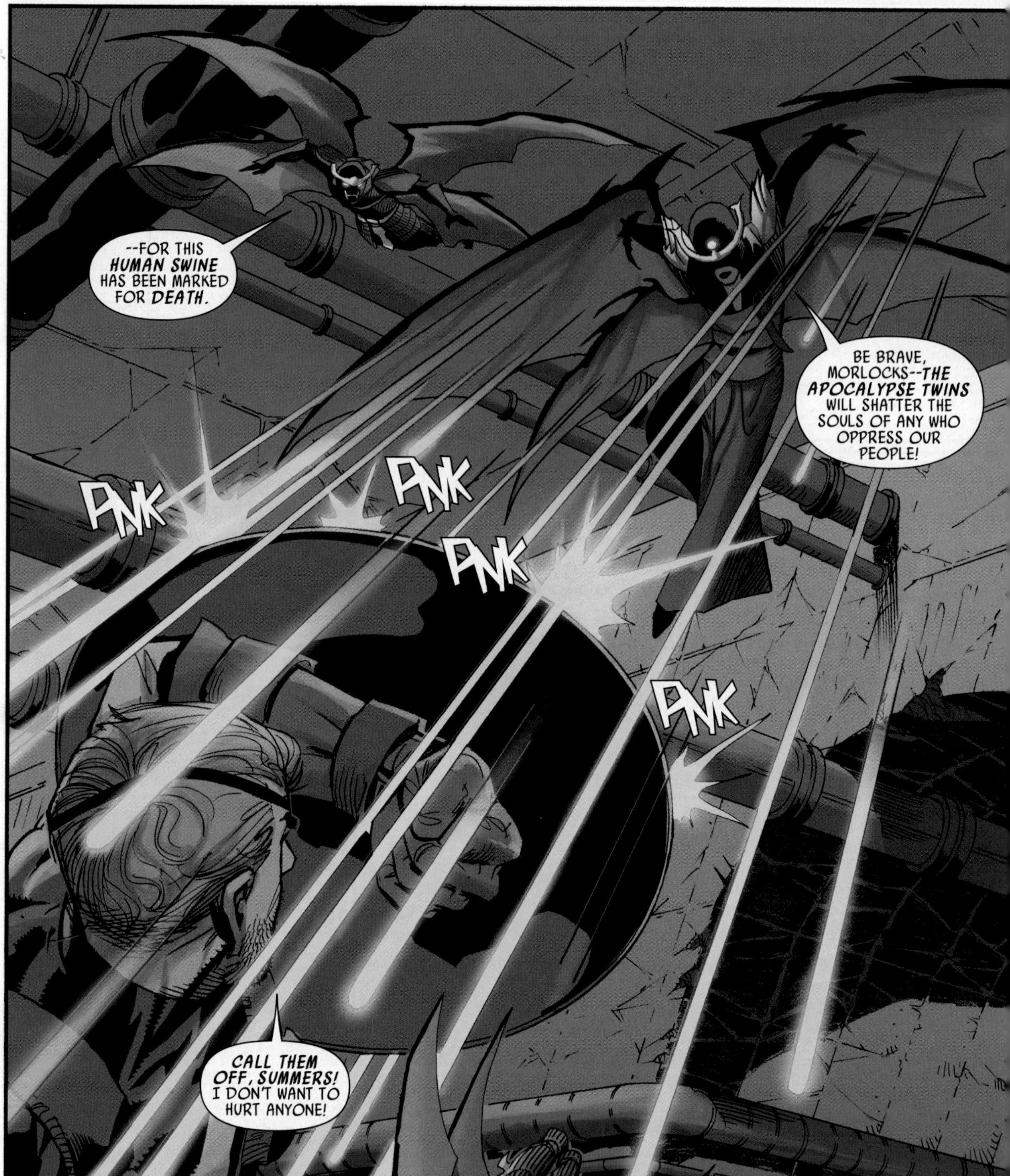
--FOR THIS HUMAN SWINE HAS BEEN MARKED FOR DEATH.
BE BRAVE, MORLOCKS--THE APOCALYPSE TWINS WILL SHATTER THE SOULS OF ANY WHO OPPRESS OUR PEOPLE!
PNK
PNK
PNK
PNK
CALL THEM OFF, SUMMERS! I DON'T WANT TO HURT ANYONE!
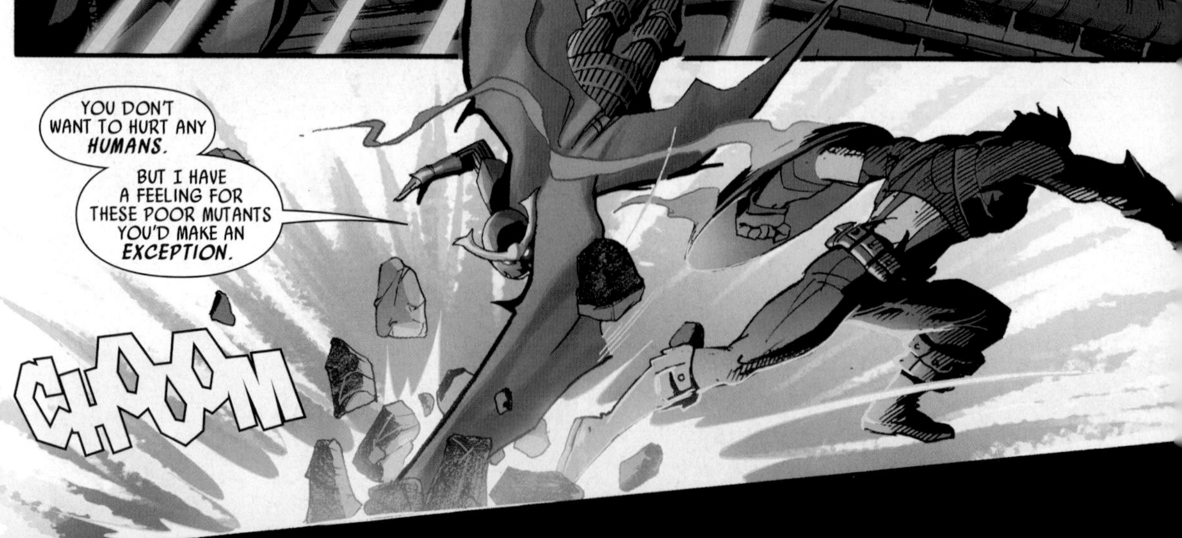
YOU DON'T WANT TO HURT ANY HUMANS.
BUT I HAVE A FEELING FOR THESE POOR MUTANTS YOU'D MAKE AN EXCEPTION.
CHOOOM

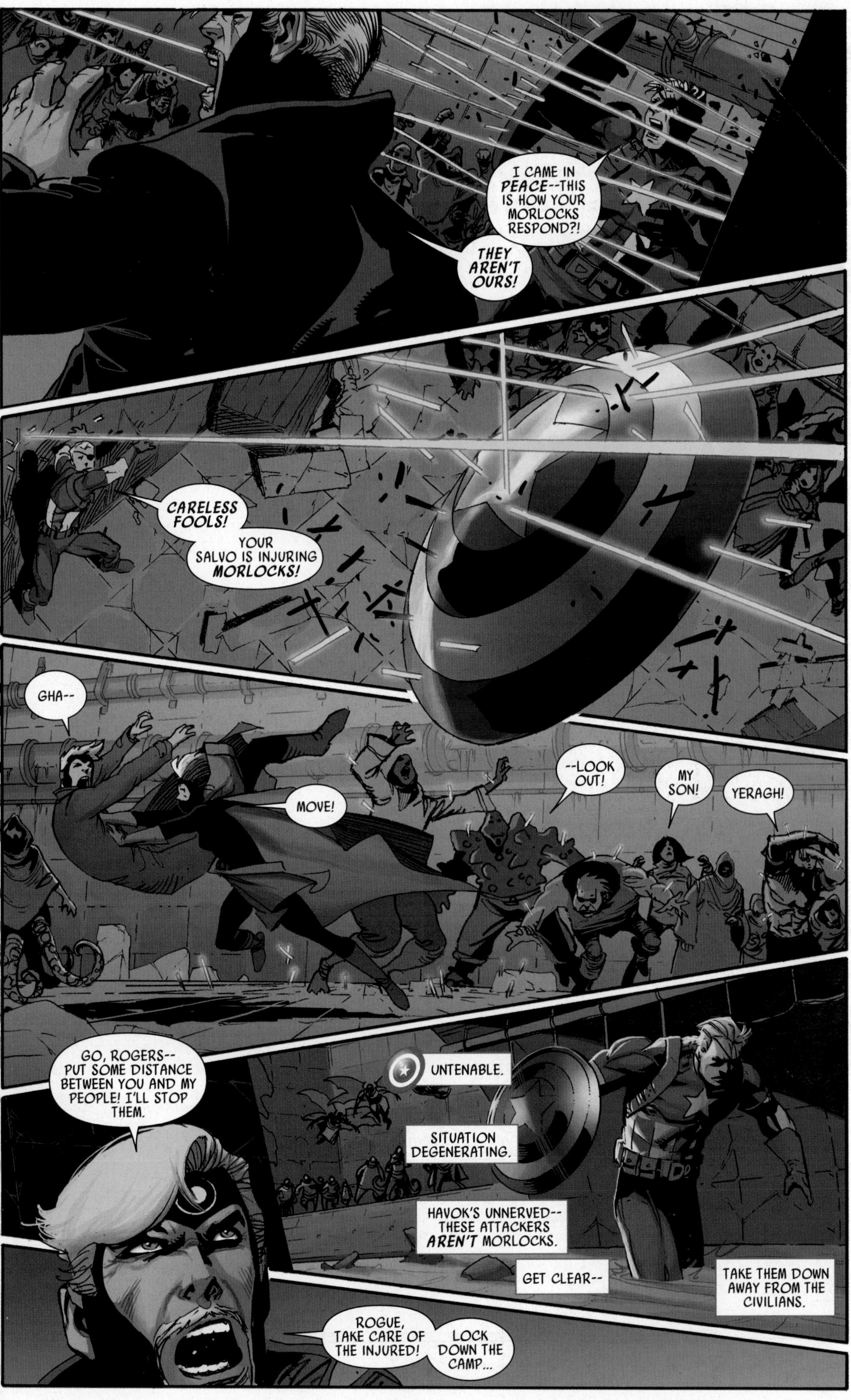
I CAME IN PEACE--THIS IS HOW YOUR MORLOCKS RESPOND?!
THEY AREN'T OURS!
CARELESS FOOLS!
YOUR SALVO IS INJURING MORLOCKS!
GHA--
MOVE!
--LOOK OUT!
MY SON!
YERAGH!
GO, ROGERS--PUT SOME DISTANCE BETWEEN YOU AND MY PEOPLE! I'LL STOP THEM.
UNTENABLE.
SITUATION DEGENERATING.
HAVOK'S UNNERVED--THESE ATTACKERS AREN'T MORLOCKS.
GET CLEAR--
TAKE THEM DOWN AWAY FROM THE CIVILIANS.
ROGUE, TAKE CARE OF THE INJURED!
LOCK DOWN THE CAMP...

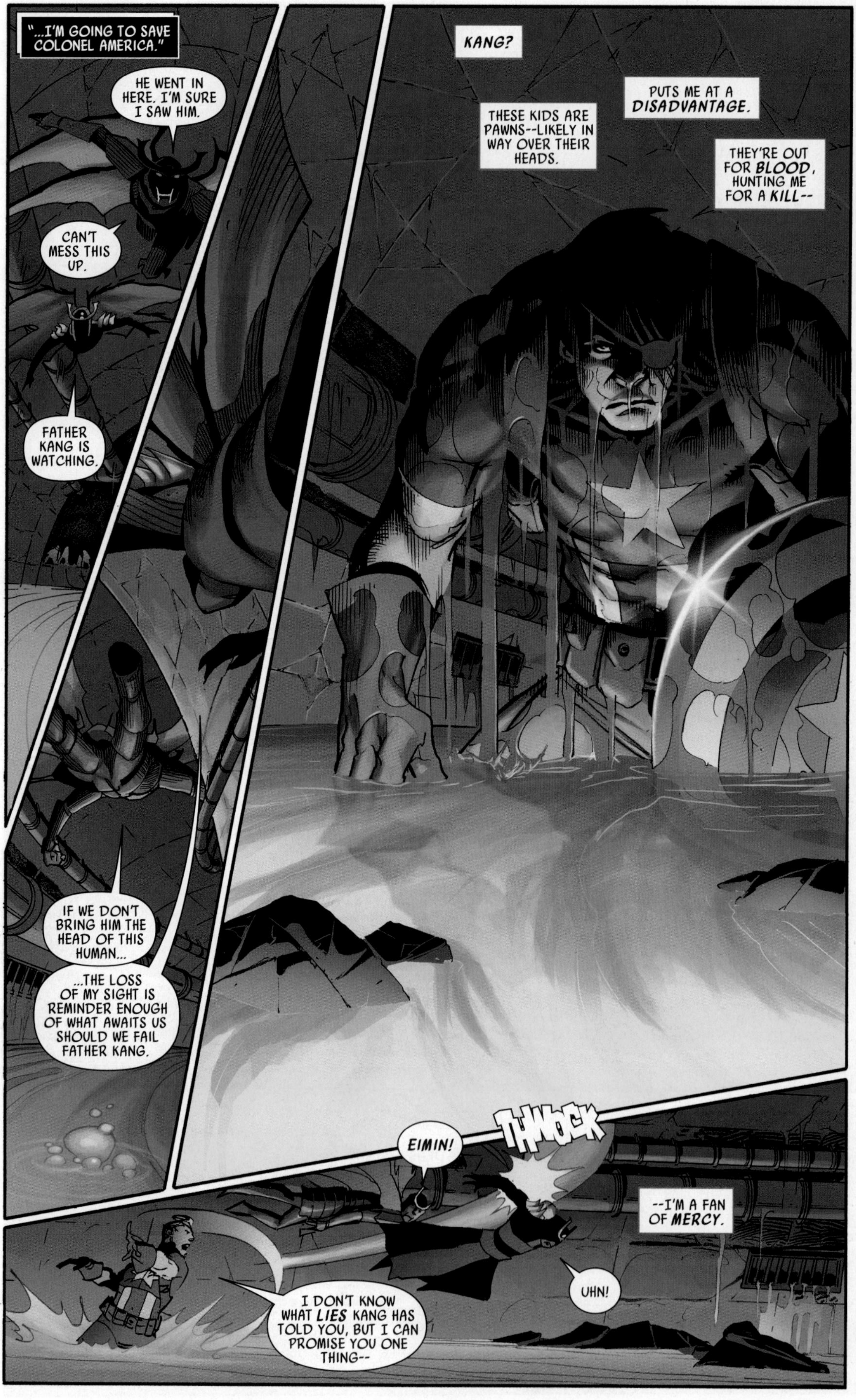
"...I'M GOING TO SAVE COLONEL AMERICA."
HE WENT IN HERE. I'M SURE I SAW HIM.
CAN'T MESS THIS UP.
FATHER KANG IS WATCHING.
IF WE DON'T BRING HIM THE HEAD OF THIS HUMAN...
...THE LOSS OF MY SIGHT IS REMINDER ENOUGH OF WHAT AWAITS US SHOULD WE FAIL FATHER KANG.
KANG?
THESE KIDS ARE PAWNS--LIKELY IN WAY OVER THEIR HEADS.
PUTS ME AT A DISADVANTAGE.
THEY'RE OUT FOR BLOOD, HUNTING ME FOR A KILL--
I DON'T KNOW WHAT LIES KANG HAS TOLD YOU, BUT I CAN PROMISE YOU ONE THING--
EIMIN!
THWOCK
UHN!
--I'M A FAN OF MERCY.

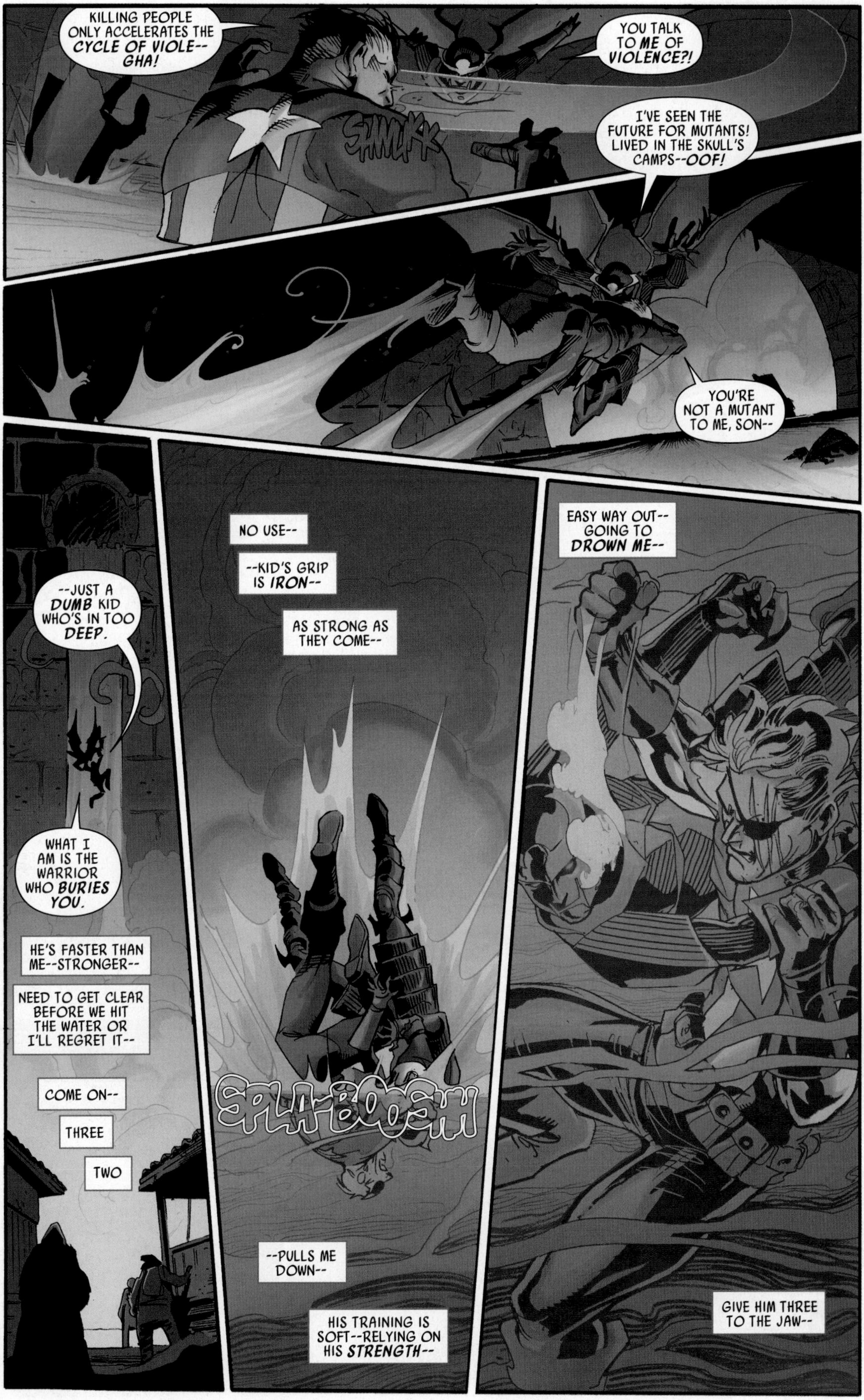
KILLING PEOPLE ONLY ACCELERATES THE CYCLE OF VIOLE--GHA!
SHNLKK
YOU TALK TO ME OF VIOLENCE?!
I'VE SEEN THE FUTURE FOR MUTANTS! LIVED IN THE SKULL'S CAMPS--OOF!
YOU'RE NOT A MUTANT TO ME, SON--
--JUST A DUMB KID WHO'S IN TOO DEEP.
WHAT I AM IS THE WARRIOR WHO BURIES YOU.
HE'S FASTER THAN ME--STRONGER--
NEED TO GET CLEAR BEFORE WE HIT THE WATER OR I'LL REGRET IT--
COME ON--
THREE
TWO
NO USE--
--KID'S GRIP IS IRON--
AS STRONG AS THEY COME--
SPLA-BOOSH
--PULLS ME DOWN--
HIS TRAINING IS SOFT--RELYING ON HIS STRENGTH--
EASY WAY OUT--GOING TO DROWN ME--
GIVE HIM THREE TO THE JAW--

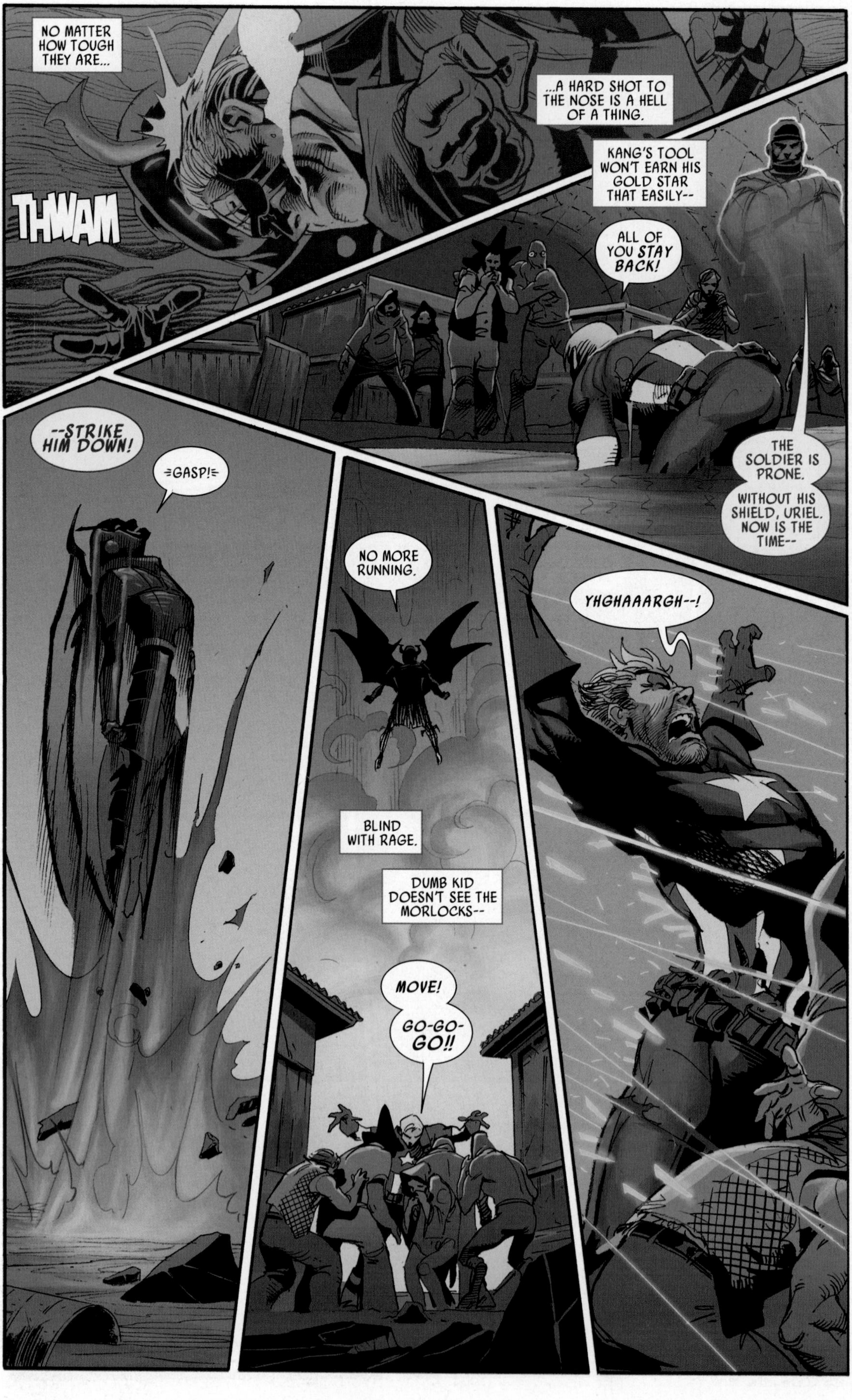
NO MATTER HOW TOUGH THEY ARE...
THWAM
...A HARD SHOT TO THE NOSE IS A HELL OF A THING.
KANG'S TOOL WON'T EARN HIS GOLD STAR THAT EASILY--
ALL OF YOU STAY BACK!
THE SOLDIER IS PRONE.
WITHOUT HIS SHIELD, URIEL, NOW IS THE TIME--
--STRIKE HIM DOWN!
=GASP!=
NO MORE RUNNING.
BLIND WITH RAGE.
DUMB KID DOESN'T SEE THE MORLOCKS--
MOVE!
GO-GO-GO!!
YHGHAAARGH--!

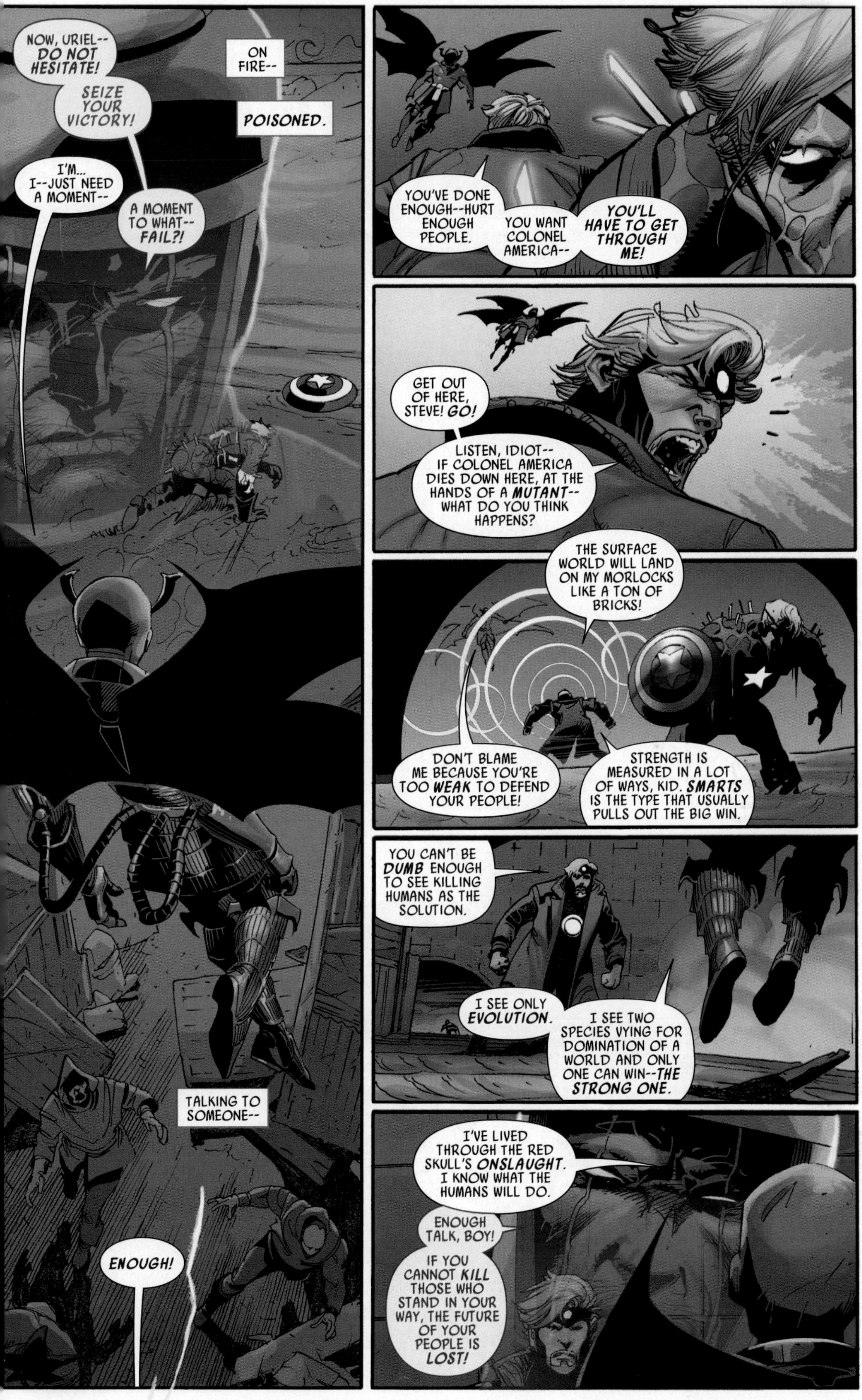
NOW, URIEL-- DO NOT HESITATE!
SEIZE YOUR VICTORY!
ON FIRE--
POISONED.
I'M... I--JUST NEED A MOMENT--
A MOMENT TO WHAT-- FAIL?!
TALKING TO SOMEONE--
ENOUGH!
YOU'VE DONE ENOUGH--HURT ENOUGH PEOPLE.
YOU WANT COLONEL AMERICA--
YOU'LL HAVE TO GET THROUGH ME!
GET OUT OF HERE, STEVE! GO!
LISTEN, IDIOT-- IF COLONEL AMERICA DIES DOWN HERE, AT THE HANDS OF A MUTANT-- WHAT DO YOU THINK HAPPENS?
THE SURFACE WORLD WILL LAND ON MY MORLOCKS LIKE A TON OF BRICKS!
DON'T BLAME ME BECAUSE YOU'RE TOO WEAK TO DEFEND YOUR PEOPLE!
STRENGTH IS MEASURED IN A LOT OF WAYS, KID. SMARTS IS THE TYPE THAT USUALLY PULLS OUT THE BIG WIN.
YOU CAN'T BE DUMB ENOUGH TO SEE KILLING HUMANS AS THE SOLUTION.
I SEE ONLY EVOLUTION.
I SEE TWO SPECIES VYING FOR DOMINATION OF A WORLD AND ONLY ONE CAN WIN--THE STRONG ONE.
I'VE LIVED THROUGH THE RED SKULL'S ONSLAUGHT. I KNOW WHAT THE HUMANS WILL DO.
ENOUGH TALK, BOY!
IF YOU CANNOT KILL THOSE WHO STAND IN YOUR WAY, THE FUTURE OF YOUR PEOPLE IS LOST!

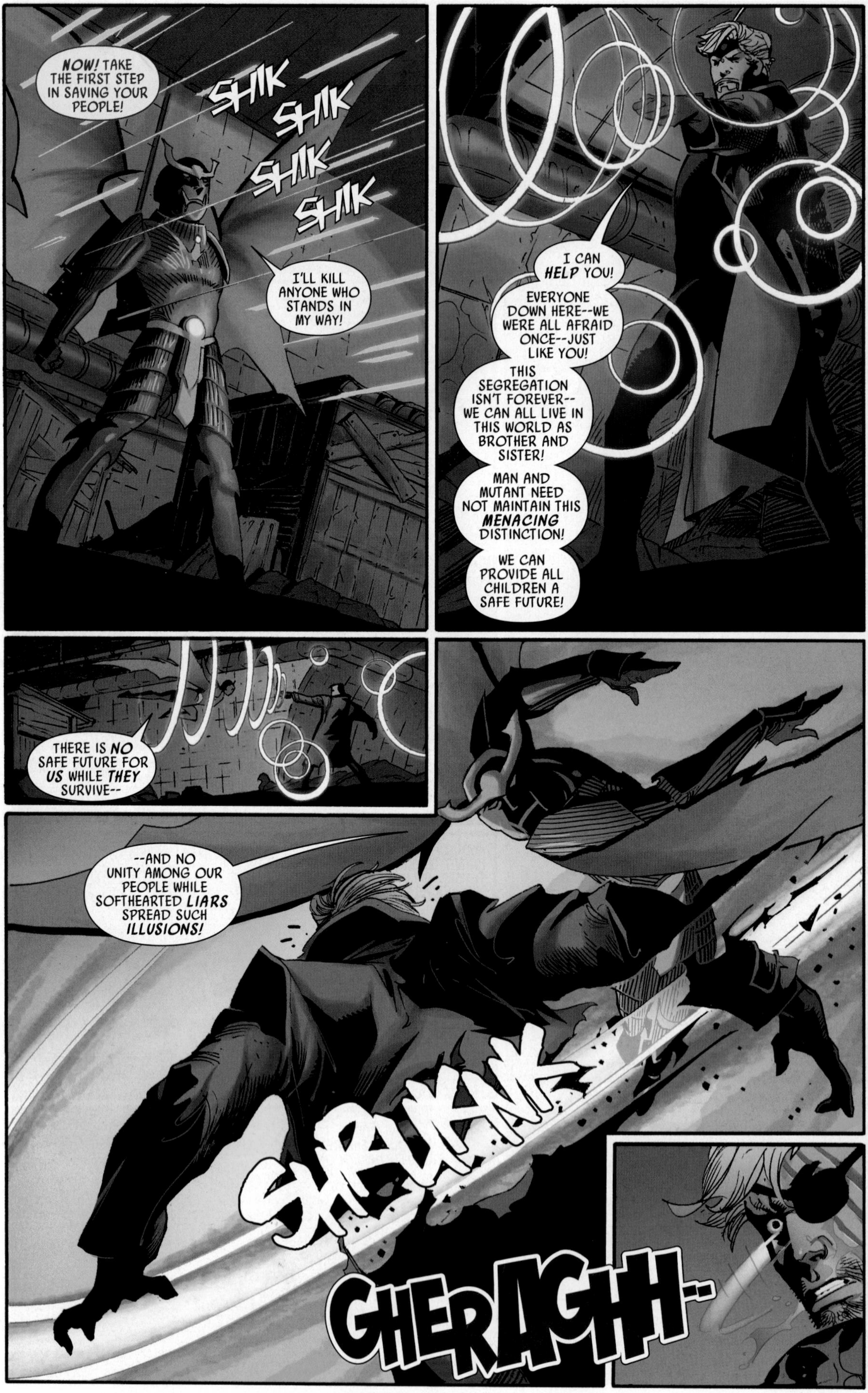
NOW! TAKE THE FIRST STEP IN SAVING YOUR PEOPLE!
SHIK SHIK SHIK SHIK
I'LL KILL ANYONE WHO STANDS IN MY WAY!
I CAN HELP YOU!
EVERYONE DOWN HERE--WE WERE ALL AFRAID ONCE--JUST LIKE YOU!
THIS SEGREGATION ISN'T FOREVER--WE CAN ALL LIVE IN THIS WORLD AS BROTHER AND SISTER!
MAN AND MUTANT NEED NOT MAINTAIN THIS MENACING DISTINCTION!
WE CAN PROVIDE ALL CHILDREN A SAFE FUTURE!
THERE IS NO SAFE FUTURE FOR US WHILE THEY SURVIVE--
--AND NO UNITY AMONG OUR PEOPLE WHILE SOFTHEARTED LIARS SPREAD SUCH ILLUSIONS!
SHRUKNK
GHERAGHH-

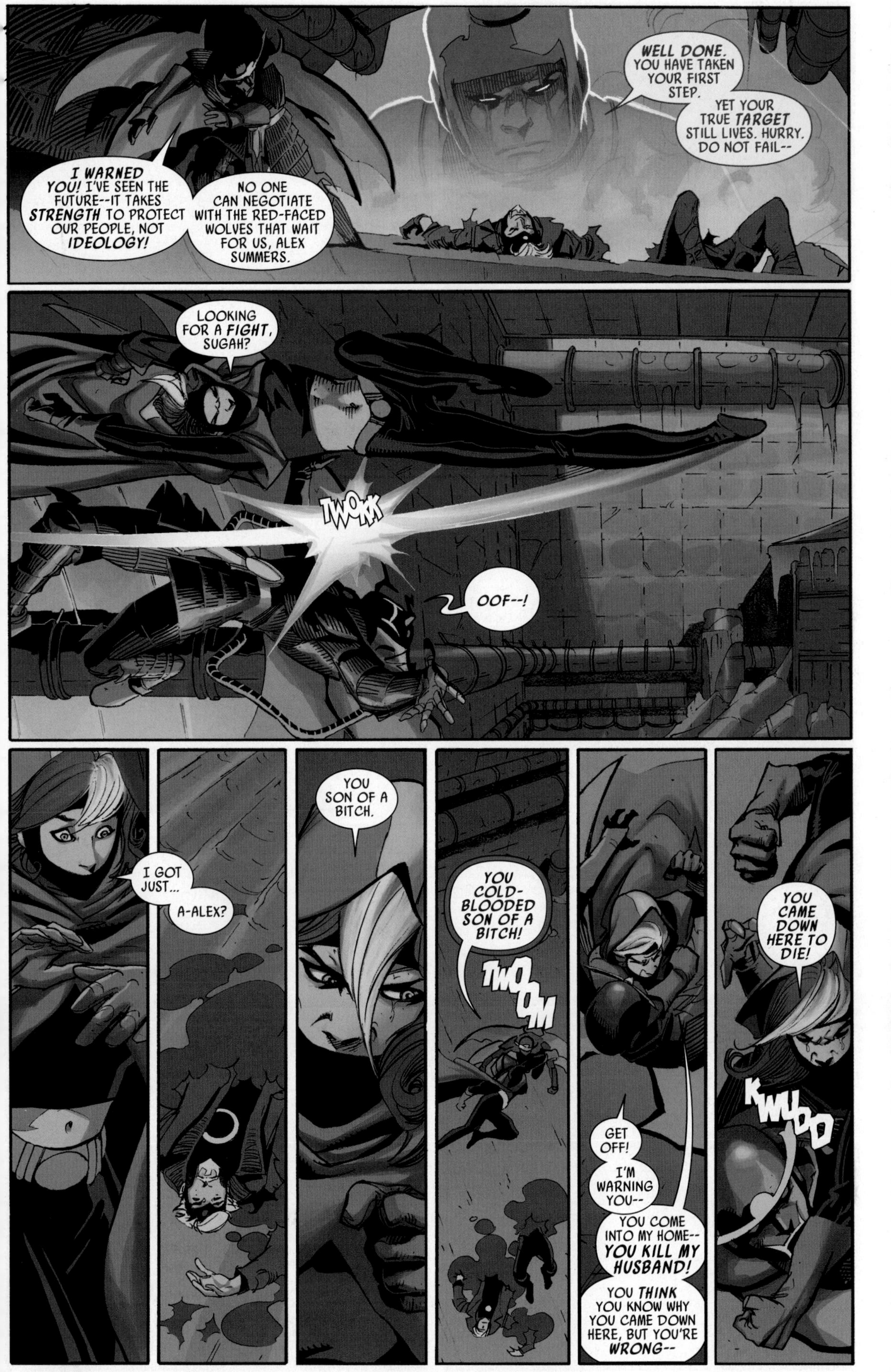
WELL DONE. YOU HAVE TAKEN YOUR FIRST STEP.
YET YOUR TRUE TARGET STILL LIVES. HURRY. DO NOT FAIL--
I WARNED YOU! I'VE SEEN THE FUTURE--IT TAKES STRENGTH TO PROTECT OUR PEOPLE, NOT IDEOLOGY!
NO ONE CAN NEGOTIATE WITH THE RED-FACED WOLVES THAT WAIT FOR US, ALEX SUMMERS.
LOOKING FOR A FIGHT, SUGAH?
TWOKK
OOF--!
I GOT JUST...
A-ALEX?
YOU SON OF A BITCH.
YOU COLD-BLOODED SON OF A BITCH!
TWOOM
GET OFF!
I'M WARNING YOU--
YOU COME INTO MY HOME-- YOU KILL MY HUSBAND!
YOU THINK YOU KNOW WHY YOU CAME DOWN HERE, BUT YOU'RE WRONG--
YOU CAME DOWN HERE TO DIE!
KWUDD

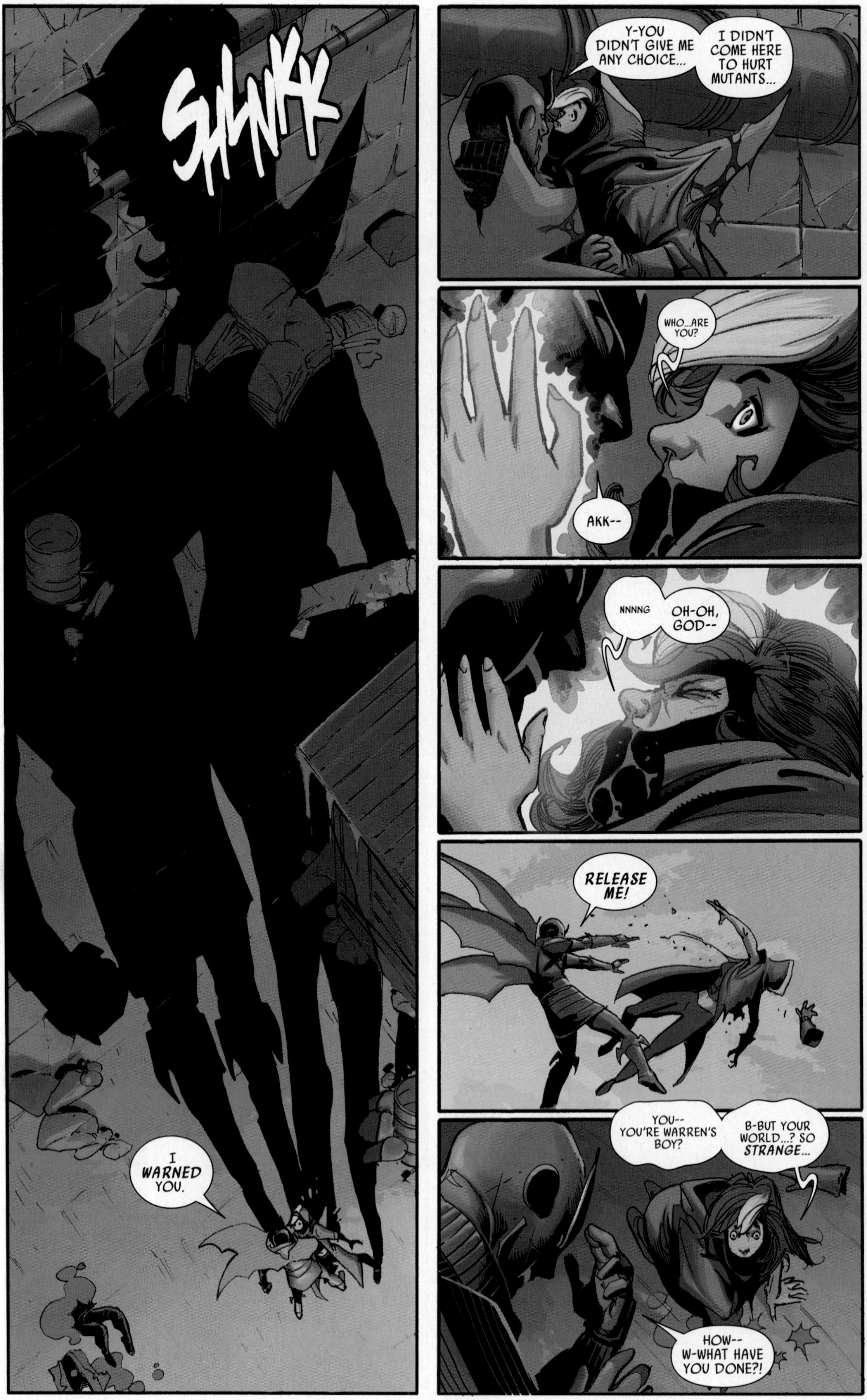
SHNKK
I WARNED YOU.
Y-YOU DIDN'T GIVE ME ANY CHOICE...
I DIDN'T COME HERE TO HURT MUTANTS...
WHO...ARE YOU?
AKK--
NNNNG
OH-OH, GOD--
RELEASE ME!
YOU-- YOU'RE WARREN'S BOY?
B-BUT YOUR WORLD...? SO STRANGE...
HOW-- W-WHAT HAVE YOU DONE?!

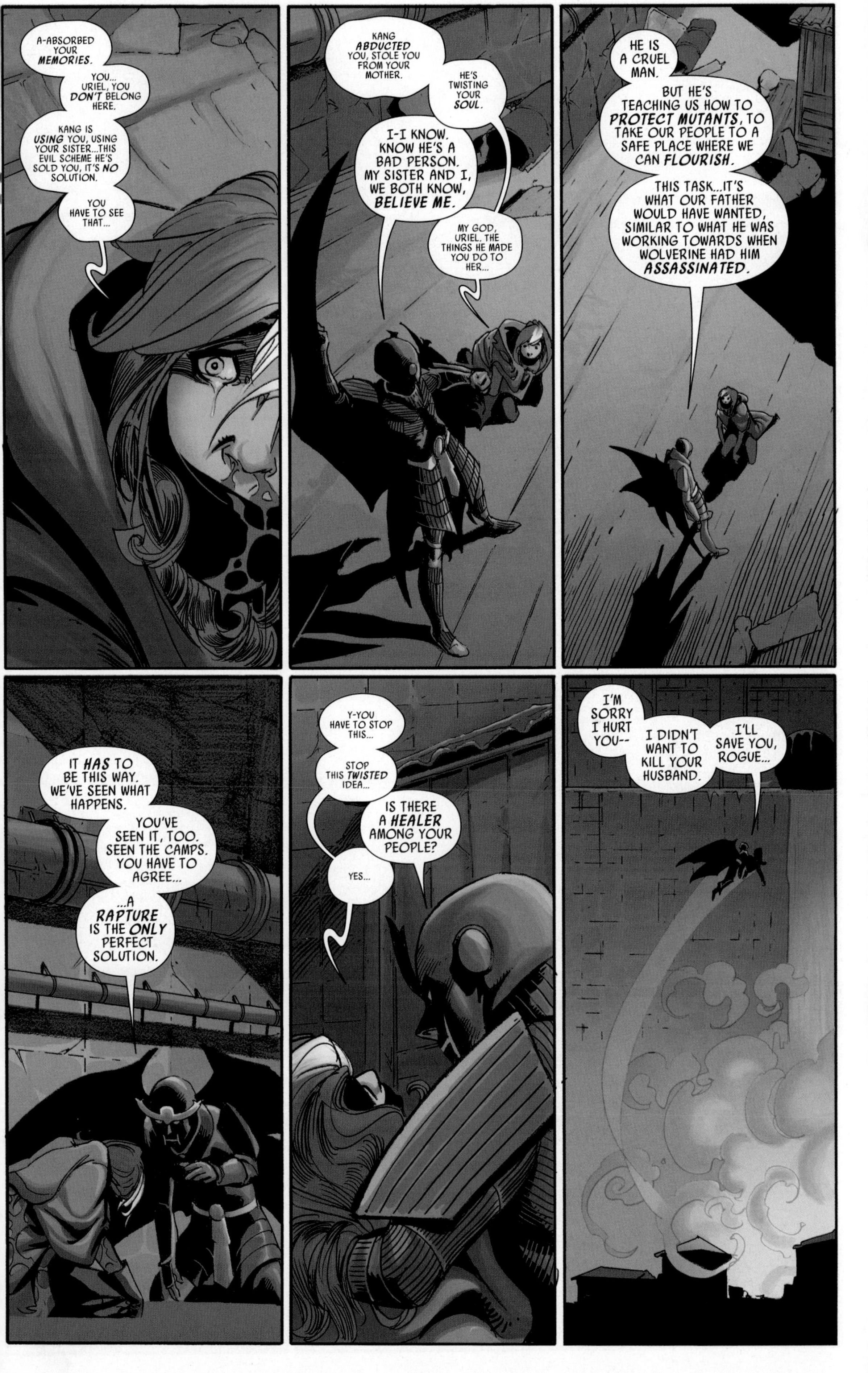
A-ABSORBED YOUR MEMORIES.
YOU... URIEL, YOU DON'T BELONG HERE.
KANG IS USING YOU, USING YOUR SISTER...THIS EVIL SCHEME HE'S SOLD YOU, IT'S NO SOLUTION.
YOU HAVE TO SEE THAT...
KANG ABDUCTED YOU, STOLE YOU FROM YOUR MOTHER.
HE'S TWISTING YOUR SOUL.
I-I KNOW. KNOW HE'S A BAD PERSON. MY SISTER AND I, WE BOTH KNOW, BELIEVE ME.
MY GOD, URIEL, THE THINGS HE MADE YOU DO TO HER...
HE IS A CRUEL MAN.
BUT HE'S TEACHING US HOW TO PROTECT MUTANTS, TO TAKE OUR PEOPLE TO A SAFE PLACE WHERE WE CAN FLOURISH.
THIS TASK...IT'S WHAT OUR FATHER WOULD HAVE WANTED, SIMILAR TO WHAT HE WAS WORKING TOWARDS WHEN WOLVERINE HAD HIM ASSASSINATED.
IT HAS TO BE THIS WAY. WE'VE SEEN WHAT HAPPENS.
YOU'VE SEEN IT, TOO. SEEN THE CAMPS. YOU HAVE TO AGREE...
...A RAPTURE IS THE ONLY PERFECT SOLUTION.
Y-YOU HAVE TO STOP THIS...
STOP THIS TWISTED IDEA...
IS THERE A HEALER AMONG YOUR PEOPLE?
YES...
I'M SORRY I HURT YOU--
I DIDN'T WANT TO KILL YOUR HUSBAND.
I'LL SAVE YOU, ROGUE...

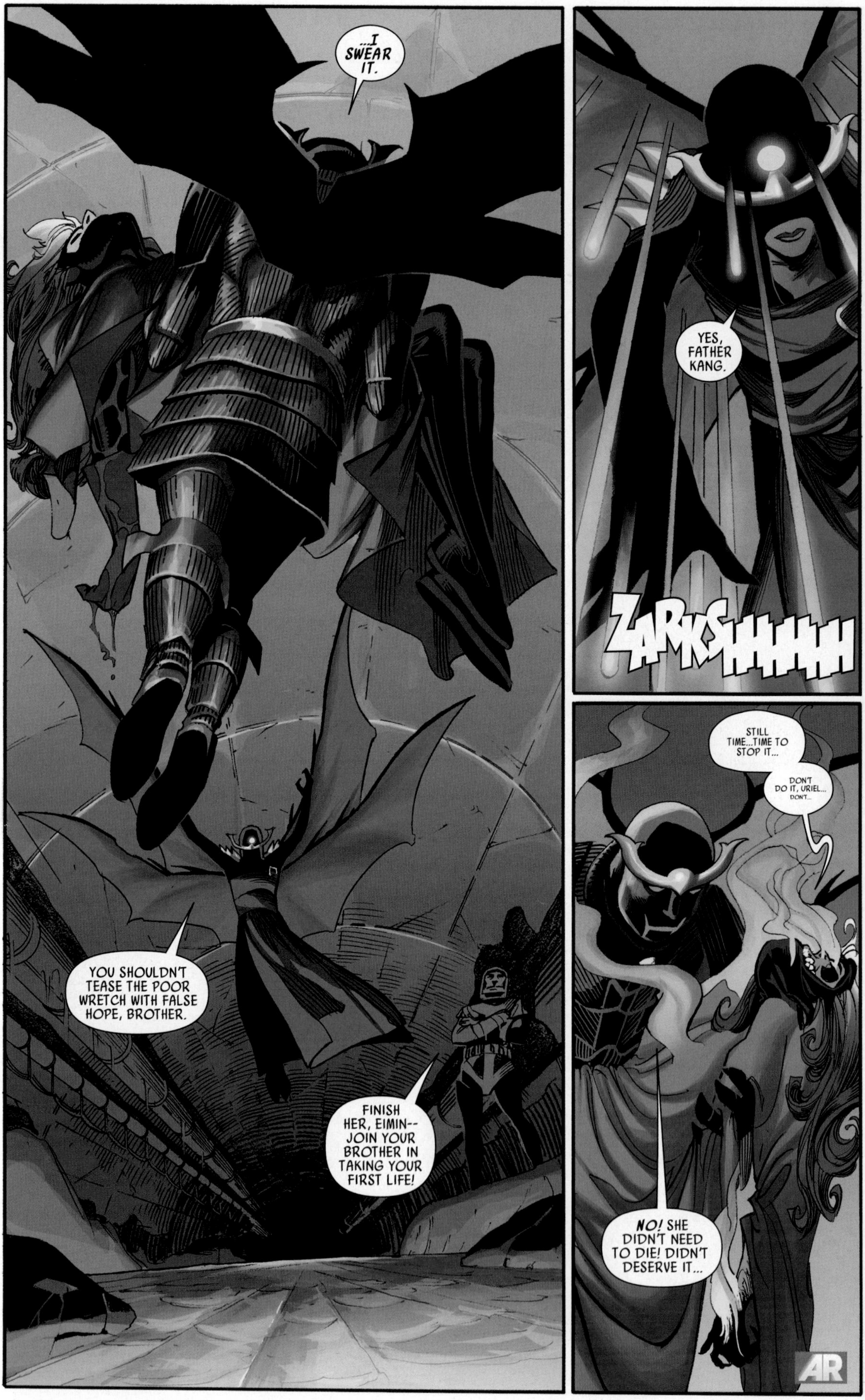

...I SWEAR IT.
YOU SHOULDN'T TEASE THE POOR WRETCH WITH FALSE HOPE, BROTHER.
FINISH HER, EIMIN-- JOIN YOUR BROTHER IN TAKING YOUR FIRST LIFE!
YES, FATHER KANG.
ZARKSHHHHHH
STILL TIME...TIME TO STOP IT...
DON'T DO IT, URIEL... DON'T...
NO! SHE DIDN'T NEED TO DIE! DIDN'T DESERVE IT...

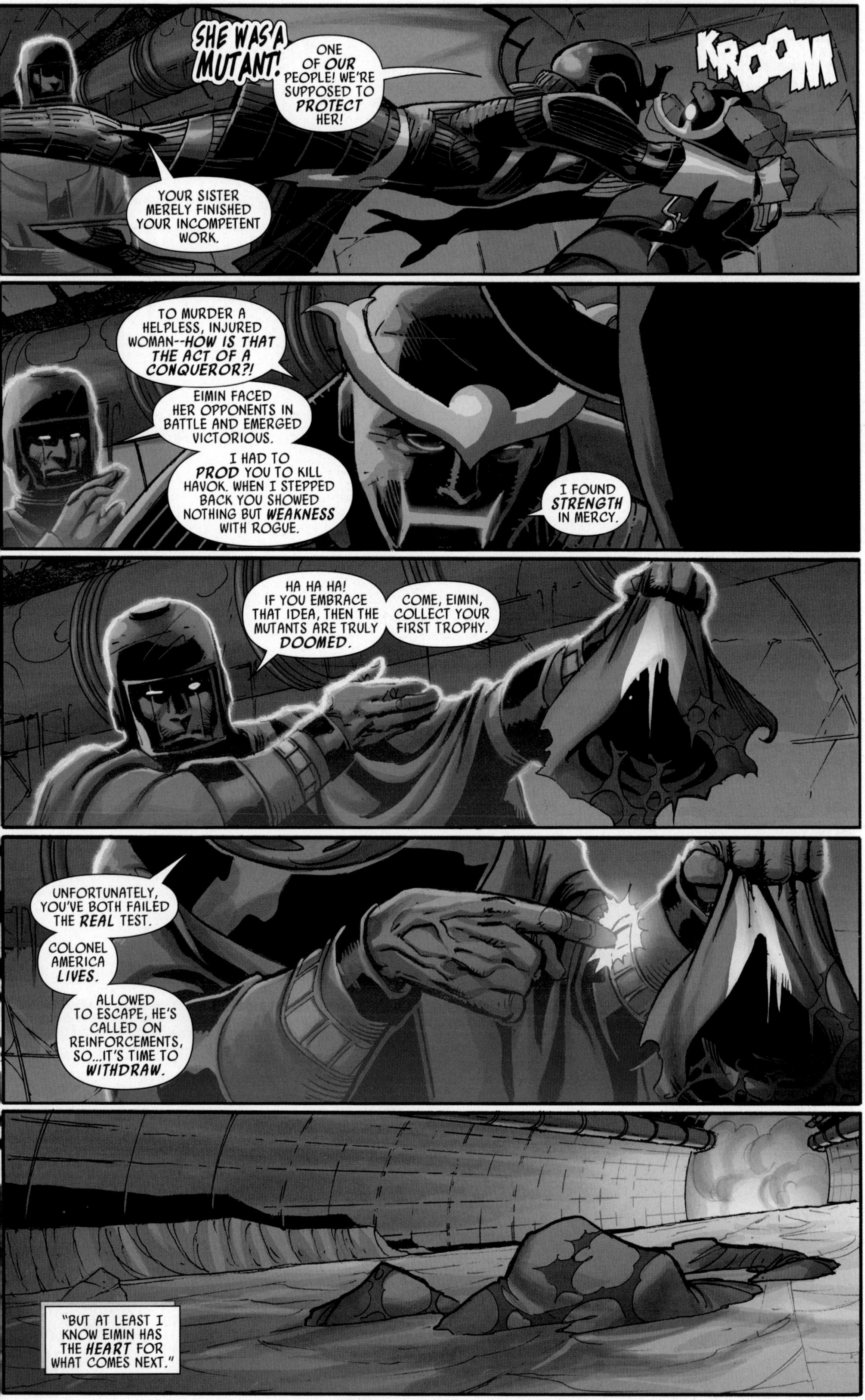
SHE WAS A MUTANT!
ONE OF OUR PEOPLE! WE'RE SUPPOSED TO PROTECT HER!
KROOM
YOUR SISTER MERELY FINISHED YOUR INCOMPETENT WORK.
TO MURDER A HELPLESS, INJURED WOMAN--HOW IS THAT THE ACT OF A CONQUEROR?!
EIMIN FACED HER OPPONENTS IN BATTLE AND EMERGED VICTORIOUS.
I HAD TO PROD YOU TO KILL HAVOK. WHEN I STEPPED BACK YOU SHOWED NOTHING BUT WEAKNESS WITH ROGUE.
I FOUND STRENGTH IN MERCY.
HA HA HA! IF YOU EMBRACE THAT IDEA, THEN THE MUTANTS ARE TRULY DOOMED.
COME, EIMIN, COLLECT YOUR FIRST TROPHY.
UNFORTUNATELY, YOU'VE BOTH FAILED THE REAL TEST.
COLONEL AMERICA LIVES.
ALLOWED TO ESCAPE, HE'S CALLED ON REINFORCEMENTS, SO...IT'S TIME TO WITHDRAW.
"BUT AT LEAST I KNOW EIMIN HAS THE HEART FOR WHAT COMES NEXT."

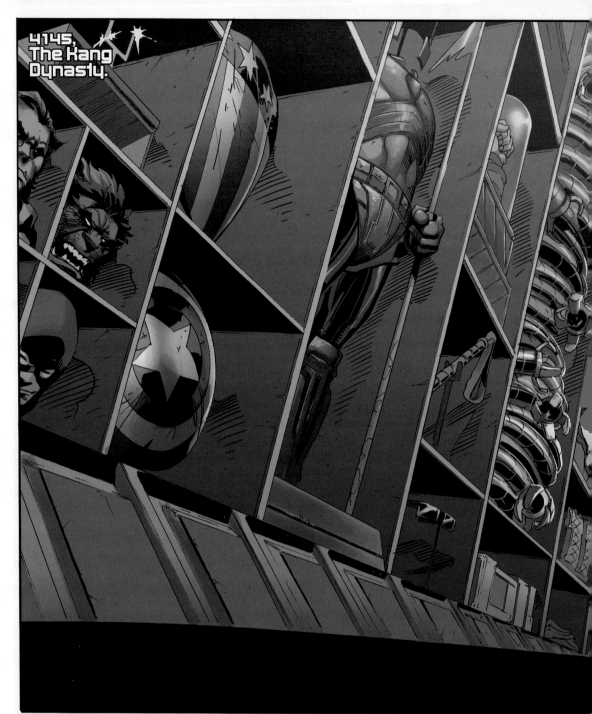

I-I'M SORRY, FATHER KANG. PLEASE...

QUIET YOUR *SNIVELING.* NEVER BE *SORRY*...

...BE *VICTORIOUS.*

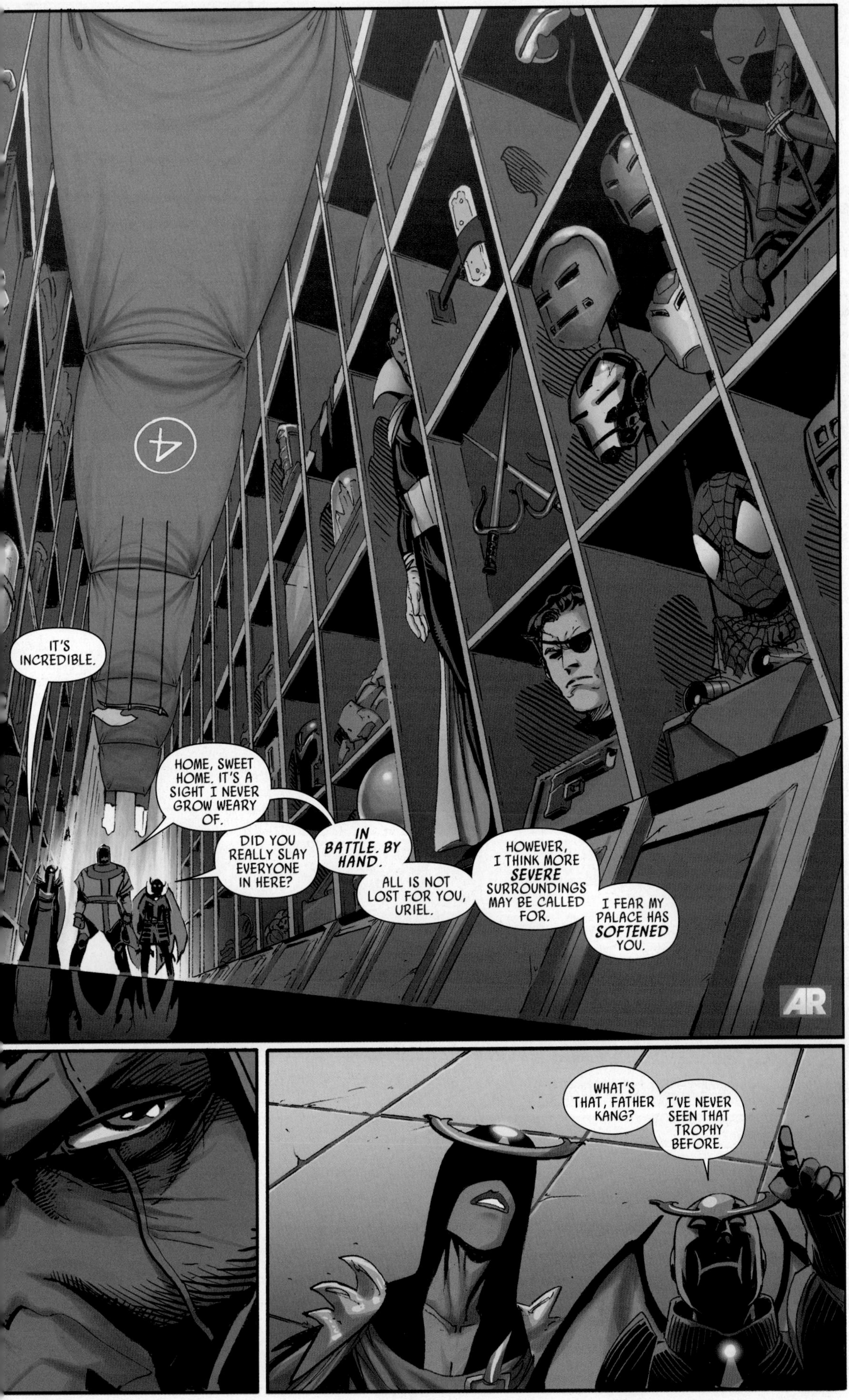
IT'S INCREDIBLE.
HOME, SWEET HOME. IT'S A SIGHT I NEVER GROW WEARY OF.
DID YOU REALLY SLAY EVERYONE IN HERE?
IN BATTLE. BY HAND.
ALL IS NOT LOST FOR YOU, URIEL.
HOWEVER, I THINK MORE ***SEVERE*** SURROUNDINGS MAY BE CALLED FOR.
I FEAR MY PALACE HAS ***SOFTENED*** YOU.
WHAT'S THAT, FATHER KANG?
I'VE NEVER SEEN THAT TROPHY BEFORE.

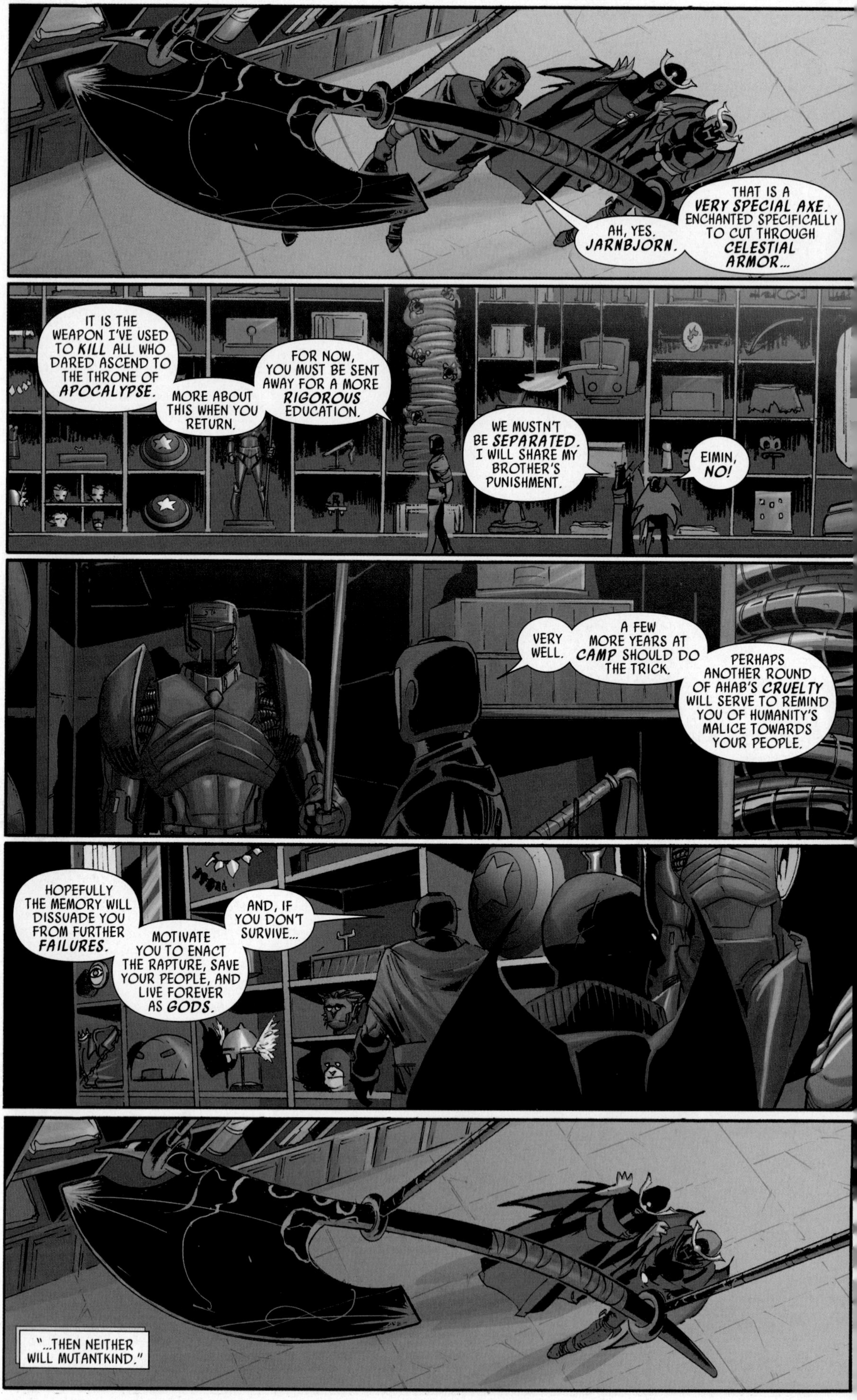
AH, YES. JARNBJORN.
THAT IS A VERY SPECIAL AXE. ENCHANTED SPECIFICALLY TO CUT THROUGH CELESTIAL ARMOR...
IT IS THE WEAPON I'VE USED TO KILL ALL WHO DARED ASCEND TO THE THRONE OF APOCALYPSE.
MORE ABOUT THIS WHEN YOU RETURN.
FOR NOW, YOU MUST BE SENT AWAY FOR A MORE RIGOROUS EDUCATION.
WE MUSTN'T BE SEPARATED. I WILL SHARE MY BROTHER'S PUNISHMENT.
EIMIN, NO!
VERY WELL.
A FEW MORE YEARS AT CAMP SHOULD DO THE TRICK.
PERHAPS ANOTHER ROUND OF AHAB'S CRUELTY WILL SERVE TO REMIND YOU OF HUMANITY'S MALICE TOWARDS YOUR PEOPLE.
HOPEFULLY THE MEMORY WILL DISSUADE YOU FROM FURTHER FAILURES.
MOTIVATE YOU TO ENACT THE RAPTURE, SAVE YOUR PEOPLE, AND LIVE FOREVER AS GODS.
AND, IF YOU DON'T SURVIVE...
"...THEN NEITHER WILL MUTANTKIND."

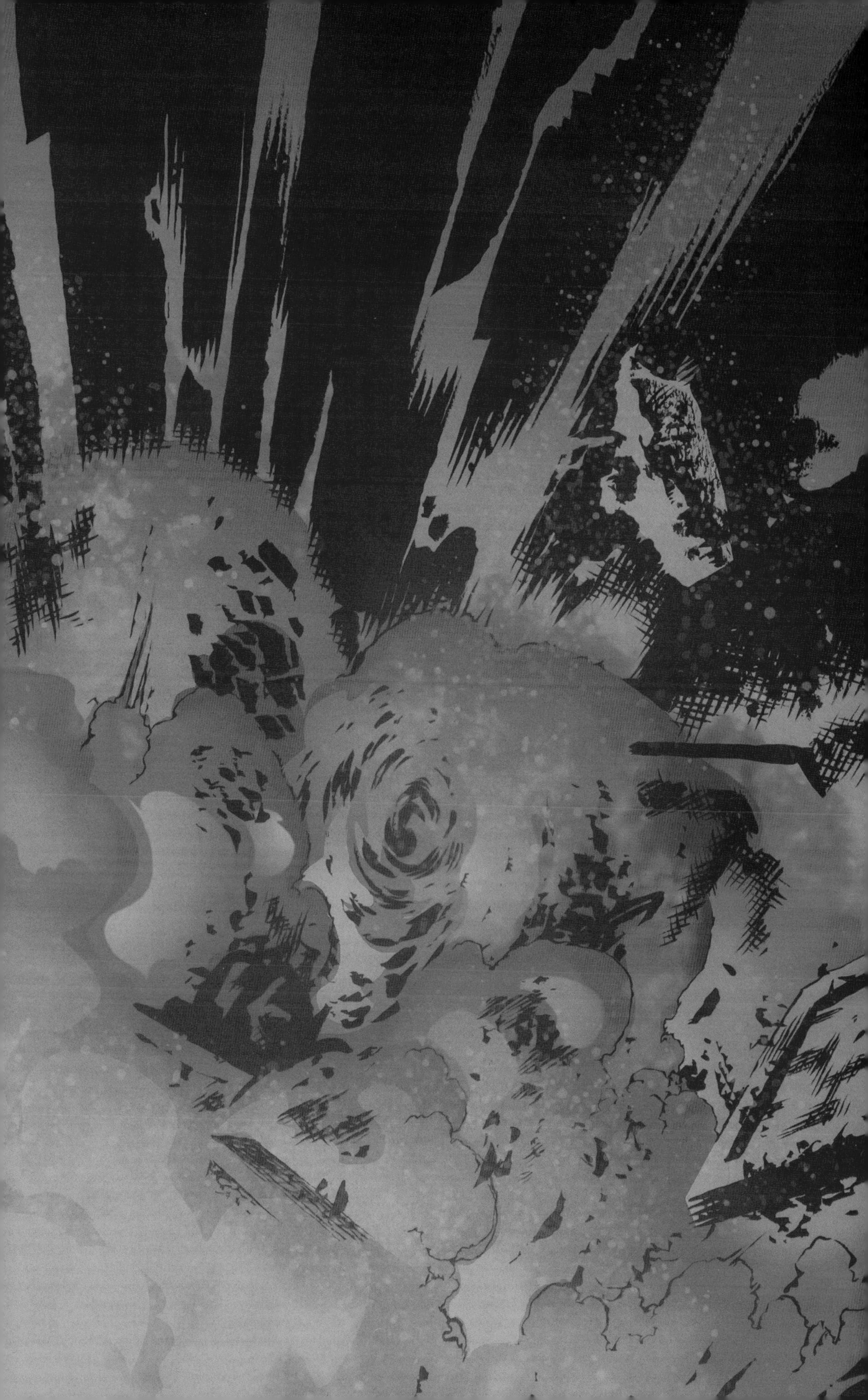

UNCANNY AVENGERS #7

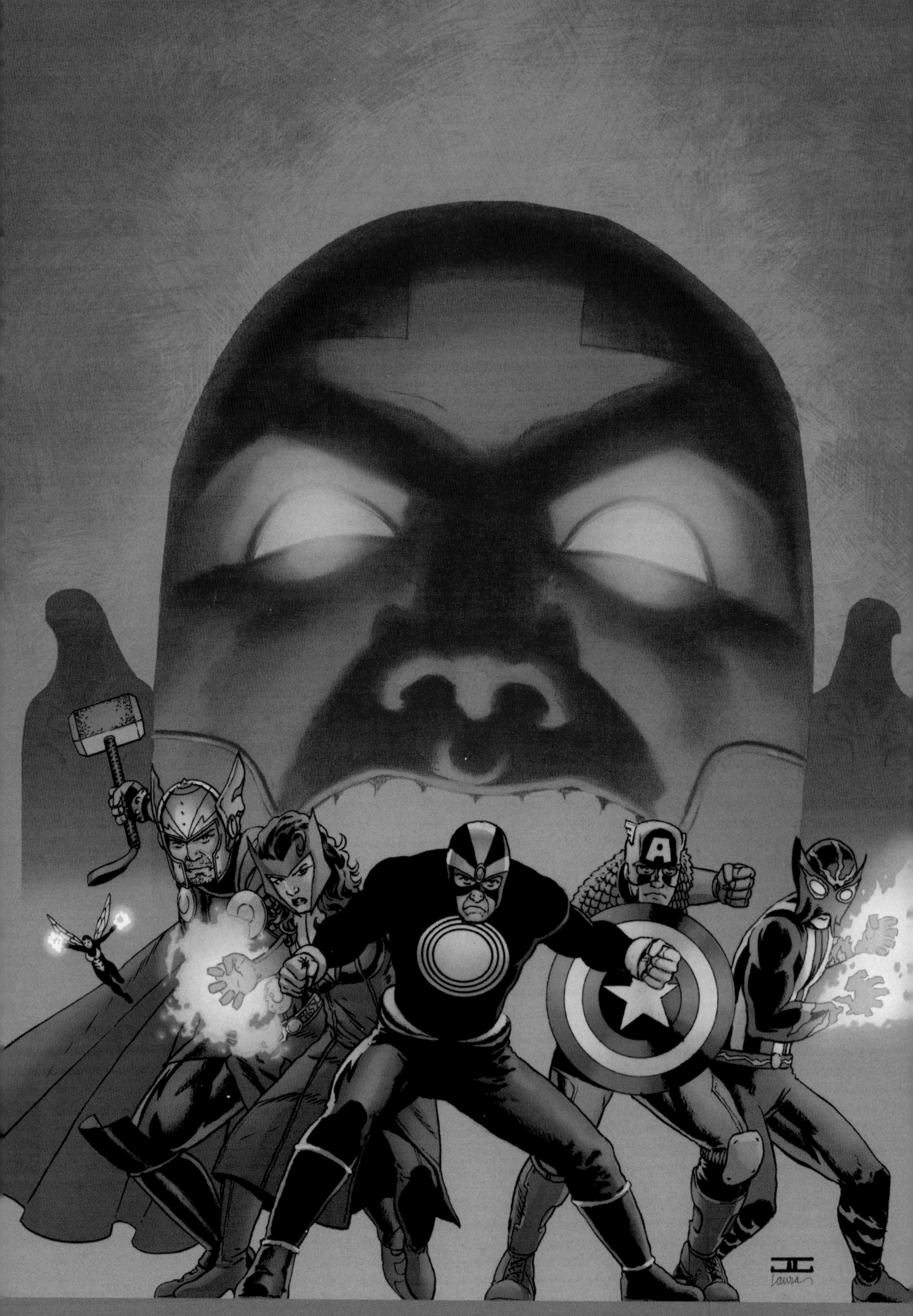

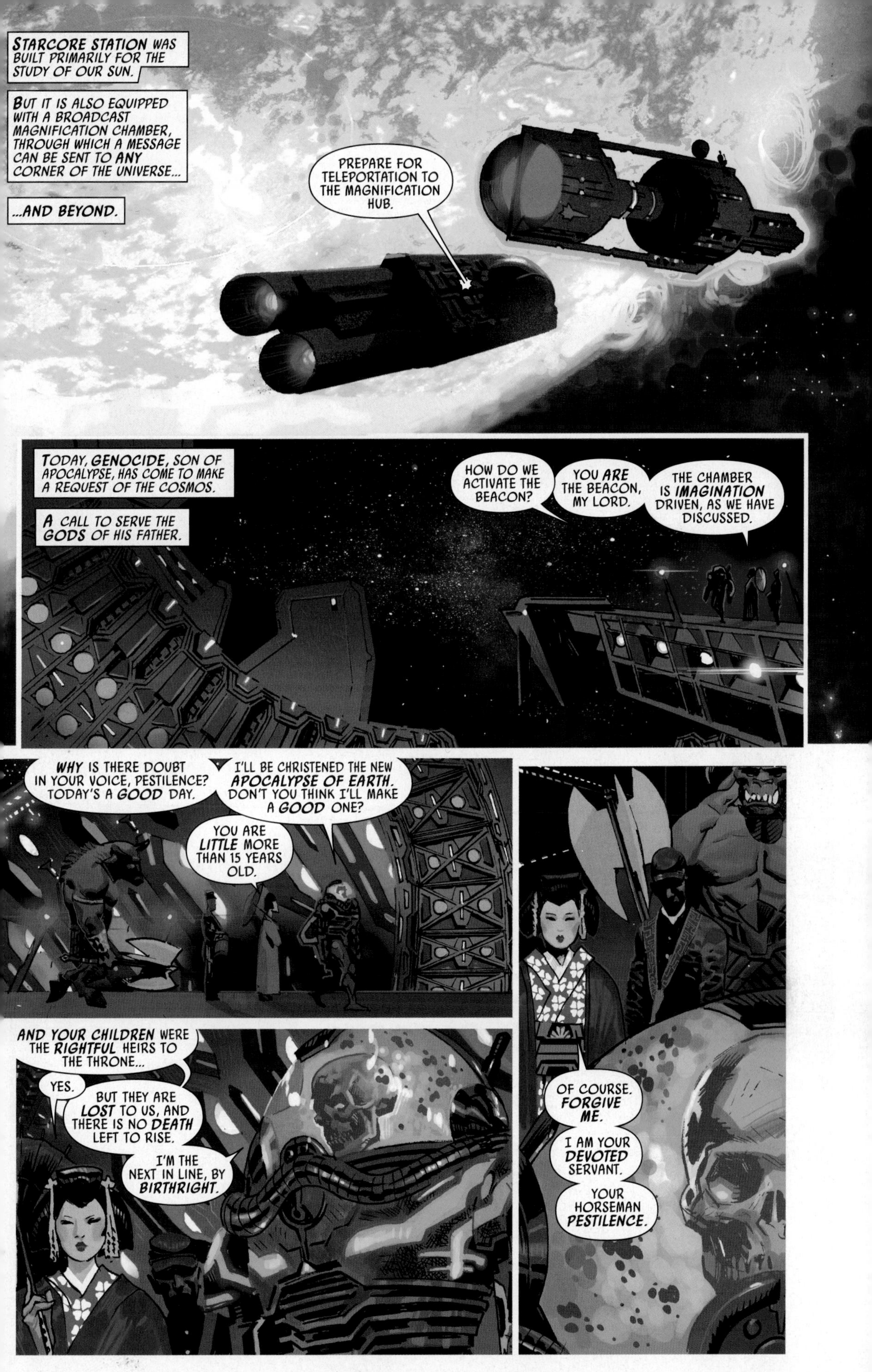
STARCORE STATION WAS BUILT PRIMARILY FOR THE STUDY OF OUR SUN.
BUT IT IS ALSO EQUIPPED WITH A BROADCAST MAGNIFICATION CHAMBER, THROUGH WHICH A MESSAGE CAN BE SENT TO ANY CORNER OF THE UNIVERSE...
...AND BEYOND.
PREPARE FOR TELEPORTATION TO THE MAGNIFICATION HUB.
TODAY, GENOCIDE, SON OF APOCALYPSE, HAS COME TO MAKE A REQUEST OF THE COSMOS.
A CALL TO SERVE THE GODS OF HIS FATHER.
HOW DO WE ACTIVATE THE BEACON?
YOU ARE THE BEACON, MY LORD.
THE CHAMBER IS IMAGINATION DRIVEN, AS WE HAVE DISCUSSED.
WHY IS THERE DOUBT IN YOUR VOICE, PESTILENCE? TODAY'S A GOOD DAY.
I'LL BE CHRISTENED THE NEW APOCALYPSE OF EARTH. DON'T YOU THINK I'LL MAKE A GOOD ONE?
YOU ARE LITTLE MORE THAN 15 YEARS OLD.
AND YOUR CHILDREN WERE THE RIGHTFUL HEIRS TO THE THRONE...
YES.
BUT THEY ARE LOST TO US, AND THERE IS NO DEATH LEFT TO RISE.
I'M THE NEXT IN LINE, BY BIRTHRIGHT.
OF COURSE. FORGIVE ME.
I AM YOUR DEVOTED SERVANT.
YOUR HORSEMAN PESTILENCE.

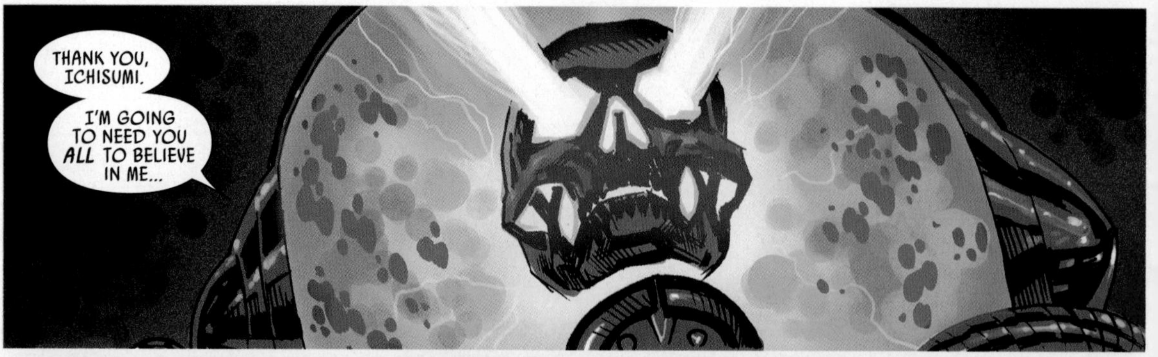
THANK YOU, ICHISUMI.
I'M GOING TO NEED YOU ALL TO BELIEVE IN ME...

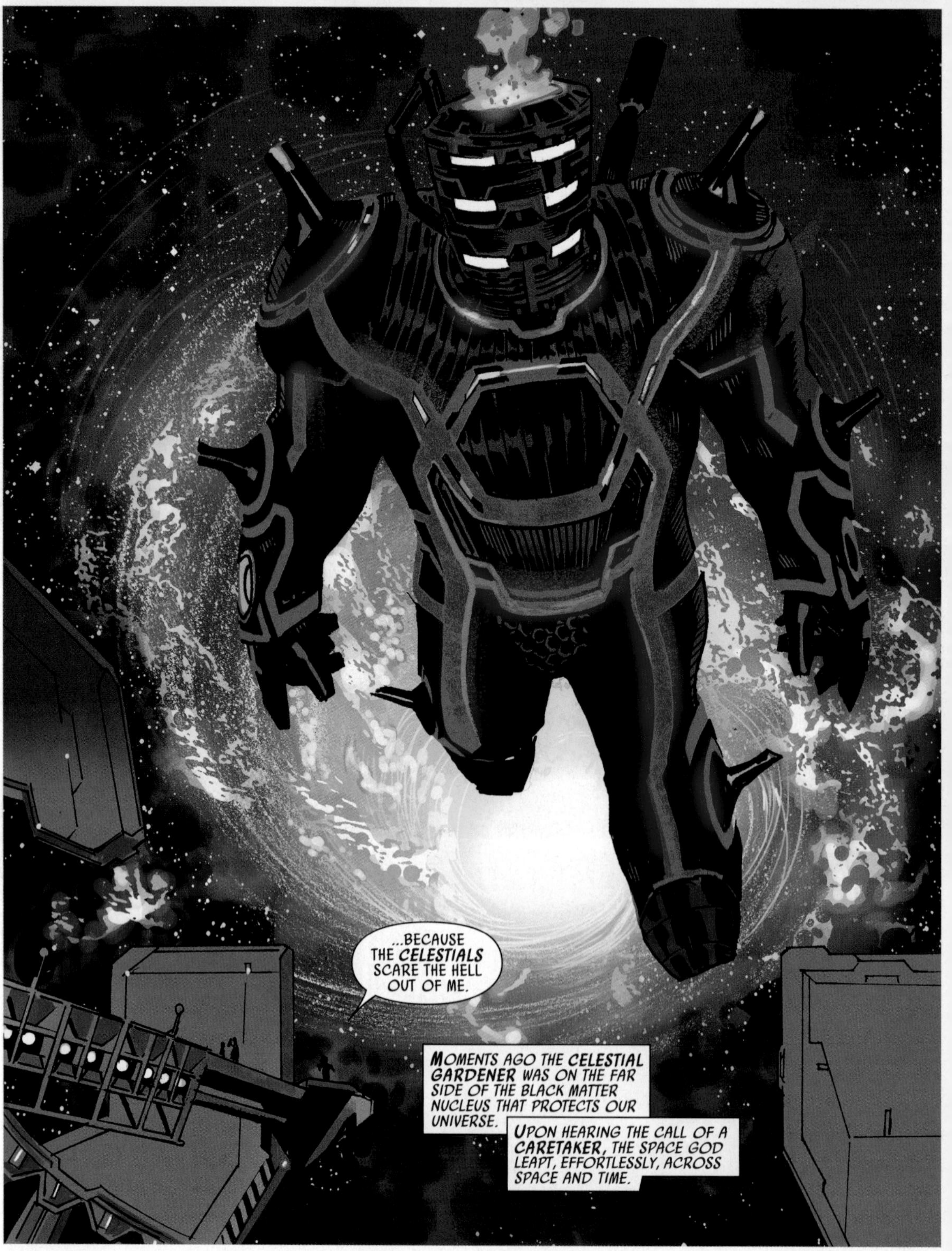
...BECAUSE THE CELESTIALS SCARE THE HELL OUT OF ME.
MOMENTS AGO THE CELESTIAL GARDENER WAS ON THE FAR SIDE OF THE BLACK MATTER NUCLEUS THAT PROTECTS OUR UNIVERSE.
UPON HEARING THE CALL OF A CARETAKER, THE SPACE GOD LEAPT, EFFORTLESSLY, ACROSS SPACE AND TIME.

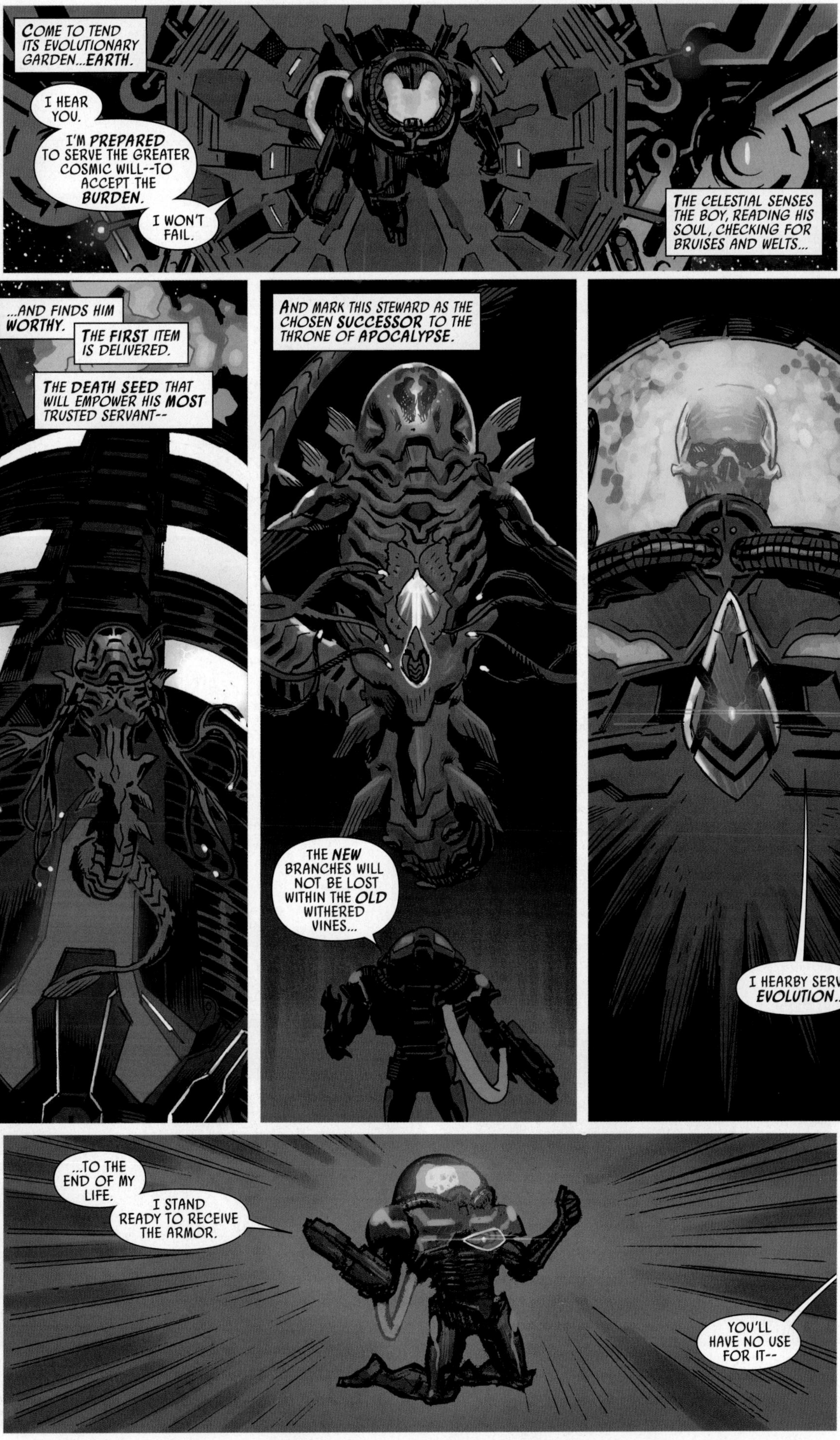

COME TO TEND ITS EVOLUTIONARY GARDEN...EARTH.
I HEAR YOU.
I'M PREPARED TO SERVE THE GREATER COSMIC WILL--TO ACCEPT THE BURDEN.
I WON'T FAIL.
THE CELESTIAL SENSES THE BOY, READING HIS SOUL, CHECKING FOR BRUISES AND WELTS...
...AND FINDS HIM WORTHY.
THE FIRST ITEM IS DELIVERED.
THE DEATH SEED THAT WILL EMPOWER HIS MOST TRUSTED SERVANT--
AND MARK THIS STEWARD AS THE CHOSEN SUCCESSOR TO THE THRONE OF APOCALYPSE.
THE NEW BRANCHES WILL NOT BE LOST WITHIN THE OLD WITHERED VINES...
I HEARBY SERVE EVOLUTION...
...TO THE END OF MY LIFE.
I STAND READY TO RECEIVE THE ARMOR.
YOU'LL HAVE NO USE FOR IT--

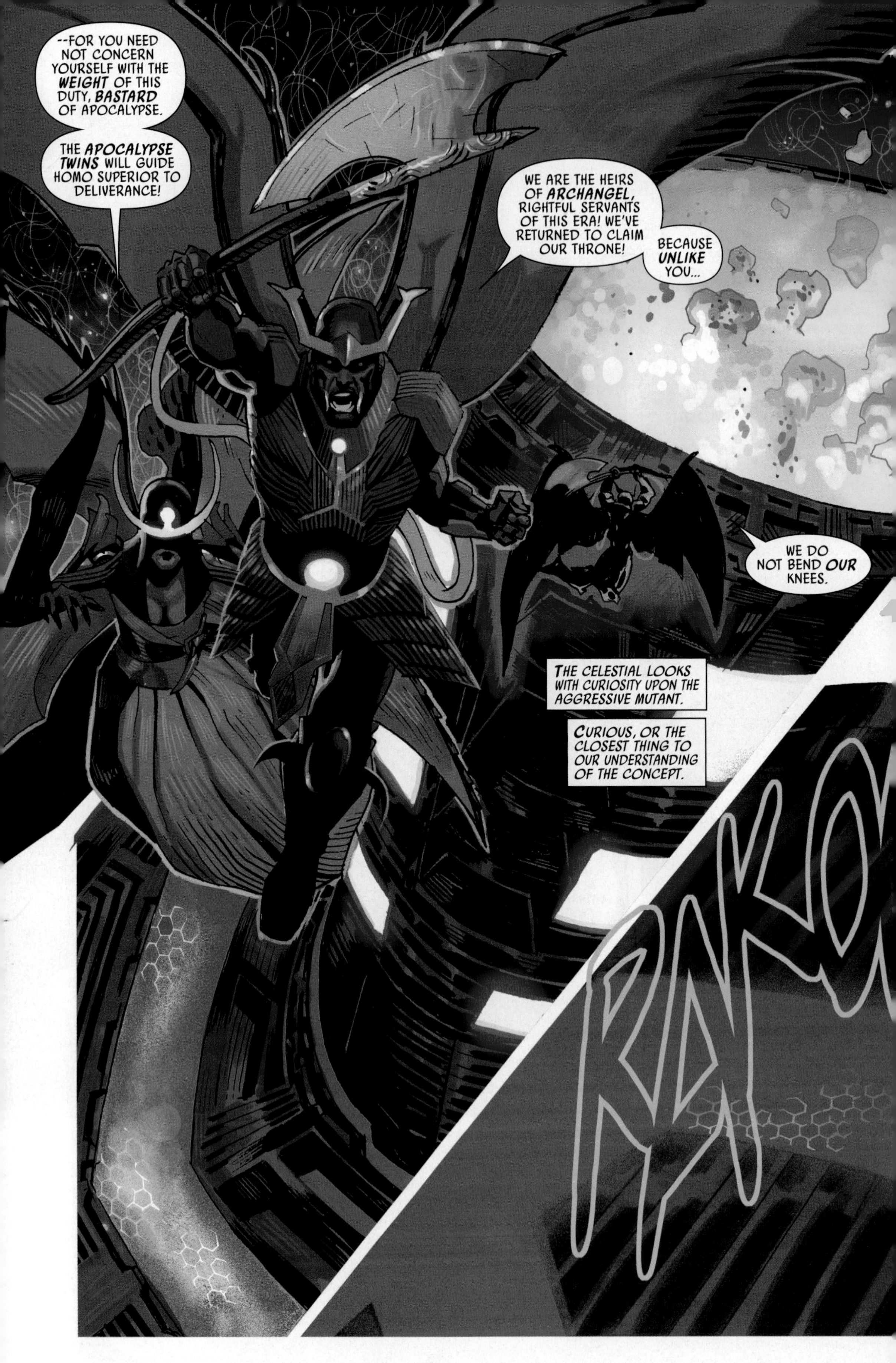
--FOR YOU NEED NOT CONCERN YOURSELF WITH THE WEIGHT OF THIS DUTY, BASTARD OF APOCALYPSE.
THE APOCALYPSE TWINS WILL GUIDE HOMO SUPERIOR TO DELIVERANCE!
WE ARE THE HEIRS OF ARCHANGEL, RIGHTFUL SERVANTS OF THIS ERA! WE'VE RETURNED TO CLAIM OUR THRONE!
BECAUSE UNLIKE YOU...
WE DO NOT BEND OUR KNEES.
THE CELESTIAL LOOKS WITH CURIOSITY UPON THE AGGRESSIVE MUTANT.
CURIOUS, OR THE CLOSEST THING TO OUR UNDERSTANDING OF THE CONCEPT.

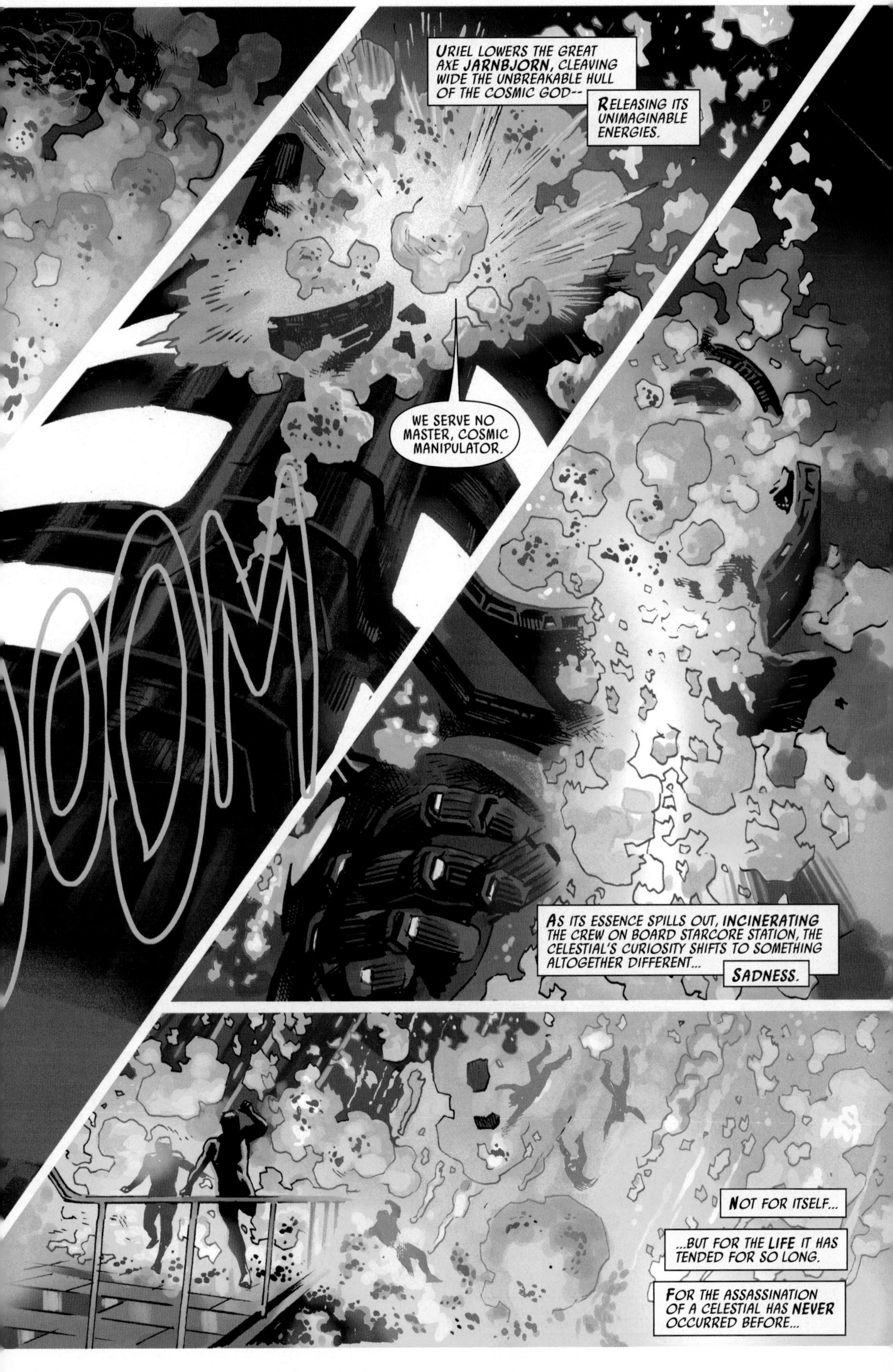
URIEL LOWERS THE GREAT AXE JARNBJORN, CLEAVING WIDE THE UNBREAKABLE HULL OF THE COSMIC GOD--
RELEASING ITS UNIMAGINABLE ENERGIES.
WE SERVE NO MASTER, COSMIC MANIPULATOR.
DOOOM
AS ITS ESSENCE SPILLS OUT, INCINERATING THE CREW ON BOARD STARCORE STATION, THE CELESTIAL'S CURIOSITY SHIFTS TO SOMETHING ALTOGETHER DIFFERENT...
SADNESS.
NOT FOR ITSELF...
...BUT FOR THE LIFE IT HAS TENDED FOR SO LONG.
FOR THE ASSASSINATION OF A CELESTIAL HAS NEVER OCCURRED BEFORE...

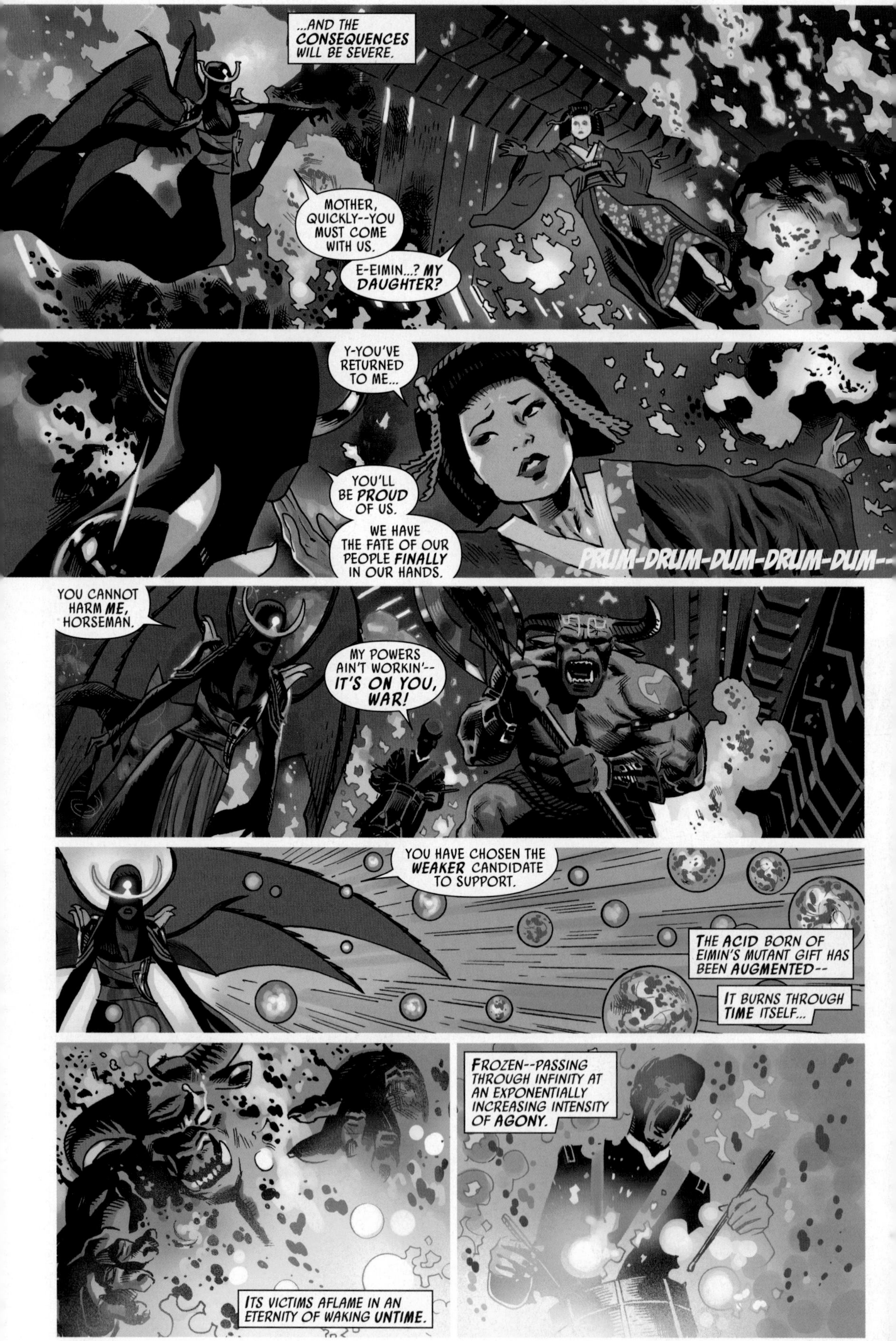
...AND THE CONSEQUENCES WILL BE SEVERE.
MOTHER, QUICKLY--YOU MUST COME WITH US.
E-EIMIN...? MY DAUGHTER?
Y-YOU'VE RETURNED TO ME...
YOU'LL BE PROUD OF US.
WE HAVE THE FATE OF OUR PEOPLE FINALLY IN OUR HANDS.
PRUM-DRUM-DUM-DRUM-DUM--
YOU CANNOT HARM ME, HORSEMAN.
MY POWERS AIN'T WORKIN'-- IT'S ON YOU, WAR!
YOU HAVE CHOSEN THE WEAKER CANDIDATE TO SUPPORT.
THE ACID BORN OF EIMIN'S MUTANT GIFT HAS BEEN AUGMENTED--
IT BURNS THROUGH TIME ITSELF...
ITS VICTIMS AFLAME IN AN ETERNITY OF WAKING UNTIME.
FROZEN--PASSING THROUGH INFINITY AT AN EXPONENTIALLY INCREASING INTENSITY OF AGONY.

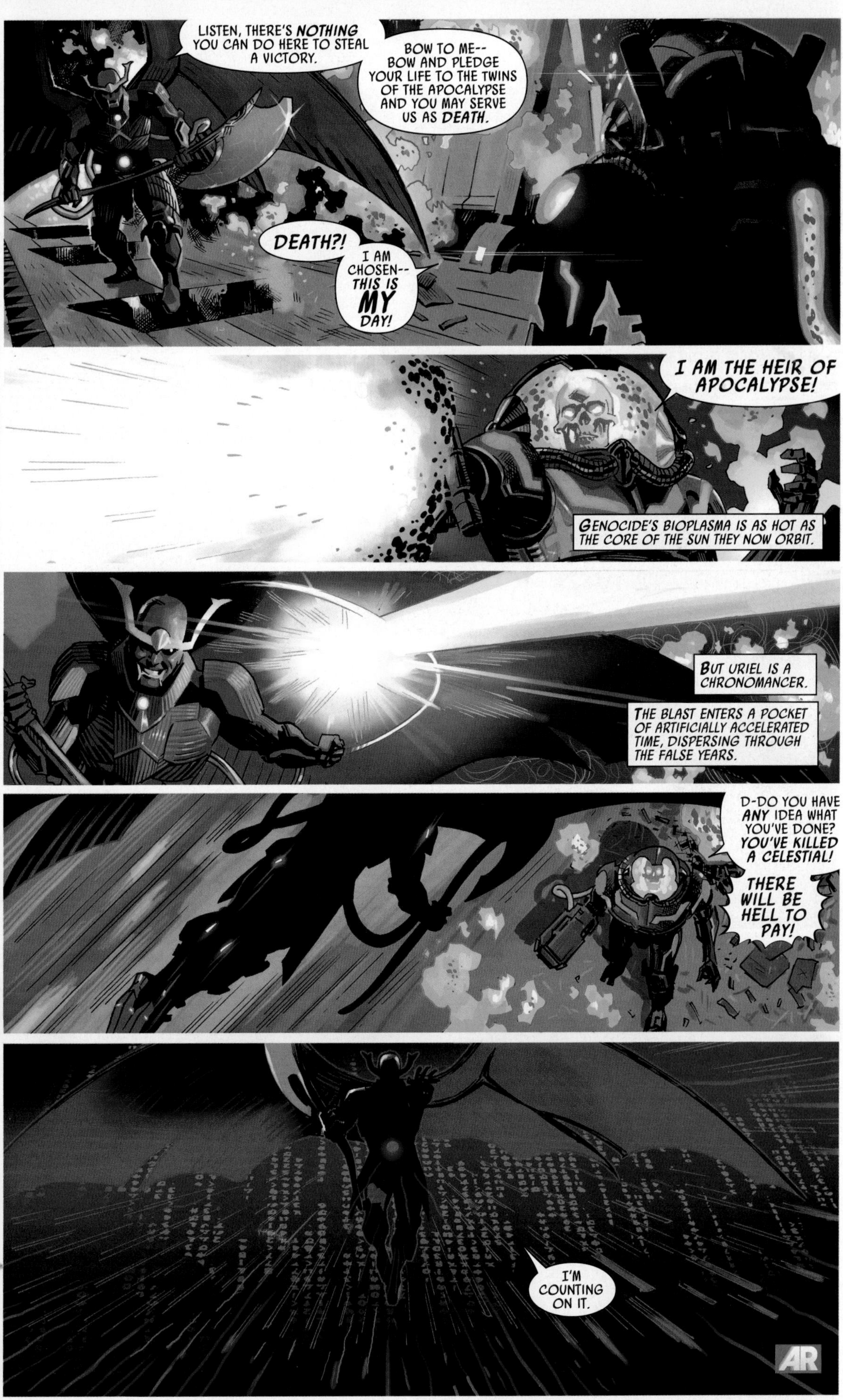
LISTEN, THERE'S NOTHING YOU CAN DO HERE TO STEAL A VICTORY.
BOW TO ME-- BOW AND PLEDGE YOUR LIFE TO THE TWINS OF THE APOCALYPSE AND YOU MAY SERVE US AS DEATH.
DEATH?!
I AM CHOSEN-- THIS IS MY DAY!
I AM THE HEIR OF APOCALYPSE!
GENOCIDE'S BIOPLASMA IS AS HOT AS THE CORE OF THE SUN THEY NOW ORBIT.
BUT URIEL IS A CHRONOMANCER.
THE BLAST ENTERS A POCKET OF ARTIFICIALLY ACCELERATED TIME, DISPERSING THROUGH THE FALSE YEARS.
D-DO YOU HAVE ANY IDEA WHAT YOU'VE DONE? YOU'VE KILLED A CELESTIAL!
THERE WILL BE HELL TO PAY!
I'M COUNTING ON IT.

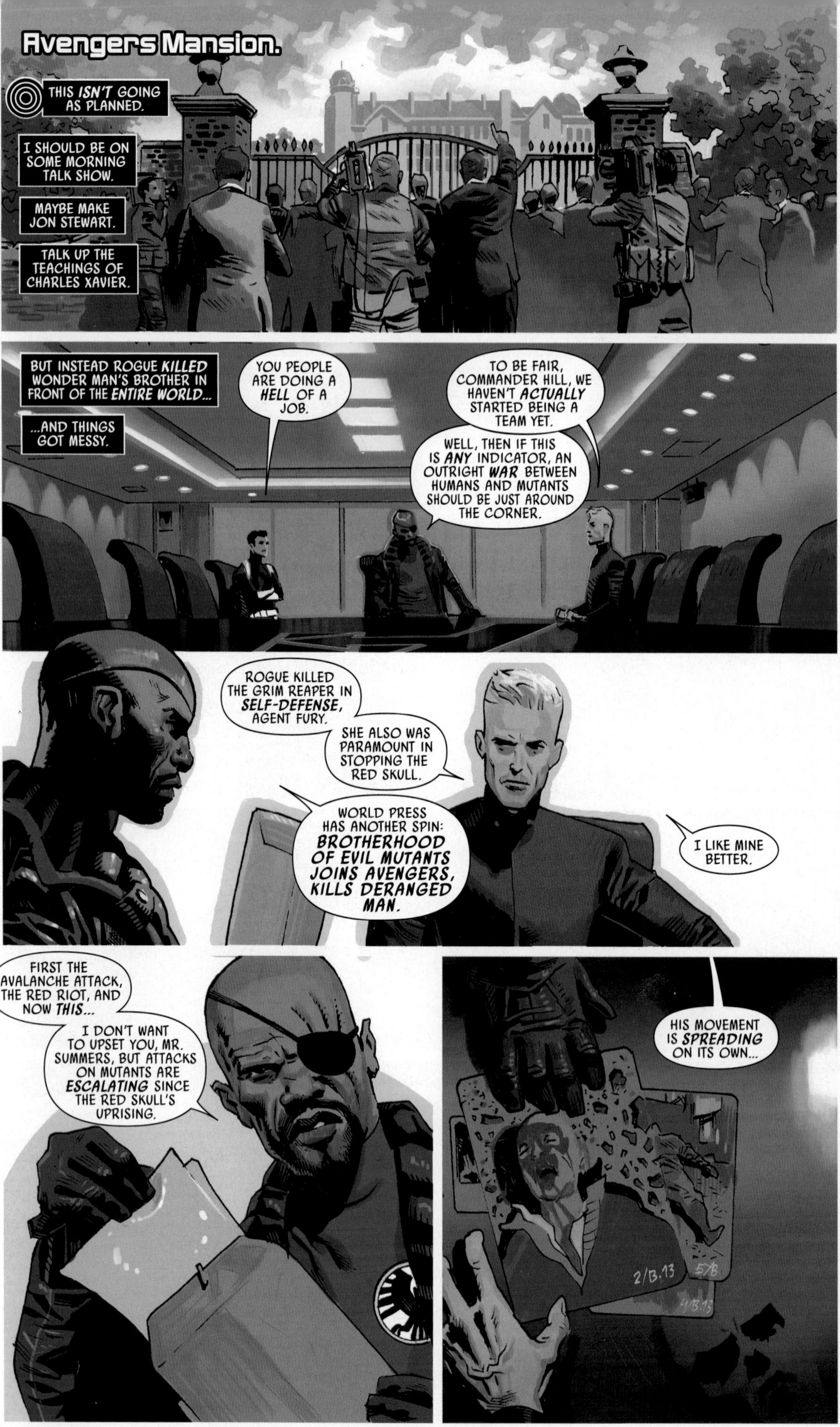
Avengers Mansion.
THIS ISN'T GOING AS PLANNED.
I SHOULD BE ON SOME MORNING TALK SHOW.
MAYBE MAKE JON STEWART.
TALK UP THE TEACHINGS OF CHARLES XAVIER.
BUT INSTEAD ROGUE KILLED WONDER MAN'S BROTHER IN FRONT OF THE ENTIRE WORLD...
...AND THINGS GOT MESSY.
YOU PEOPLE ARE DOING A HELL OF A JOB.
TO BE FAIR, COMMANDER HILL, WE HAVEN'T ACTUALLY STARTED BEING A TEAM YET.
WELL, THEN IF THIS IS ANY INDICATOR, AN OUTRIGHT WAR BETWEEN HUMANS AND MUTANTS SHOULD BE JUST AROUND THE CORNER.
ROGUE KILLED THE GRIM REAPER IN SELF-DEFENSE, AGENT FURY.
SHE ALSO WAS PARAMOUNT IN STOPPING THE RED SKULL.
WORLD PRESS HAS ANOTHER SPIN: BROTHERHOOD OF EVIL MUTANTS JOINS AVENGERS, KILLS DERANGED MAN.
I LIKE MINE BETTER.
FIRST THE AVALANCHE ATTACK, THE RED RIOT, AND NOW THIS...
I DON'T WANT TO UPSET YOU, MR. SUMMERS, BUT ATTACKS ON MUTANTS ARE ESCALATING SINCE THE RED SKULL'S UPRISING.
HIS MOVEMENT IS SPREADING ON ITS OWN...
2/B.13
5/B
4/B.13

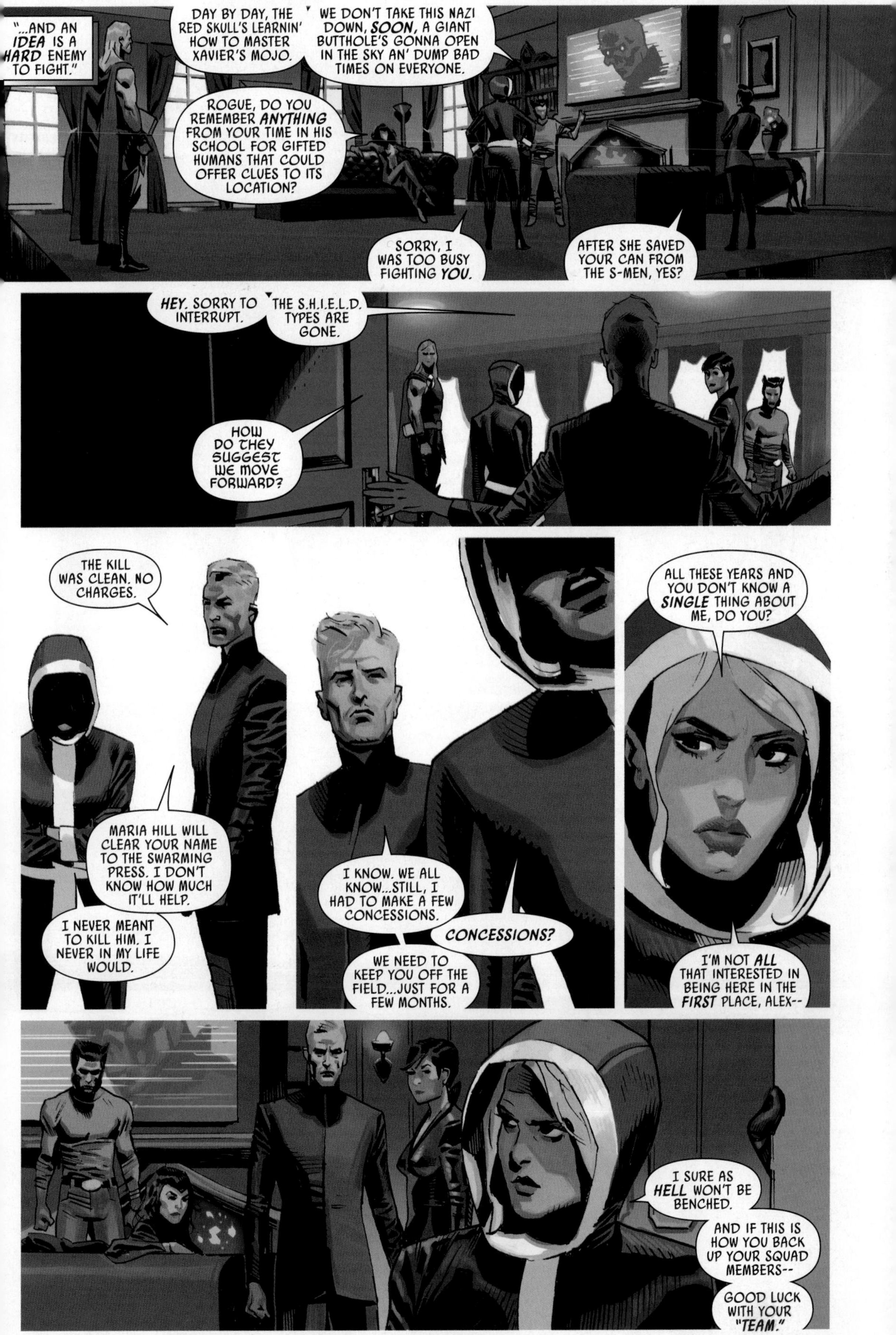
"...AND AN IDEA IS A HARD ENEMY TO FIGHT."
DAY BY DAY, THE RED SKULL'S LEARNIN' HOW TO MASTER XAVIER'S MOJO.
WE DON'T TAKE THIS NAZI DOWN, SOON, A GIANT BUTTHOLE'S GONNA OPEN IN THE SKY AN' DUMP BAD TIMES ON EVERYONE.
ROGUE, DO YOU REMEMBER ANYTHING FROM YOUR TIME IN HIS SCHOOL FOR GIFTED HUMANS THAT COULD OFFER CLUES TO ITS LOCATION?
SORRY, I WAS TOO BUSY FIGHTING YOU.
AFTER SHE SAVED YOUR CAN FROM THE S-MEN, YES?
HEY. SORRY TO INTERRUPT.
THE S.H.I.E.L.D. TYPES ARE GONE.
HOW DO THEY SUGGEST WE MOVE FORWARD?
THE KILL WAS CLEAN. NO CHARGES.
MARIA HILL WILL CLEAR YOUR NAME TO THE SWARMING PRESS. I DON'T KNOW HOW MUCH IT'LL HELP.
I NEVER MEANT TO KILL HIM. I NEVER IN MY LIFE WOULD.
I KNOW. WE ALL KNOW...STILL, I HAD TO MAKE A FEW CONCESSIONS.
CONCESSIONS?
WE NEED TO KEEP YOU OFF THE FIELD...JUST FOR A FEW MONTHS.
ALL THESE YEARS AND YOU DON'T KNOW A SINGLE THING ABOUT ME, DO YOU?
I'M NOT ALL THAT INTERESTED IN BEING HERE IN THE FIRST PLACE, ALEX--
I SURE AS HELL WON'T BE BENCHED.
AND IF THIS IS HOW YOU BACK UP YOUR SQUAD MEMBERS--
GOOD LUCK WITH YOUR "TEAM."

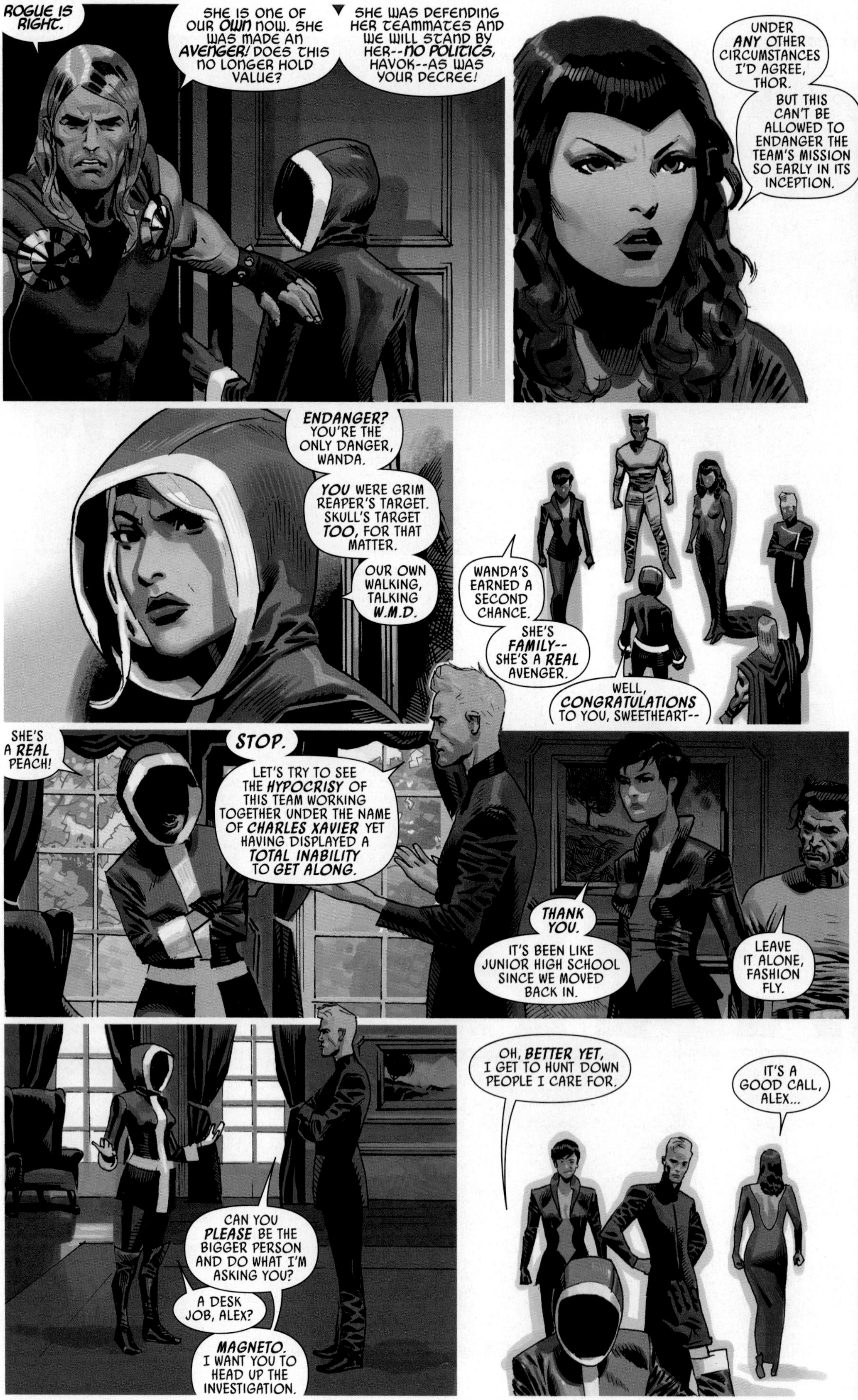
ROGUE IS RIGHT.
SHE IS ONE OF OUR OWN NOW. SHE WAS MADE AN AVENGER! DOES THIS NO LONGER HOLD VALUE?
SHE WAS DEFENDING HER TEAMMATES AND WE WILL STAND BY HER--NO POLITICS, HAVOK--AS WAS YOUR DECREE!
UNDER ANY OTHER CIRCUMSTANCES I'D AGREE, THOR.
BUT THIS CAN'T BE ALLOWED TO ENDANGER THE TEAM'S MISSION SO EARLY IN ITS INCEPTION.
ENDANGER? YOU'RE THE ONLY DANGER, WANDA.
YOU WERE GRIM REAPER'S TARGET. SKULL'S TARGET TOO, FOR THAT MATTER.
OUR OWN WALKING, TALKING W.M.D.
WANDA'S EARNED A SECOND CHANCE.
SHE'S FAMILY-- SHE'S A REAL AVENGER.
WELL, CONGRATULATIONS TO YOU, SWEETHEART--
SHE'S A REAL PEACH!
STOP.
LET'S TRY TO SEE THE HYPOCRISY OF THIS TEAM WORKING TOGETHER UNDER THE NAME OF CHARLES XAVIER YET HAVING DISPLAYED A TOTAL INABILITY TO GET ALONG.
THANK YOU.
IT'S BEEN LIKE JUNIOR HIGH SCHOOL SINCE WE MOVED BACK IN.
LEAVE IT ALONE, FASHION FLY.
CAN YOU PLEASE BE THE BIGGER PERSON AND DO WHAT I'M ASKING YOU?
A DESK JOB, ALEX?
MAGNETO. I WANT YOU TO HEAD UP THE INVESTIGATION.
OH, BETTER YET, I GET TO HUNT DOWN PEOPLE I CARE FOR.
IT'S A GOOD CALL, ALEX...

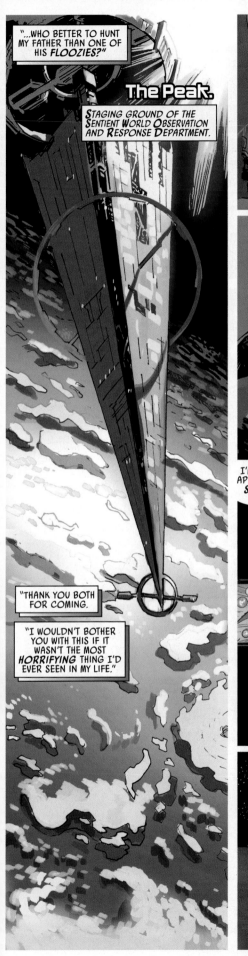

"...WHO BETTER TO HUNT MY FATHER THAN ONE OF HIS *FLOOZIES?*"

The Peak.

STAGING GROUND OF THE SENTIENT WORLD OBSERVATION AND RESPONSE DEPARTMENT.

"THANK YOU BOTH FOR COMING."

"I WOULDN'T BOTHER YOU WITH THIS IF IT WASN'T THE MOST *HORRIFYING* THING I'D EVER SEEN IN MY LIFE."

THE AVENGERS ARE ALWAYS ON CALL, AGENT BRAND.

WELL, HOLD ON TO YOUR STRIPES, CAP-- WE'VE GOT *BIG* TROUBLE.

THIS FOOTAGE CAME BACK FROM STARCORE STATION ONE HOUR BEFORE WE LOST CONTACT.

AT FIRST I THOUGHT IT MUST BE A *HOAX* OF SOME KIND, BUT THE ENERGIES WE PICKED UP CONFIRM IT.

WHAT YOU ARE WITNESSING IS THE *ASSASSINATION* OF A CELESTIAL.

GOD...

I'M GLAD YOU APPRECIATE THE *SCOPE* OF THIS.

THIS IS *"FATE OF OUR GALAXY"* BIG. ANY INFORMATION YOU MIGHT HAVE--

THE FIERY BEAST IS *GENOCIDE*, THE SON OF APOCALYPSE.

THE OTHERS, I HAVE NEVER SEEN, THOUGH THEY DO RESEMBLE--

COMMANDER BRAND!

A CELESTIAL CRAFT IS EXITING WARP...

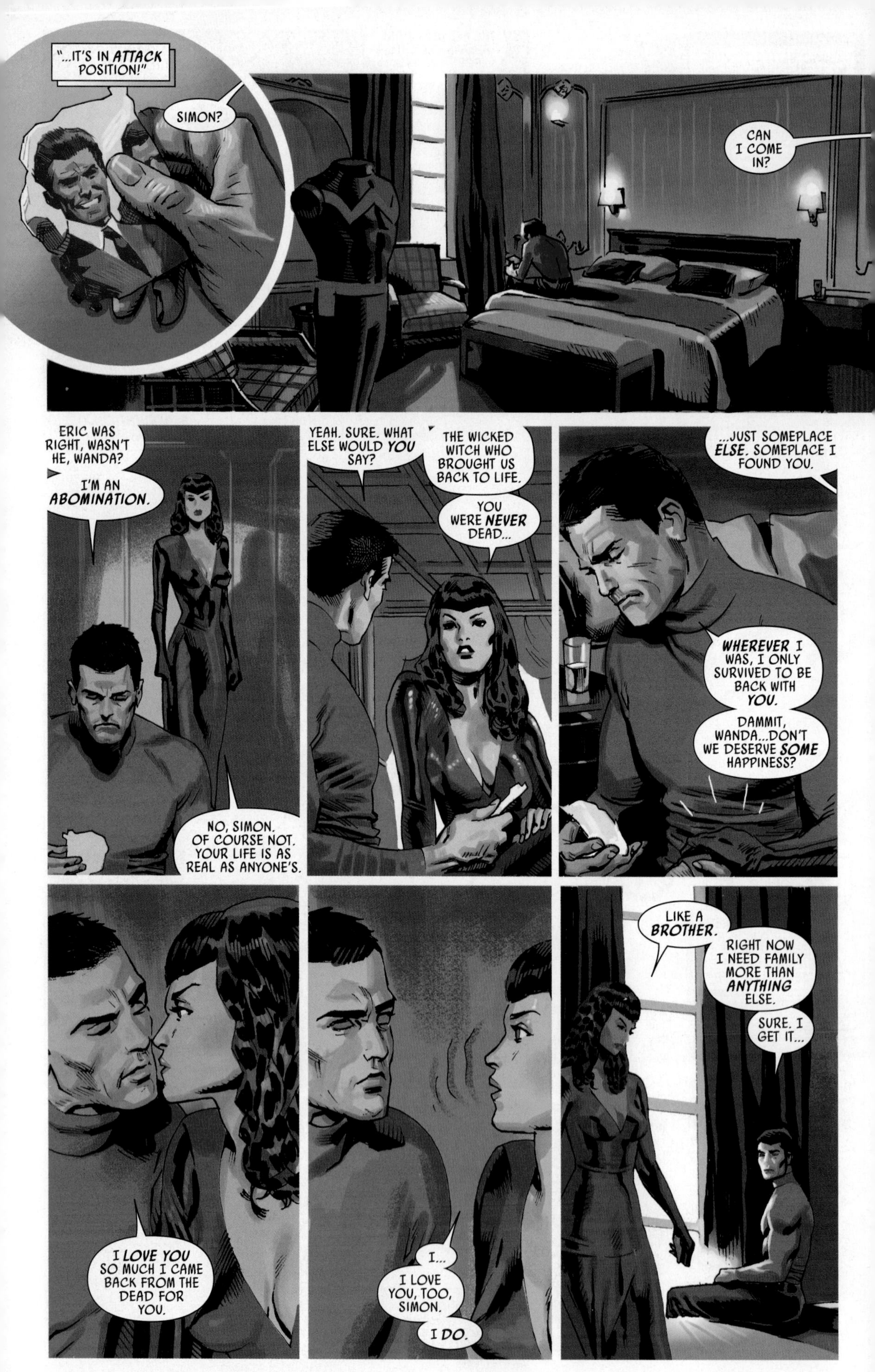

"...IT'S IN ATTACK POSITION!"
SIMON?
CAN I COME IN?
ERIC WAS RIGHT, WASN'T HE, WANDA?
I'M AN ABOMINATION.
NO, SIMON. OF COURSE NOT. YOUR LIFE IS AS REAL AS ANYONE'S.
YEAH. SURE. WHAT ELSE WOULD YOU SAY?
THE WICKED WITCH WHO BROUGHT US BACK TO LIFE.
YOU WERE NEVER DEAD...
...JUST SOMEPLACE ELSE. SOMEPLACE I FOUND YOU.
WHEREVER I WAS, I ONLY SURVIVED TO BE BACK WITH YOU.
DAMMIT, WANDA...DON'T WE DESERVE SOME HAPPINESS?
I LOVE YOU SO MUCH I CAME BACK FROM THE DEAD FOR YOU.
I...
I LOVE YOU, TOO, SIMON.
I DO.
LIKE A BROTHER.
RIGHT NOW I NEED FAMILY MORE THAN ANYTHING ELSE.
SURE. I GET IT...

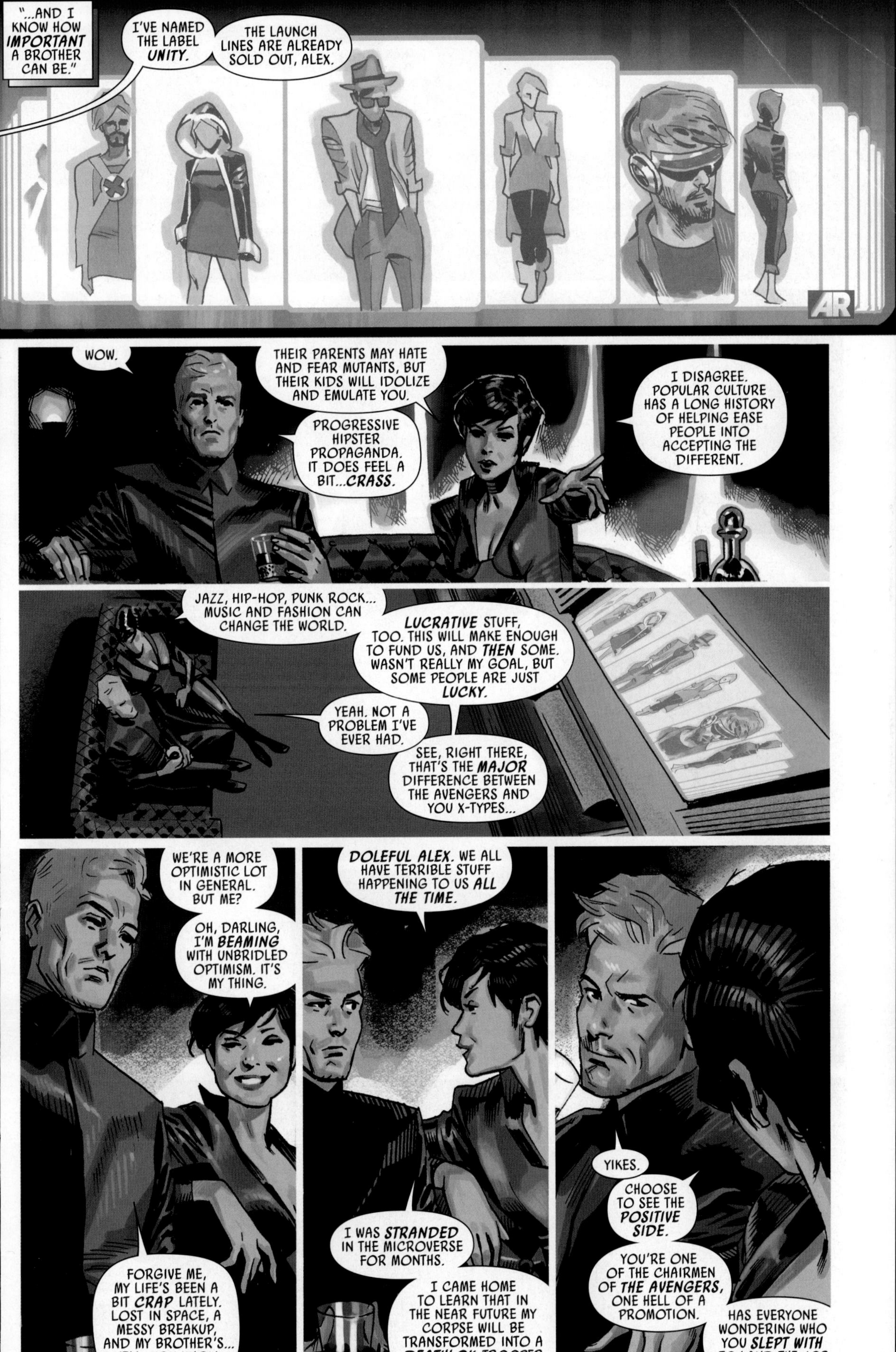
"...AND I KNOW HOW IMPORTANT A BROTHER CAN BE."
I'VE NAMED THE LABEL UNITY.
THE LAUNCH LINES ARE ALREADY SOLD OUT, ALEX.
AR
WOW.
THEIR PARENTS MAY HATE AND FEAR MUTANTS, BUT THEIR KIDS WILL IDOLIZE AND EMULATE YOU.
PROGRESSIVE HIPSTER PROPAGANDA. IT DOES FEEL A BIT...CRASS.
I DISAGREE. POPULAR CULTURE HAS A LONG HISTORY OF HELPING EASE PEOPLE INTO ACCEPTING THE DIFFERENT.
JAZZ, HIP-HOP, PUNK ROCK... MUSIC AND FASHION CAN CHANGE THE WORLD.
LUCRATIVE STUFF, TOO. THIS WILL MAKE ENOUGH TO FUND US, AND THEN SOME. WASN'T REALLY MY GOAL, BUT SOME PEOPLE ARE JUST LUCKY.
YEAH. NOT A PROBLEM I'VE EVER HAD.
SEE, RIGHT THERE, THAT'S THE MAJOR DIFFERENCE BETWEEN THE AVENGERS AND YOU X-TYPES...
WE'RE A MORE OPTIMISTIC LOT IN GENERAL. BUT ME?
OH, DARLING, I'M BEAMING WITH UNBRIDLED OPTIMISM. IT'S MY THING.
FORGIVE ME, MY LIFE'S BEEN A BIT CRAP LATELY. LOST IN SPACE, A MESSY BREAKUP, AND MY BROTHER'S... WELL, YOU KNOW.
DOLEFUL ALEX. WE ALL HAVE TERRIBLE STUFF HAPPENING TO US ALL THE TIME.
I WAS STRANDED IN THE MICROVERSE FOR MONTHS.
I CAME HOME TO LEARN THAT IN THE NEAR FUTURE MY CORPSE WILL BE TRANSFORMED INTO A DEATHLOK TROOPER.
YIKES.
CHOOSE TO SEE THE POSITIVE SIDE.
YOU'RE ONE OF THE CHAIRMEN OF THE AVENGERS, ONE HELL OF A PROMOTION.
HAS EVERYONE WONDERING WHO YOU SLEPT WITH TO LAND THE JOB.

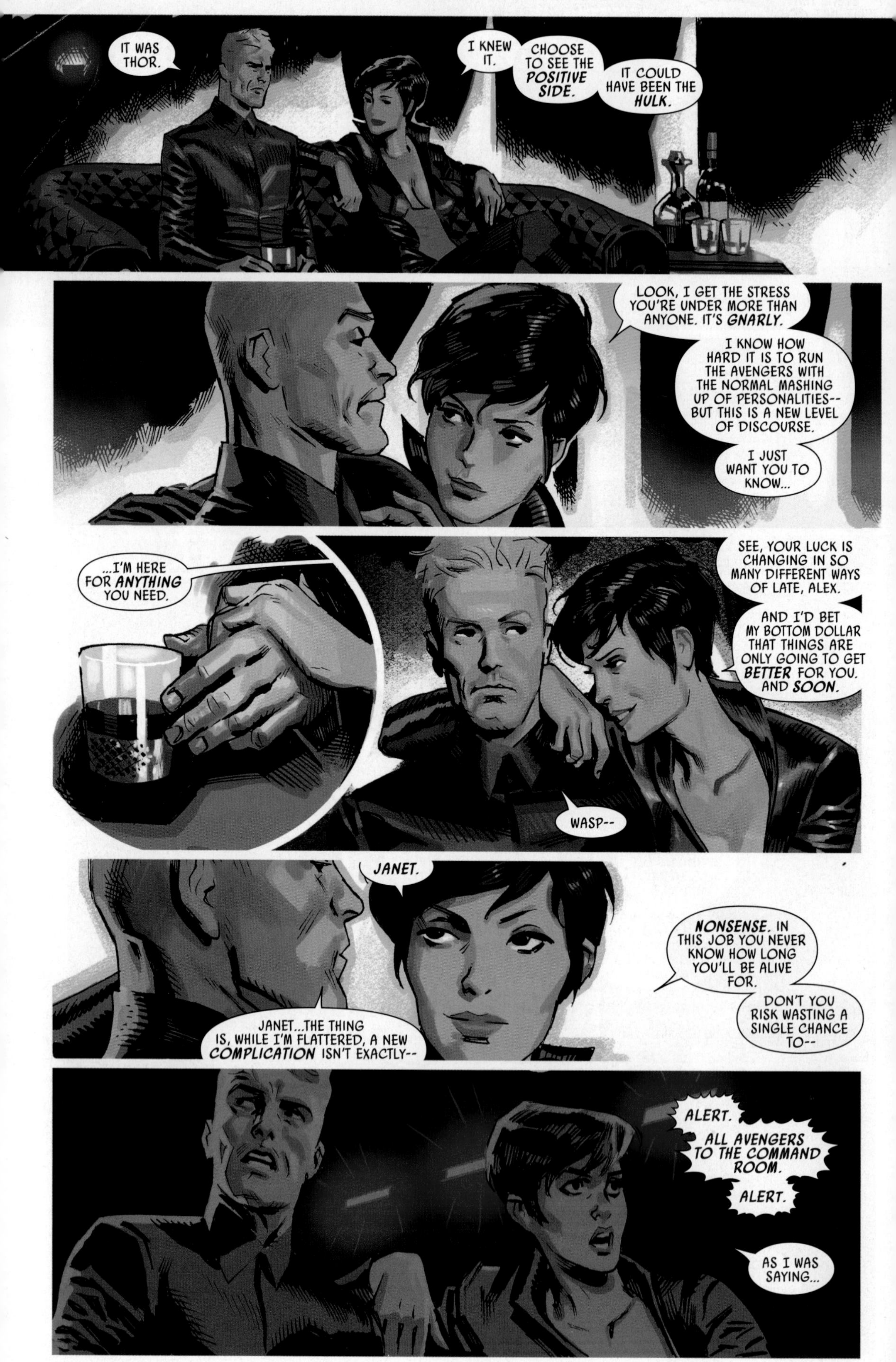

IT WAS THOR.
I KNEW IT.
CHOOSE TO SEE THE **POSITIVE SIDE.**
IT COULD HAVE BEEN THE **HULK.**
LOOK, I GET THE STRESS YOU'RE UNDER MORE THAN ANYONE. IT'S **GNARLY.**
I KNOW HOW HARD IT IS TO RUN THE AVENGERS WITH THE NORMAL MASHING UP OF PERSONALITIES-- BUT THIS IS A NEW LEVEL OF DISCOURSE.
I JUST WANT YOU TO KNOW...
...I'M HERE FOR **ANYTHING** YOU NEED.
SEE, YOUR LUCK IS CHANGING IN SO MANY DIFFERENT WAYS OF LATE, ALEX.
AND I'D BET MY BOTTOM DOLLAR THAT THINGS ARE ONLY GOING TO GET **BETTER** FOR YOU. AND **SOON.**
WASP--
JANET.
JANET...THE THING IS, WHILE I'M FLATTERED, A NEW **COMPLICATION** ISN'T EXACTLY--
NONSENSE. IN THIS JOB YOU NEVER KNOW HOW LONG YOU'LL BE ALIVE FOR.
DON'T YOU RISK WASTING A SINGLE CHANCE TO--
ALERT.
ALL AVENGERS TO THE COMMAND ROOM.
ALERT.
AS I WAS SAYING...

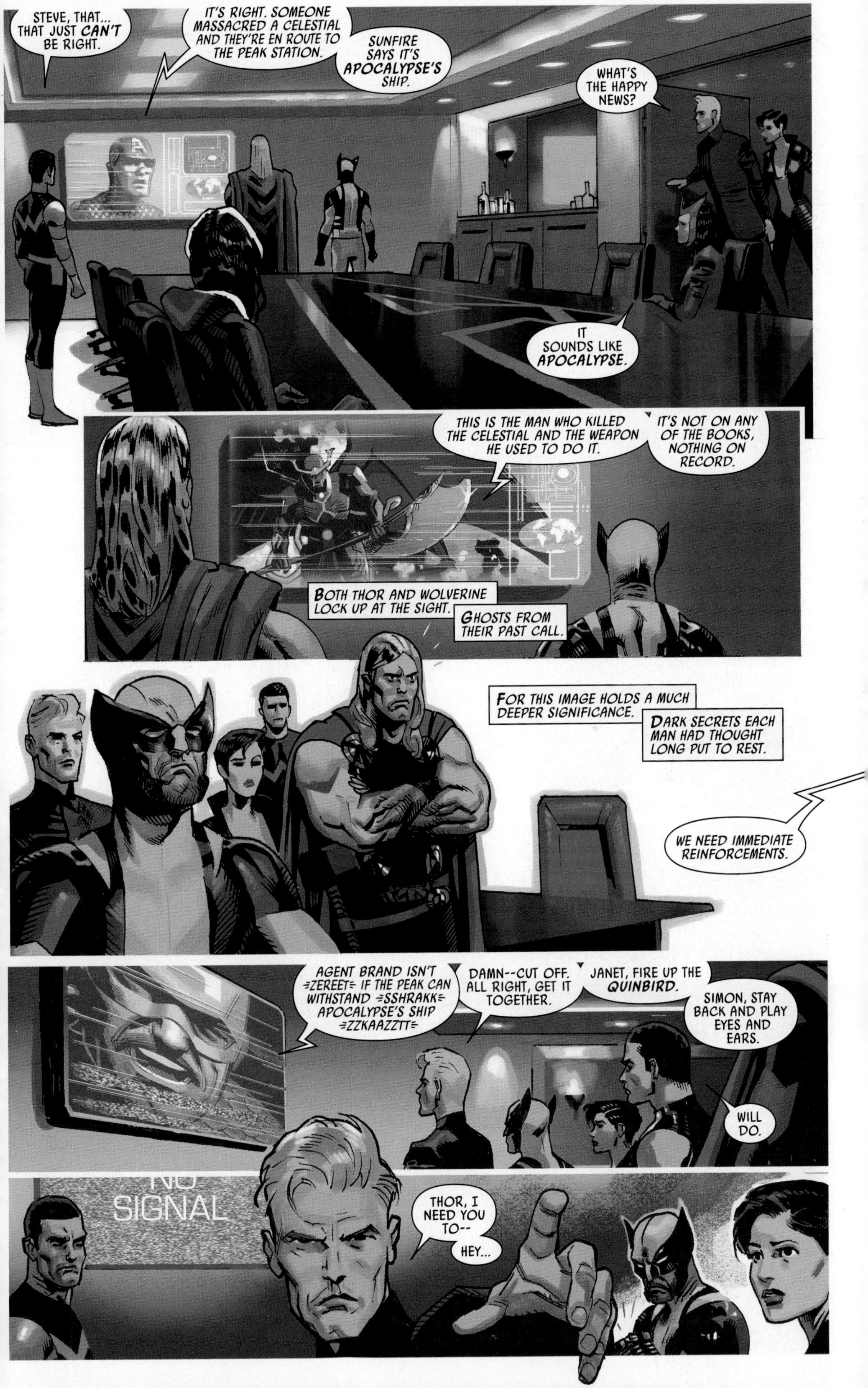
STEVE, THAT... THAT JUST CAN'T BE RIGHT.
IT'S RIGHT. SOMEONE MASSACRED A CELESTIAL AND THEY'RE EN ROUTE TO THE PEAK STATION.
SUNFIRE SAYS IT'S APOCALYPSE'S SHIP.
WHAT'S THE HAPPY NEWS?
IT SOUNDS LIKE APOCALYPSE.
THIS IS THE MAN WHO KILLED THE CELESTIAL AND THE WEAPON HE USED TO DO IT.
IT'S NOT ON ANY OF THE BOOKS, NOTHING ON RECORD.
BOTH THOR AND WOLVERINE LOCK UP AT THE SIGHT.
GHOSTS FROM THEIR PAST CALL.
FOR THIS IMAGE HOLDS A MUCH DEEPER SIGNIFICANCE.
DARK SECRETS EACH MAN HAD THOUGHT LONG PUT TO REST.
WE NEED IMMEDIATE REINFORCEMENTS.
AGENT BRAND ISN'T =ZEREET= IF THE PEAK CAN WITHSTAND =SSHRAKK= APOCALYPSE'S SHIP =ZZKAAZZTT=
DAMN--CUT OFF. ALL RIGHT, GET IT TOGETHER.
JANET, FIRE UP THE QUINBIRD.
SIMON, STAY BACK AND PLAY EYES AND EARS.
WILL DO.
NO SIGNAL
THOR, I NEED YOU TO--
HEY...

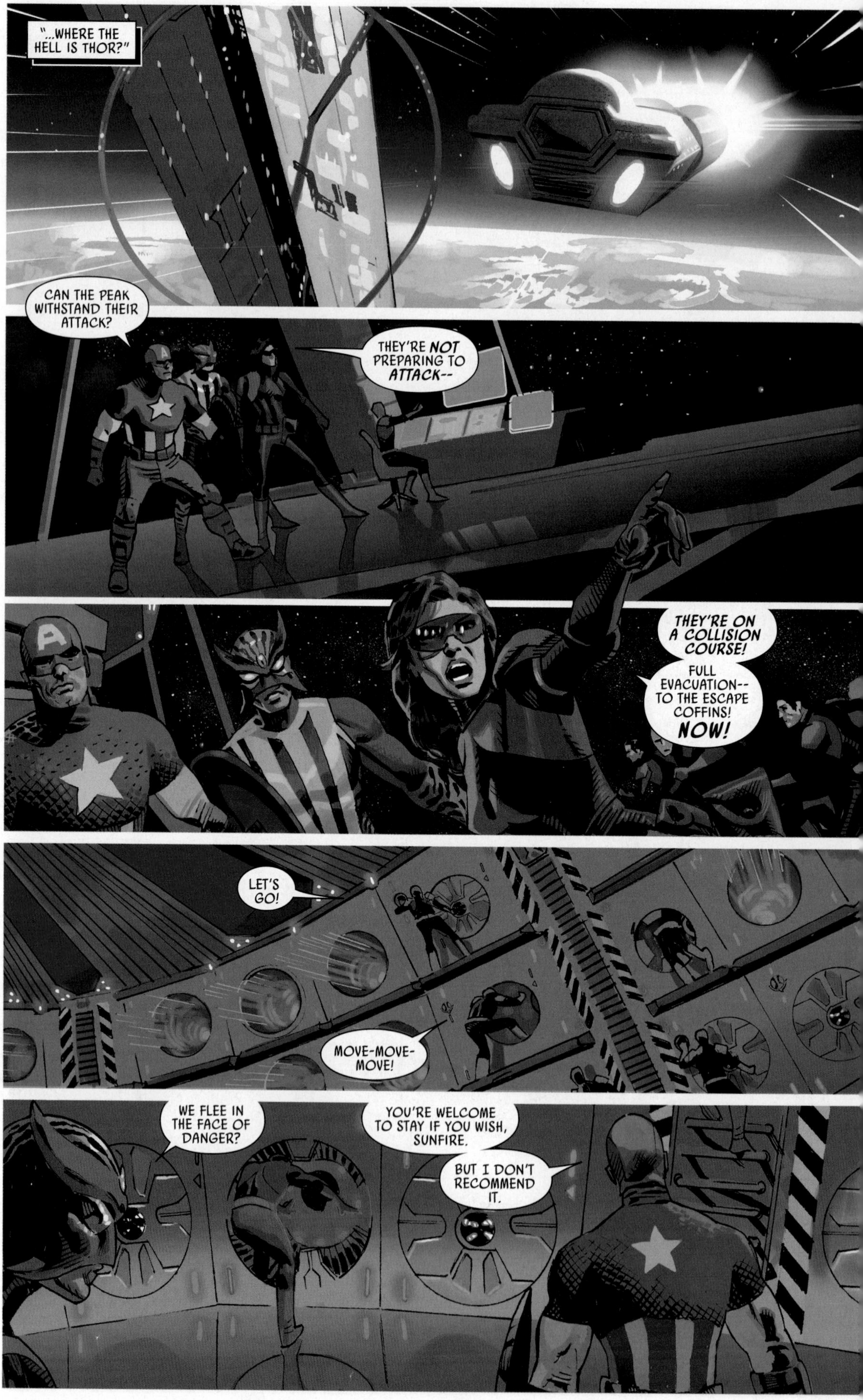
"...WHERE THE HELL IS THOR?"
CAN THE PEAK WITHSTAND THEIR ATTACK?
THEY'RE *NOT* PREPARING TO *ATTACK*--
THEY'RE ON A COLLISION COURSE!
FULL EVACUATION-- TO THE ESCAPE COFFINS! **NOW!**
LET'S GO!
MOVE-MOVE-MOVE!
WE FLEE IN THE FACE OF DANGER?
YOU'RE WELCOME TO STAY IF YOU WISH, SUNFIRE.
BUT I DON'T RECOMMEND IT.

LOCKED! THING WON'T OPEN!

THEN IT LOOKS LIKE I'LL GET MY WISH.

SUNFIRE!

SHIRO! OPEN THIS DOO--

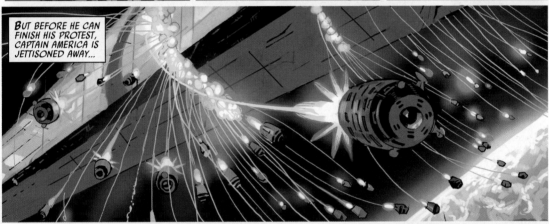

BUT BEFORE HE CAN FINISH HIS PROTEST, CAPTAIN AMERICA IS JETTISONED AWAY...

...LEAVING THE SOLAR SAMURAI ALONE TO PONDER HIS SPLIT SECOND GALLANTRY...

BY AMERATSU'S LIGHT...

SUDDENLY REGRETTING THIS.

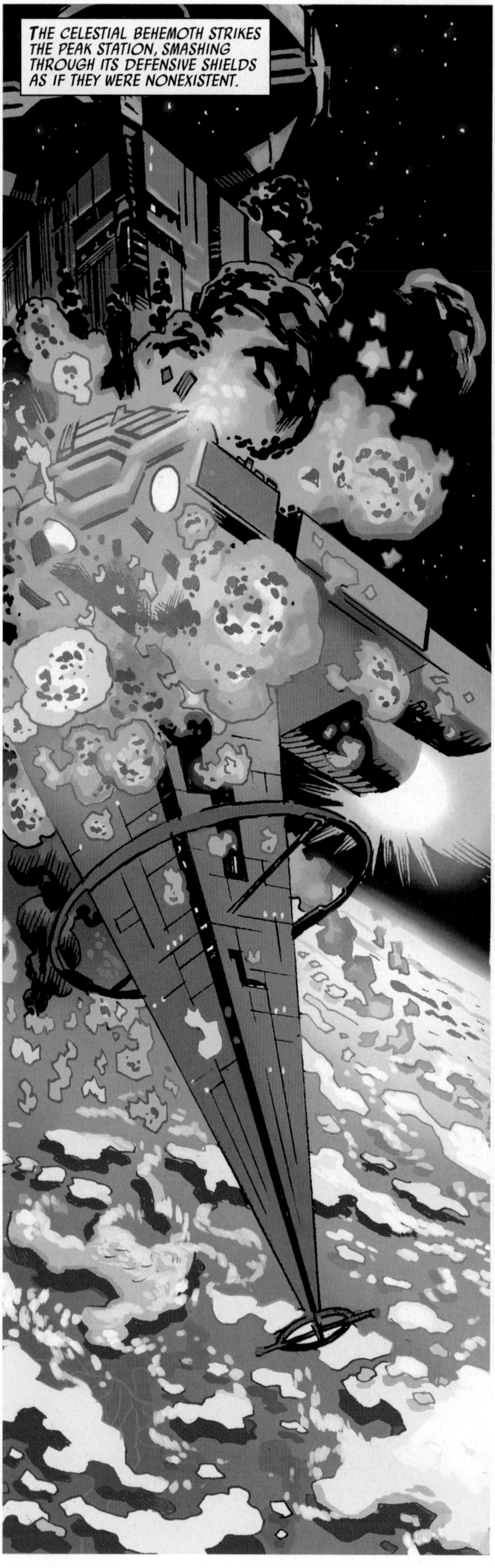
THE CELESTIAL BEHEMOTH STRIKES THE PEAK STATION, SMASHING THROUGH ITS DEFENSIVE SHIELDS AS IF THEY WERE NONEXISTENT.
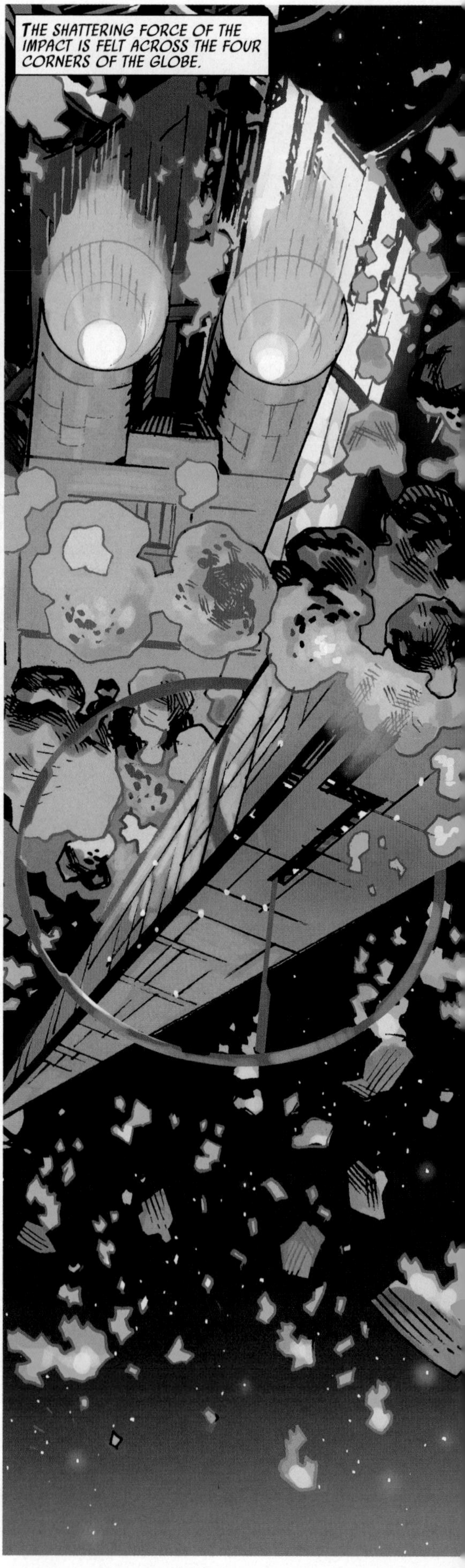
THE SHATTERING FORCE OF THE IMPACT IS FELT ACROSS THE FOUR CORNERS OF THE GLOBE.

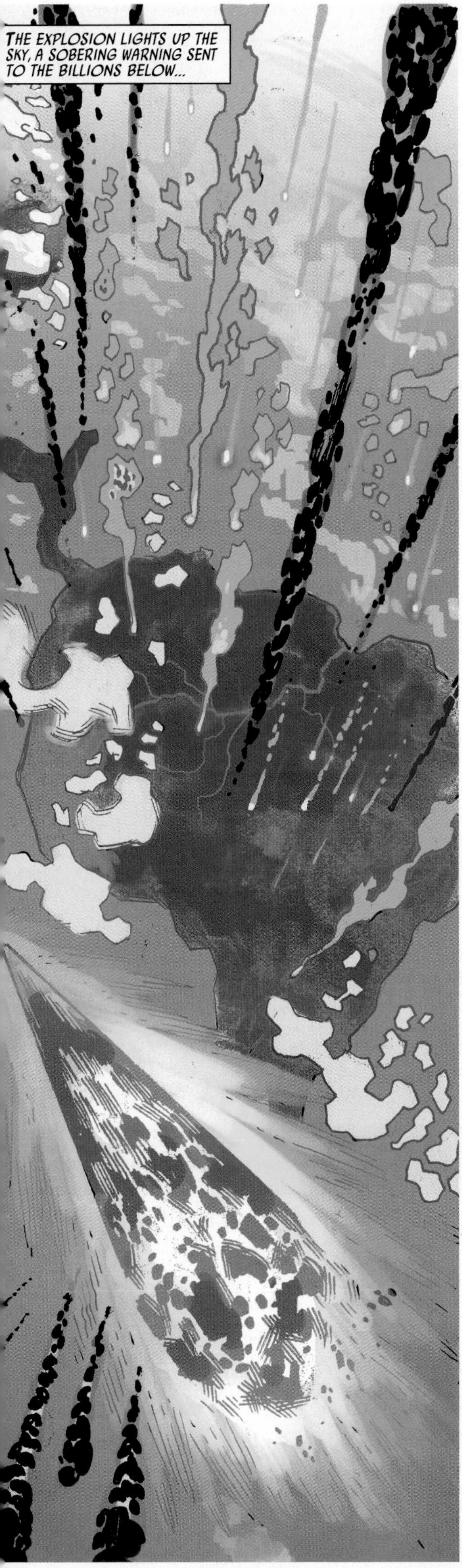
THE EXPLOSION LIGHTS UP THE SKY, A SOBERING WARNING SENT TO THE BILLIONS BELOW...
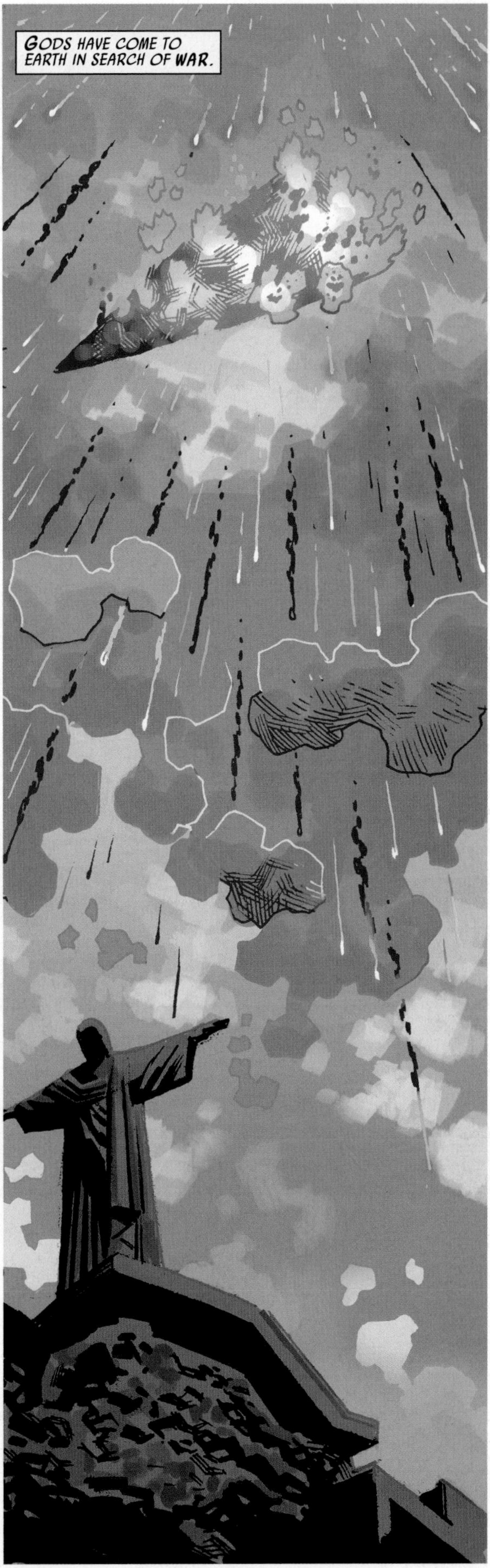
GODS HAVE COME TO EARTH IN SEARCH OF WAR.

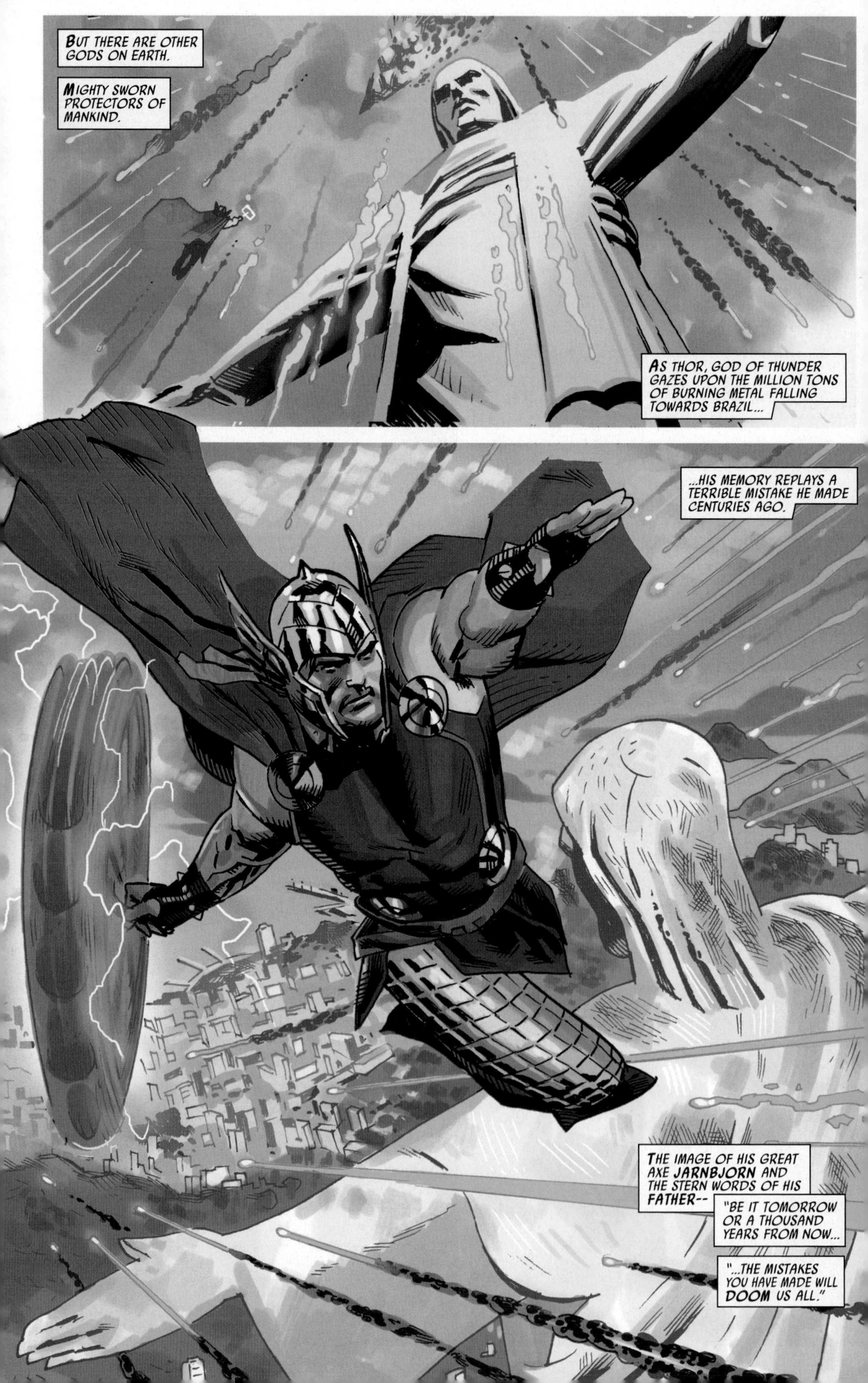

BUT THERE ARE OTHER GODS ON EARTH.
MIGHTY SWORN PROTECTORS OF MANKIND.
AS THOR, GOD OF THUNDER GAZES UPON THE MILLION TONS OF BURNING METAL FALLING TOWARDS BRAZIL...
...HIS MEMORY REPLAYS A TERRIBLE MISTAKE HE MADE CENTURIES AGO.
THE IMAGE OF HIS GREAT AXE JARNBJORN AND THE STERN WORDS OF HIS FATHER--
"BE IT TOMORROW OR A THOUSAND YEARS FROM NOW...
"...THE MISTAKES YOU HAVE MADE WILL DOOM US ALL."

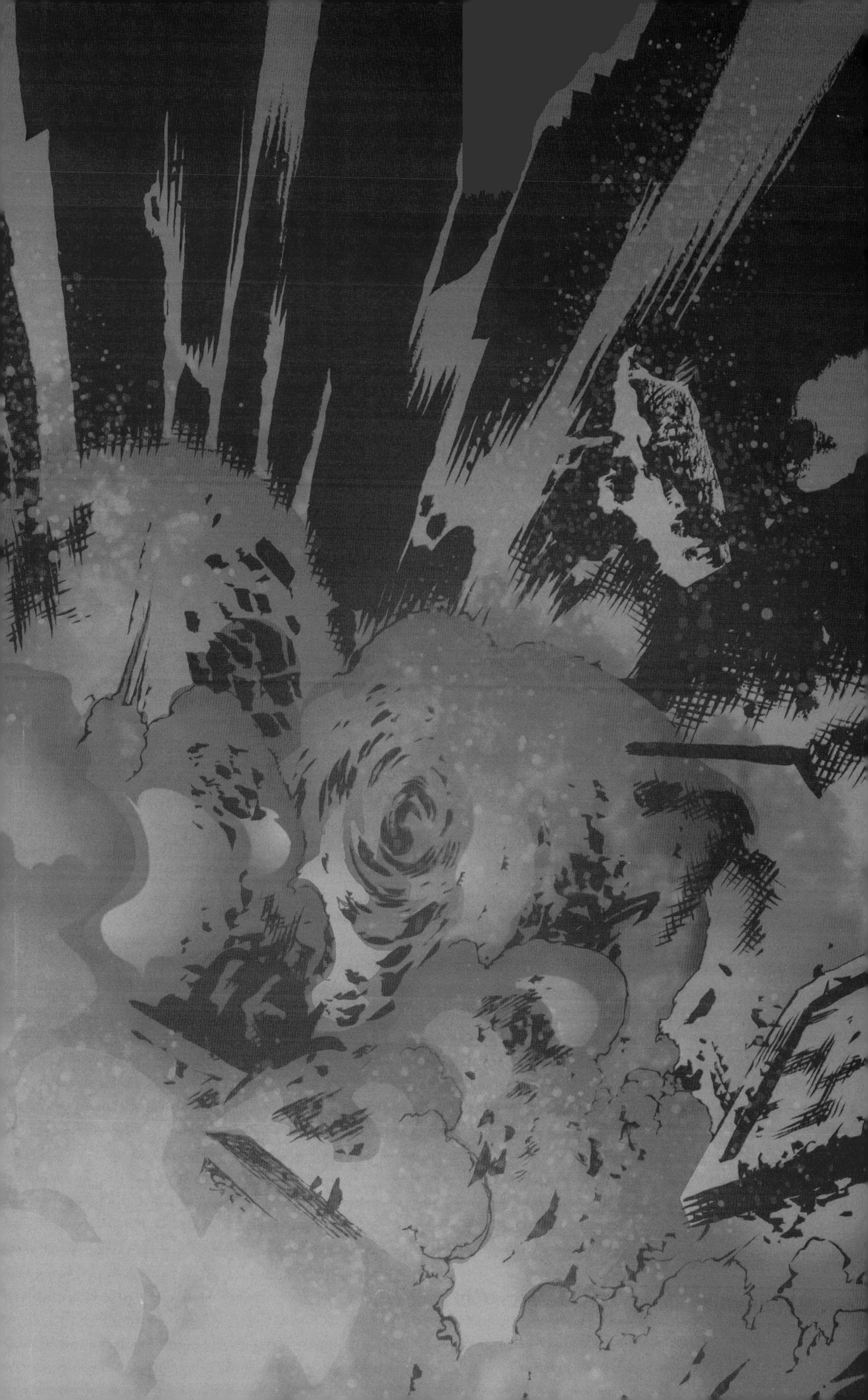

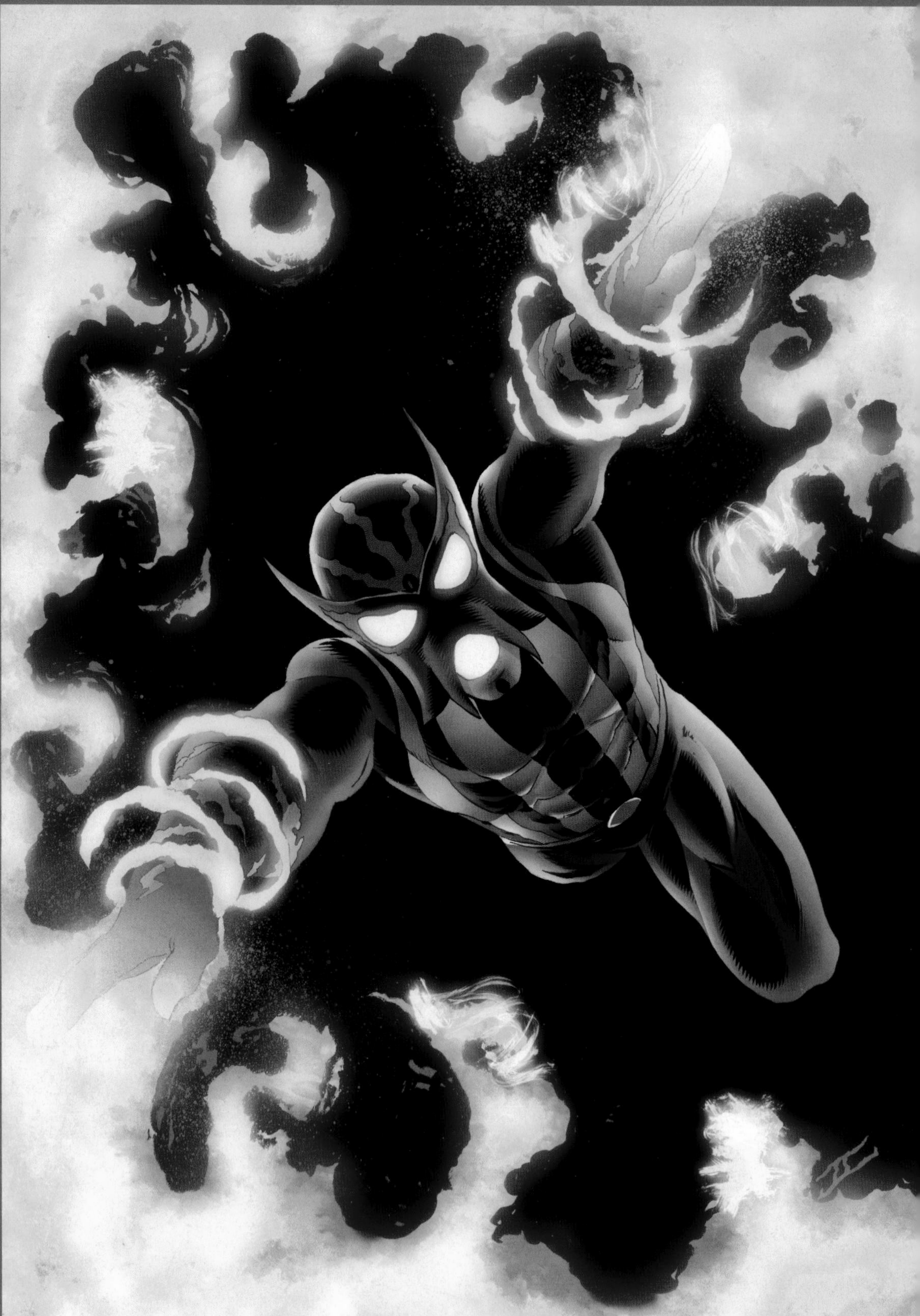

UNCANNY AVENGERS #8

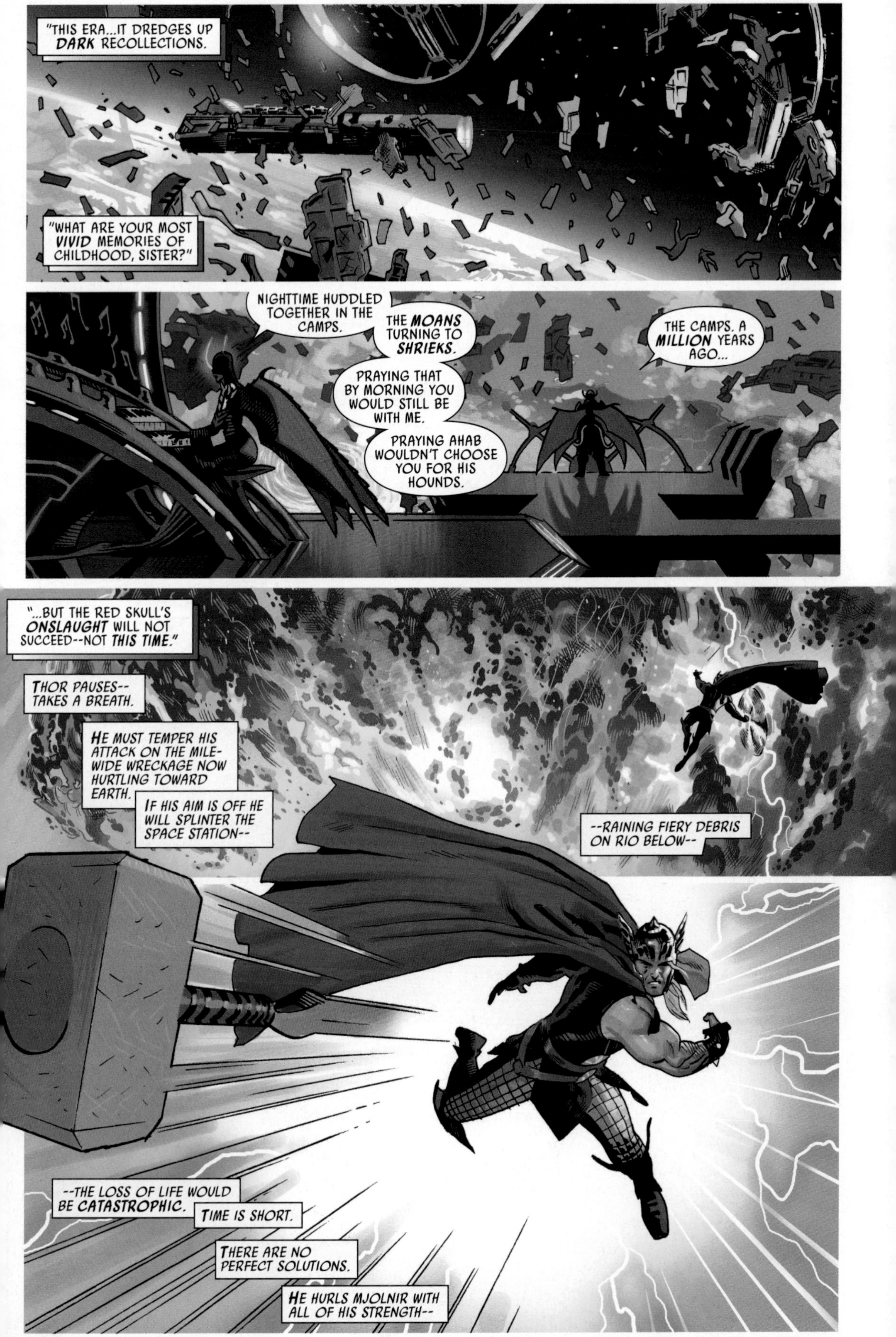
"THIS ERA...IT DREDGES UP DARK RECOLLECTIONS.
"WHAT ARE YOUR MOST VIVID MEMORIES OF CHILDHOOD, SISTER?"
NIGHTTIME HUDDLED TOGETHER IN THE CAMPS.
THE MOANS TURNING TO SHRIEKS.
PRAYING THAT BY MORNING YOU WOULD STILL BE WITH ME.
PRAYING AHAB WOULDN'T CHOOSE YOU FOR HIS HOUNDS.
THE CAMPS. A MILLION YEARS AGO...
"...BUT THE RED SKULL'S ONSLAUGHT WILL NOT SUCCEED--NOT THIS TIME."
THOR PAUSES-- TAKES A BREATH.
HE MUST TEMPER HIS ATTACK ON THE MILE-WIDE WRECKAGE NOW HURTLING TOWARD EARTH.
IF HIS AIM IS OFF HE WILL SPLINTER THE SPACE STATION--
--RAINING FIERY DEBRIS ON RIO BELOW--
--THE LOSS OF LIFE WOULD BE CATASTROPHIC.
TIME IS SHORT.
THERE ARE NO PERFECT SOLUTIONS.
HE HURLS MJOLNIR WITH ALL OF HIS STRENGTH--

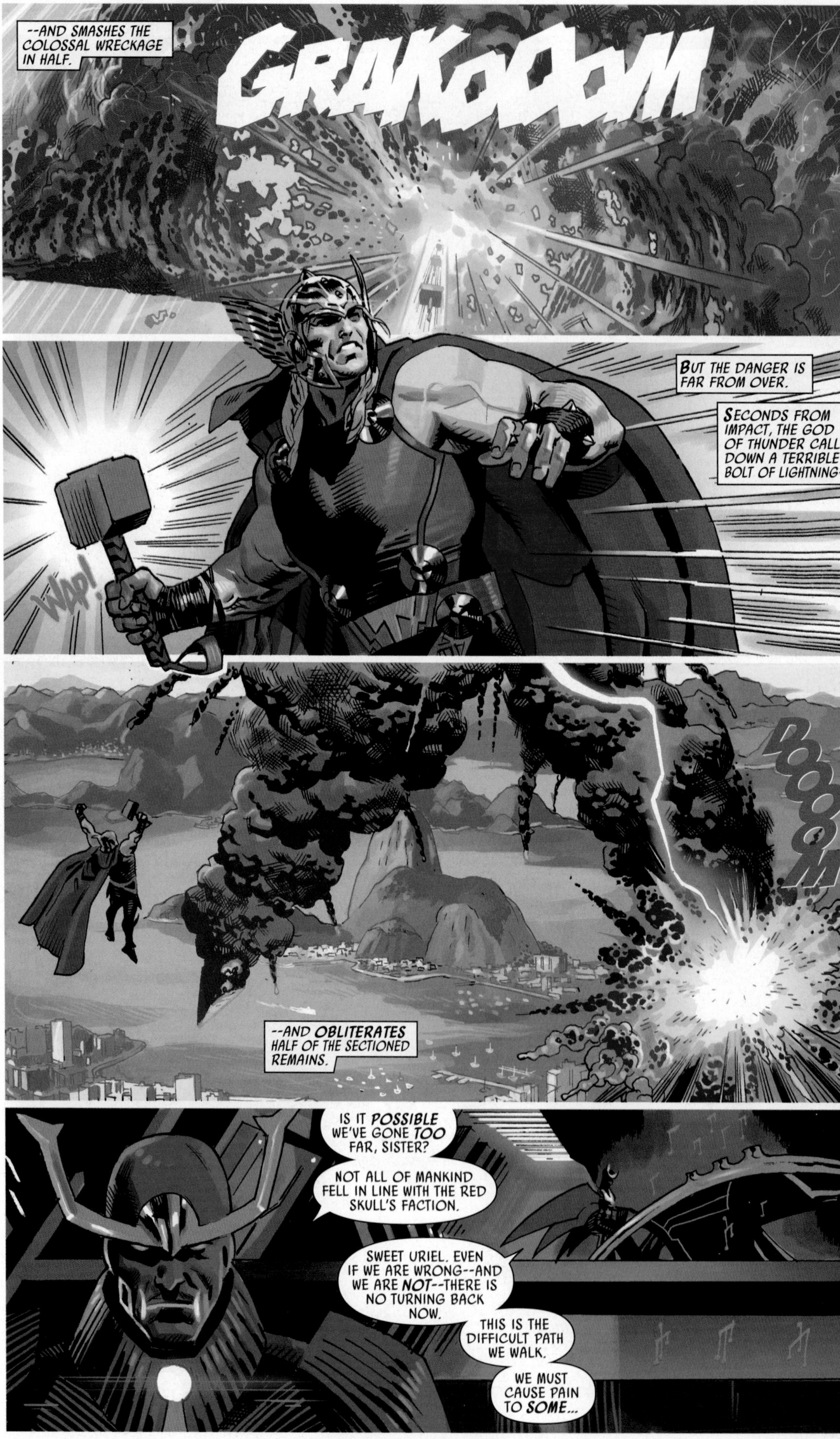
--AND SMASHES THE COLOSSAL WRECKAGE IN HALF.
GRAKOOOM
BUT THE DANGER IS FAR FROM OVER.
SECONDS FROM IMPACT, THE GOD OF THUNDER CALLS DOWN A TERRIBLE BOLT OF LIGHTNING--
WAP!
DOOOOOM
--AND OBLITERATES HALF OF THE SECTIONED REMAINS.
IS IT POSSIBLE WE'VE GONE TOO FAR, SISTER?
NOT ALL OF MANKIND FELL IN LINE WITH THE RED SKULL'S FACTION.
SWEET URIEL. EVEN IF WE ARE WRONG--AND WE ARE NOT--THERE IS NO TURNING BACK NOW.
THIS IS THE DIFFICULT PATH WE WALK.
WE MUST CAUSE PAIN TO SOME...

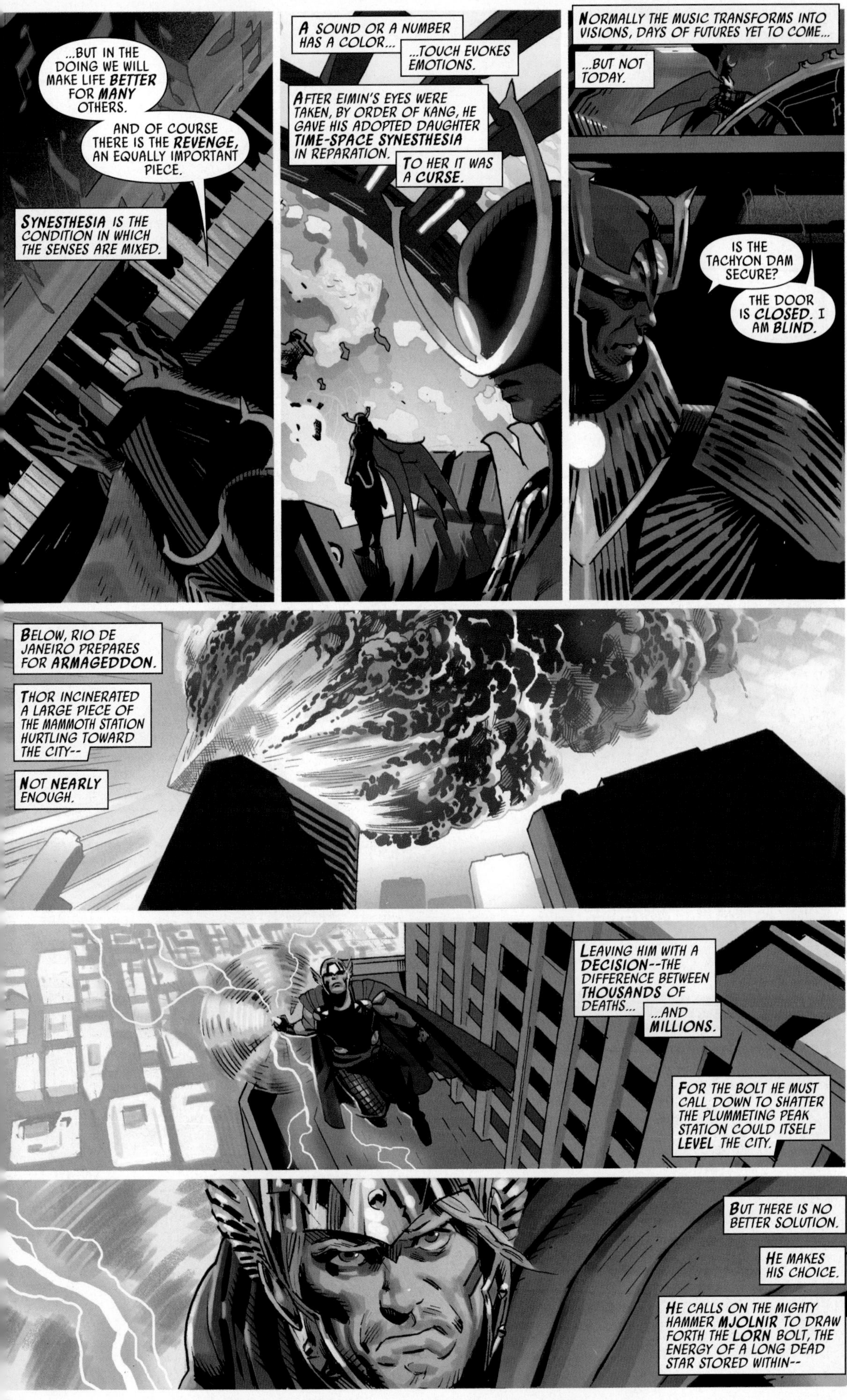
...BUT IN THE DOING WE WILL MAKE LIFE BETTER FOR MANY OTHERS.
AND OF COURSE THERE IS THE REVENGE, AN EQUALLY IMPORTANT PIECE.
SYNESTHESIA IS THE CONDITION IN WHICH THE SENSES ARE MIXED.
A SOUND OR A NUMBER HAS A COLOR...
...TOUCH EVOKES EMOTIONS.
AFTER EIMIN'S EYES WERE TAKEN, BY ORDER OF KANG, HE GAVE HIS ADOPTED DAUGHTER TIME-SPACE SYNESTHESIA IN REPARATION.
TO HER IT WAS A CURSE.
NORMALLY THE MUSIC TRANSFORMS INTO VISIONS, DAYS OF FUTURES YET TO COME...
...BUT NOT TODAY.
IS THE TACHYON DAM SECURE?
THE DOOR IS CLOSED. I AM BLIND.
BELOW, RIO DE JANEIRO PREPARES FOR ARMAGEDDON.
THOR INCINERATED A LARGE PIECE OF THE MAMMOTH STATION HURTLING TOWARD THE CITY--
NOT NEARLY ENOUGH.
LEAVING HIM WITH A DECISION--THE DIFFERENCE BETWEEN THOUSANDS OF DEATHS...
...AND MILLIONS.
FOR THE BOLT HE MUST CALL DOWN TO SHATTER THE PLUMMETING PEAK STATION COULD ITSELF LEVEL THE CITY.
BUT THERE IS NO BETTER SOLUTION.
HE MAKES HIS CHOICE.
HE CALLS ON THE MIGHTY HAMMER MJOLNIR TO DRAW FORTH THE LORN BOLT, THE ENERGY OF A LONG DEAD STAR STORED WITHIN--

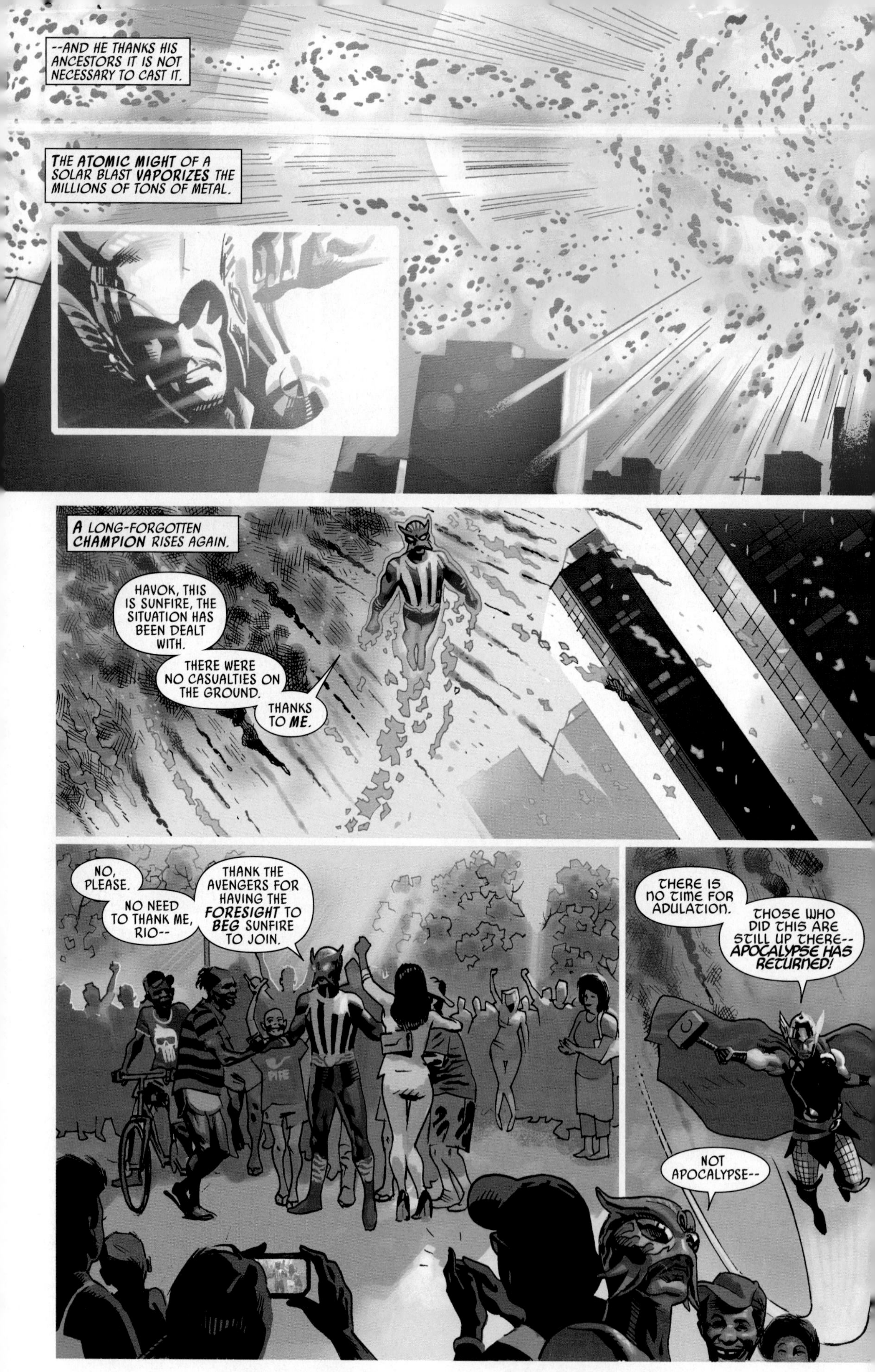
--AND HE THANKS HIS ANCESTORS IT IS NOT NECESSARY TO CAST IT.
THE ATOMIC MIGHT OF A SOLAR BLAST VAPORIZES THE MILLIONS OF TONS OF METAL.
A LONG-FORGOTTEN CHAMPION RISES AGAIN.
HAVOK, THIS IS SUNFIRE, THE SITUATION HAS BEEN DEALT WITH.
THERE WERE NO CASUALTIES ON THE GROUND.
THANKS TO ME.
NO, PLEASE.
NO NEED TO THANK ME, RIO--
THANK THE AVENGERS FOR HAVING THE FORESIGHT TO BEG SUNFIRE TO JOIN.
THERE IS NO TIME FOR ADULATION.
THOSE WHO DID THIS ARE STILL UP THERE-- APOCALYPSE HAS RETURNED!
NOT APOCALYPSE--

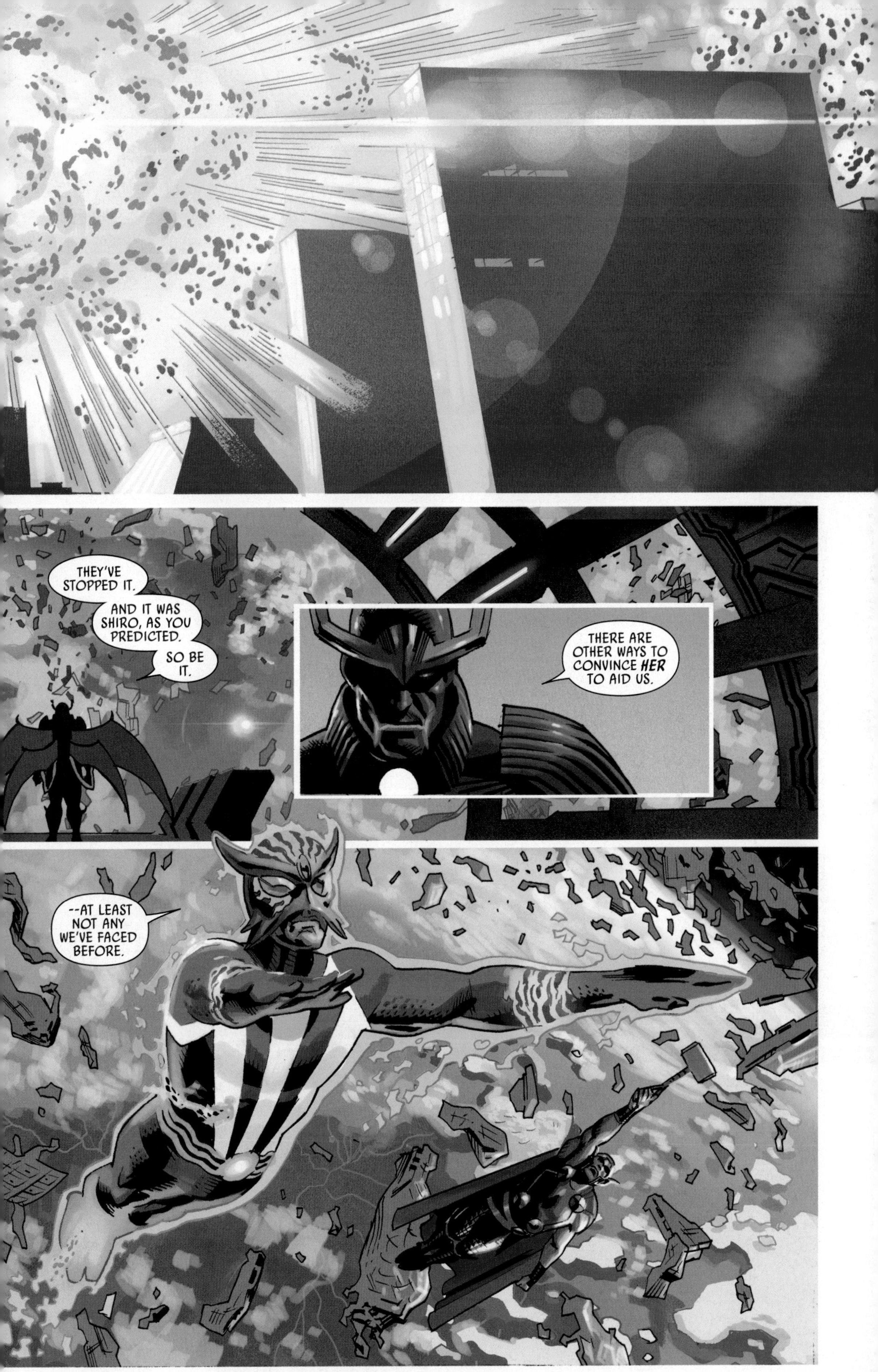
THEY'VE STOPPED IT.
AND IT WAS SHIRO, AS YOU PREDICTED.
SO BE IT.
THERE ARE OTHER WAYS TO CONVINCE **HER** TO AID US.
--AT LEAST NOT ANY WE'VE FACED BEFORE.

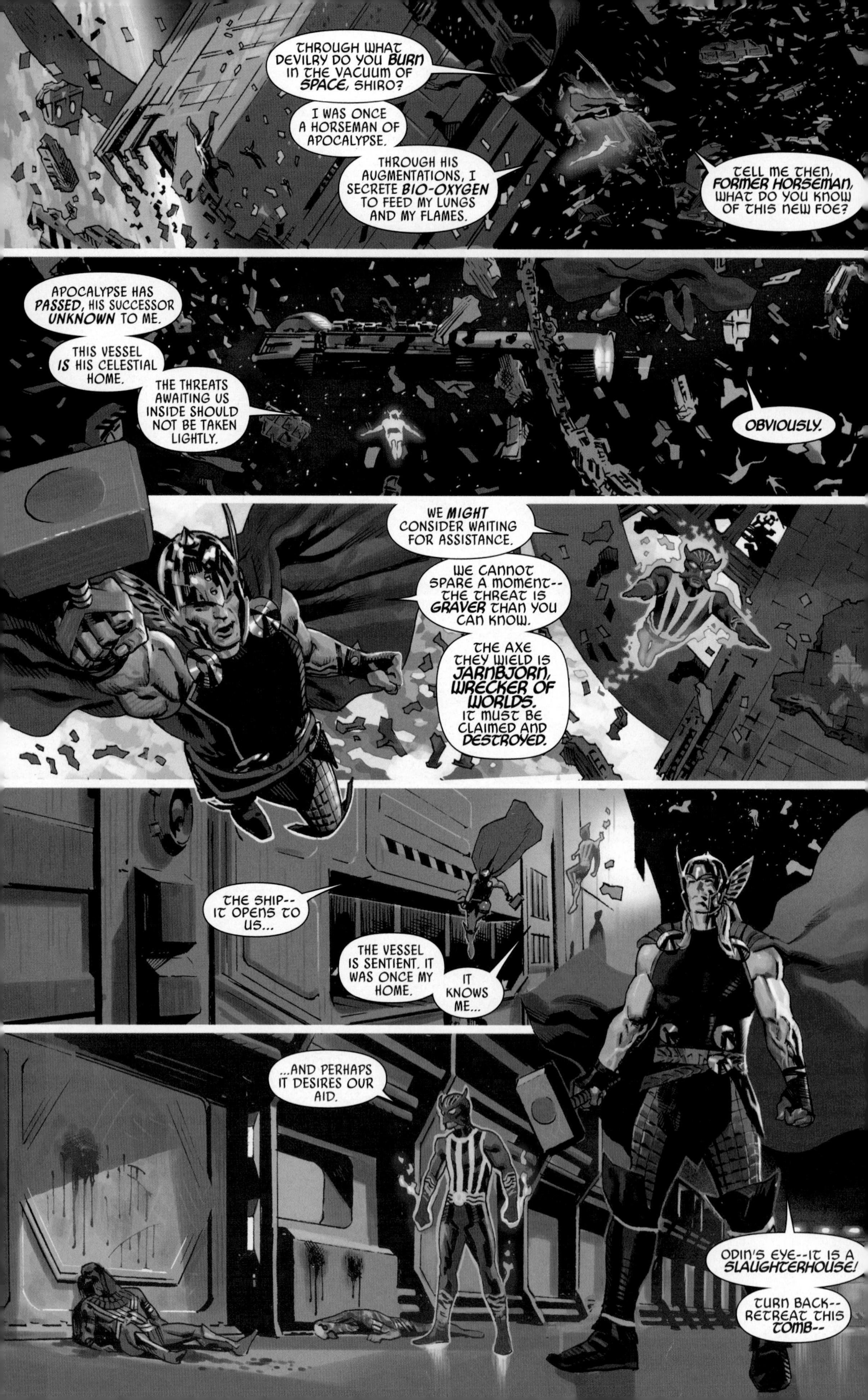
THROUGH WHAT DEVILRY DO YOU BURN IN THE VACUUM OF SPACE, SHIRO?
I WAS ONCE A HORSEMAN OF APOCALYPSE.
THROUGH HIS AUGMENTATIONS, I SECRETE BIO-OXYGEN TO FEED MY LUNGS AND MY FLAMES.
TELL ME THEN, FORMER HORSEMAN, WHAT DO YOU KNOW OF THIS NEW FOE?
APOCALYPSE HAS PASSED, HIS SUCCESSOR UNKNOWN TO ME.
THIS VESSEL IS HIS CELESTIAL HOME.
THE THREATS AWAITING US INSIDE SHOULD NOT BE TAKEN LIGHTLY.
OBVIOUSLY.
WE MIGHT CONSIDER WAITING FOR ASSISTANCE.
WE CANNOT SPARE A MOMENT--THE THREAT IS GRAVER THAN YOU CAN KNOW.
THE AXE THEY WIELD IS JARNBJORN, WRECKER OF WORLDS. IT MUST BE CLAIMED AND DESTROYED.
THE SHIP--IT OPENS TO US...
THE VESSEL IS SENTIENT. IT WAS ONCE MY HOME.
IT KNOWS ME...
...AND PERHAPS IT DESIRES OUR AID.
ODIN'S EYE--IT IS A SLAUGHTERHOUSE!
TURN BACK--RETREAT THIS TOMB--

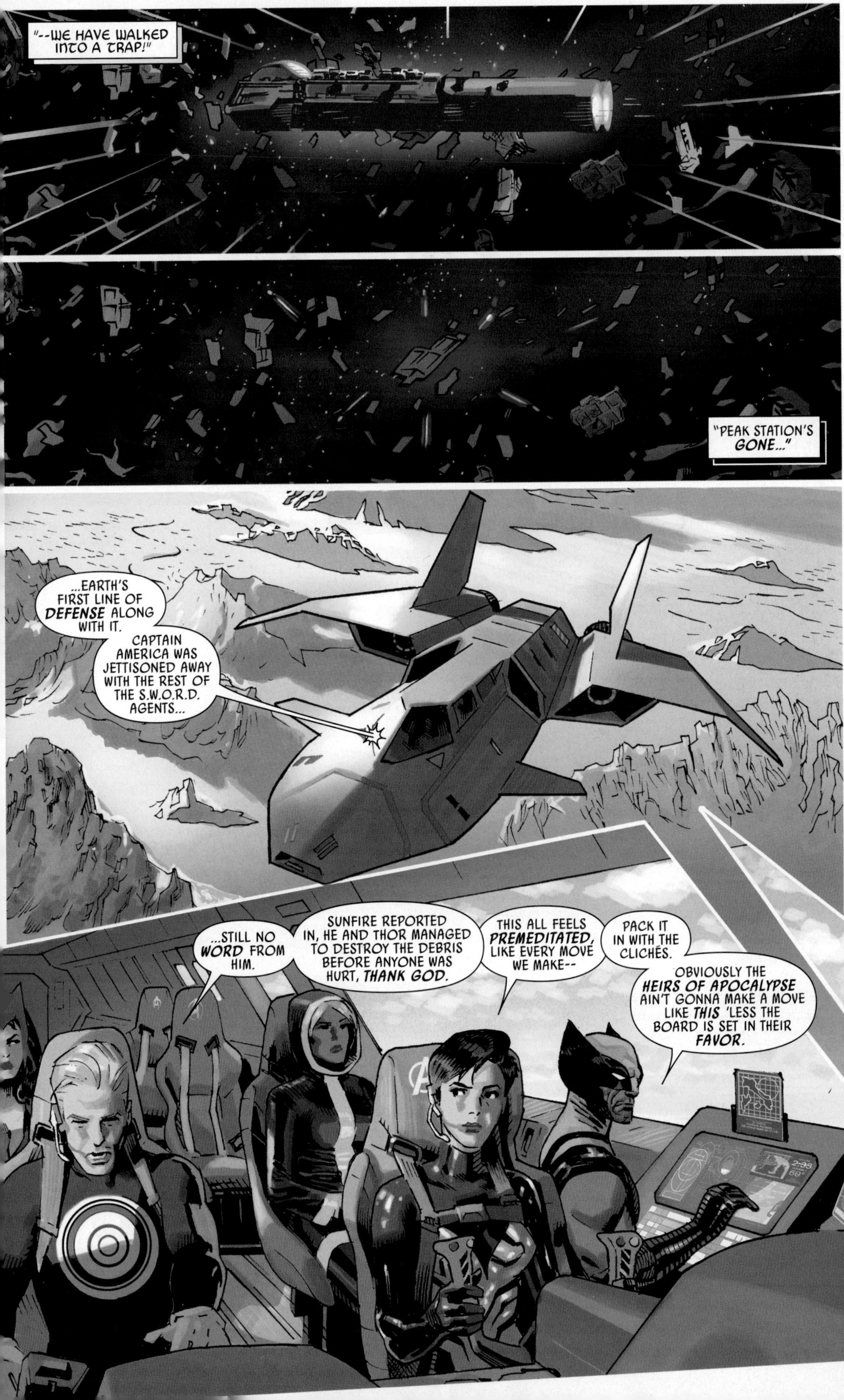
"--WE HAVE WALKED INTO A TRAP!"
"PEAK STATION'S GONE..."
...EARTH'S FIRST LINE OF DEFENSE ALONG WITH IT.
CAPTAIN AMERICA WAS JETTISONED AWAY WITH THE REST OF THE S.W.O.R.D. AGENTS...
...STILL NO WORD FROM HIM.
SUNFIRE REPORTED IN, HE AND THOR MANAGED TO DESTROY THE DEBRIS BEFORE ANYONE WAS HURT, THANK GOD.
THIS ALL FEELS PREMEDITATED, LIKE EVERY MOVE WE MAKE--
PACK IT IN WITH THE CLICHÉS.
OBVIOUSLY THE HEIRS OF APOCALYPSE AIN'T GONNA MAKE A MOVE LIKE THIS 'LESS THE BOARD IS SET IN THEIR FAVOR.

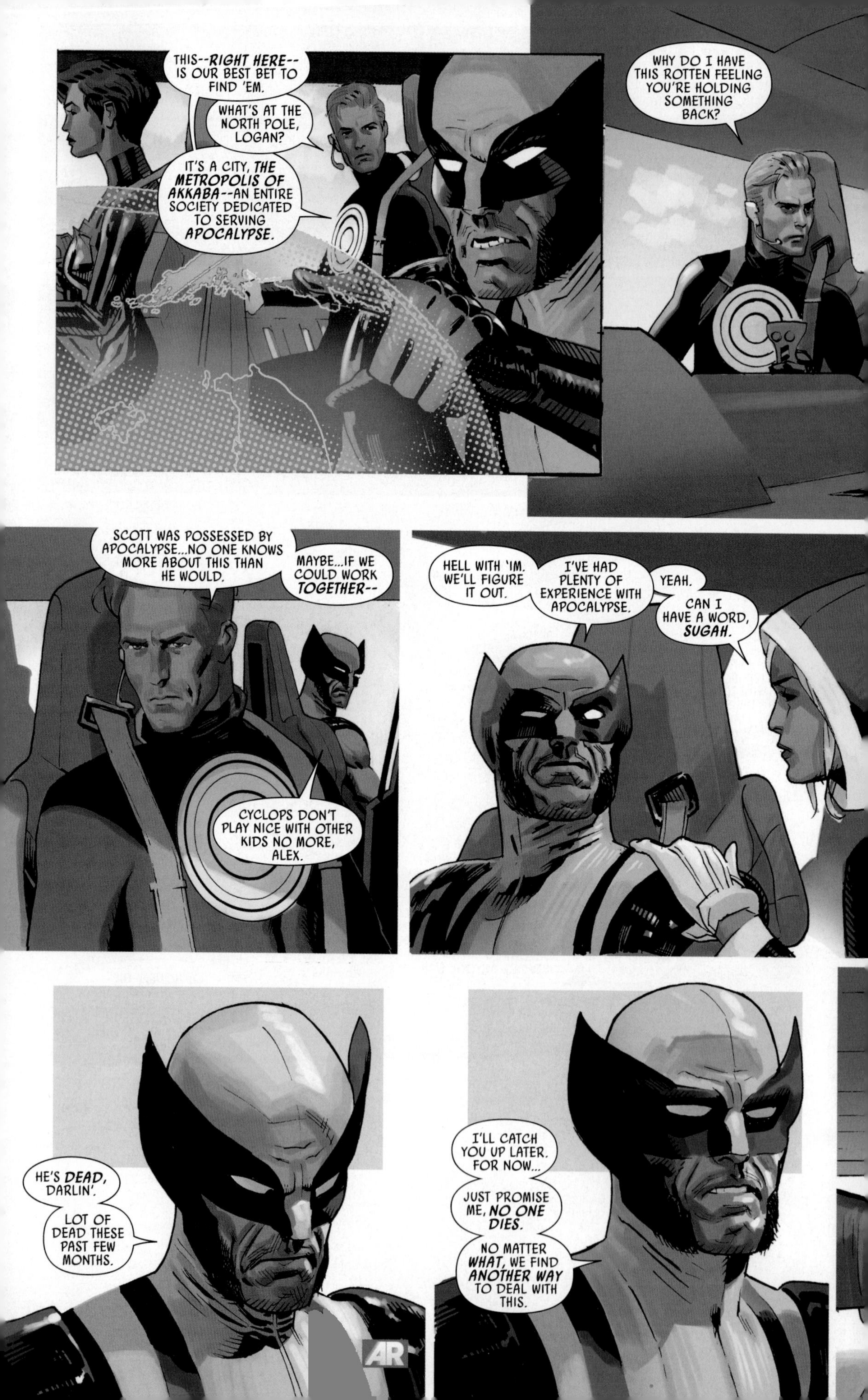
THIS--RIGHT HERE--IS OUR BEST BET TO FIND 'EM.
WHAT'S AT THE NORTH POLE, LOGAN?
IT'S A CITY, THE METROPOLIS OF AKKABA--AN ENTIRE SOCIETY DEDICATED TO SERVING APOCALYPSE.
WHY DO I HAVE THIS ROTTEN FEELING YOU'RE HOLDING SOMETHING BACK?
SCOTT WAS POSSESSED BY APOCALYPSE...NO ONE KNOWS MORE ABOUT THIS THAN HE WOULD.
MAYBE...IF WE COULD WORK TOGETHER--
CYCLOPS DON'T PLAY NICE WITH OTHER KIDS NO MORE, ALEX.
HELL WITH 'IM. WE'LL FIGURE IT OUT.
I'VE HAD PLENTY OF EXPERIENCE WITH APOCALYPSE.
YEAH.
CAN I HAVE A WORD, SUGAH.
HE'S DEAD, DARLIN'.
LOT OF DEAD THESE PAST FEW MONTHS.
I'LL CATCH YOU UP LATER. FOR NOW...
JUST PROMISE ME, NO ONE DIES.
NO MATTER WHAT, WE FIND ANOTHER WAY TO DEAL WITH THIS.

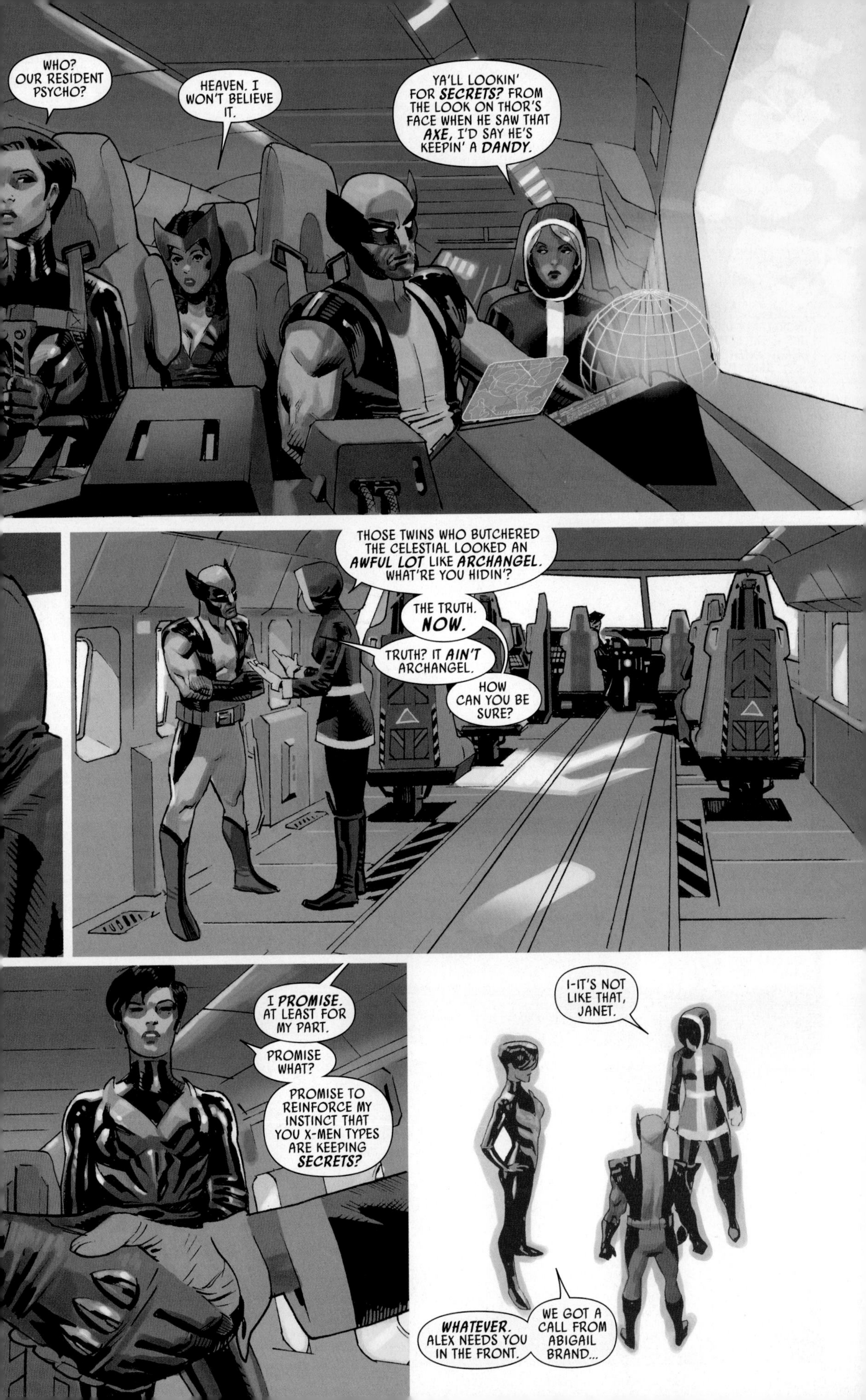

WHO? OUR RESIDENT PSYCHO?
HEAVEN. I WON'T BELIEVE IT.
YA'LL LOOKIN' FOR SECRETS? FROM THE LOOK ON THOR'S FACE WHEN HE SAW THAT AXE, I'D SAY HE'S KEEPIN' A DANDY.
THOSE TWINS WHO BUTCHERED THE CELESTIAL LOOKED AN AWFUL LOT LIKE ARCHANGEL. WHAT'RE YOU HIDIN'?
THE TRUTH. NOW.
TRUTH? IT AIN'T ARCHANGEL.
HOW CAN YOU BE SURE?
I PROMISE. AT LEAST FOR MY PART.
PROMISE WHAT?
PROMISE TO REINFORCE MY INSTINCT THAT YOU X-MEN TYPES ARE KEEPING SECRETS?
I-IT'S NOT LIKE THAT, JANET.
WE GOT A CALL FROM ABIGAIL BRAND...
WHATEVER. ALEX NEEDS YOU IN THE FRONT.

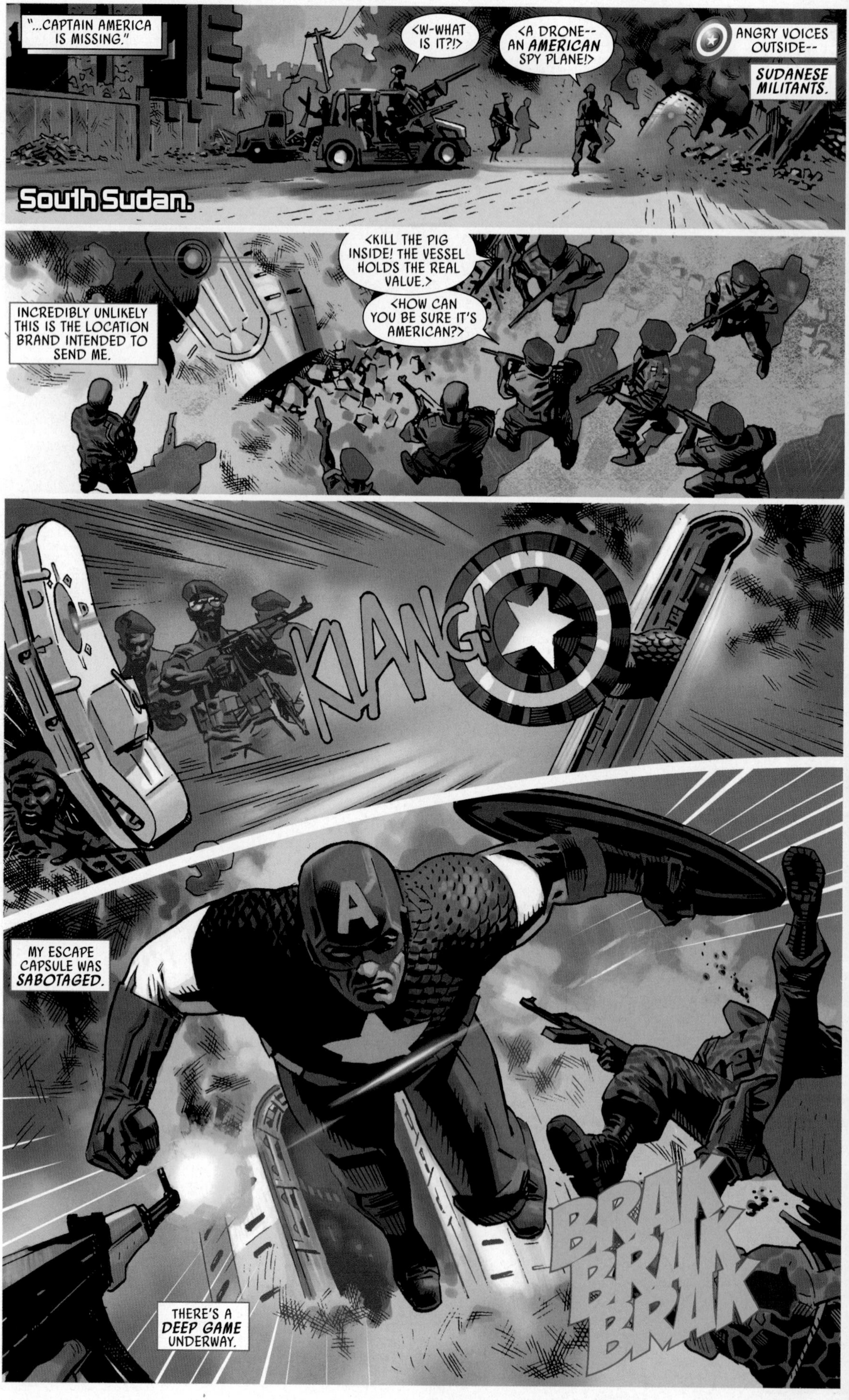
"...CAPTAIN AMERICA IS MISSING."
<W-WHAT IS IT?!>
<A DRONE-- AN AMERICAN SPY PLANE!>
ANGRY VOICES OUTSIDE--
SUDANESE MILITANTS.
South Sudan.
<KILL THE PIG INSIDE! THE VESSEL HOLDS THE REAL VALUE.>
INCREDIBLY UNLIKELY THIS IS THE LOCATION BRAND INTENDED TO SEND ME.
<HOW CAN YOU BE SURE IT'S AMERICAN?>
KLANG!
MY ESCAPE CAPSULE WAS SABOTAGED.
BRAK BRAK BRAK
THERE'S A DEEP GAME UNDERWAY.

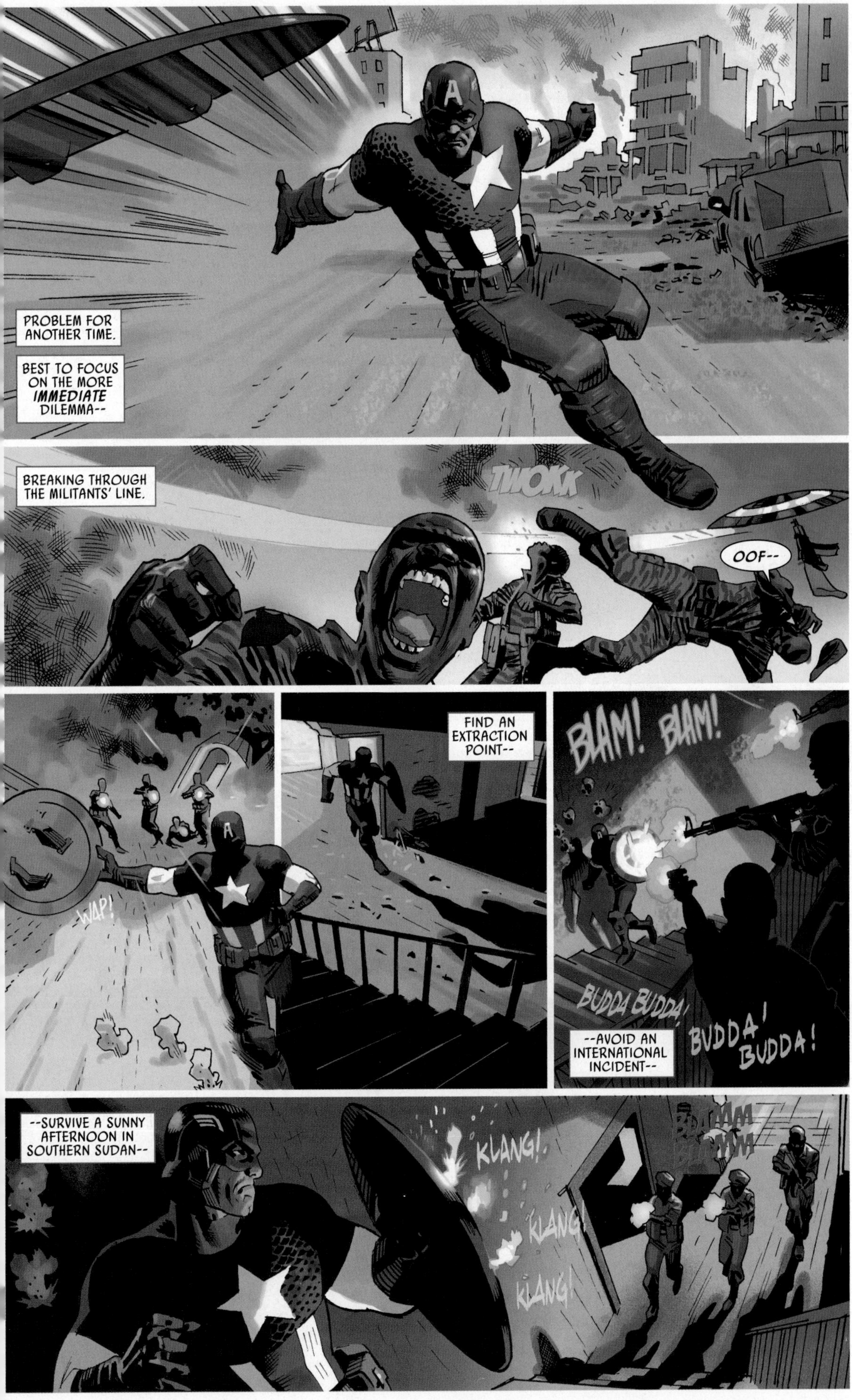
PROBLEM FOR ANOTHER TIME.
BEST TO FOCUS ON THE MORE IMMEDIATE DILEMMA--
BREAKING THROUGH THE MILITANTS' LINE.
TWOKK
OOF--
WAP!
FIND AN EXTRACTION POINT--
BLAM! BLAM!
BUDDA BUDDA!
BUDDA! BUDDA!
--AVOID AN INTERNATIONAL INCIDENT--
--SURVIVE A SUNNY AFTERNOON IN SOUTHERN SUDAN--
KLANG!
KLANG!
KLANG!

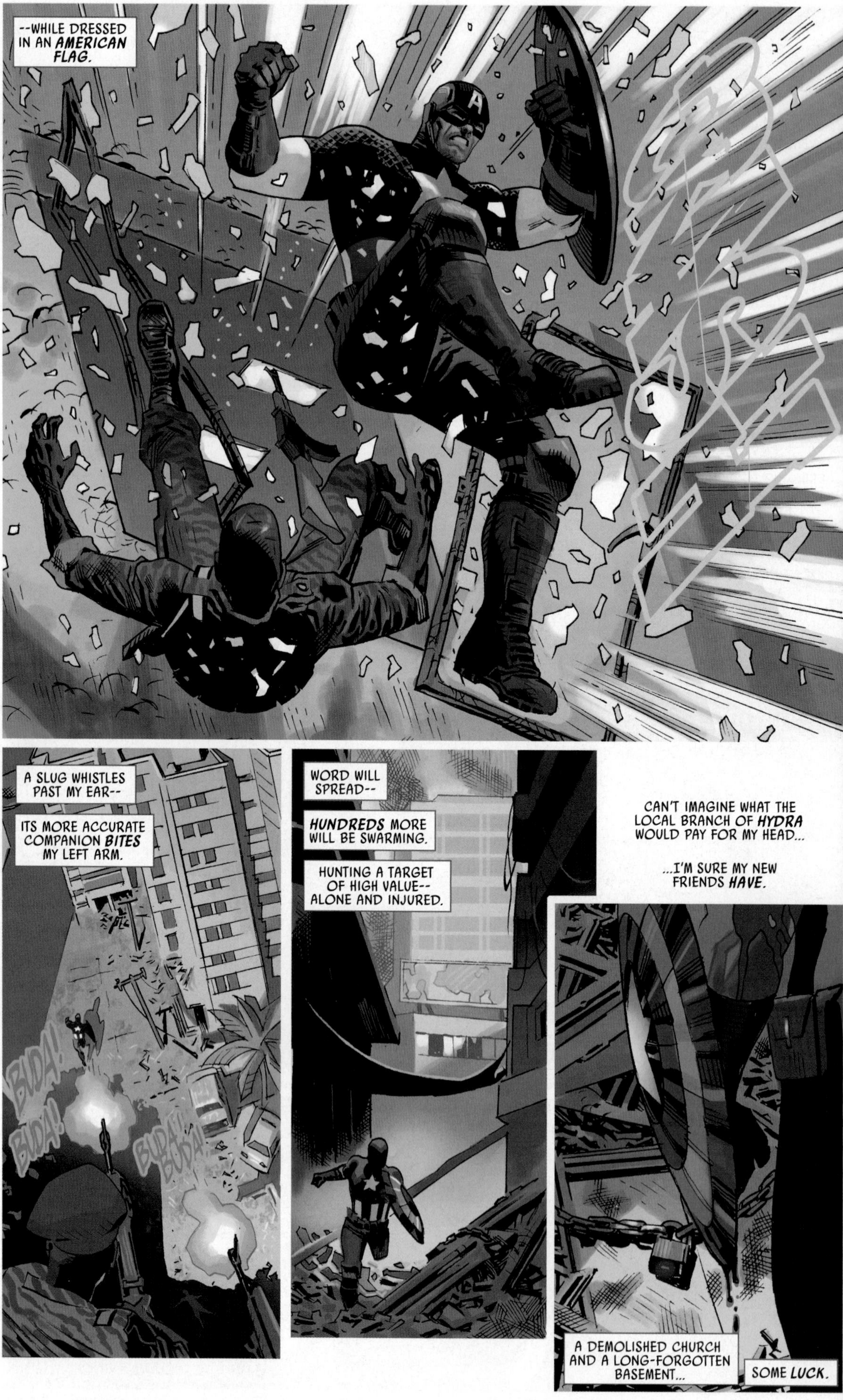

--WHILE DRESSED IN AN *AMERICAN FLAG.*
A SLUG WHISTLES PAST MY EAR--
ITS MORE ACCURATE COMPANION *BITES* MY LEFT ARM.
BUDA! BUDA!
BUDA! BUDA!
WORD WILL SPREAD--
HUNDREDS MORE WILL BE SWARMING.
HUNTING A TARGET OF HIGH VALUE-- ALONE AND INJURED.
CAN'T IMAGINE WHAT THE LOCAL BRANCH OF *HYDRA* WOULD PAY FOR MY HEAD...
...I'M SURE MY NEW FRIENDS *HAVE.*
A DEMOLISHED CHURCH AND A LONG-FORGOTTEN BASEMENT...
SOME *LUCK.*

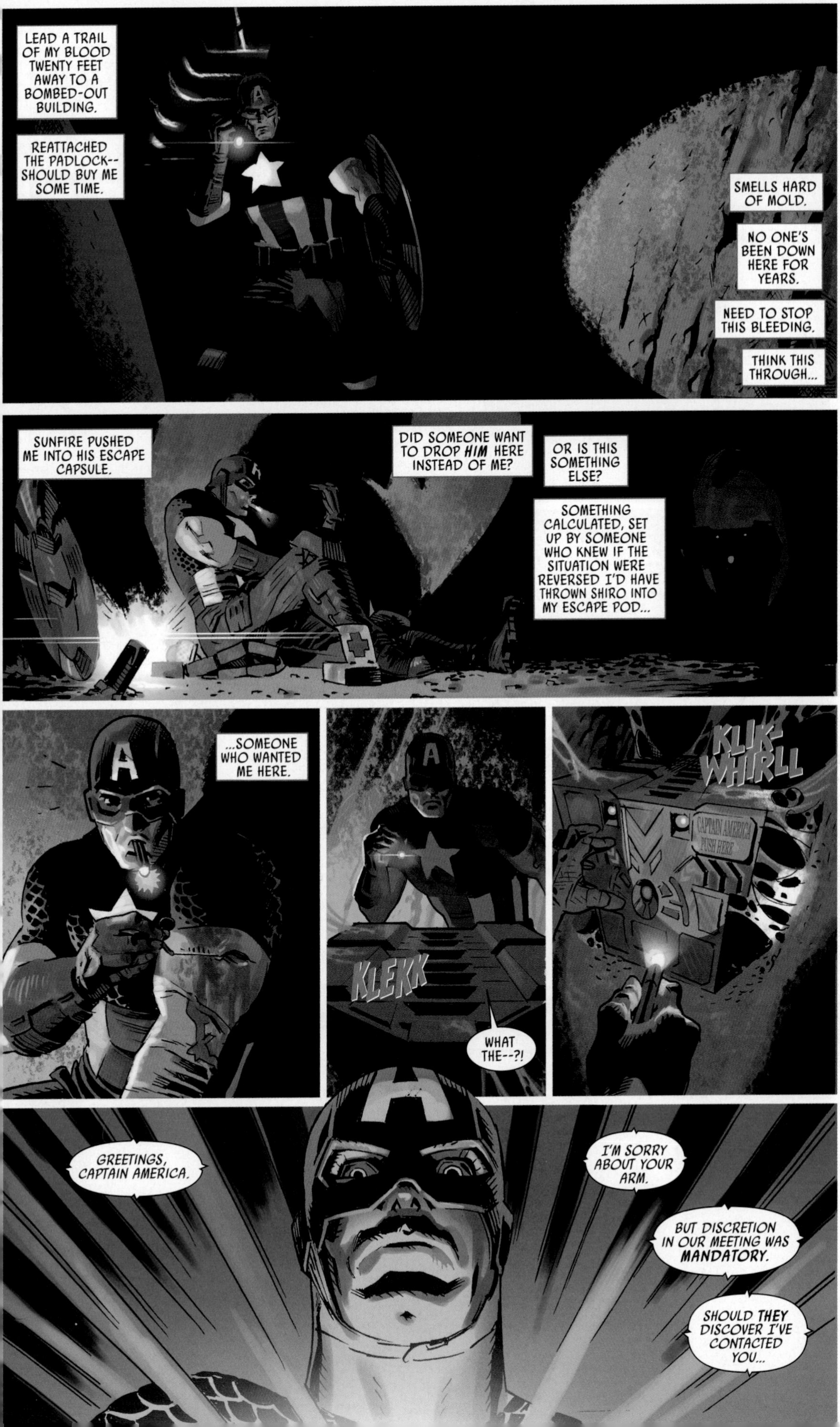
LEAD A TRAIL OF MY BLOOD TWENTY FEET AWAY TO A BOMBED-OUT BUILDING.
REATTACHED THE PADLOCK--SHOULD BUY ME SOME TIME.
SMELLS HARD OF MOLD.
NO ONE'S BEEN DOWN HERE FOR YEARS.
NEED TO STOP THIS BLEEDING.
THINK THIS THROUGH...
SUNFIRE PUSHED ME INTO HIS ESCAPE CAPSULE.
DID SOMEONE WANT TO DROP HIM HERE INSTEAD OF ME?
OR IS THIS SOMETHING ELSE?
SOMETHING CALCULATED, SET UP BY SOMEONE WHO KNEW IF THE SITUATION WERE REVERSED I'D HAVE THROWN SHIRO INTO MY ESCAPE POD...
...SOMEONE WHO WANTED ME HERE.
KLEKK
WHAT THE--?!
KLIK-WHIRLL
CAPTAIN AMERICA PUSH HERE
GREETINGS, CAPTAIN AMERICA.
I'M SORRY ABOUT YOUR ARM.
BUT DISCRETION IN OUR MEETING WAS MANDATORY.
SHOULD THEY DISCOVER I'VE CONTACTED YOU...

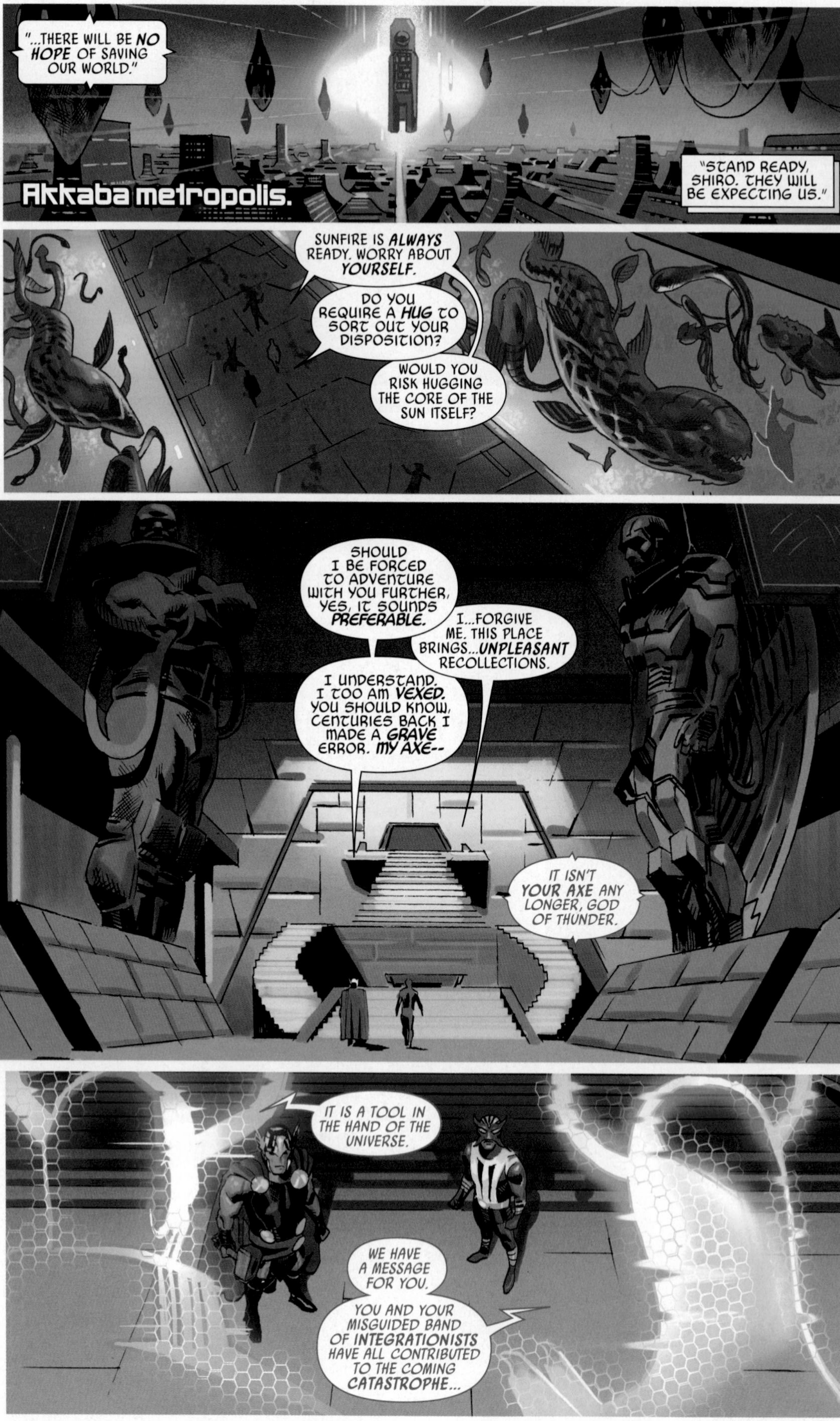
"...THERE WILL BE NO HOPE OF SAVING OUR WORLD."
Akkaba metropolis.
"STAND READY, SHIRO. THEY WILL BE EXPECTING US."
SUNFIRE IS ALWAYS READY. WORRY ABOUT YOURSELF.
DO YOU REQUIRE A HUG TO SORT OUT YOUR DISPOSITION?
WOULD YOU RISK HUGGING THE CORE OF THE SUN ITSELF?
SHOULD I BE FORCED TO ADVENTURE WITH YOU FURTHER, YES, IT SOUNDS PREFERABLE.
I...FORGIVE ME. THIS PLACE BRINGS...UNPLEASANT RECOLLECTIONS.
I UNDERSTAND. I TOO AM VEXED. YOU SHOULD KNOW, CENTURIES BACK I MADE A GRAVE ERROR. MY AXE--
IT ISN'T YOUR AXE ANY LONGER, GOD OF THUNDER.
IT IS A TOOL IN THE HAND OF THE UNIVERSE.
WE HAVE A MESSAGE FOR YOU.
YOU AND YOUR MISGUIDED BAND OF INTEGRATIONISTS HAVE ALL CONTRIBUTED TO THE COMING CATASTROPHE...

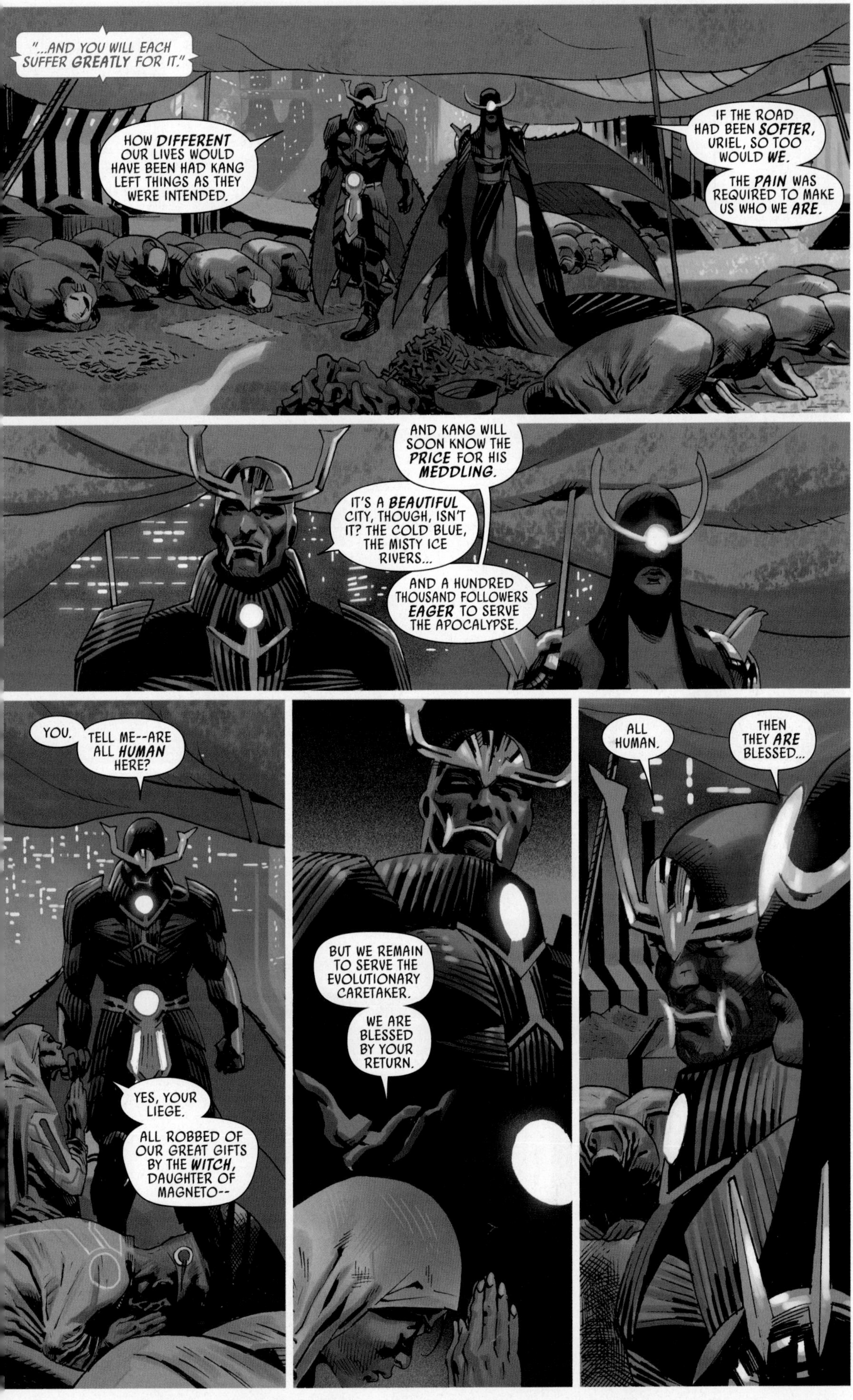
"...AND YOU WILL EACH SUFFER GREATLY FOR IT."
HOW DIFFERENT OUR LIVES WOULD HAVE BEEN HAD KANG LEFT THINGS AS THEY WERE INTENDED.
IF THE ROAD HAD BEEN SOFTER, URIEL, SO TOO WOULD WE.
THE PAIN WAS REQUIRED TO MAKE US WHO WE ARE.
AND KANG WILL SOON KNOW THE PRICE FOR HIS MEDDLING.
IT'S A BEAUTIFUL CITY, THOUGH, ISN'T IT? THE COLD BLUE, THE MISTY ICE RIVERS...
AND A HUNDRED THOUSAND FOLLOWERS EAGER TO SERVE THE APOCALYPSE.
YOU.
TELL ME--ARE ALL HUMAN HERE?
YES, YOUR LIEGE.
ALL ROBBED OF OUR GREAT GIFTS BY THE WITCH, DAUGHTER OF MAGNETO--
BUT WE REMAIN TO SERVE THE EVOLUTIONARY CARETAKER.
WE ARE BLESSED BY YOUR RETURN.
ALL HUMAN.
THEN THEY ARE BLESSED...

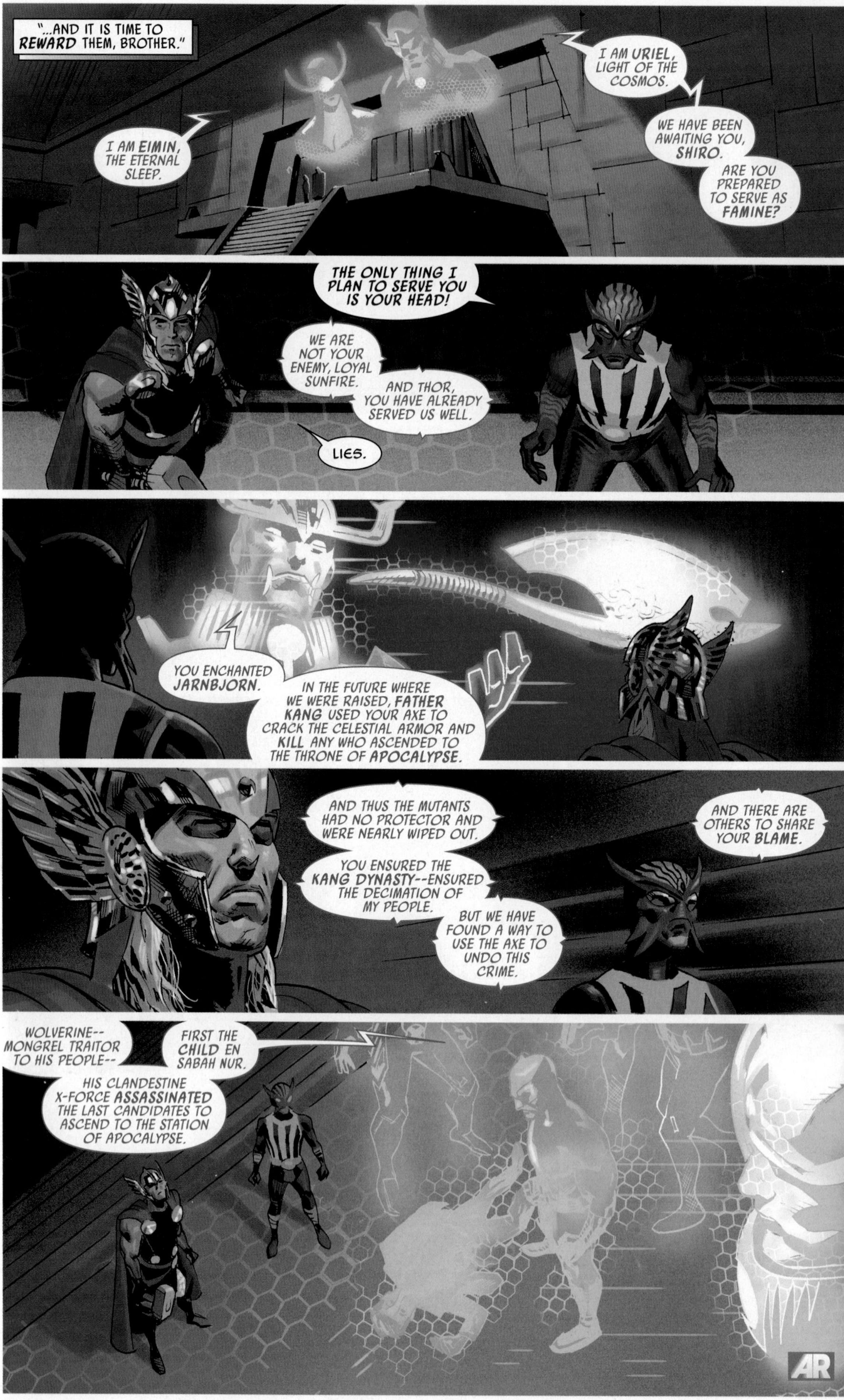
"...AND IT IS TIME TO REWARD THEM, BROTHER."
I AM URIEL, LIGHT OF THE COSMOS.
I AM EIMIN, THE ETERNAL SLEEP.
WE HAVE BEEN AWAITING YOU, SHIRO.
ARE YOU PREPARED TO SERVE AS FAMINE?
THE ONLY THING I PLAN TO SERVE YOU IS YOUR HEAD!
WE ARE NOT YOUR ENEMY, LOYAL SUNFIRE.
AND THOR, YOU HAVE ALREADY SERVED US WELL.
LIES.
YOU ENCHANTED JARNBJORN.
IN THE FUTURE WHERE WE WERE RAISED, FATHER KANG USED YOUR AXE TO CRACK THE CELESTIAL ARMOR AND KILL ANY WHO ASCENDED TO THE THRONE OF APOCALYPSE.
AND THUS THE MUTANTS HAD NO PROTECTOR AND WERE NEARLY WIPED OUT.
YOU ENSURED THE KANG DYNASTY--ENSURED THE DECIMATION OF MY PEOPLE.
BUT WE HAVE FOUND A WAY TO USE THE AXE TO UNDO THIS CRIME.
AND THERE ARE OTHERS TO SHARE YOUR BLAME.
FIRST THE CHILD EN SABAH NUR.
WOLVERINE-- MONGREL TRAITOR TO HIS PEOPLE--
HIS CLANDESTINE X-FORCE ASSASSINATED THE LAST CANDIDATES TO ASCEND TO THE STATION OF APOCALYPSE.
AR

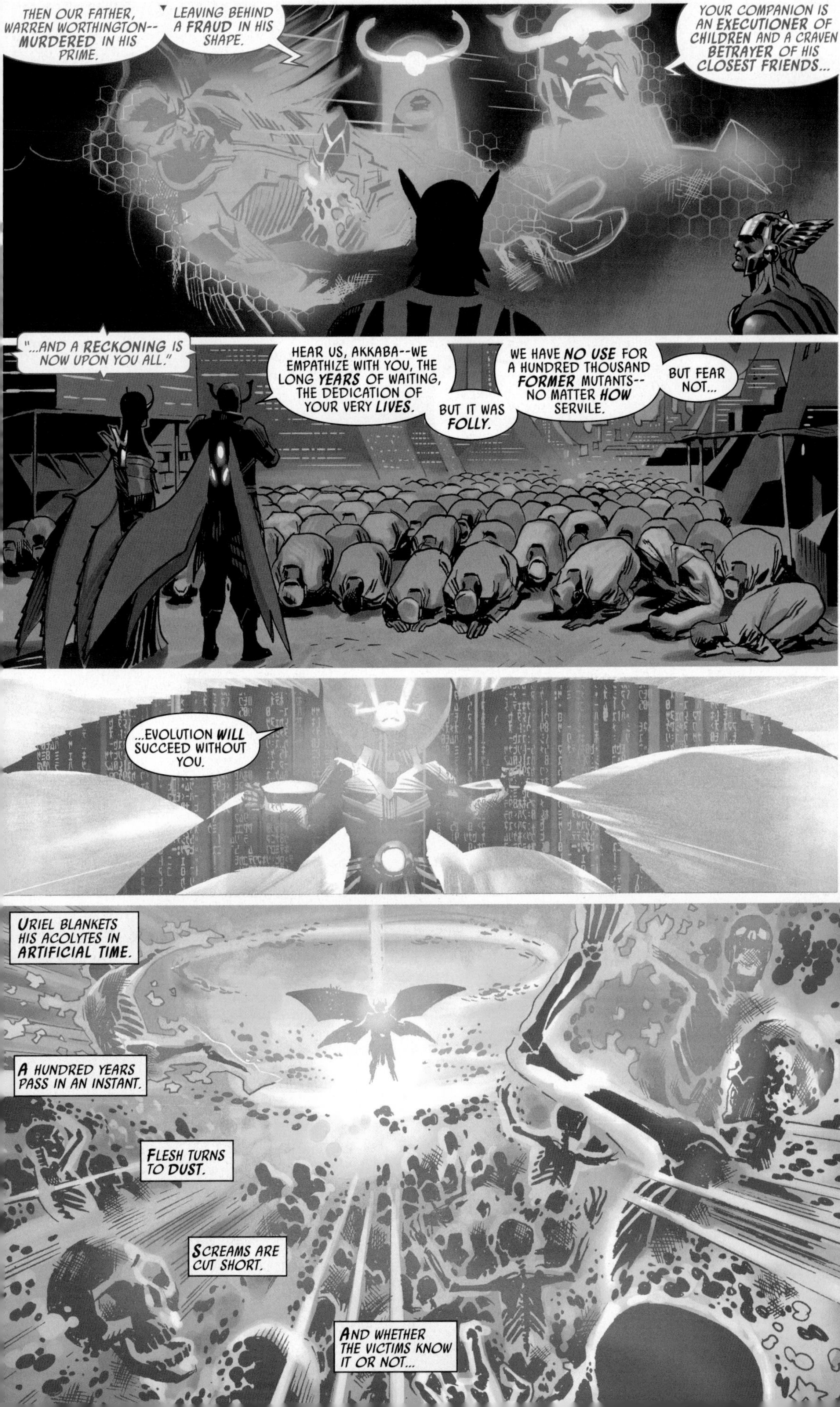
THEN OUR FATHER, WARREN WORTHINGTON-- MURDERED IN HIS PRIME.
LEAVING BEHIND A FRAUD IN HIS SHAPE.
YOUR COMPANION IS AN EXECUTIONER OF CHILDREN AND A CRAVEN BETRAYER OF HIS CLOSEST FRIENDS...
"...AND A RECKONING IS NOW UPON YOU ALL."
HEAR US, AKKABA--WE EMPATHIZE WITH YOU, THE LONG YEARS OF WAITING, THE DEDICATION OF YOUR VERY LIVES.
BUT IT WAS FOLLY.
WE HAVE NO USE FOR A HUNDRED THOUSAND FORMER MUTANTS-- NO MATTER HOW SERVILE.
BUT FEAR NOT...
...EVOLUTION WILL SUCCEED WITHOUT YOU.
URIEL BLANKETS HIS ACOLYTES IN ARTIFICIAL TIME.
A HUNDRED YEARS PASS IN AN INSTANT.
FLESH TURNS TO DUST.
SCREAMS ARE CUT SHORT.
AND WHETHER THE VICTIMS KNOW IT OR NOT...

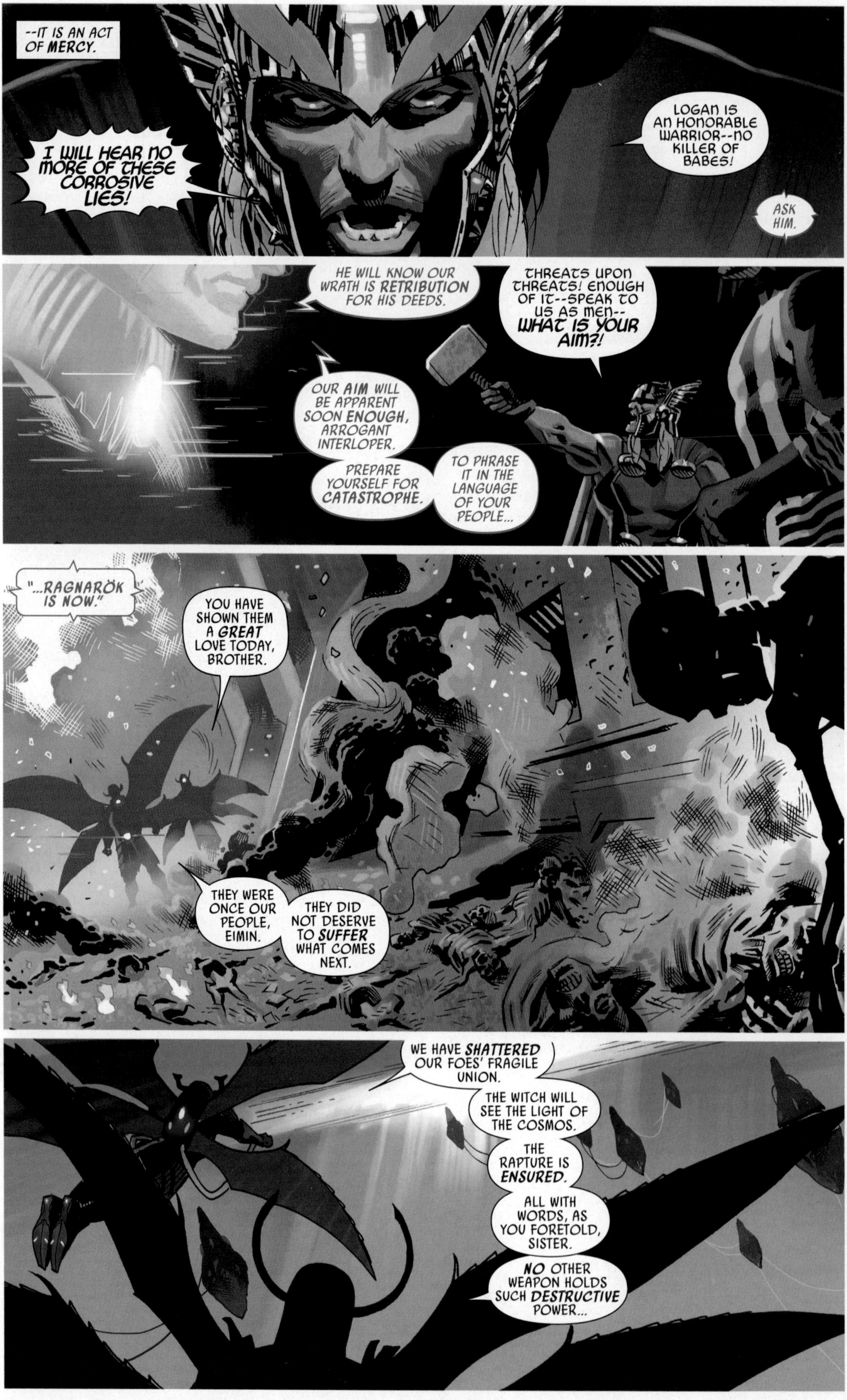
--IT IS AN ACT OF MERCY.
I WILL HEAR NO MORE OF THESE CORROSIVE LIES!
LOGAN IS AN HONORABLE WARRIOR--NO KILLER OF BABES!
ASK HIM.
HE WILL KNOW OUR WRATH IS RETRIBUTION FOR HIS DEEDS.
THREATS UPON THREATS! ENOUGH OF IT--SPEAK TO US AS MEN--WHAT IS YOUR AIM?!
OUR AIM WILL BE APPARENT SOON ENOUGH, ARROGANT INTERLOPER.
PREPARE YOURSELF FOR CATASTROPHE.
TO PHRASE IT IN THE LANGUAGE OF YOUR PEOPLE...
"...RAGNARÖK IS NOW."
YOU HAVE SHOWN THEM A GREAT LOVE TODAY, BROTHER.
THEY WERE ONCE OUR PEOPLE, EIMIN.
THEY DID NOT DESERVE TO SUFFER WHAT COMES NEXT.
WE HAVE SHATTERED OUR FOES' FRAGILE UNION.
THE WITCH WILL SEE THE LIGHT OF THE COSMOS.
THE RAPTURE IS ENSURED.
ALL WITH WORDS, AS YOU FORETOLD, SISTER.
NO OTHER WEAPON HOLDS SUCH DESTRUCTIVE POWER...

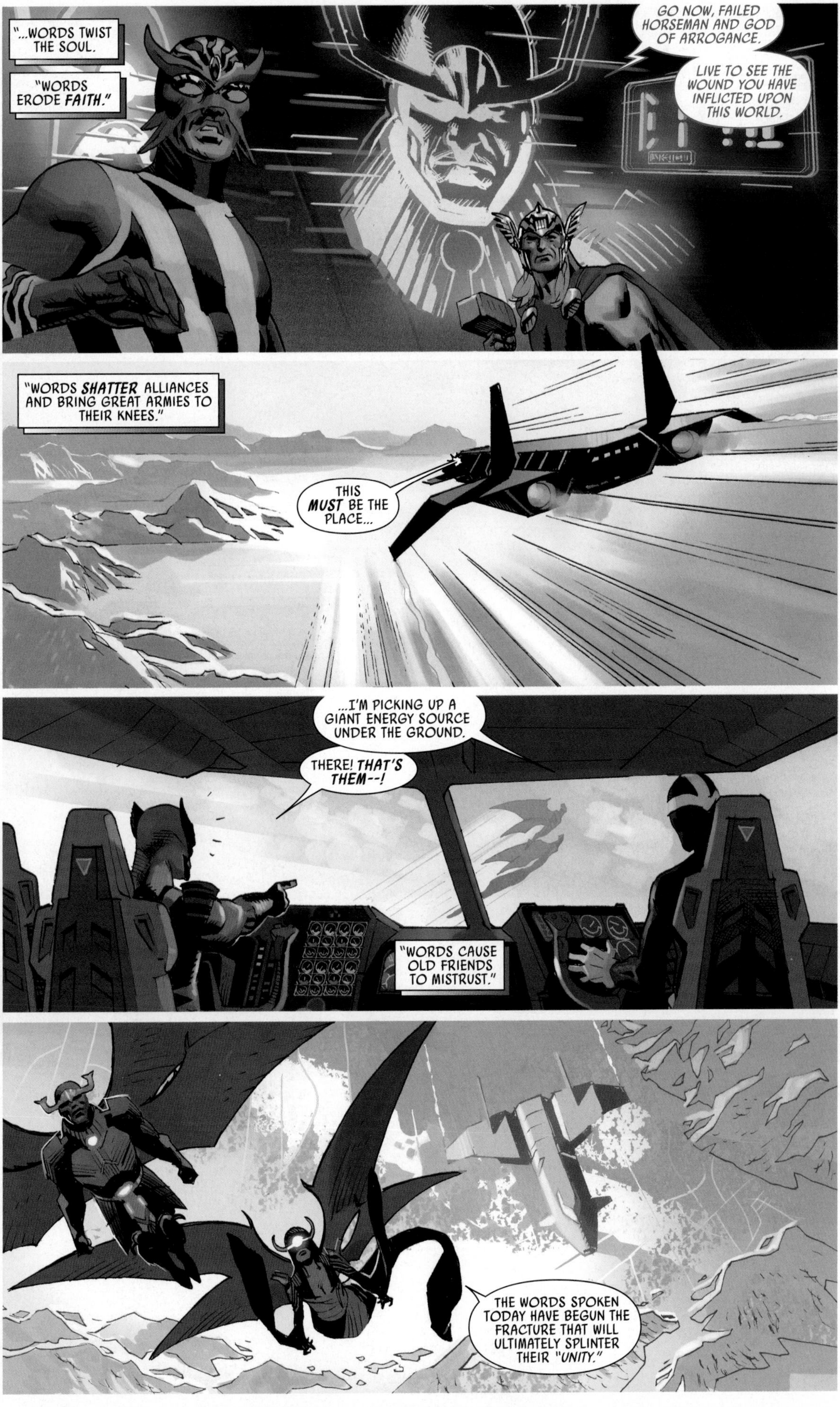

"...WORDS TWIST THE SOUL.
"WORDS ERODE FAITH."
GO NOW, FAILED HORSEMAN AND GOD OF ARROGANCE.
LIVE TO SEE THE WOUND YOU HAVE INFLICTED UPON THIS WORLD.
"WORDS SHATTER ALLIANCES AND BRING GREAT ARMIES TO THEIR KNEES."
THIS MUST BE THE PLACE...
...I'M PICKING UP A GIANT ENERGY SOURCE UNDER THE GROUND.
THERE! THAT'S THEM--!
"WORDS CAUSE OLD FRIENDS TO MISTRUST."
THE WORDS SPOKEN TODAY HAVE BEGUN THE FRACTURE THAT WILL ULTIMATELY SPLINTER THEIR "UNITY."

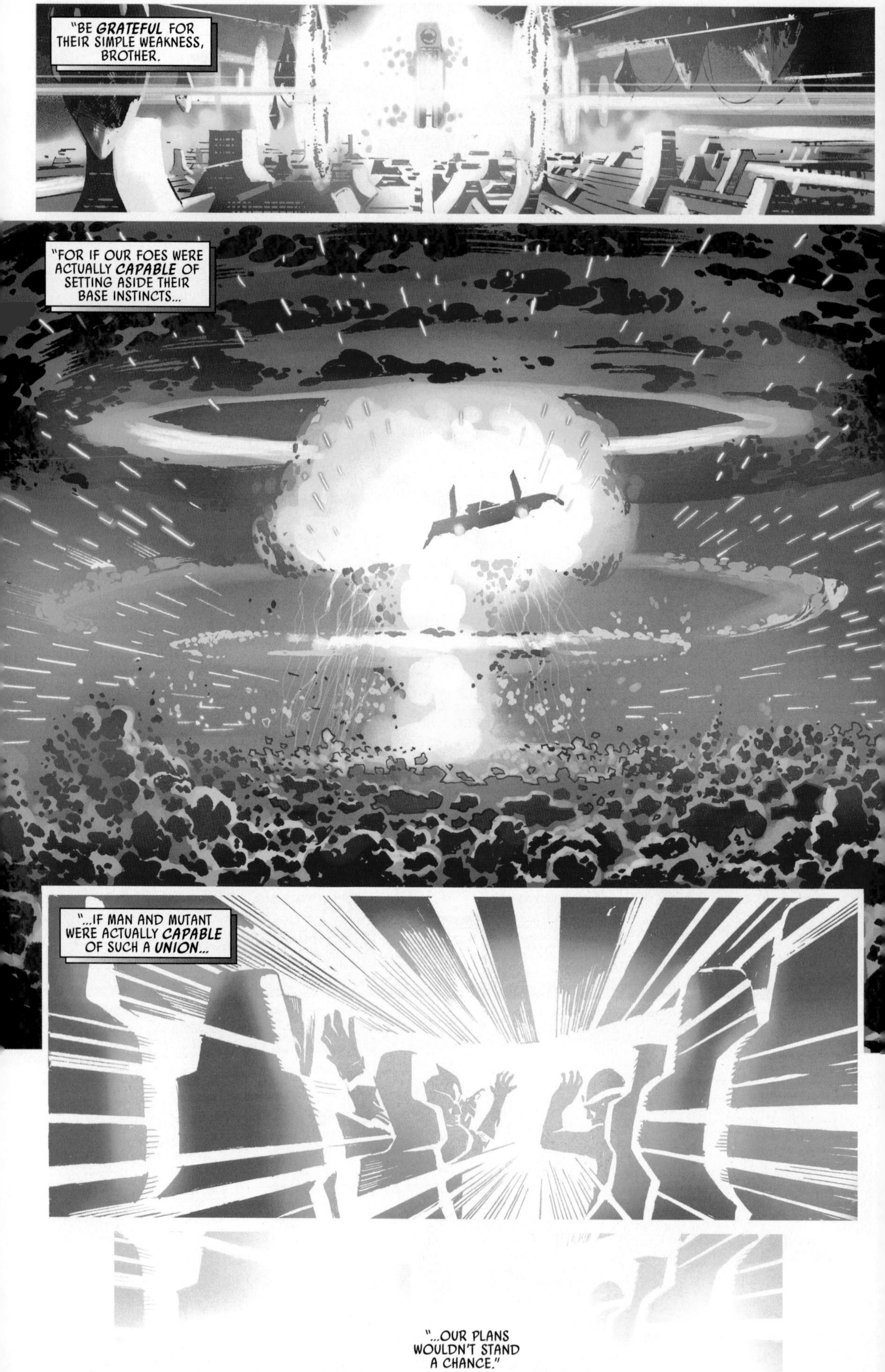
"BE GRATEFUL FOR THEIR SIMPLE WEAKNESS, BROTHER.
"FOR IF OUR FOES WERE ACTUALLY CAPABLE OF SETTING ASIDE THEIR BASE INSTINCTS...
"...IF MAN AND MUTANT WERE ACTUALLY CAPABLE OF SUCH A UNION...
"...OUR PLANS WOULDN'T STAND A CHANCE."

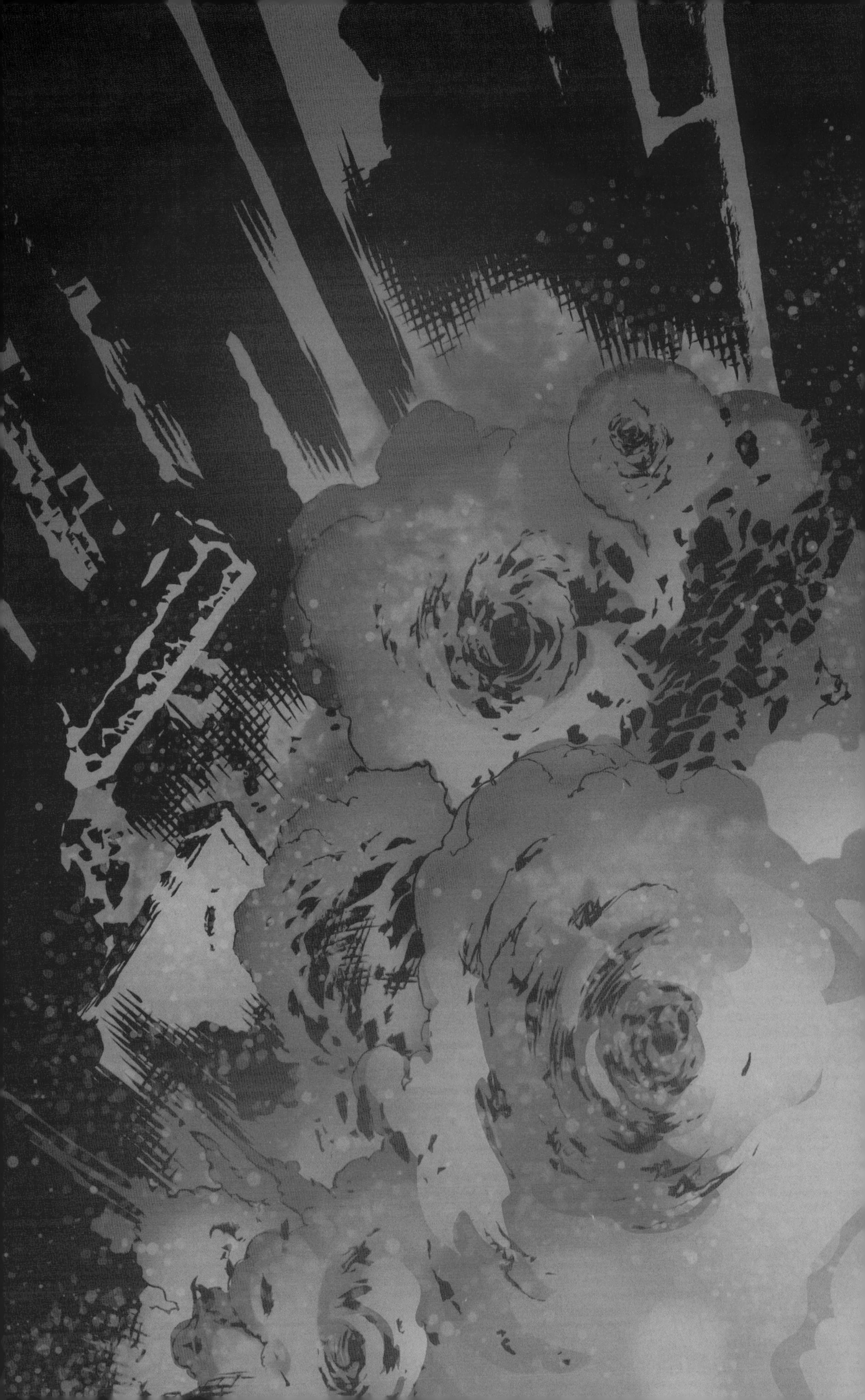

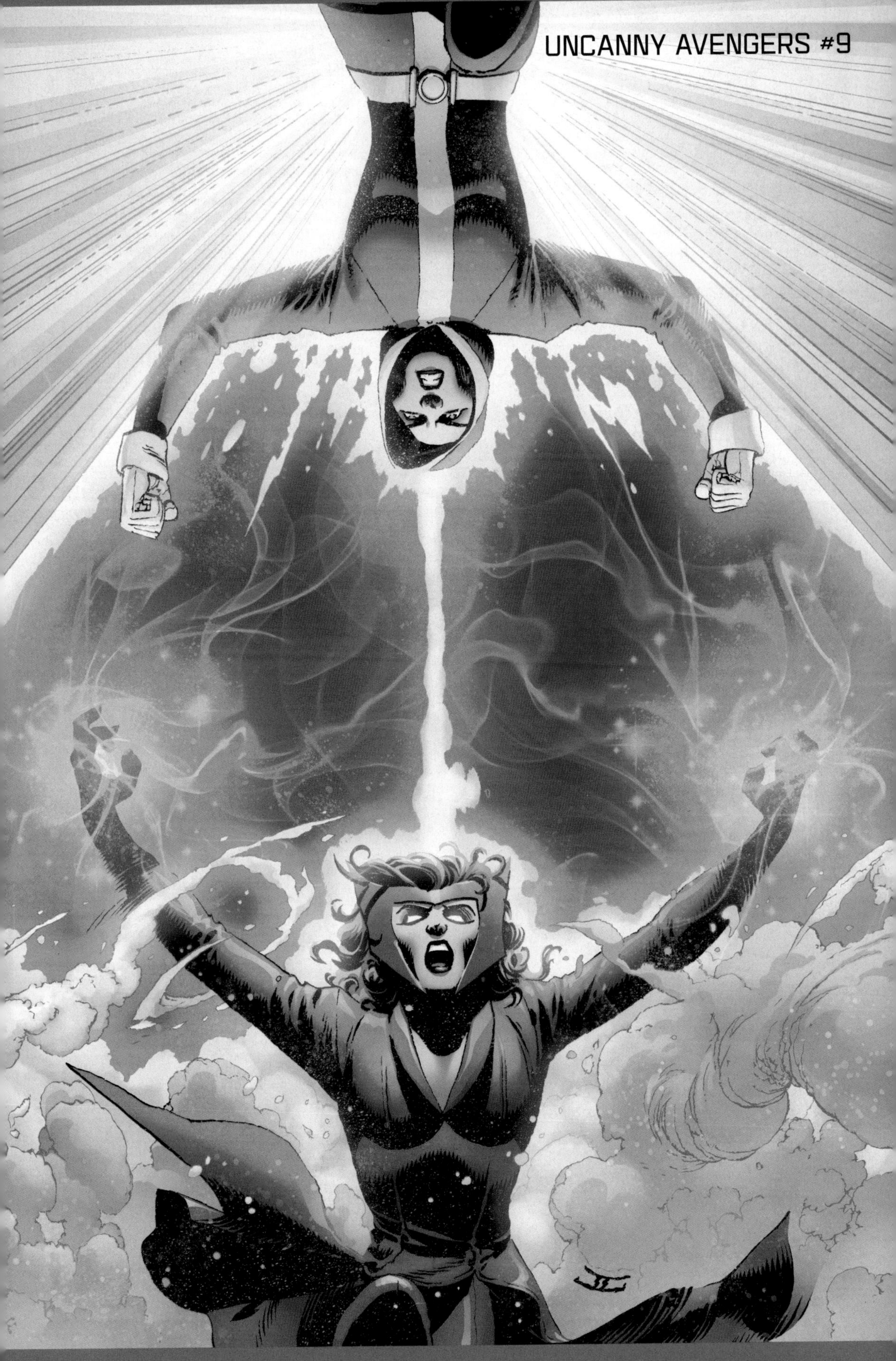
UNCANNY AVENGERS #9

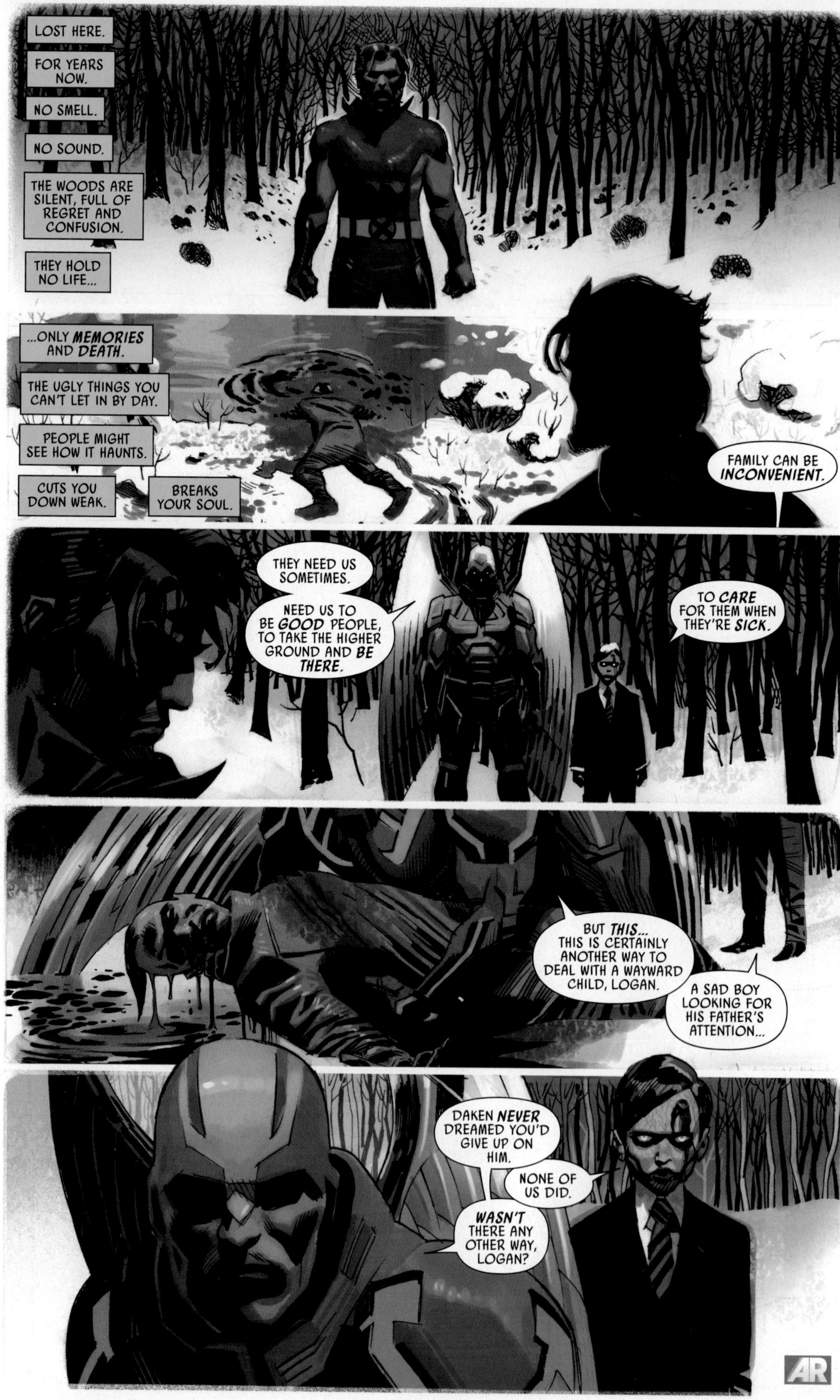
LOST HERE.
FOR YEARS NOW.
NO SMELL.
NO SOUND.
THE WOODS ARE SILENT, FULL OF REGRET AND CONFUSION.
THEY HOLD NO LIFE...
...ONLY MEMORIES AND DEATH.
THE UGLY THINGS YOU CAN'T LET IN BY DAY.
PEOPLE MIGHT SEE HOW IT HAUNTS.
CUTS YOU DOWN WEAK.
BREAKS YOUR SOUL.
FAMILY CAN BE INCONVENIENT.
THEY NEED US SOMETIMES.
NEED US TO BE GOOD PEOPLE, TO TAKE THE HIGHER GROUND AND BE THERE.
TO CARE FOR THEM WHEN THEY'RE SICK.
BUT THIS... THIS IS CERTAINLY ANOTHER WAY TO DEAL WITH A WAYWARD CHILD, LOGAN.
A SAD BOY LOOKING FOR HIS FATHER'S ATTENTION...
DAKEN NEVER DREAMED YOU'D GIVE UP ON HIM.
NONE OF US DID.
WASN'T THERE ANY OTHER WAY, LOGAN?

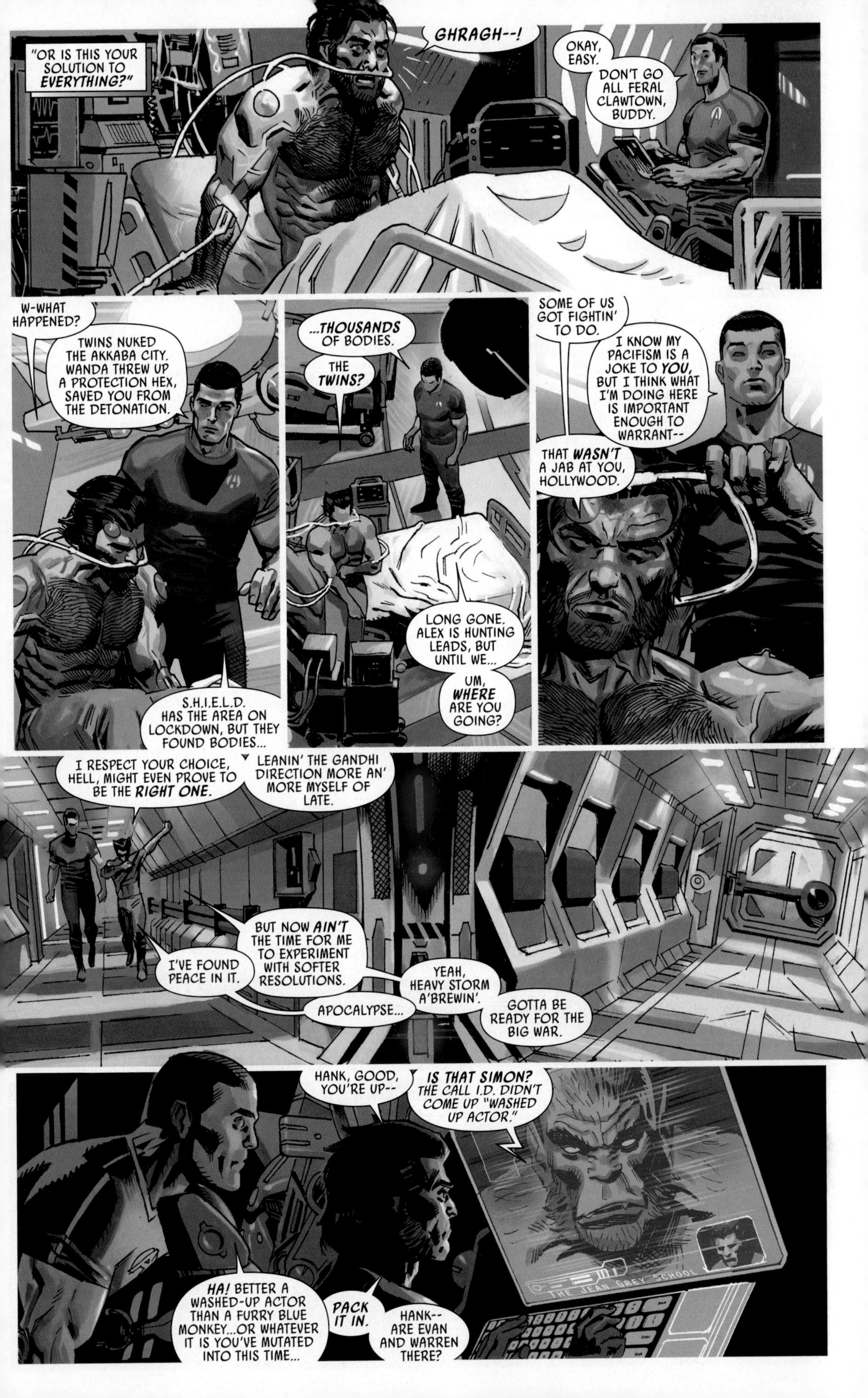

"OR IS THIS YOUR SOLUTION TO EVERYTHING?"
GHRAGH--!
OKAY, EASY.
DON'T GO ALL FERAL CLAWTOWN, BUDDY.
W-WHAT HAPPENED?
TWINS NUKED THE AKKABA CITY. WANDA THREW UP A PROTECTION HEX, SAVED YOU FROM THE DETONATION.
S.H.I.E.L.D. HAS THE AREA ON LOCKDOWN, BUT THEY FOUND BODIES...
...THOUSANDS OF BODIES.
THE TWINS?
LONG GONE. ALEX IS HUNTING LEADS, BUT UNTIL WE...
UM, WHERE ARE YOU GOING?
SOME OF US GOT FIGHTIN' TO DO.
I KNOW MY PACIFISM IS A JOKE TO YOU, BUT I THINK WHAT I'M DOING HERE IS IMPORTANT ENOUGH TO WARRANT--
THAT WASN'T A JAB AT YOU, HOLLYWOOD.
I RESPECT YOUR CHOICE, HELL, MIGHT EVEN PROVE TO BE THE RIGHT ONE.
LEANIN' THE GANDHI DIRECTION MORE AN' MORE MYSELF OF LATE.
I'VE FOUND PEACE IN IT.
BUT NOW AIN'T THE TIME FOR ME TO EXPERIMENT WITH SOFTER RESOLUTIONS.
YEAH, HEAVY STORM A'BREWIN'.
APOCALYPSE...
GOTTA BE READY FOR THE BIG WAR.
HANK, GOOD, YOU'RE UP--
IS THAT SIMON? THE CALL I.D. DIDN'T COME UP "WASHED UP ACTOR."
THE JEAN GREY SCHOOL
HA! BETTER A WASHED-UP ACTOR THAN A FURRY BLUE MONKEY...OR WHATEVER IT IS YOU'VE MUTATED INTO THIS TIME...
PACK IT IN.
HANK-- ARE EVAN AND WARREN THERE?

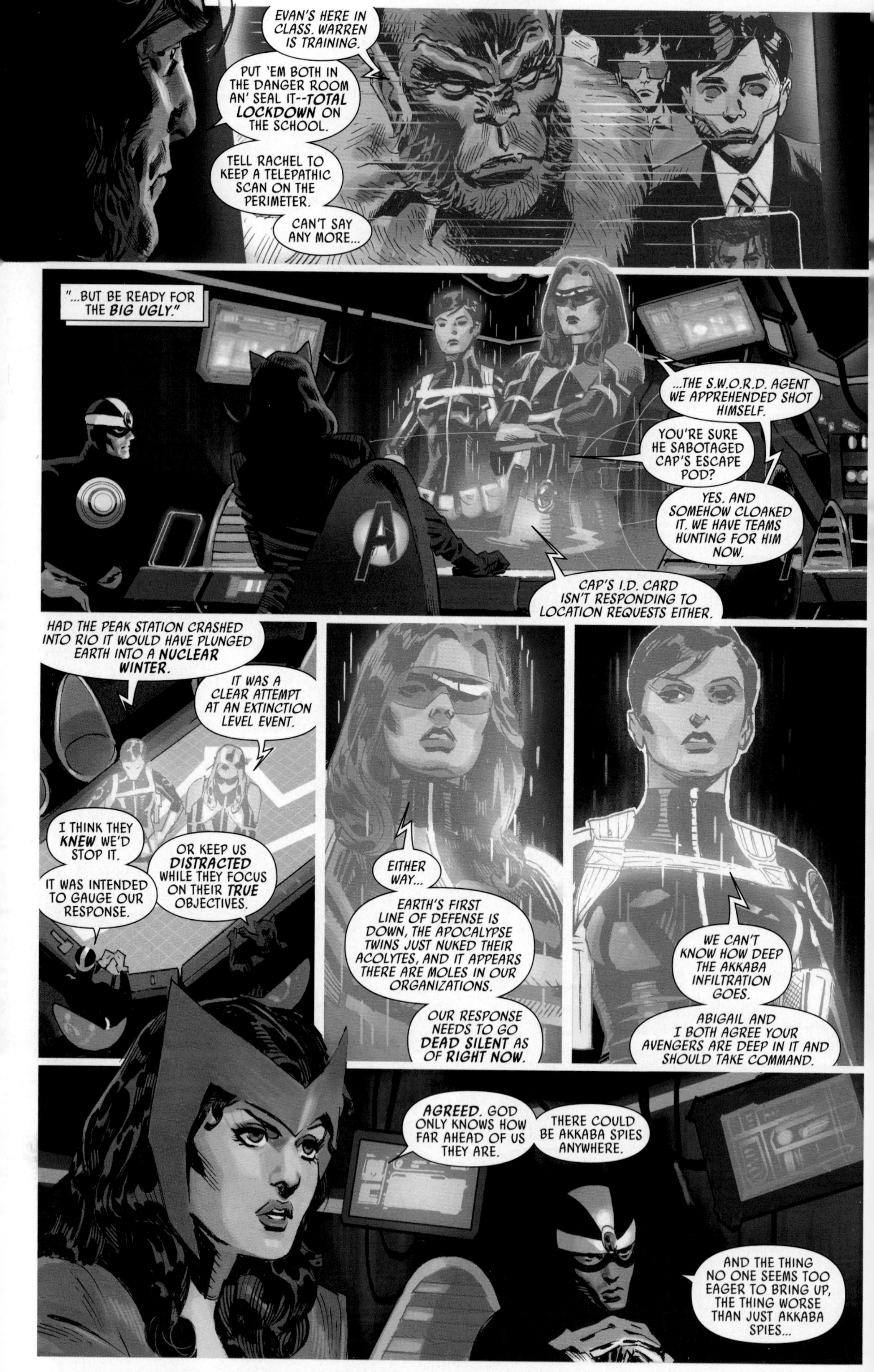
EVAN'S HERE IN CLASS. WARREN IS TRAINING.
PUT 'EM BOTH IN THE DANGER ROOM AN' SEAL IT--TOTAL LOCKDOWN ON THE SCHOOL.
TELL RACHEL TO KEEP A TELEPATHIC SCAN ON THE PERIMETER.
CAN'T SAY ANY MORE...
"...BUT BE READY FOR THE BIG UGLY."
...THE S.W.O.R.D. AGENT WE APPREHENDED SHOT HIMSELF.
YOU'RE SURE HE SABOTAGED CAP'S ESCAPE POD?
YES. AND SOMEHOW CLOAKED IT. WE HAVE TEAMS HUNTING FOR HIM NOW.
CAP'S I.D. CARD ISN'T RESPONDING TO LOCATION REQUESTS EITHER.
HAD THE PEAK STATION CRASHED INTO RIO IT WOULD HAVE PLUNGED EARTH INTO A NUCLEAR WINTER.
IT WAS A CLEAR ATTEMPT AT AN EXTINCTION LEVEL EVENT.
I THINK THEY KNEW WE'D STOP IT.
IT WAS INTENDED TO GAUGE OUR RESPONSE.
OR KEEP US DISTRACTED WHILE THEY FOCUS ON THEIR TRUE OBJECTIVES.
EITHER WAY...
EARTH'S FIRST LINE OF DEFENSE IS DOWN, THE APOCALYPSE TWINS JUST NUKED THEIR ACOLYTES, AND IT APPEARS THERE ARE MOLES IN OUR ORGANIZATIONS.
OUR RESPONSE NEEDS TO GO DEAD SILENT AS OF RIGHT NOW.
WE CAN'T KNOW HOW DEEP THE AKKABA INFILTRATION GOES.
ABIGAIL AND I BOTH AGREE YOUR AVENGERS ARE DEEP IN IT AND SHOULD TAKE COMMAND.
AGREED. GOD ONLY KNOWS HOW FAR AHEAD OF US THEY ARE.
THERE COULD BE AKKABA SPIES ANYWHERE.
AND THE THING NO ONE SEEMS TOO EAGER TO BRING UP, THE THING WORSE THAN JUST AKKABA SPIES...

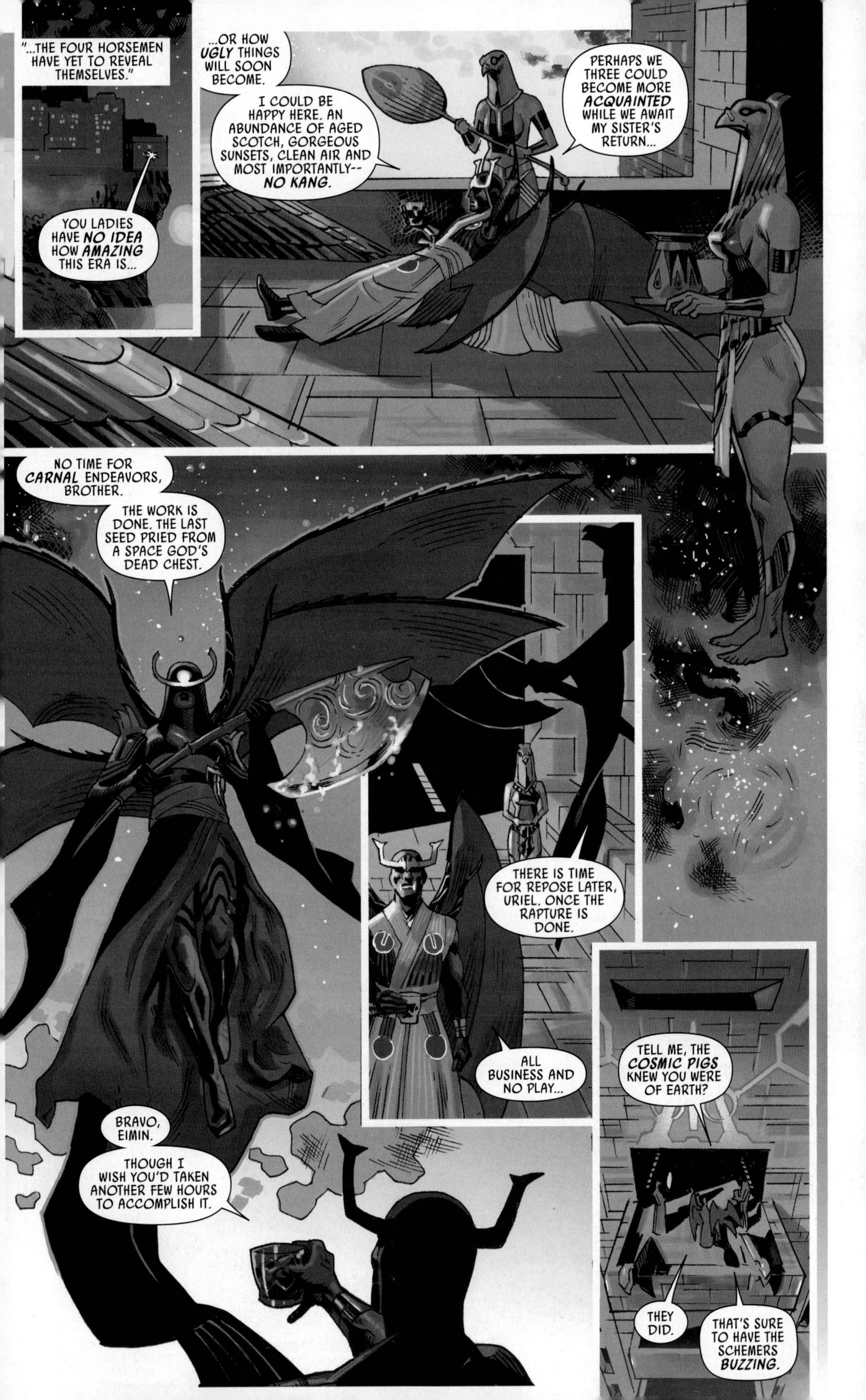
"...THE FOUR HORSEMEN HAVE YET TO REVEAL THEMSELVES."
YOU LADIES HAVE NO IDEA HOW AMAZING THIS ERA IS...
...OR HOW UGLY THINGS WILL SOON BECOME.
I COULD BE HAPPY HERE. AN ABUNDANCE OF AGED SCOTCH, GORGEOUS SUNSETS, CLEAN AIR AND MOST IMPORTANTLY-- NO KANG.
PERHAPS WE THREE COULD BECOME MORE ACQUAINTED WHILE WE AWAIT MY SISTER'S RETURN...
NO TIME FOR CARNAL ENDEAVORS, BROTHER.
THE WORK IS DONE. THE LAST SEED PRIED FROM A SPACE GOD'S DEAD CHEST.
THERE IS TIME FOR REPOSE LATER, URIEL. ONCE THE RAPTURE IS DONE.
ALL BUSINESS AND NO PLAY...
BRAVO, EIMIN.
THOUGH I WISH YOU'D TAKEN ANOTHER FEW HOURS TO ACCOMPLISH IT.
TELL ME, THE COSMIC PIGS KNEW YOU WERE OF EARTH?
THEY DID.
THAT'S SURE TO HAVE THE SCHEMERS BUZZING.

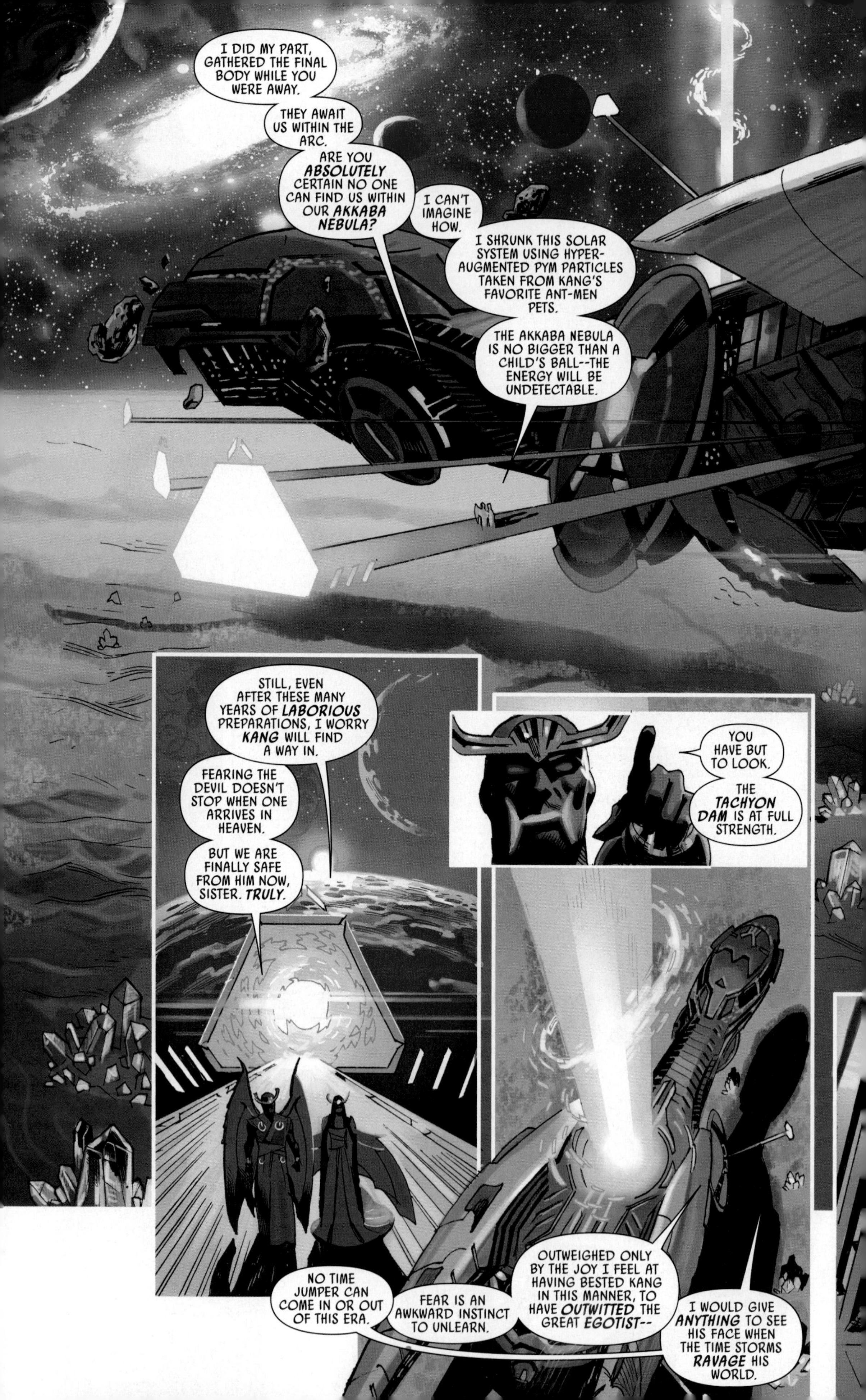
I DID MY PART, GATHERED THE FINAL BODY WHILE YOU WERE AWAY.
THEY AWAIT US WITHIN THE ARC.
ARE YOU ABSOLUTELY CERTAIN NO ONE CAN FIND US WITHIN OUR AKKABA NEBULA?
I CAN'T IMAGINE HOW.
I SHRUNK THIS SOLAR SYSTEM USING HYPER-AUGMENTED PYM PARTICLES TAKEN FROM KANG'S FAVORITE ANT-MEN PETS.
THE AKKABA NEBULA IS NO BIGGER THAN A CHILD'S BALL--THE ENERGY WILL BE UNDETECTABLE.
STILL, EVEN AFTER THESE MANY YEARS OF LABORIOUS PREPARATIONS, I WORRY KANG WILL FIND A WAY IN.
FEARING THE DEVIL DOESN'T STOP WHEN ONE ARRIVES IN HEAVEN.
BUT WE ARE FINALLY SAFE FROM HIM NOW, SISTER. TRULY.
YOU HAVE BUT TO LOOK.
THE TACHYON DAM IS AT FULL STRENGTH.
NO TIME JUMPER CAN COME IN OR OUT OF THIS ERA.
FEAR IS AN AWKWARD INSTINCT TO UNLEARN.
OUTWEIGHED ONLY BY THE JOY I FEEL AT HAVING BESTED KANG IN THIS MANNER, TO HAVE OUTWITTED THE GREAT EGOTIST--
I WOULD GIVE ANYTHING TO SEE HIS FACE WHEN THE TIME STORMS RAVAGE HIS WORLD.

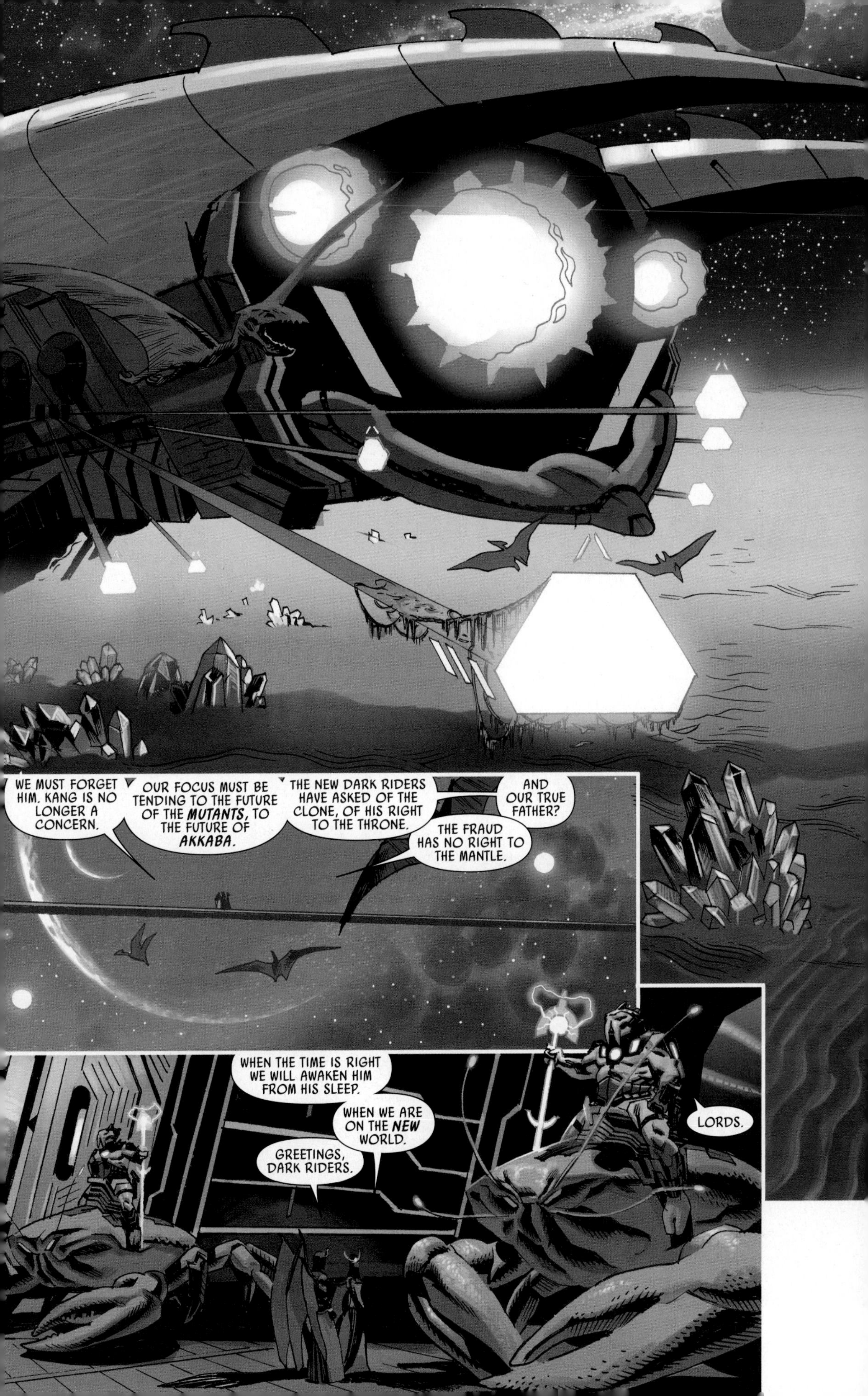
WE MUST FORGET HIM. KANG IS NO LONGER A CONCERN.
OUR FOCUS MUST BE TENDING TO THE FUTURE OF THE *MUTANTS*, TO THE FUTURE OF *AKKABA*.
THE NEW DARK RIDERS HAVE ASKED OF THE CLONE, OF HIS RIGHT TO THE THRONE.
AND OUR TRUE FATHER?
THE FRAUD HAS NO RIGHT TO THE MANTLE.
WHEN THE TIME IS RIGHT WE WILL AWAKEN HIM FROM HIS SLEEP.
WHEN WE ARE ON THE *NEW* WORLD.
GREETINGS, DARK RIDERS.
LORDS.

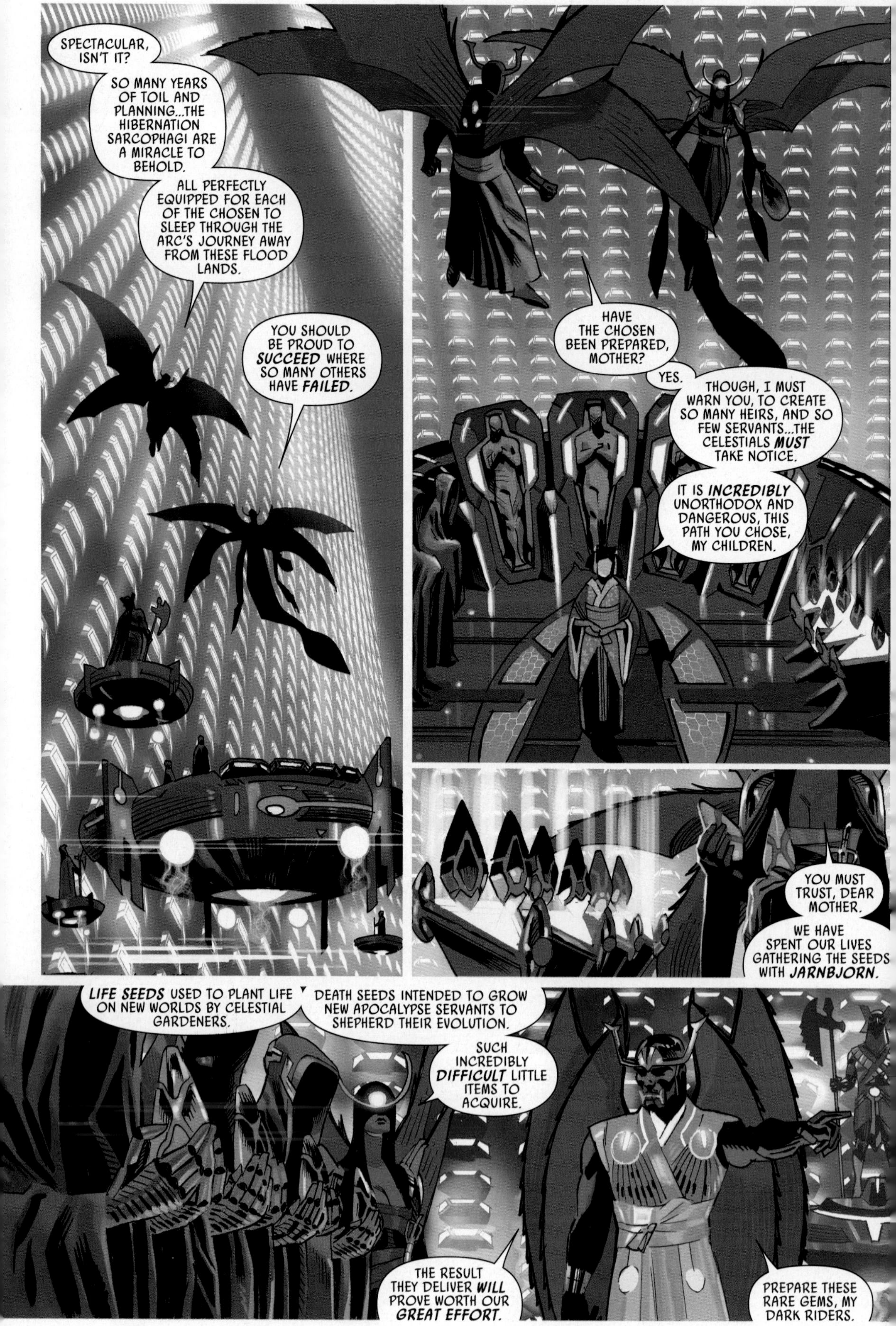

SPECTACULAR, ISN'T IT?
SO MANY YEARS OF TOIL AND PLANNING...THE HIBERNATION SARCOPHAGI ARE A MIRACLE TO BEHOLD.
ALL PERFECTLY EQUIPPED FOR EACH OF THE CHOSEN TO SLEEP THROUGH THE ARC'S JOURNEY AWAY FROM THESE FLOOD LANDS.
YOU SHOULD BE PROUD TO SUCCEED WHERE SO MANY OTHERS HAVE FAILED.
HAVE THE CHOSEN BEEN PREPARED, MOTHER?
YES.
THOUGH, I MUST WARN YOU, TO CREATE SO MANY HEIRS, AND SO FEW SERVANTS...THE CELESTIALS MUST TAKE NOTICE.
IT IS INCREDIBLY UNORTHODOX AND DANGEROUS, THIS PATH YOU CHOSE, MY CHILDREN.
YOU MUST TRUST, DEAR MOTHER.
WE HAVE SPENT OUR LIVES GATHERING THE SEEDS WITH JARNBJORN.
LIFE SEEDS USED TO PLANT LIFE ON NEW WORLDS BY CELESTIAL GARDENERS.
DEATH SEEDS INTENDED TO GROW NEW APOCALYPSE SERVANTS TO SHEPHERD THEIR EVOLUTION.
SUCH INCREDIBLY DIFFICULT LITTLE ITEMS TO ACQUIRE.
THE RESULT THEY DELIVER WILL PROVE WORTH OUR GREAT EFFORT.
PREPARE THESE RARE GEMS, MY DARK RIDERS.

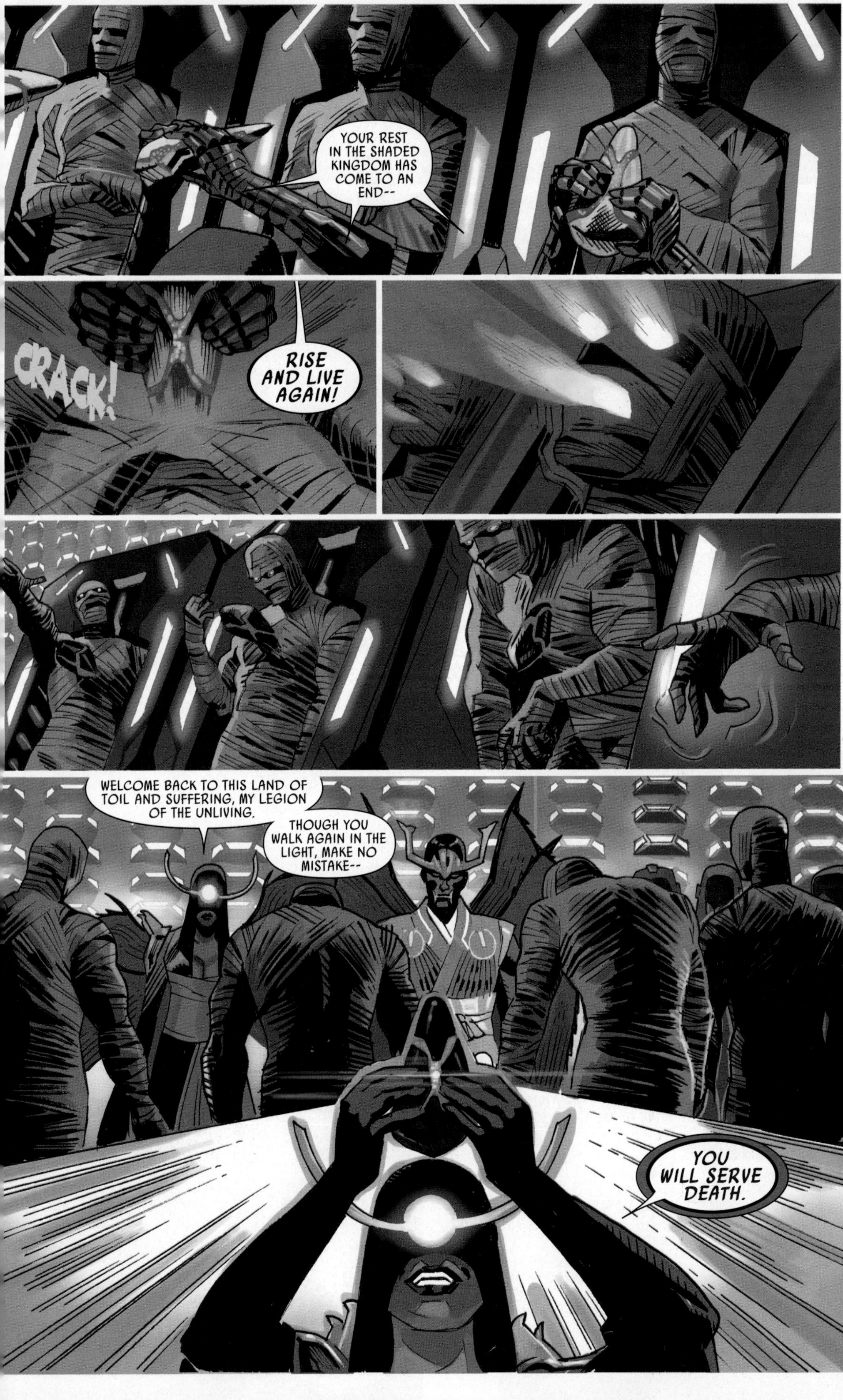
YOUR REST IN THE SHADED KINGDOM HAS COME TO AN END--
CRACK!
RISE AND LIVE AGAIN!
WELCOME BACK TO THIS LAND OF TOIL AND SUFFERING, MY LEGION OF THE UNLIVING.
THOUGH YOU WALK AGAIN IN THE LIGHT, MAKE NO MISTAKE--
YOU WILL SERVE DEATH.

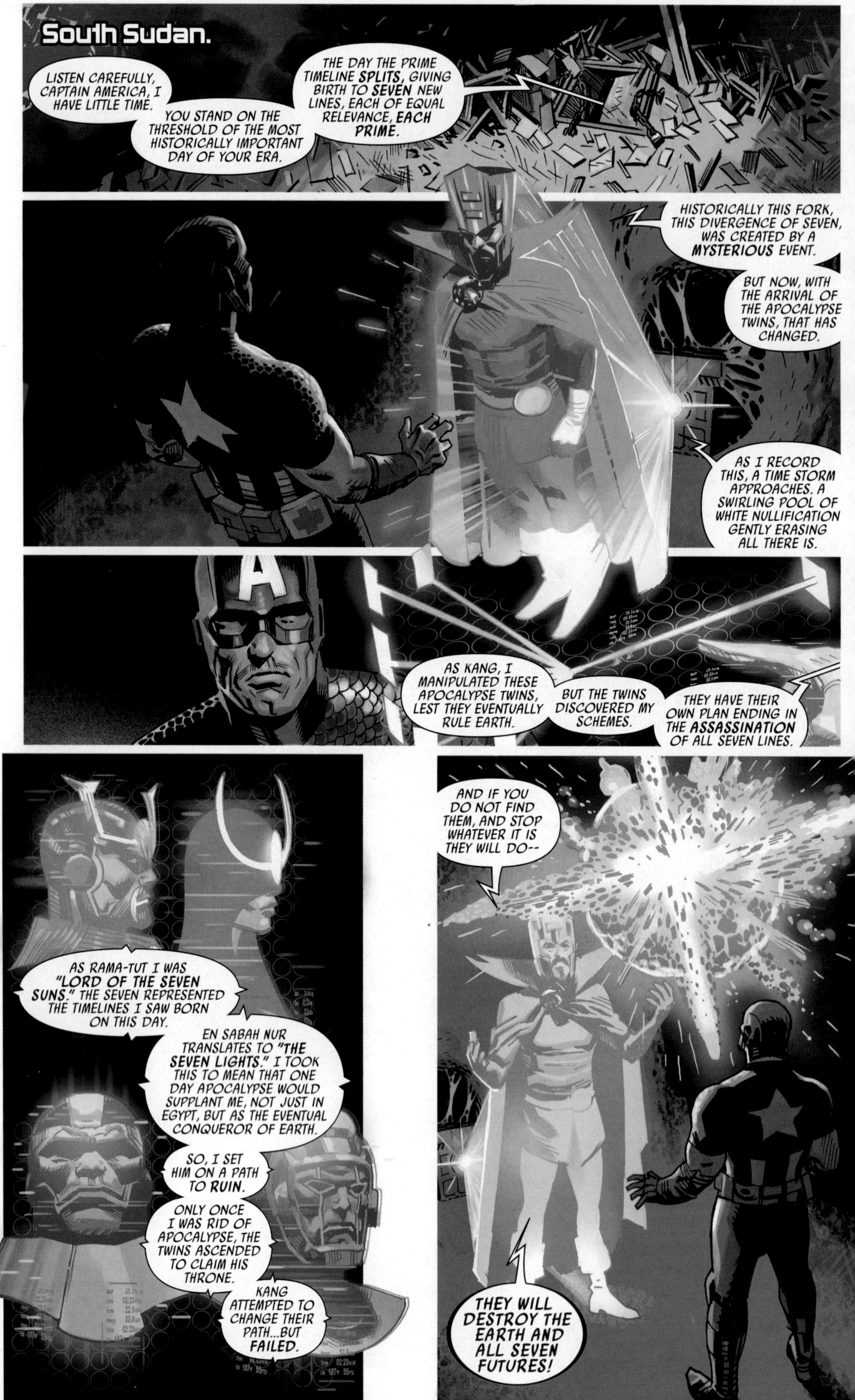
South Sudan.
LISTEN CAREFULLY, CAPTAIN AMERICA, I HAVE LITTLE TIME.
YOU STAND ON THE THRESHOLD OF THE MOST HISTORICALLY IMPORTANT DAY OF YOUR ERA.
THE DAY THE PRIME TIMELINE SPLITS, GIVING BIRTH TO SEVEN NEW LINES, EACH OF EQUAL RELEVANCE, EACH PRIME.
HISTORICALLY THIS FORK, THIS DIVERGENCE OF SEVEN, WAS CREATED BY A MYSTERIOUS EVENT.
BUT NOW, WITH THE ARRIVAL OF THE APOCALYPSE TWINS, THAT HAS CHANGED.
AS I RECORD THIS, A TIME STORM APPROACHES. A SWIRLING POOL OF WHITE NULLIFICATION GENTLY ERASING ALL THERE IS.
AS KANG, I MANIPULATED THESE APOCALYPSE TWINS, LEST THEY EVENTUALLY RULE EARTH.
BUT THE TWINS DISCOVERED MY SCHEMES.
THEY HAVE THEIR OWN PLAN ENDING IN THE ASSASSINATION OF ALL SEVEN LINES.
AS RAMA-TUT I WAS "LORD OF THE SEVEN SUNS." THE SEVEN REPRESENTED THE TIMELINES I SAW BORN ON THIS DAY.
EN SABAH NUR TRANSLATES TO "THE SEVEN LIGHTS." I TOOK THIS TO MEAN THAT ONE DAY APOCALYPSE WOULD SUPPLANT ME, NOT JUST IN EGYPT, BUT AS THE EVENTUAL CONQUEROR OF EARTH.
SO, I SET HIM ON A PATH TO RUIN.
ONLY ONCE I WAS RID OF APOCALYPSE, THE TWINS ASCENDED TO CLAIM HIS THRONE.
KANG ATTEMPTED TO CHANGE THEIR PATH...BUT FAILED.
AND IF YOU DO NOT FIND THEM, AND STOP WHATEVER IT IS THEY WILL DO--
THEY WILL DESTROY THE EARTH AND ALL SEVEN FUTURES!

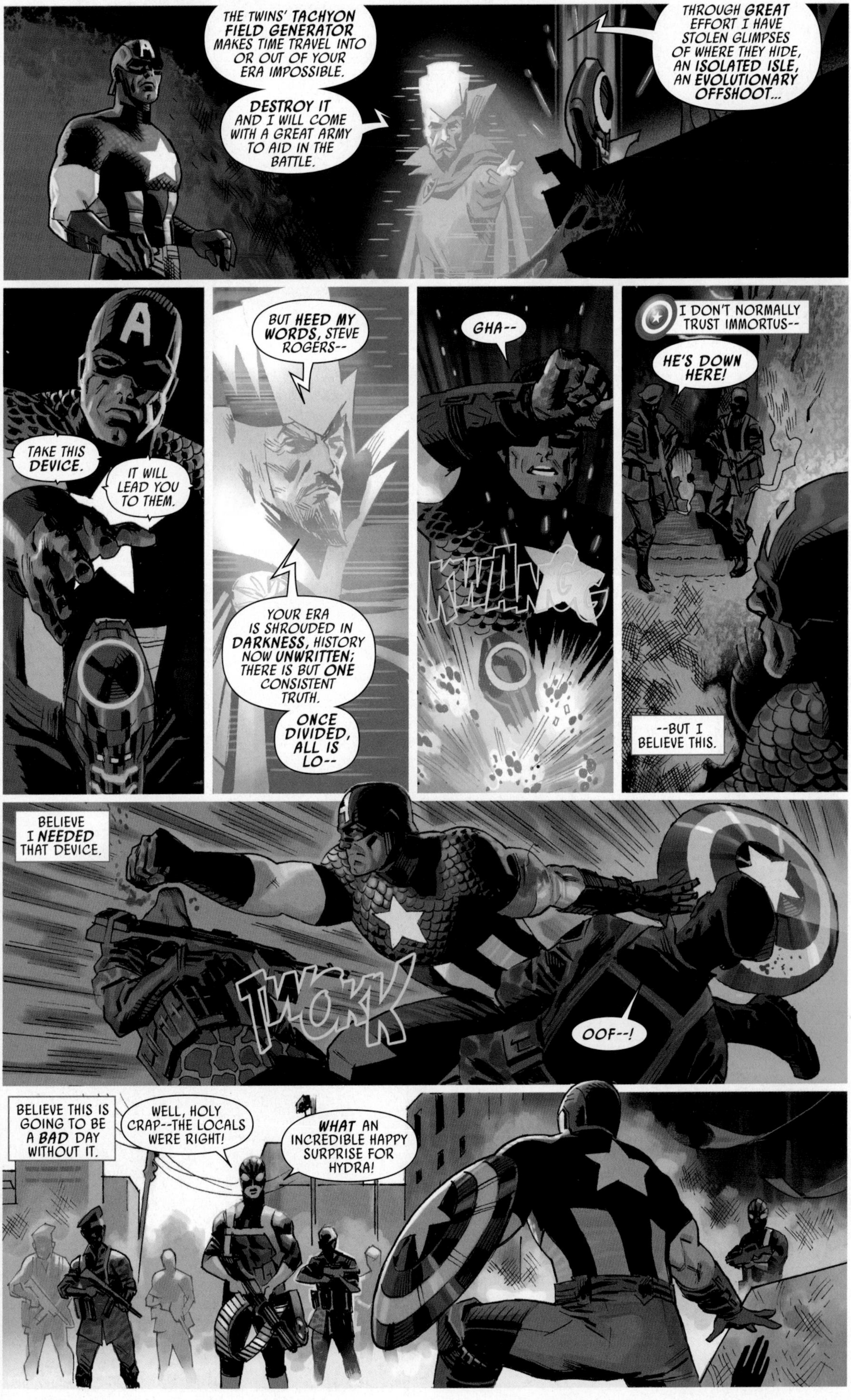

THE TWINS' TACHYON FIELD GENERATOR MAKES TIME TRAVEL INTO OR OUT OF YOUR ERA IMPOSSIBLE.
DESTROY IT AND I WILL COME WITH A GREAT ARMY TO AID IN THE BATTLE.
THROUGH GREAT EFFORT I HAVE STOLEN GLIMPSES OF WHERE THEY HIDE, AN ISOLATED ISLE, AN EVOLUTIONARY OFFSHOOT...
TAKE THIS DEVICE.
IT WILL LEAD YOU TO THEM.
BUT HEED MY WORDS, STEVE ROGERS--
YOUR ERA IS SHROUDED IN DARKNESS, HISTORY NOW UNWRITTEN; THERE IS BUT ONE CONSISTENT TRUTH.
ONCE DIVIDED, ALL IS LO--
GHA--
KWANG
I DON'T NORMALLY TRUST IMMORTUS--
HE'S DOWN HERE!
--BUT I BELIEVE THIS.
BELIEVE I NEEDED THAT DEVICE.
TWOK
OOF--!
BELIEVE THIS IS GOING TO BE A BAD DAY WITHOUT IT.
WELL, HOLY CRAP--THE LOCALS WERE RIGHT!
WHAT AN INCREDIBLE HAPPY SURPRISE FOR HYDRA!

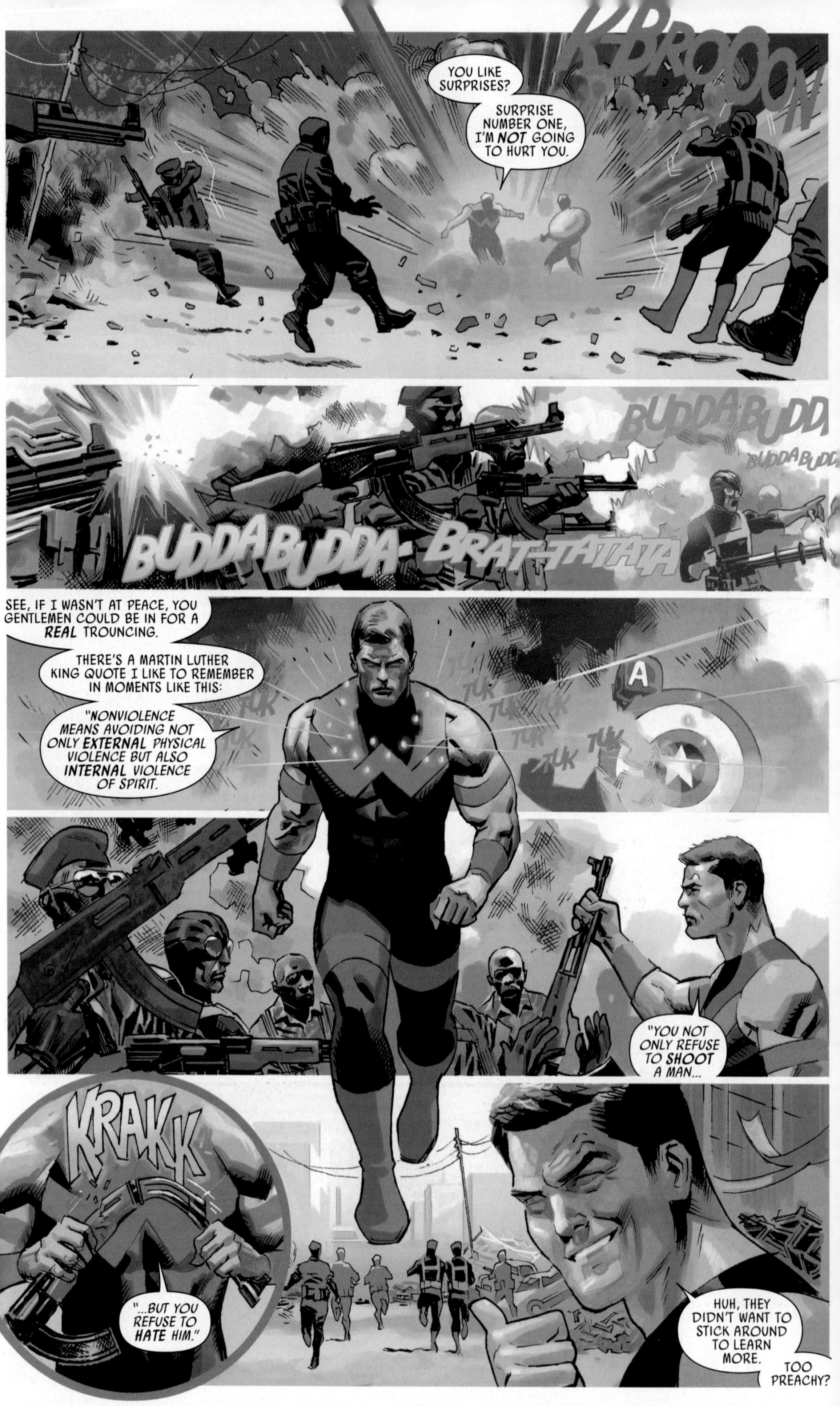
KBROOOON
YOU LIKE SURPRISES?
SURPRISE NUMBER ONE, I'M NOT GOING TO HURT YOU.
BUDDA BUDD
BUDDA BUDD
BUDDA BUDDA- BRAT-TATATA
SEE, IF I WASN'T AT PEACE, YOU GENTLEMEN COULD BE IN FOR A REAL TROUNCING.
THERE'S A MARTIN LUTHER KING QUOTE I LIKE TO REMEMBER IN MOMENTS LIKE THIS:
"NONVIOLENCE MEANS AVOIDING NOT ONLY EXTERNAL PHYSICAL VIOLENCE BUT ALSO INTERNAL VIOLENCE OF SPIRIT.
TUK TUK TUK TUK TUK TUK TUK
"YOU NOT ONLY REFUSE TO SHOOT A MAN...
KRAKK
"...BUT YOU REFUSE TO HATE HIM."
HUH, THEY DIDN'T WANT TO STICK AROUND TO LEARN MORE.
TOO PREACHY?

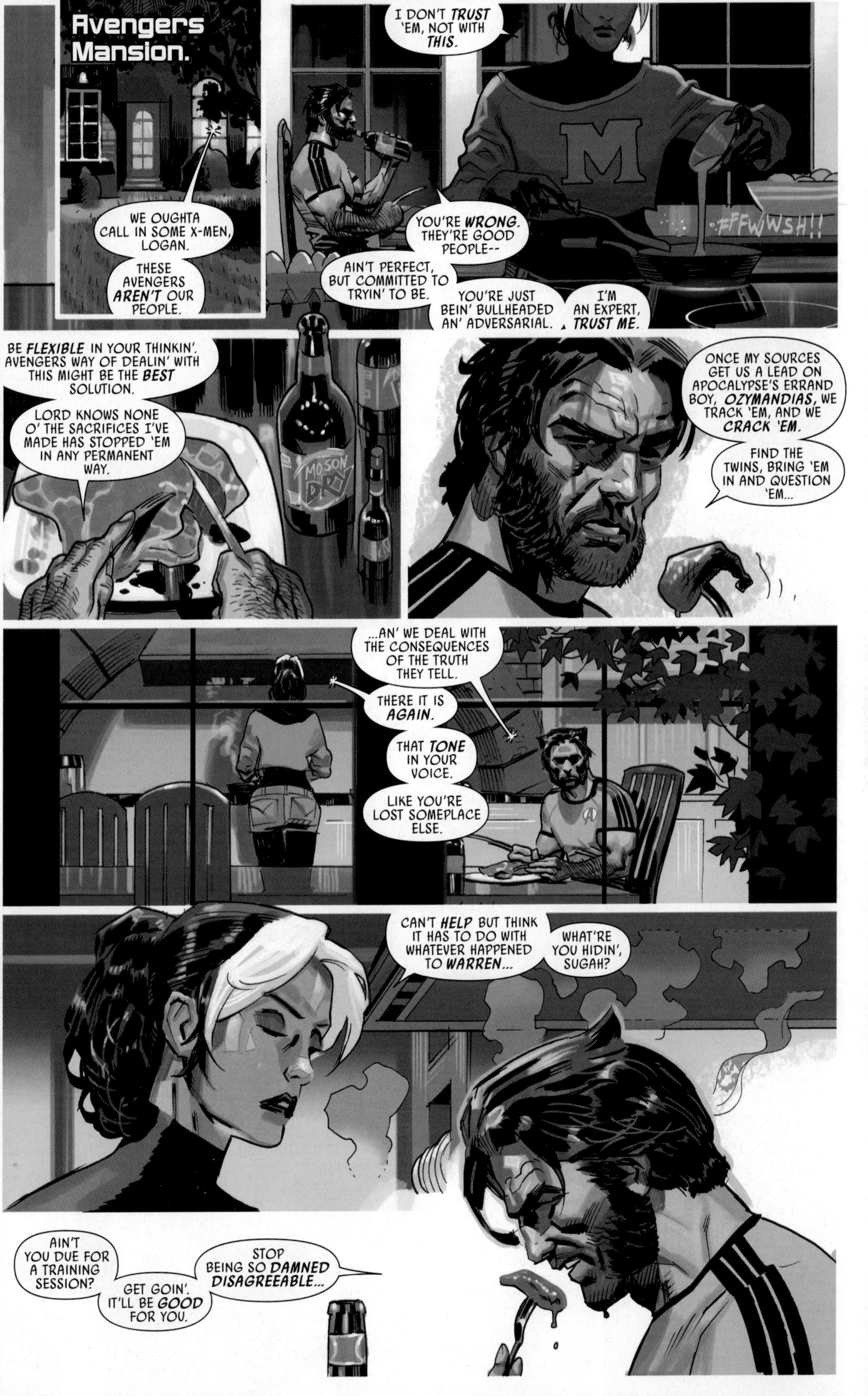
Avengers Mansion.
WE OUGHTA CALL IN SOME X-MEN, LOGAN.
THESE AVENGERS AREN'T OUR PEOPLE.
I DON'T TRUST 'EM, NOT WITH THIS.
YOU'RE WRONG. THEY'RE GOOD PEOPLE--
AIN'T PERFECT, BUT COMMITTED TO TRYIN' TO BE.
YOU'RE JUST BEIN' BULLHEADED AN' ADVERSARIAL.
I'M AN EXPERT, TRUST ME.
FFFWWSH!!
BE FLEXIBLE IN YOUR THINKIN'. AVENGERS WAY OF DEALIN' WITH THIS MIGHT BE THE BEST SOLUTION.
LORD KNOWS NONE O' THE SACRIFICES I'VE MADE HAS STOPPED 'EM IN ANY PERMANENT WAY.
MOSON DRY
ONCE MY SOURCES GET US A LEAD ON APOCALYPSE'S ERRAND BOY, OZYMANDIAS, WE TRACK 'EM, AND WE CRACK 'EM.
FIND THE TWINS, BRING 'EM IN AND QUESTION 'EM...
...AN' WE DEAL WITH THE CONSEQUENCES OF THE TRUTH THEY TELL.
THERE IT IS AGAIN.
THAT TONE IN YOUR VOICE.
LIKE YOU'RE LOST SOMEPLACE ELSE.
CAN'T HELP BUT THINK IT HAS TO DO WITH WHATEVER HAPPENED TO WARREN...
WHAT'RE YOU HIDIN', SUGAH?
AIN'T YOU DUE FOR A TRAINING SESSION?
GET GOIN'. IT'LL BE GOOD FOR YOU.
STOP BEING SO DAMNED DISAGREEABLE...

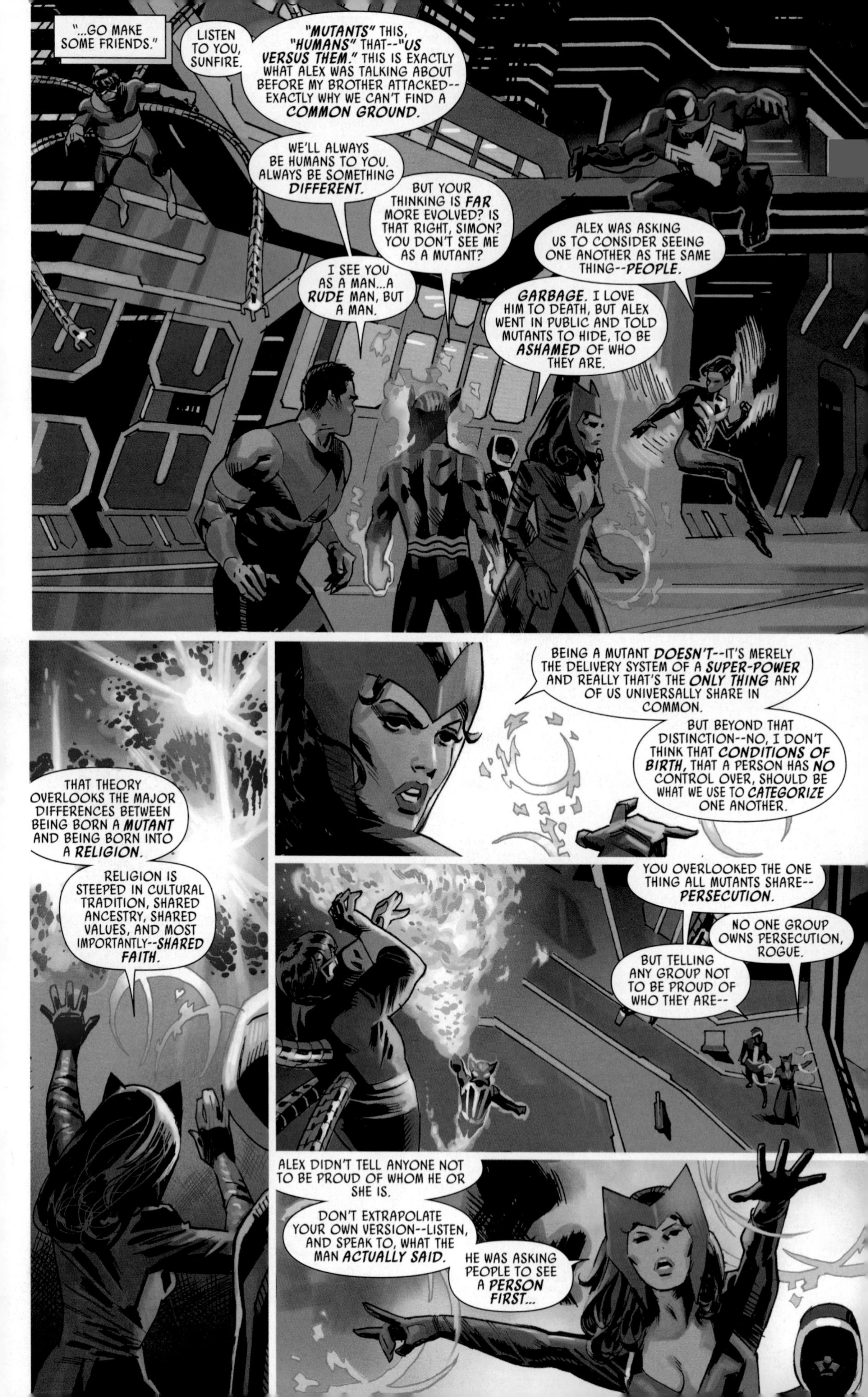
"...GO MAKE SOME FRIENDS."
LISTEN TO YOU, SUNFIRE.
"MUTANTS" THIS, "HUMANS" THAT--"US VERSUS THEM." THIS IS EXACTLY WHAT ALEX WAS TALKING ABOUT BEFORE MY BROTHER ATTACKED--EXACTLY WHY WE CAN'T FIND A COMMON GROUND.
WE'LL ALWAYS BE HUMANS TO YOU. ALWAYS BE SOMETHING DIFFERENT.
BUT YOUR THINKING IS FAR MORE EVOLVED? IS THAT RIGHT, SIMON? YOU DON'T SEE ME AS A MUTANT?
I SEE YOU AS A MAN...A RUDE MAN, BUT A MAN.
ALEX WAS ASKING US TO CONSIDER SEEING ONE ANOTHER AS THE SAME THING--PEOPLE.
GARBAGE. I LOVE HIM TO DEATH, BUT ALEX WENT IN PUBLIC AND TOLD MUTANTS TO HIDE, TO BE ASHAMED OF WHO THEY ARE.
THAT THEORY OVERLOOKS THE MAJOR DIFFERENCES BETWEEN BEING BORN A MUTANT AND BEING BORN INTO A RELIGION.
RELIGION IS STEEPED IN CULTURAL TRADITION, SHARED ANCESTRY, SHARED VALUES, AND MOST IMPORTANTLY--SHARED FAITH.
BEING A MUTANT DOESN'T--IT'S MERELY THE DELIVERY SYSTEM OF A SUPER-POWER AND REALLY THAT'S THE ONLY THING ANY OF US UNIVERSALLY SHARE IN COMMON.
BUT BEYOND THAT DISTINCTION--NO, I DON'T THINK THAT CONDITIONS OF BIRTH, THAT A PERSON HAS NO CONTROL OVER, SHOULD BE WHAT WE USE TO CATEGORIZE ONE ANOTHER.
YOU OVERLOOKED THE ONE THING ALL MUTANTS SHARE--PERSECUTION.
NO ONE GROUP OWNS PERSECUTION, ROGUE.
BUT TELLING ANY GROUP NOT TO BE PROUD OF WHO THEY ARE--
ALEX DIDN'T TELL ANYONE NOT TO BE PROUD OF WHOM HE OR SHE IS.
DON'T EXTRAPOLATE YOUR OWN VERSION--LISTEN, AND SPEAK TO, WHAT THE MAN ACTUALLY SAID.
HE WAS ASKING PEOPLE TO SEE A PERSON FIRST...

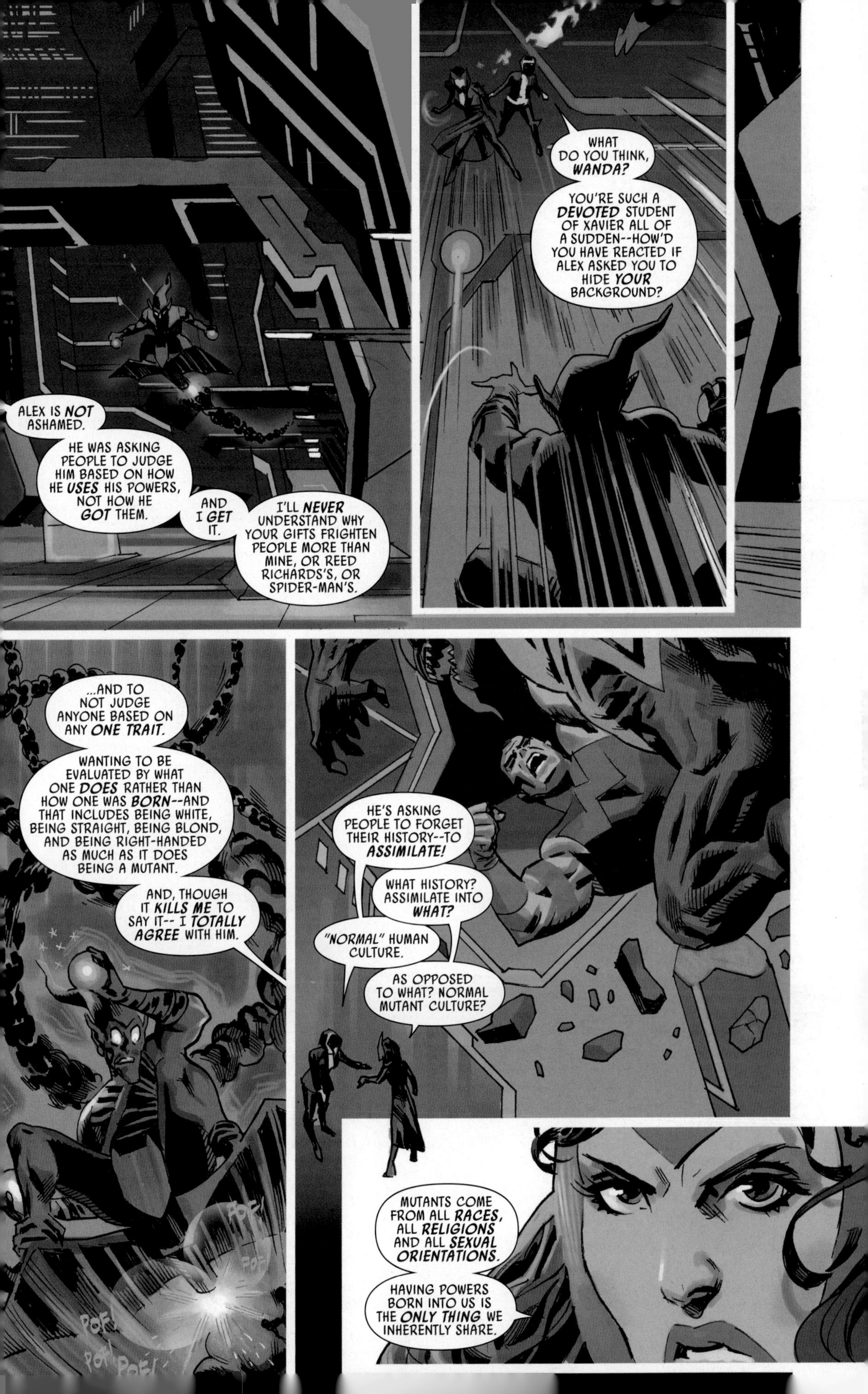

WHAT DO YOU THINK, WANDA?
YOU'RE SUCH A DEVOTED STUDENT OF XAVIER ALL OF A SUDDEN--HOW'D YOU HAVE REACTED IF ALEX ASKED YOU TO HIDE YOUR BACKGROUND?
ALEX IS NOT ASHAMED.
HE WAS ASKING PEOPLE TO JUDGE HIM BASED ON HOW HE USES HIS POWERS, NOT HOW HE GOT THEM.
AND I GET IT.
I'LL NEVER UNDERSTAND WHY YOUR GIFTS FRIGHTEN PEOPLE MORE THAN MINE, OR REED RICHARDS'S, OR SPIDER-MAN'S.
...AND TO NOT JUDGE ANYONE BASED ON ANY ONE TRAIT.
WANTING TO BE EVALUATED BY WHAT ONE DOES RATHER THAN HOW ONE WAS BORN--AND THAT INCLUDES BEING WHITE, BEING STRAIGHT, BEING BLOND, AND BEING RIGHT-HANDED AS MUCH AS IT DOES BEING A MUTANT.
AND, THOUGH IT KILLS ME TO SAY IT-- I TOTALLY AGREE WITH HIM.
POF! POF! POF!
HE'S ASKING PEOPLE TO FORGET THEIR HISTORY--TO ASSIMILATE!
WHAT HISTORY? ASSIMILATE INTO WHAT?
"NORMAL" HUMAN CULTURE.
AS OPPOSED TO WHAT? NORMAL MUTANT CULTURE?
MUTANTS COME FROM ALL RACES, ALL RELIGIONS AND ALL SEXUAL ORIENTATIONS.
HAVING POWERS BORN INTO US IS THE ONLY THING WE INHERENTLY SHARE.

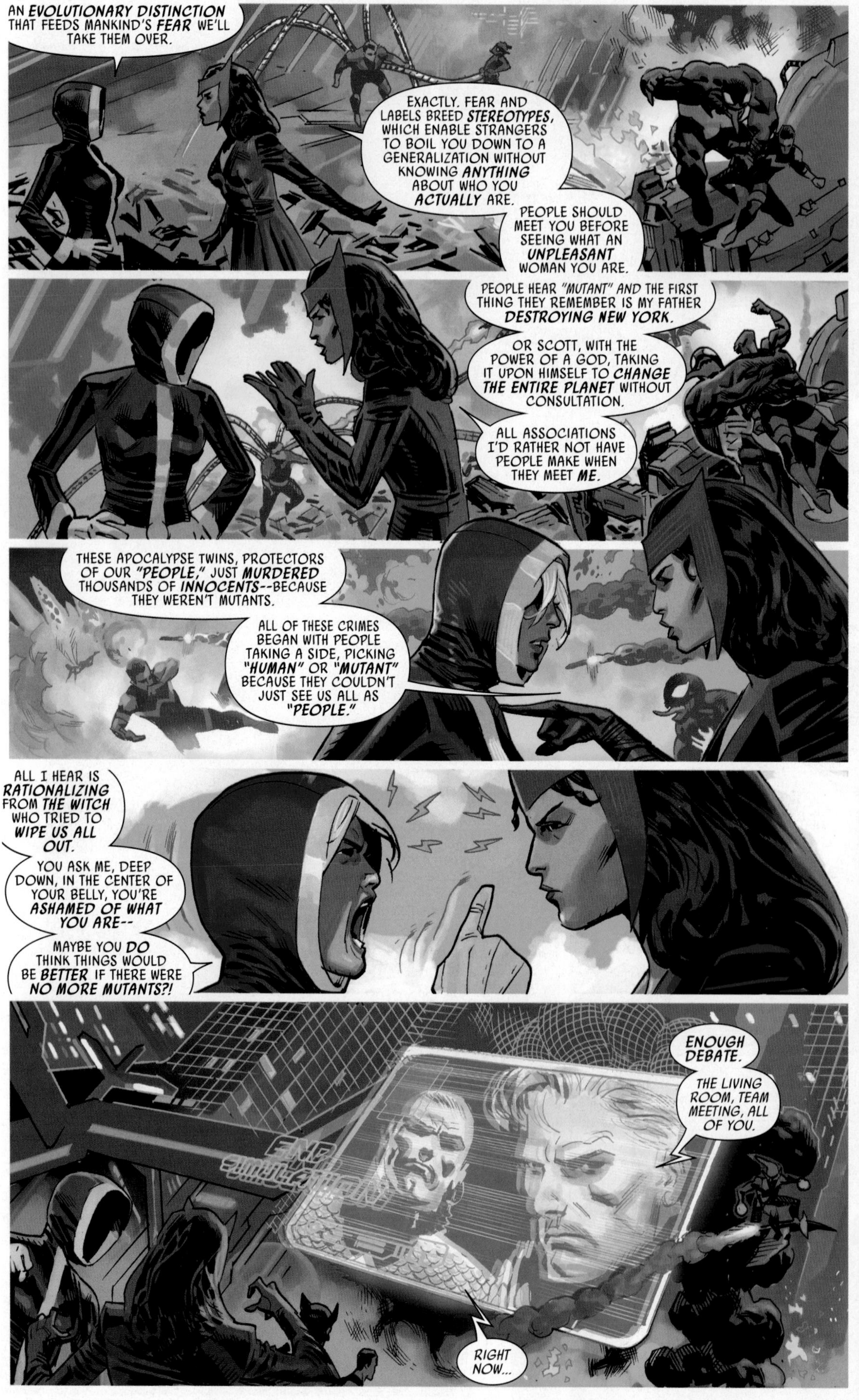
AN EVOLUTIONARY DISTINCTION THAT FEEDS MANKIND'S FEAR WE'LL TAKE THEM OVER.
EXACTLY. FEAR AND LABELS BREED STEREOTYPES, WHICH ENABLE STRANGERS TO BOIL YOU DOWN TO A GENERALIZATION WITHOUT KNOWING ANYTHING ABOUT WHO YOU ACTUALLY ARE.
PEOPLE SHOULD MEET YOU BEFORE SEEING WHAT AN UNPLEASANT WOMAN YOU ARE.
PEOPLE HEAR "MUTANT" AND THE FIRST THING THEY REMEMBER IS MY FATHER DESTROYING NEW YORK.
OR SCOTT, WITH THE POWER OF A GOD, TAKING IT UPON HIMSELF TO CHANGE THE ENTIRE PLANET WITHOUT CONSULTATION.
ALL ASSOCIATIONS I'D RATHER NOT HAVE PEOPLE MAKE WHEN THEY MEET ME.
THESE APOCALYPSE TWINS, PROTECTORS OF OUR "PEOPLE," JUST MURDERED THOUSANDS OF INNOCENTS--BECAUSE THEY WEREN'T MUTANTS.
ALL OF THESE CRIMES BEGAN WITH PEOPLE TAKING A SIDE, PICKING "HUMAN" OR "MUTANT" BECAUSE THEY COULDN'T JUST SEE US ALL AS "PEOPLE."
ALL I HEAR IS RATIONALIZING FROM THE WITCH WHO TRIED TO WIPE US ALL OUT.
YOU ASK ME, DEEP DOWN, IN THE CENTER OF YOUR BELLY, YOU'RE ASHAMED OF WHAT YOU ARE--
MAYBE YOU DO THINK THINGS WOULD BE BETTER IF THERE WERE NO MORE MUTANTS?!
ENOUGH DEBATE.
THE LIVING ROOM, TEAM MEETING, ALL OF YOU.
RIGHT NOW...

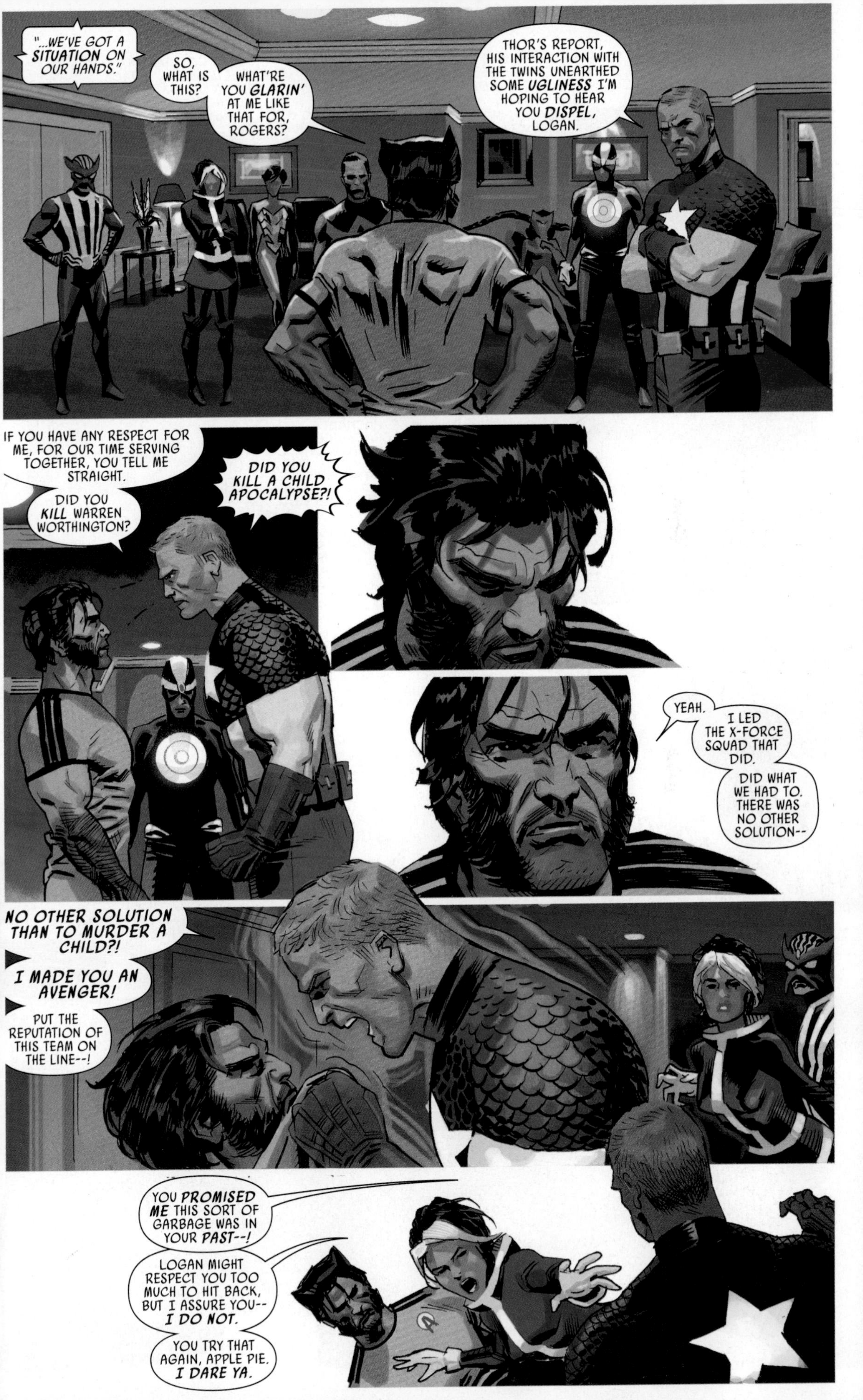
"...WE'VE GOT A SITUATION ON OUR HANDS."
SO, WHAT IS THIS?
WHAT'RE YOU GLARIN' AT ME LIKE THAT FOR, ROGERS?
THOR'S REPORT, HIS INTERACTION WITH THE TWINS UNEARTHED SOME UGLINESS I'M HOPING TO HEAR YOU DISPEL, LOGAN.
IF YOU HAVE ANY RESPECT FOR ME, FOR OUR TIME SERVING TOGETHER, YOU TELL ME STRAIGHT.
DID YOU KILL WARREN WORTHINGTON?
DID YOU KILL A CHILD APOCALYPSE?!
YEAH.
I LED THE X-FORCE SQUAD THAT DID.
DID WHAT WE HAD TO. THERE WAS NO OTHER SOLUTION--
NO OTHER SOLUTION THAN TO MURDER A CHILD?!
I MADE YOU AN AVENGER!
PUT THE REPUTATION OF THIS TEAM ON THE LINE--!
YOU PROMISED ME THIS SORT OF GARBAGE WAS IN YOUR PAST--!
LOGAN MIGHT RESPECT YOU TOO MUCH TO HIT BACK, BUT I ASSURE YOU-- I DO NOT.
YOU TRY THAT AGAIN, APPLE PIE. I DARE YA.

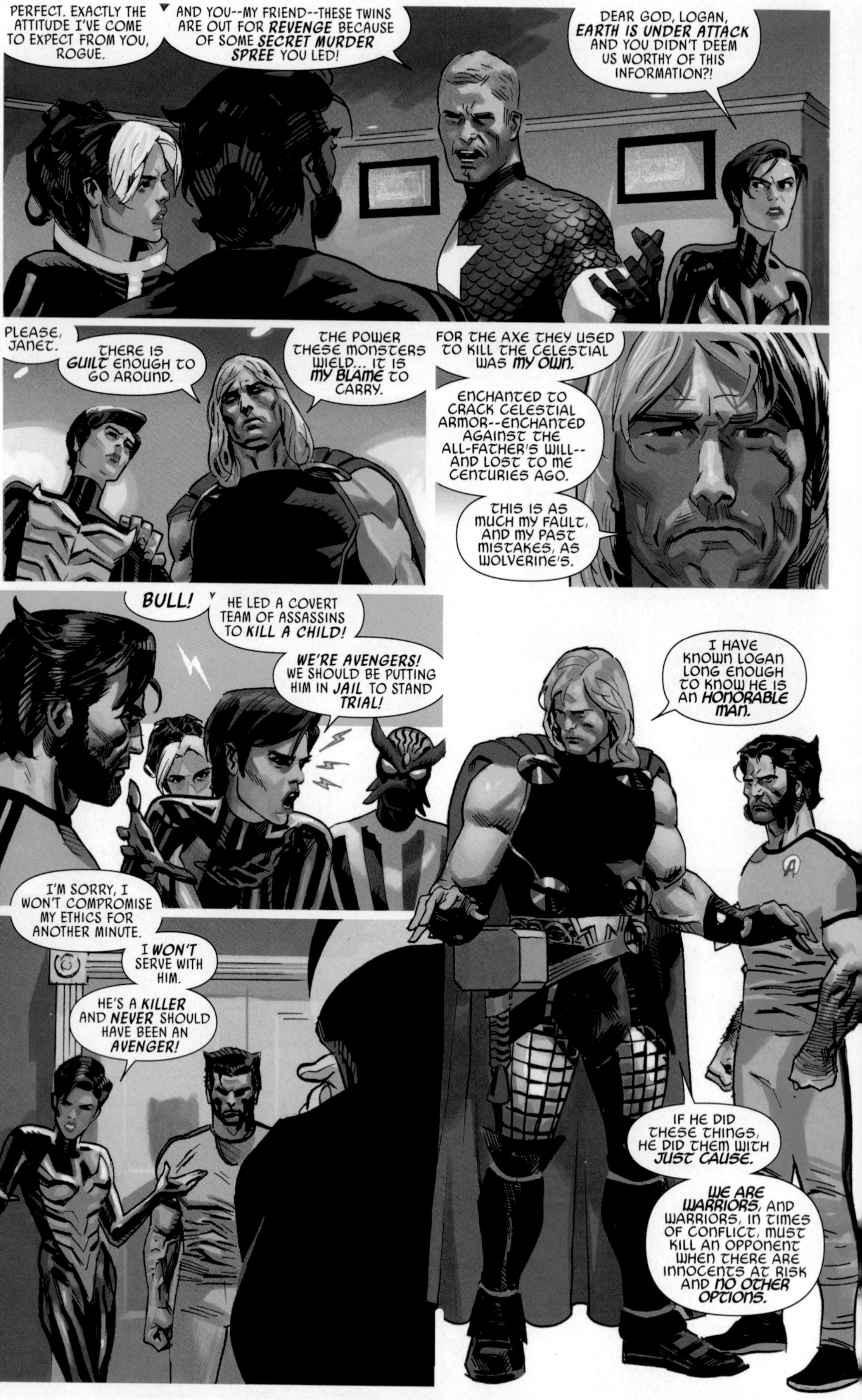
PERFECT. EXACTLY THE ATTITUDE I'VE COME TO EXPECT FROM YOU, ROGUE.
AND YOU--MY FRIEND--THESE TWINS ARE OUT FOR REVENGE BECAUSE OF SOME SECRET MURDER SPREE YOU LED!
DEAR GOD, LOGAN, EARTH IS UNDER ATTACK AND YOU DIDN'T DEEM US WORTHY OF THIS INFORMATION?!
PLEASE, JANET.
THERE IS GUILT ENOUGH TO GO AROUND.
THE POWER THESE MONSTERS WIELD... IT IS MY BLAME TO CARRY.
FOR THE AXE THEY USED TO KILL THE CELESTIAL WAS MY OWN.
ENCHANTED TO CRACK CELESTIAL ARMOR--ENCHANTED AGAINST THE ALL-FATHER'S WILL--AND LOST TO ME CENTURIES AGO.
THIS IS AS MUCH MY FAULT, AND MY PAST MISTAKES, AS WOLVERINE'S.
BULL!
HE LED A COVERT TEAM OF ASSASSINS TO KILL A CHILD!
WE'RE AVENGERS! WE SHOULD BE PUTTING HIM IN JAIL TO STAND TRIAL!
I HAVE KNOWN LOGAN LONG ENOUGH TO KNOW HE IS AN HONORABLE MAN.
I'M SORRY, I WON'T COMPROMISE MY ETHICS FOR ANOTHER MINUTE.
I WON'T SERVE WITH HIM.
HE'S A KILLER AND NEVER SHOULD HAVE BEEN AN AVENGER!
IF HE DID THESE THINGS, HE DID THEM WITH JUST CAUSE.
WE ARE WARRIORS, AND WARRIORS, IN TIMES OF CONFLICT, MUST KILL AN OPPONENT WHEN THERE ARE INNOCENTS AT RISK AND NO OTHER OPTIONS.

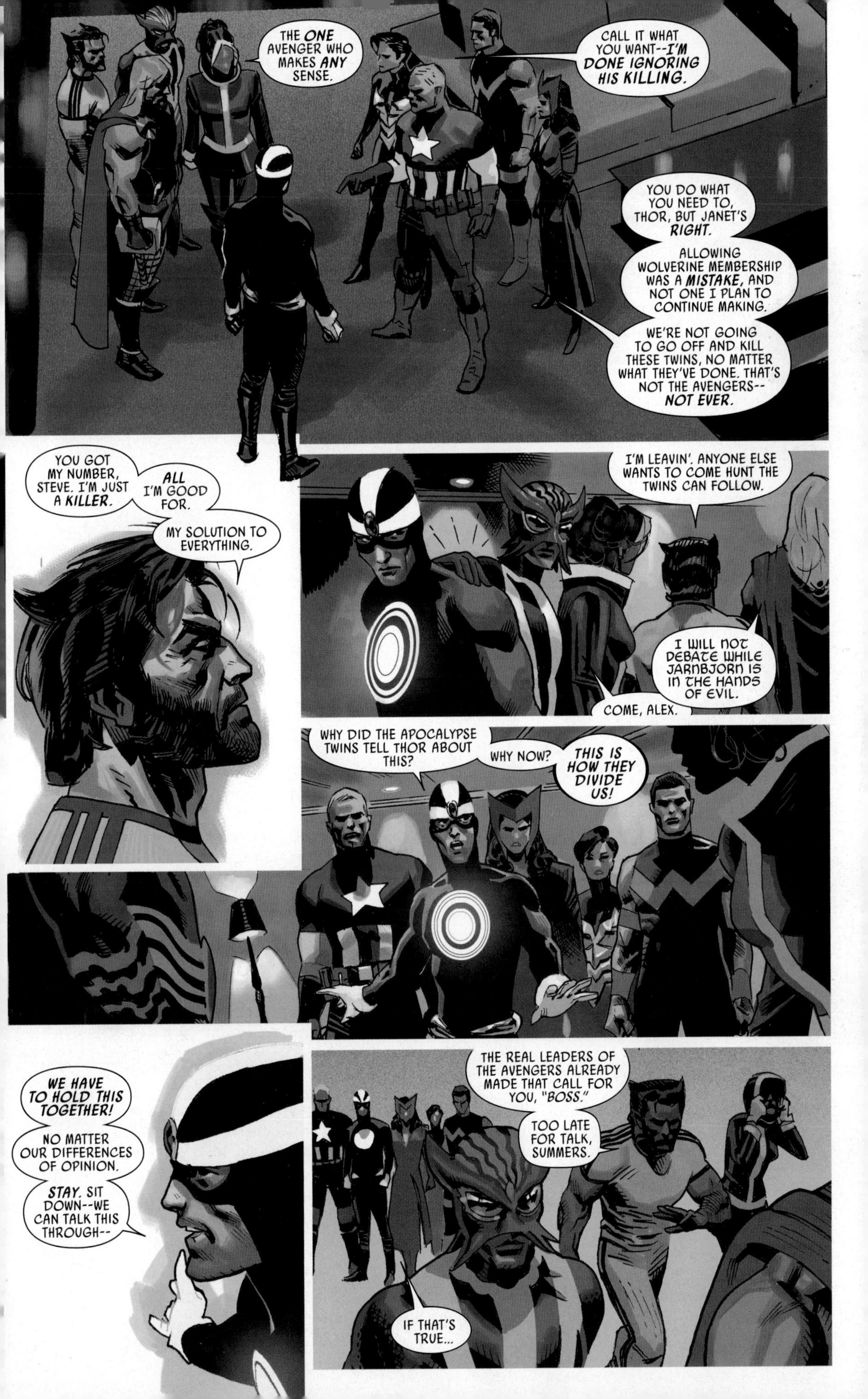
THE *ONE* AVENGER WHO MAKES *ANY* SENSE.
CALL IT WHAT YOU WANT--*I'M DONE IGNORING HIS KILLING.*
YOU DO WHAT YOU NEED TO, THOR, BUT JANET'S *RIGHT.*
ALLOWING WOLVERINE MEMBERSHIP WAS A *MISTAKE,* AND NOT ONE I PLAN TO CONTINUE MAKING.
WE'RE NOT GOING TO GO OFF AND KILL THESE TWINS, NO MATTER WHAT THEY'VE DONE. THAT'S NOT THE AVENGERS-- *NOT EVER.*
YOU GOT MY NUMBER, STEVE. I'M JUST A *KILLER.*
ALL I'M GOOD FOR.
MY SOLUTION TO EVERYTHING.
I'M LEAVIN'. ANYONE ELSE WANTS TO COME HUNT THE TWINS CAN FOLLOW.
I WILL NOT DEBATE WHILE JARNBJORN IS IN THE HANDS OF EVIL.
COME, ALEX.
WHY DID THE APOCALYPSE TWINS TELL THOR ABOUT THIS?
WHY NOW?
THIS IS HOW THEY DIVIDE US!
WE HAVE TO HOLD THIS TOGETHER!
NO MATTER OUR DIFFERENCES OF OPINION.
STAY. SIT DOWN--WE CAN TALK THIS THROUGH--
THE REAL LEADERS OF THE AVENGERS ALREADY MADE THAT CALL FOR YOU, "*BOSS.*"
TOO LATE FOR TALK, SUMMERS.
IF THAT'S TRUE...

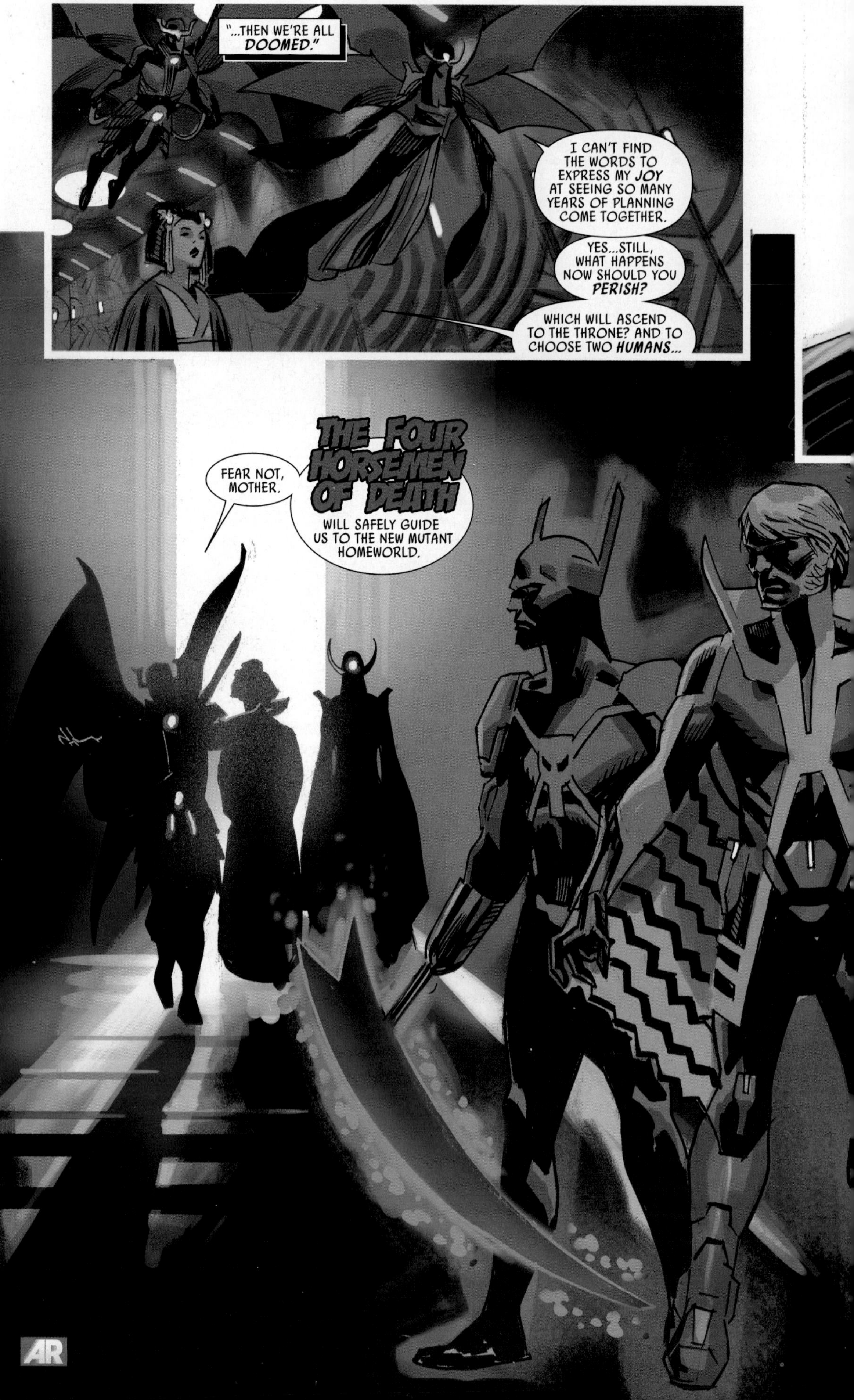

"...THEN WE'RE ALL DOOMED."
I CAN'T FIND THE WORDS TO EXPRESS MY JOY AT SEEING SO MANY YEARS OF PLANNING COME TOGETHER.
YES...STILL, WHAT HAPPENS NOW SHOULD YOU PERISH?
WHICH WILL ASCEND TO THE THRONE? AND TO CHOOSE TWO HUMANS...
FEAR NOT, MOTHER.
THE FOUR HORSEMEN OF DEATH WILL SAFELY GUIDE US TO THE NEW MUTANT HOMEWORLD.
AR

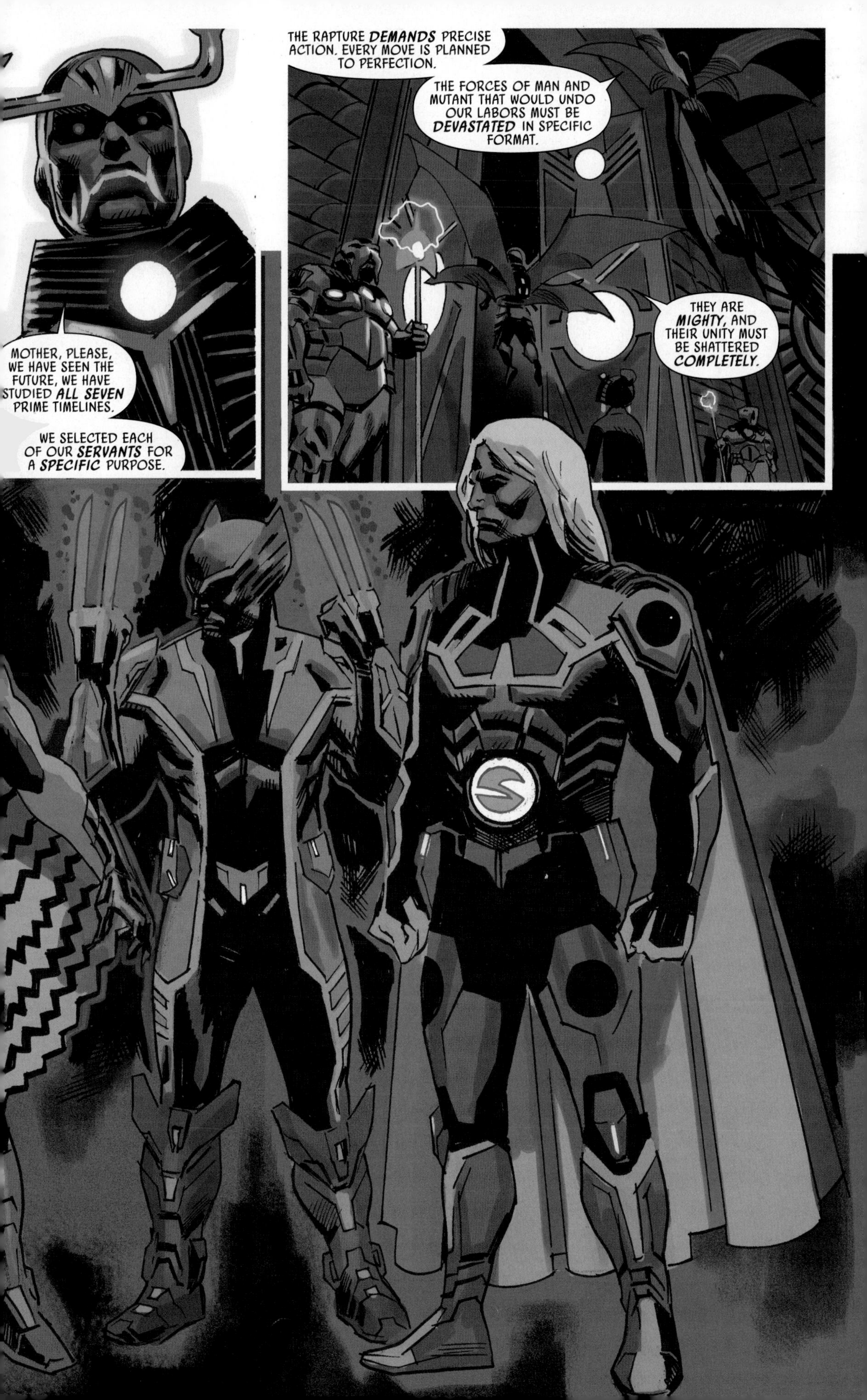
MOTHER, PLEASE, WE HAVE SEEN THE FUTURE, WE HAVE STUDIED ALL SEVEN PRIME TIMELINES.
WE SELECTED EACH OF OUR SERVANTS FOR A SPECIFIC PURPOSE.
THE RAPTURE DEMANDS PRECISE ACTION. EVERY MOVE IS PLANNED TO PERFECTION.
THE FORCES OF MAN AND MUTANT THAT WOULD UNDO OUR LABORS MUST BE DEVASTATED IN SPECIFIC FORMAT.
THEY ARE MIGHTY, AND THEIR UNITY MUST BE SHATTERED COMPLETELY.

UNCANNY AVENGERS #10

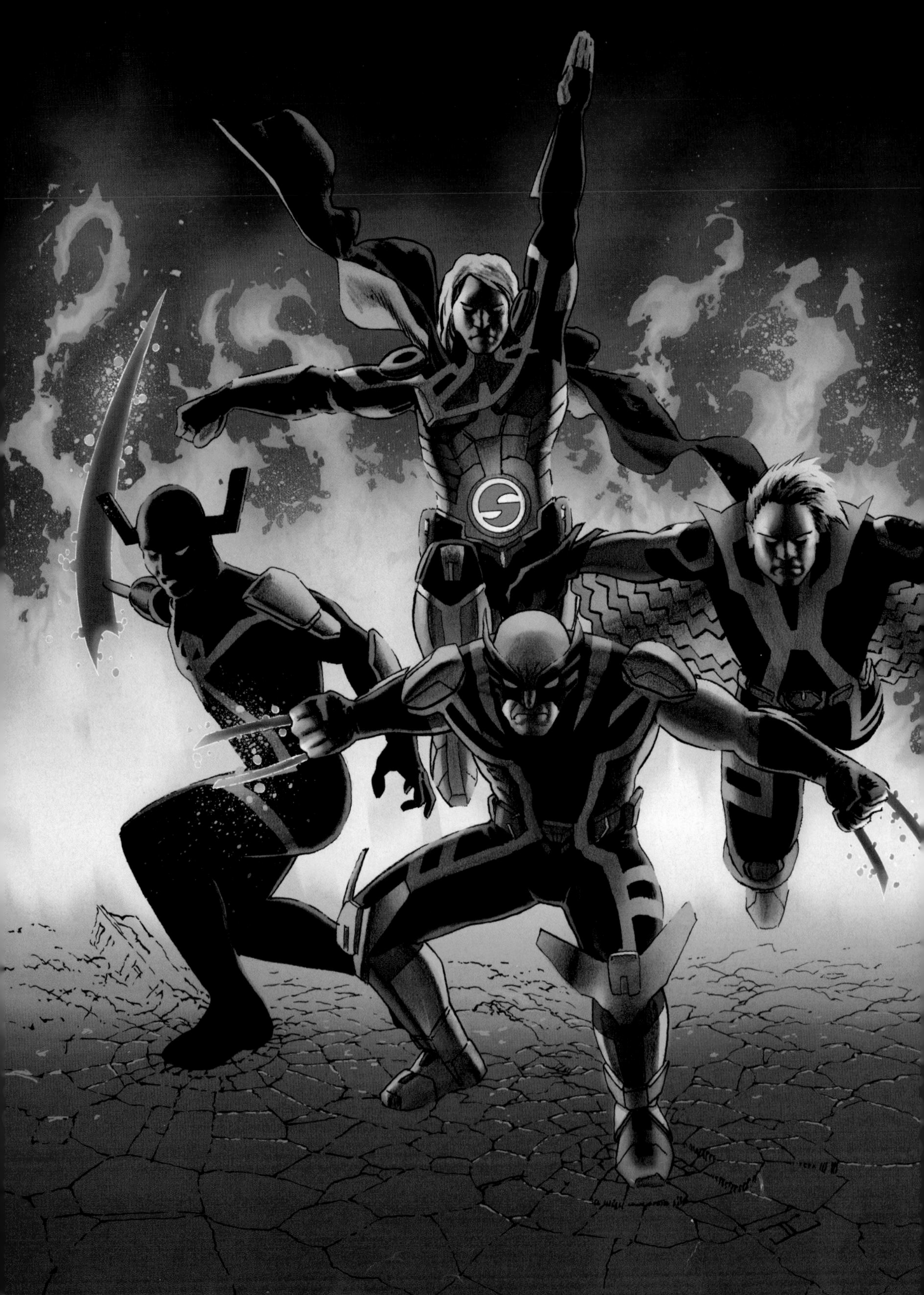

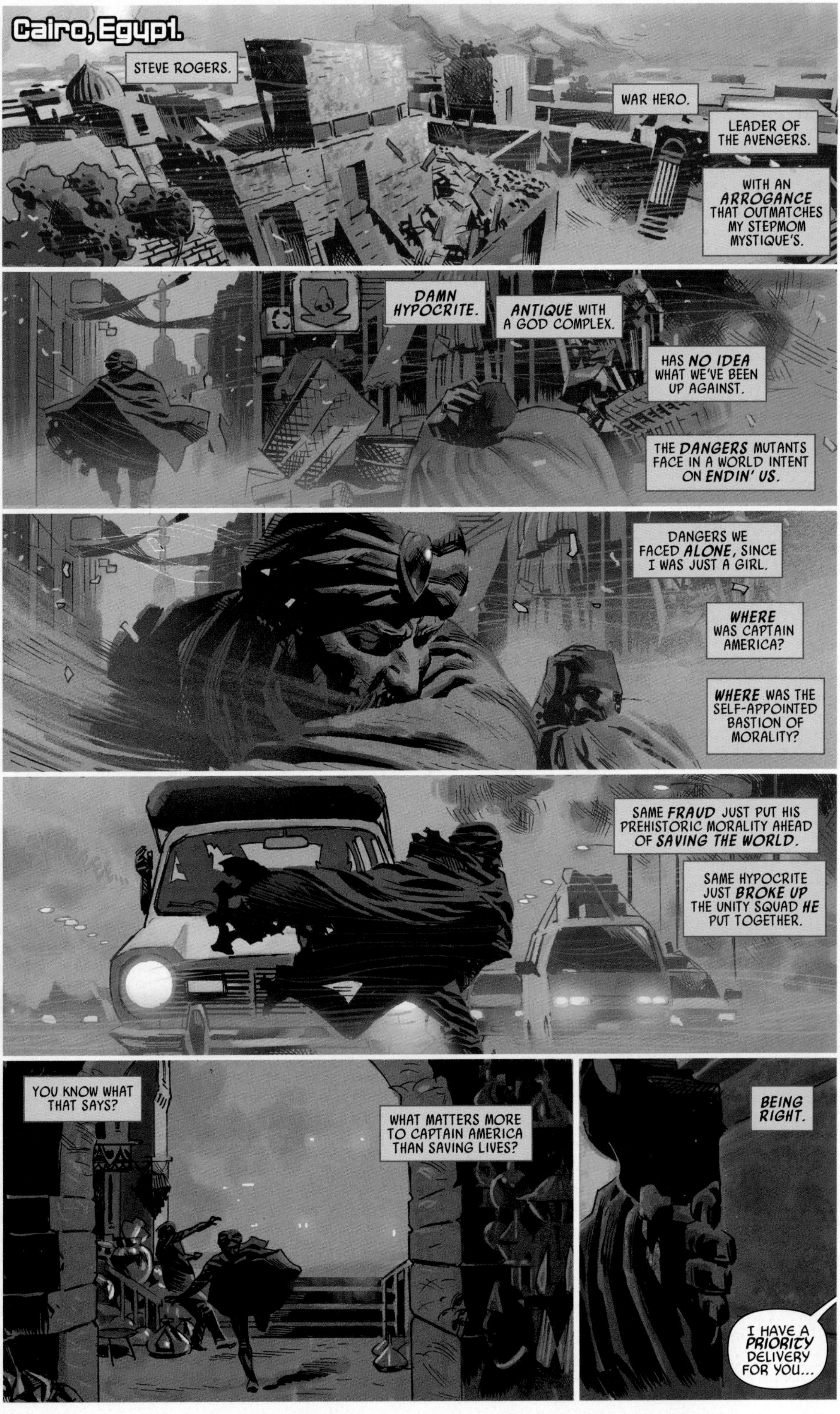
Cairo, Egypt.
STEVE ROGERS.
WAR HERO.
LEADER OF THE AVENGERS.
WITH AN ARROGANCE THAT OUTMATCHES MY STEPMOM MYSTIQUE'S.
DAMN HYPOCRITE.
ANTIQUE WITH A GOD COMPLEX.
HAS NO IDEA WHAT WE'VE BEEN UP AGAINST.
THE DANGERS MUTANTS FACE IN A WORLD INTENT ON ENDIN' US.
DANGERS WE FACED ALONE, SINCE I WAS JUST A GIRL.
WHERE WAS CAPTAIN AMERICA?
WHERE WAS THE SELF-APPOINTED BASTION OF MORALITY?
SAME FRAUD JUST PUT HIS PREHISTORIC MORALITY AHEAD OF SAVING THE WORLD.
SAME HYPOCRITE JUST BROKE UP THE UNITY SQUAD HE PUT TOGETHER.
YOU KNOW WHAT THAT SAYS?
WHAT MATTERS MORE TO CAPTAIN AMERICA THAN SAVING LIVES?
BEING RIGHT.
I HAVE A PRIORITY DELIVERY FOR YOU...

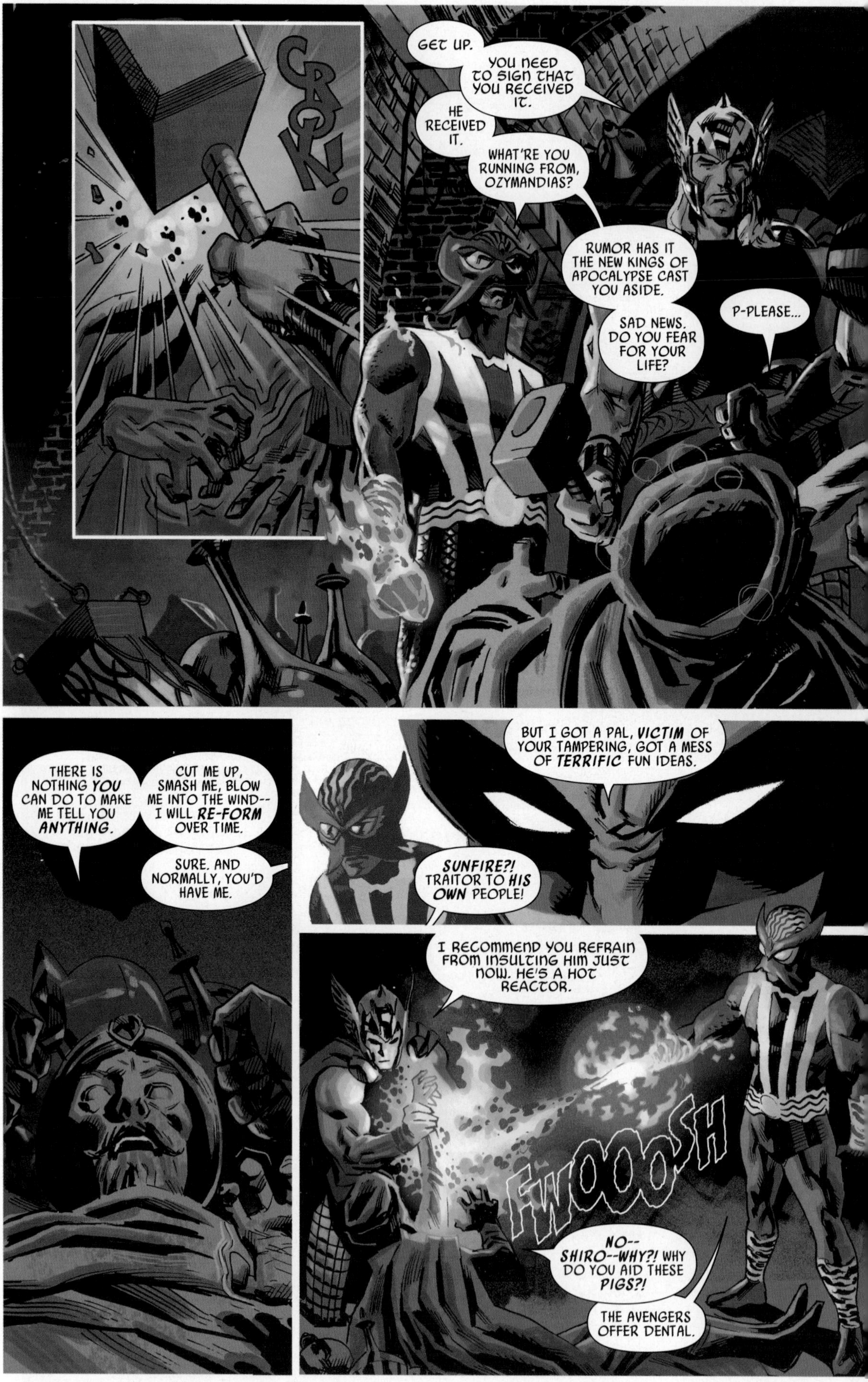
CRACK!
GET UP.
YOU NEED TO SIGN THAT YOU RECEIVED IT.
HE RECEIVED IT.
WHAT'RE YOU RUNNING FROM, OZYMANDIAS?
RUMOR HAS IT THE NEW KINGS OF APOCALYPSE CAST YOU ASIDE.
SAD NEWS. DO YOU FEAR FOR YOUR LIFE?
P-PLEASE...
THERE IS NOTHING YOU CAN DO TO MAKE ME TELL YOU ANYTHING.
CUT ME UP, SMASH ME, BLOW ME INTO THE WIND-- I WILL RE-FORM OVER TIME.
SURE. AND NORMALLY, YOU'D HAVE ME.
BUT I GOT A PAL, VICTIM OF YOUR TAMPERING, GOT A MESS OF TERRIFIC FUN IDEAS.
SUNFIRE?! TRAITOR TO HIS OWN PEOPLE!
I RECOMMEND YOU REFRAIN FROM INSULTING HIM JUST NOW. HE'S A HOT REACTOR.
FWOOOOSH
NO-- SHIRO--WHY?! WHY DO YOU AID THESE PIGS?!
THE AVENGERS OFFER DENTAL.

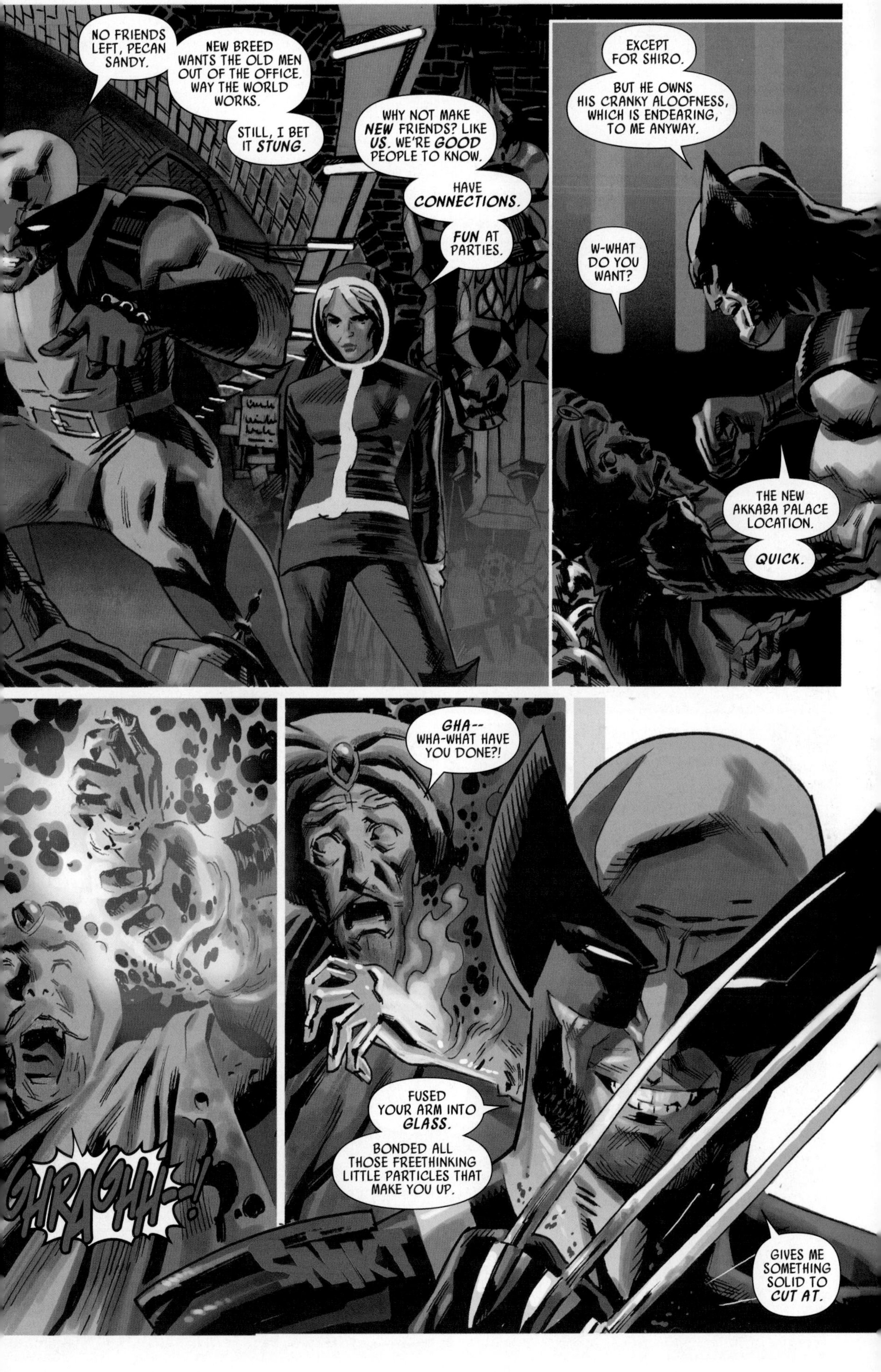
NO FRIENDS LEFT, PECAN SANDY.
NEW BREED WANTS THE OLD MEN OUT OF THE OFFICE. WAY THE WORLD WORKS.
STILL, I BET IT STUNG.
WHY NOT MAKE NEW FRIENDS? LIKE US. WE'RE GOOD PEOPLE TO KNOW.
HAVE CONNECTIONS.
FUN AT PARTIES.
EXCEPT FOR SHIRO.
BUT HE OWNS HIS CRANKY ALOOFNESS, WHICH IS ENDEARING, TO ME ANYWAY.
W-WHAT DO YOU WANT?
THE NEW AKKABA PALACE LOCATION.
QUICK.
GHRAGHH--!
GHA-- WHA-WHAT HAVE YOU DONE?!
FUSED YOUR ARM INTO GLASS.
BONDED ALL THOSE FREETHINKING LITTLE PARTICLES THAT MAKE YOU UP.
GIVES ME SOMETHING SOLID TO CUT AT.

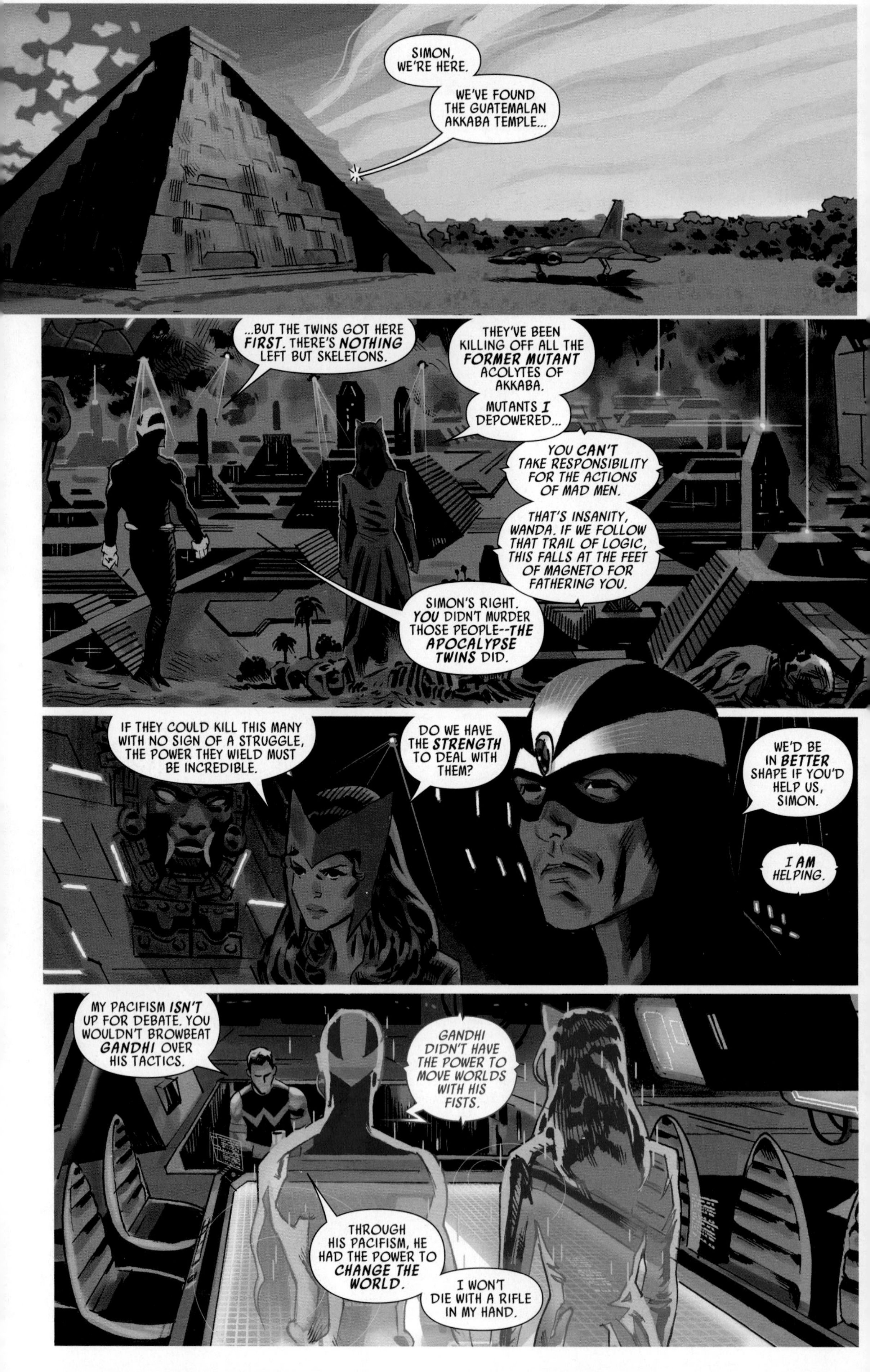
SIMON, WE'RE HERE.
WE'VE FOUND THE GUATEMALAN AKKABA TEMPLE...
...BUT THE TWINS GOT HERE FIRST. THERE'S NOTHING LEFT BUT SKELETONS.
THEY'VE BEEN KILLING OFF ALL THE FORMER MUTANT ACOLYTES OF AKKABA.
MUTANTS I DEPOWERED...
YOU CAN'T TAKE RESPONSIBILITY FOR THE ACTIONS OF MAD MEN.
THAT'S INSANITY, WANDA. IF WE FOLLOW THAT TRAIL OF LOGIC, THIS FALLS AT THE FEET OF MAGNETO FOR FATHERING YOU.
SIMON'S RIGHT. YOU DIDN'T MURDER THOSE PEOPLE--THE APOCALYPSE TWINS DID.
IF THEY COULD KILL THIS MANY WITH NO SIGN OF A STRUGGLE, THE POWER THEY WIELD MUST BE INCREDIBLE.
DO WE HAVE THE STRENGTH TO DEAL WITH THEM?
WE'D BE IN BETTER SHAPE IF YOU'D HELP US, SIMON.
I AM HELPING.
MY PACIFISM ISN'T UP FOR DEBATE. YOU WOULDN'T BROWBEAT GANDHI OVER HIS TACTICS.
GANDHI DIDN'T HAVE THE POWER TO MOVE WORLDS WITH HIS FISTS.
THROUGH HIS PACIFISM, HE HAD THE POWER TO CHANGE THE WORLD.
I WON'T DIE WITH A RIFLE IN MY HAND.

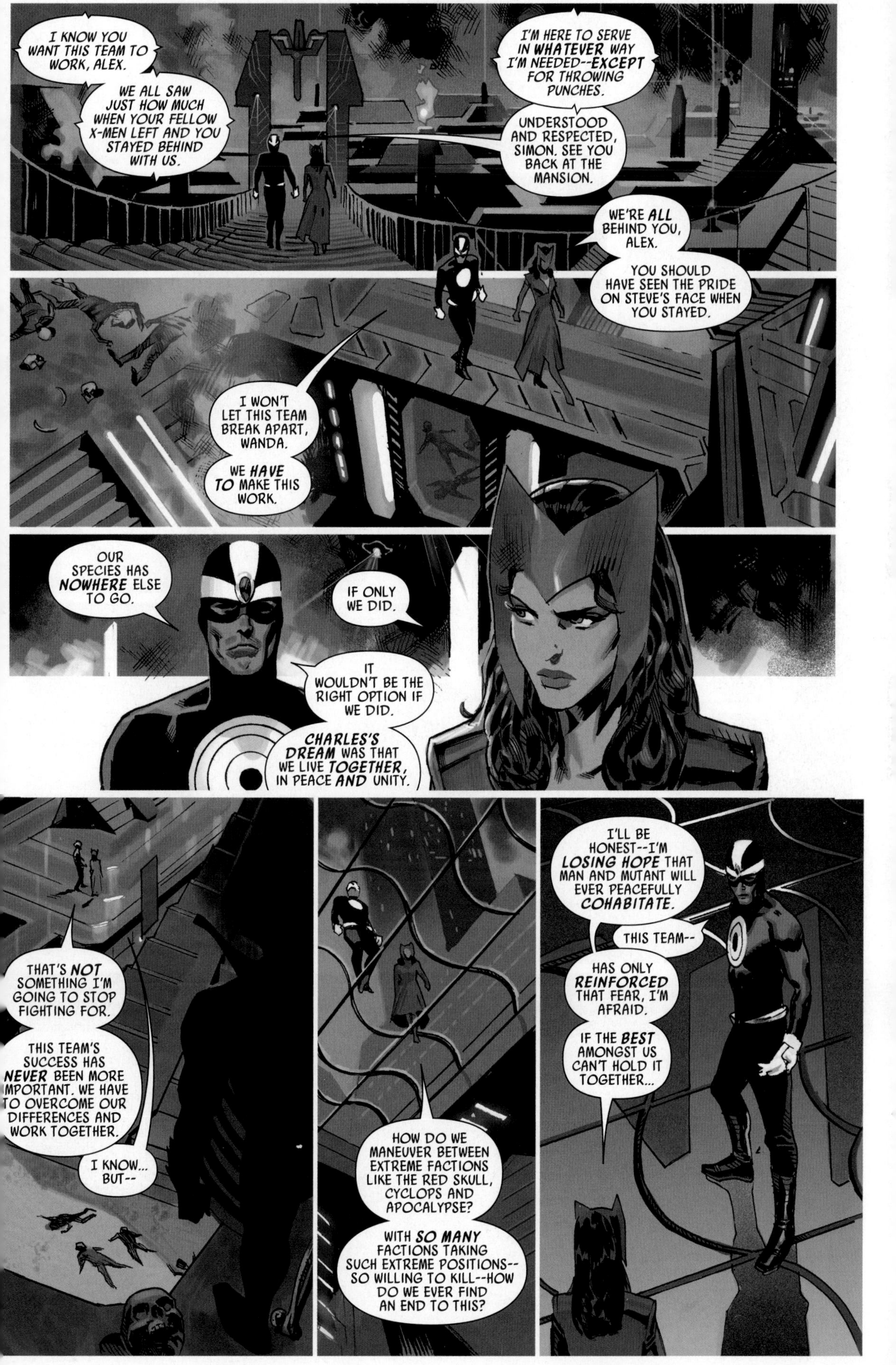
I KNOW YOU WANT THIS TEAM TO WORK, ALEX.
WE ALL SAW JUST HOW MUCH WHEN YOUR FELLOW X-MEN LEFT AND YOU STAYED BEHIND WITH US.
I'M HERE TO SERVE IN WHATEVER WAY I'M NEEDED--EXCEPT FOR THROWING PUNCHES.
UNDERSTOOD AND RESPECTED, SIMON. SEE YOU BACK AT THE MANSION.
WE'RE ALL BEHIND YOU, ALEX.
YOU SHOULD HAVE SEEN THE PRIDE ON STEVE'S FACE WHEN YOU STAYED.
I WON'T LET THIS TEAM BREAK APART, WANDA.
WE HAVE TO MAKE THIS WORK.
OUR SPECIES HAS NOWHERE ELSE TO GO.
IF ONLY WE DID.
IT WOULDN'T BE THE RIGHT OPTION IF WE DID.
CHARLES'S DREAM WAS THAT WE LIVE TOGETHER, IN PEACE AND UNITY.
THAT'S NOT SOMETHING I'M GOING TO STOP FIGHTING FOR.
THIS TEAM'S SUCCESS HAS NEVER BEEN MORE IMPORTANT. WE HAVE TO OVERCOME OUR DIFFERENCES AND WORK TOGETHER.
I KNOW... BUT--
HOW DO WE MANEUVER BETWEEN EXTREME FACTIONS LIKE THE RED SKULL, CYCLOPS AND APOCALYPSE?
WITH SO MANY FACTIONS TAKING SUCH EXTREME POSITIONS--SO WILLING TO KILL--HOW DO WE EVER FIND AN END TO THIS?
I'LL BE HONEST--I'M LOSING HOPE THAT MAN AND MUTANT WILL EVER PEACEFULLY COHABITATE.
THIS TEAM--
HAS ONLY REINFORCED THAT FEAR, I'M AFRAID.
IF THE BEST AMONGST US CAN'T HOLD IT TOGETHER...

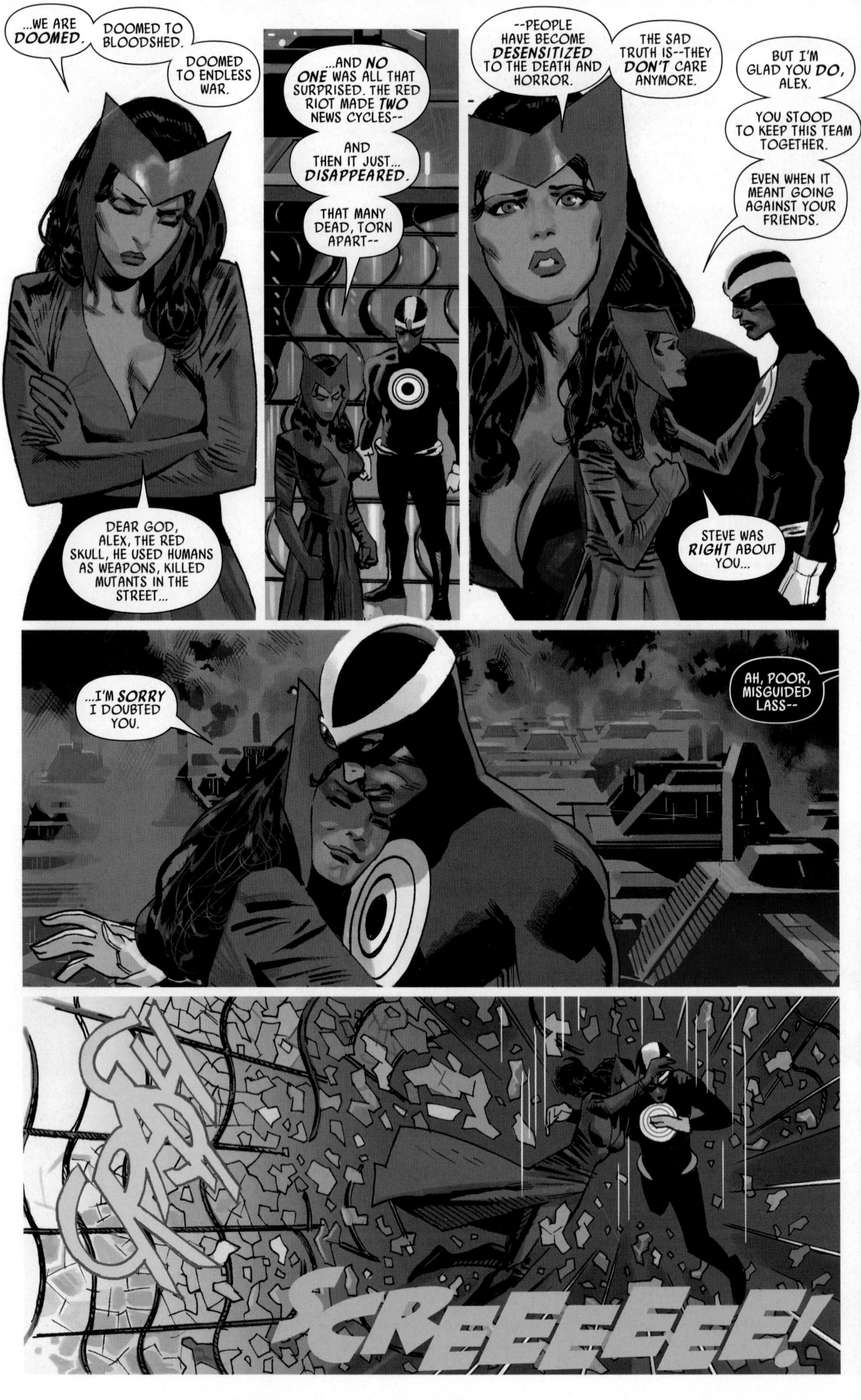
...WE ARE DOOMED.
DOOMED TO BLOODSHED.
DOOMED TO ENDLESS WAR.
DEAR GOD, ALEX, THE RED SKULL, HE USED HUMANS AS WEAPONS, KILLED MUTANTS IN THE STREET...
...AND NO ONE WAS ALL THAT SURPRISED. THE RED RIOT MADE TWO NEWS CYCLES--
AND THEN IT JUST... DISAPPEARED.
THAT MANY DEAD, TORN APART--
--PEOPLE HAVE BECOME DESENSITIZED TO THE DEATH AND HORROR.
THE SAD TRUTH IS--THEY DON'T CARE ANYMORE.
BUT I'M GLAD YOU DO, ALEX.
YOU STOOD TO KEEP THIS TEAM TOGETHER.
EVEN WHEN IT MEANT GOING AGAINST YOUR FRIENDS.
STEVE WAS RIGHT ABOUT YOU...
...I'M SORRY I DOUBTED YOU.
AH, POOR, MISGUIDED LASS--
SCREEEEEE!

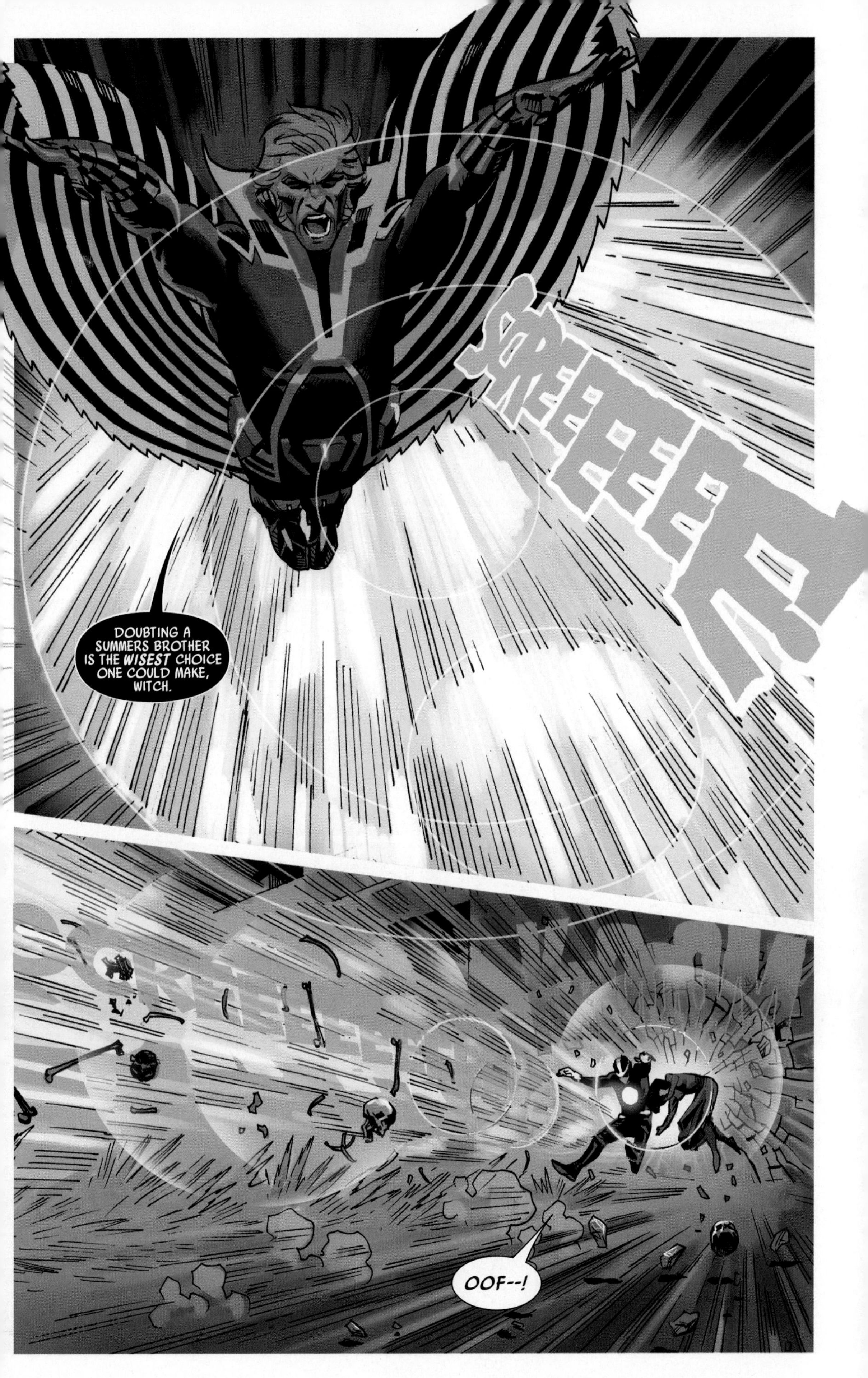
SCREEEEEE!
DOUBTING A SUMMERS BROTHER IS THE WISEST CHOICE ONE COULD MAKE, WITCH.
OOF--!

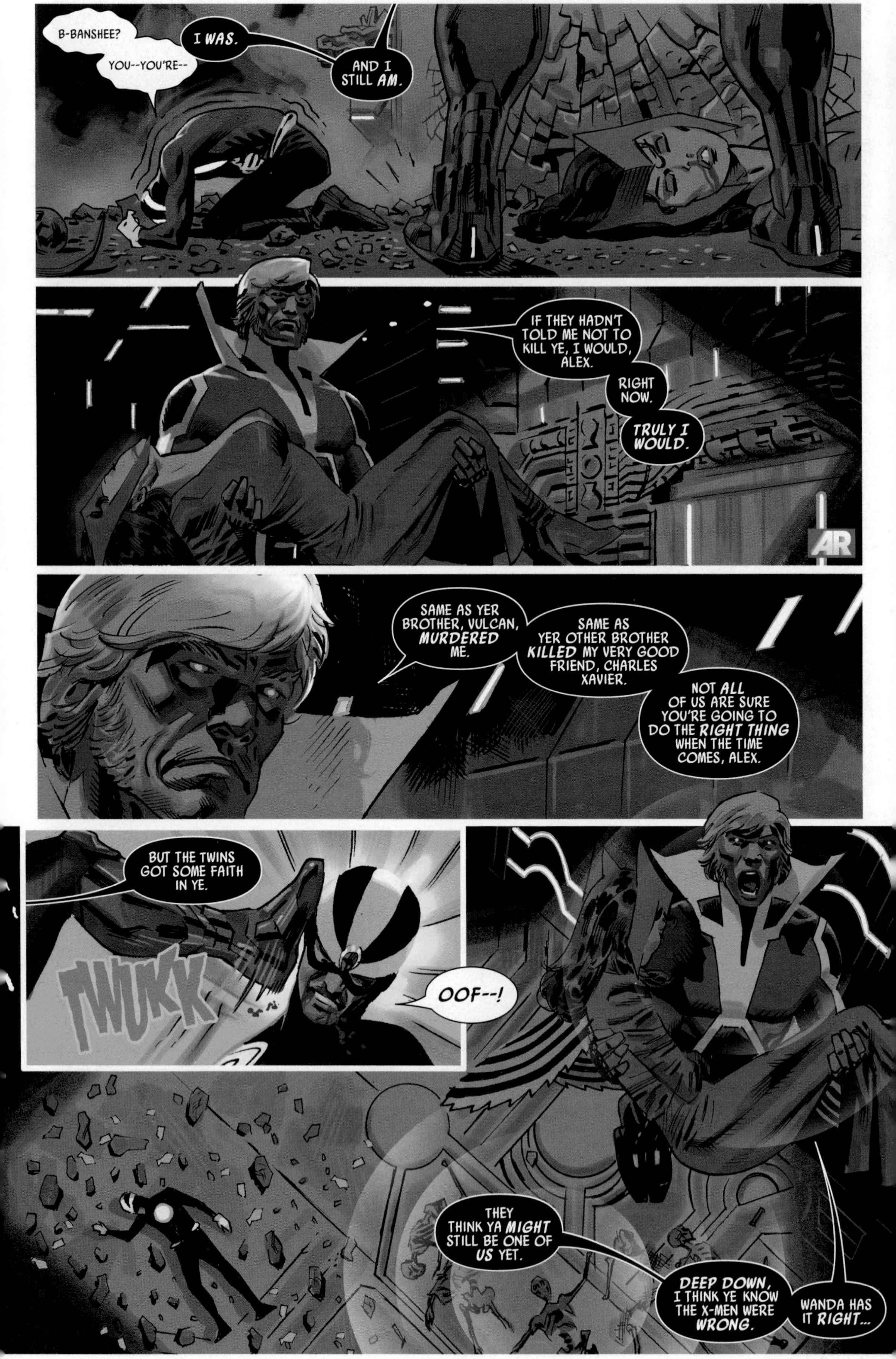
B-BANSHEE?
YOU--YOU'RE--
I WAS.
AND I STILL AM.
IF THEY HADN'T TOLD ME NOT TO KILL YE, I WOULD, ALEX.
RIGHT NOW.
TRULY I WOULD.
AR
SAME AS YER BROTHER, VULCAN, MURDERED ME.
SAME AS YER OTHER BROTHER KILLED MY VERY GOOD FRIEND, CHARLES XAVIER.
NOT ALL OF US ARE SURE YOU'RE GOING TO DO THE RIGHT THING WHEN THE TIME COMES, ALEX.
BUT THE TWINS GOT SOME FAITH IN YE.
TWUKK
OOF--!
THEY THINK YA MIGHT STILL BE ONE OF US YET.
DEEP DOWN, I THINK YE KNOW THE X-MEN WERE WRONG.
WANDA HAS IT RIGHT...

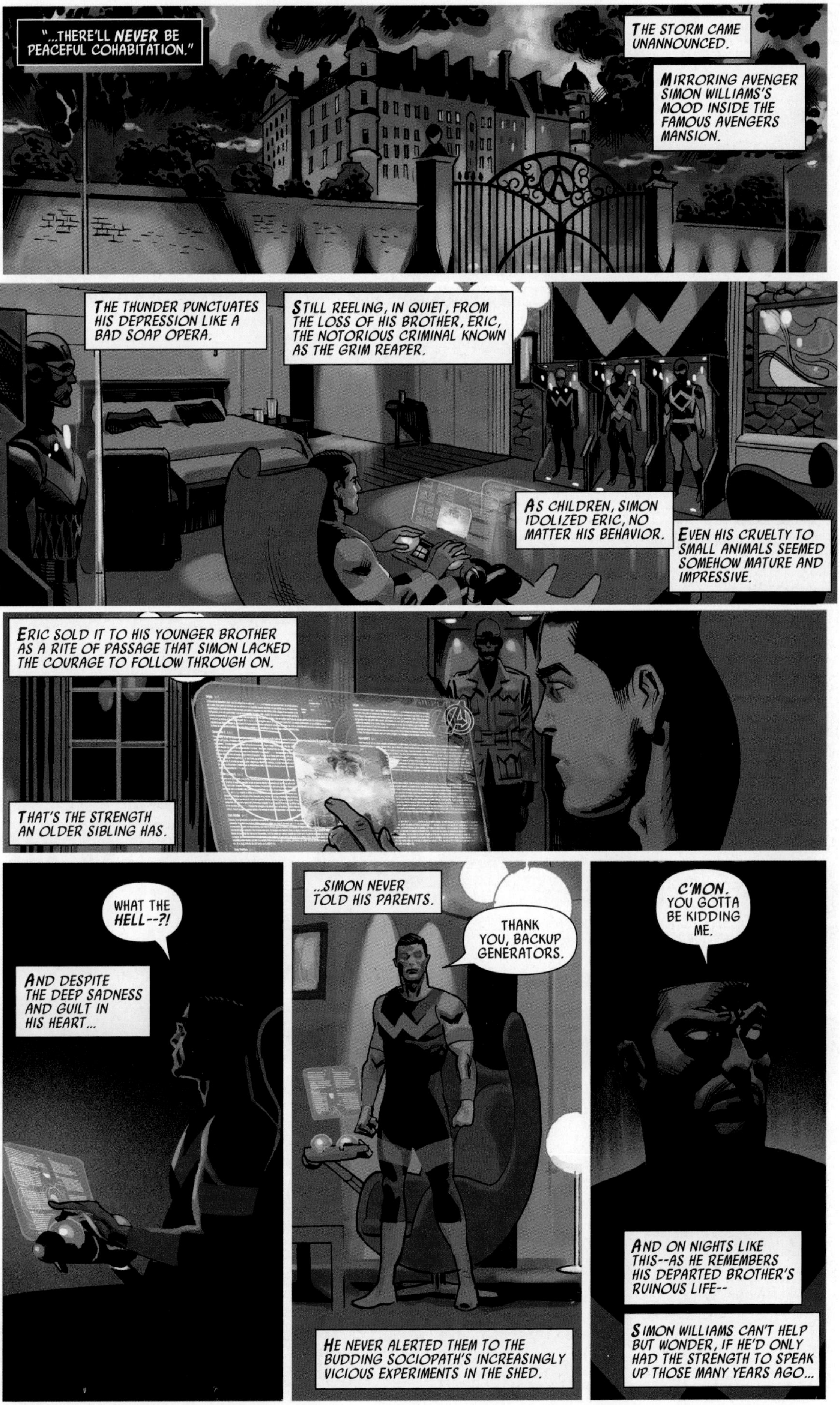
"...THERE'LL NEVER BE PEACEFUL COHABITATION."
THE STORM CAME UNANNOUNCED.
MIRRORING AVENGER SIMON WILLIAMS'S MOOD INSIDE THE FAMOUS AVENGERS MANSION.
THE THUNDER PUNCTUATES HIS DEPRESSION LIKE A BAD SOAP OPERA.
STILL REELING, IN QUIET, FROM THE LOSS OF HIS BROTHER, ERIC, THE NOTORIOUS CRIMINAL KNOWN AS THE GRIM REAPER.
AS CHILDREN, SIMON IDOLIZED ERIC, NO MATTER HIS BEHAVIOR.
EVEN HIS CRUELTY TO SMALL ANIMALS SEEMED SOMEHOW MATURE AND IMPRESSIVE.
ERIC SOLD IT TO HIS YOUNGER BROTHER AS A RITE OF PASSAGE THAT SIMON LACKED THE COURAGE TO FOLLOW THROUGH ON.
THAT'S THE STRENGTH AN OLDER SIBLING HAS.
WHAT THE HELL--?!
AND DESPITE THE DEEP SADNESS AND GUILT IN HIS HEART...
...SIMON NEVER TOLD HIS PARENTS.
THANK YOU, BACKUP GENERATORS.
HE NEVER ALERTED THEM TO THE BUDDING SOCIOPATH'S INCREASINGLY VICIOUS EXPERIMENTS IN THE SHED.
C'MON. YOU GOTTA BE KIDDING ME.
AND ON NIGHTS LIKE THIS--AS HE REMEMBERS HIS DEPARTED BROTHER'S RUINOUS LIFE--
SIMON WILLIAMS CAN'T HELP BUT WONDER, IF HE'D ONLY HAD THE STRENGTH TO SPEAK UP THOSE MANY YEARS AGO...

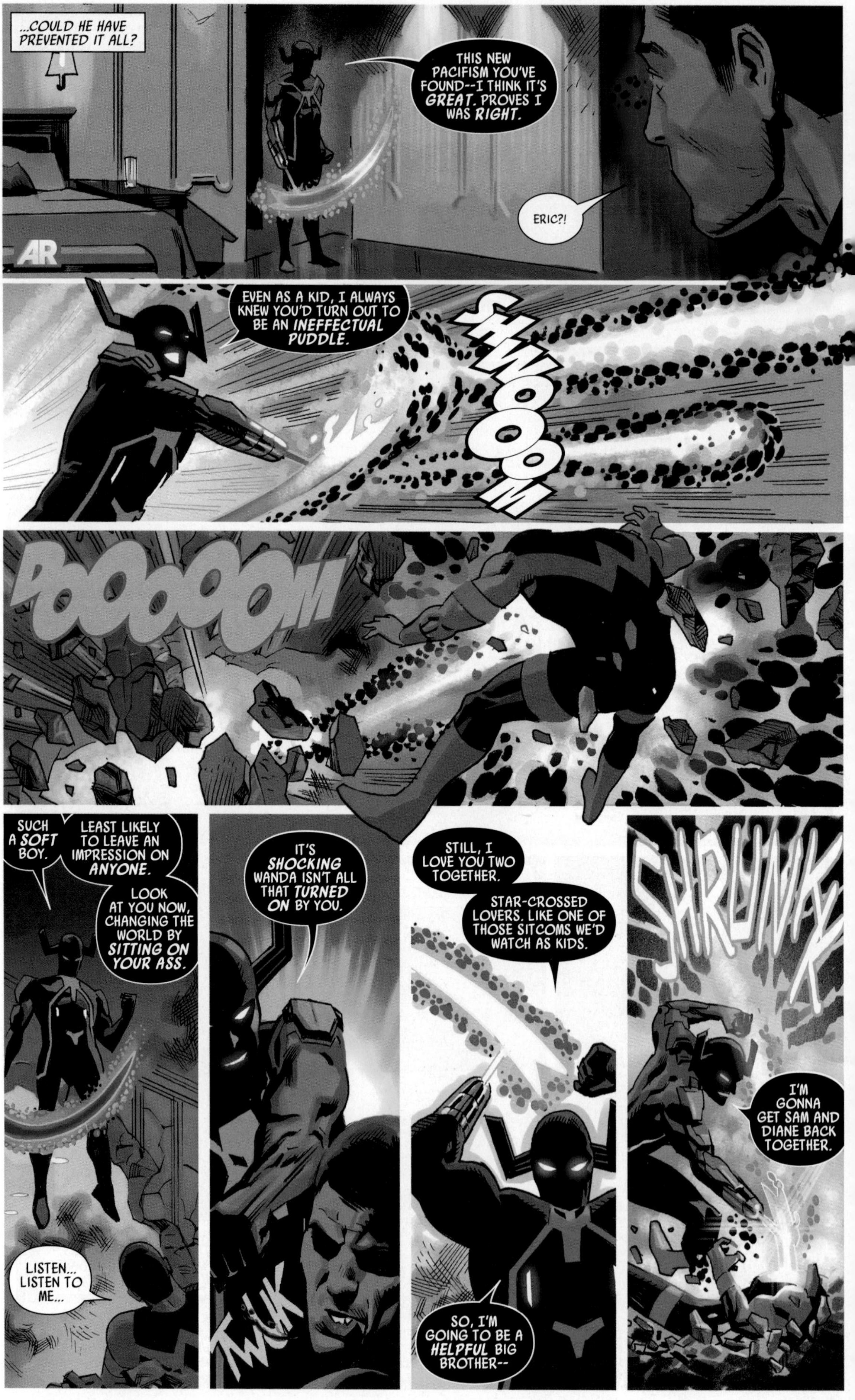
...COULD HE HAVE PREVENTED IT ALL?
THIS NEW PACIFISM YOU'VE FOUND--I THINK IT'S GREAT. PROVES I WAS RIGHT.
ERIC?!
EVEN AS A KID, I ALWAYS KNEW YOU'D TURN OUT TO BE AN INEFFECTUAL PUDDLE.
SHWOOOOM
POOOOOOM
SUCH A SOFT BOY.
LEAST LIKELY TO LEAVE AN IMPRESSION ON ANYONE.
LOOK AT YOU NOW, CHANGING THE WORLD BY SITTING ON YOUR ASS.
LISTEN... LISTEN TO ME...
IT'S SHOCKING WANDA ISN'T ALL THAT TURNED ON BY YOU.
TWUK
STILL, I LOVE YOU TWO TOGETHER.
STAR-CROSSED LOVERS. LIKE ONE OF THOSE SITCOMS WE'D WATCH AS KIDS.
SO, I'M GOING TO BE A HELPFUL BIG BROTHER--
SHRUNK
I'M GONNA GET SAM AND DIANE BACK TOGETHER.

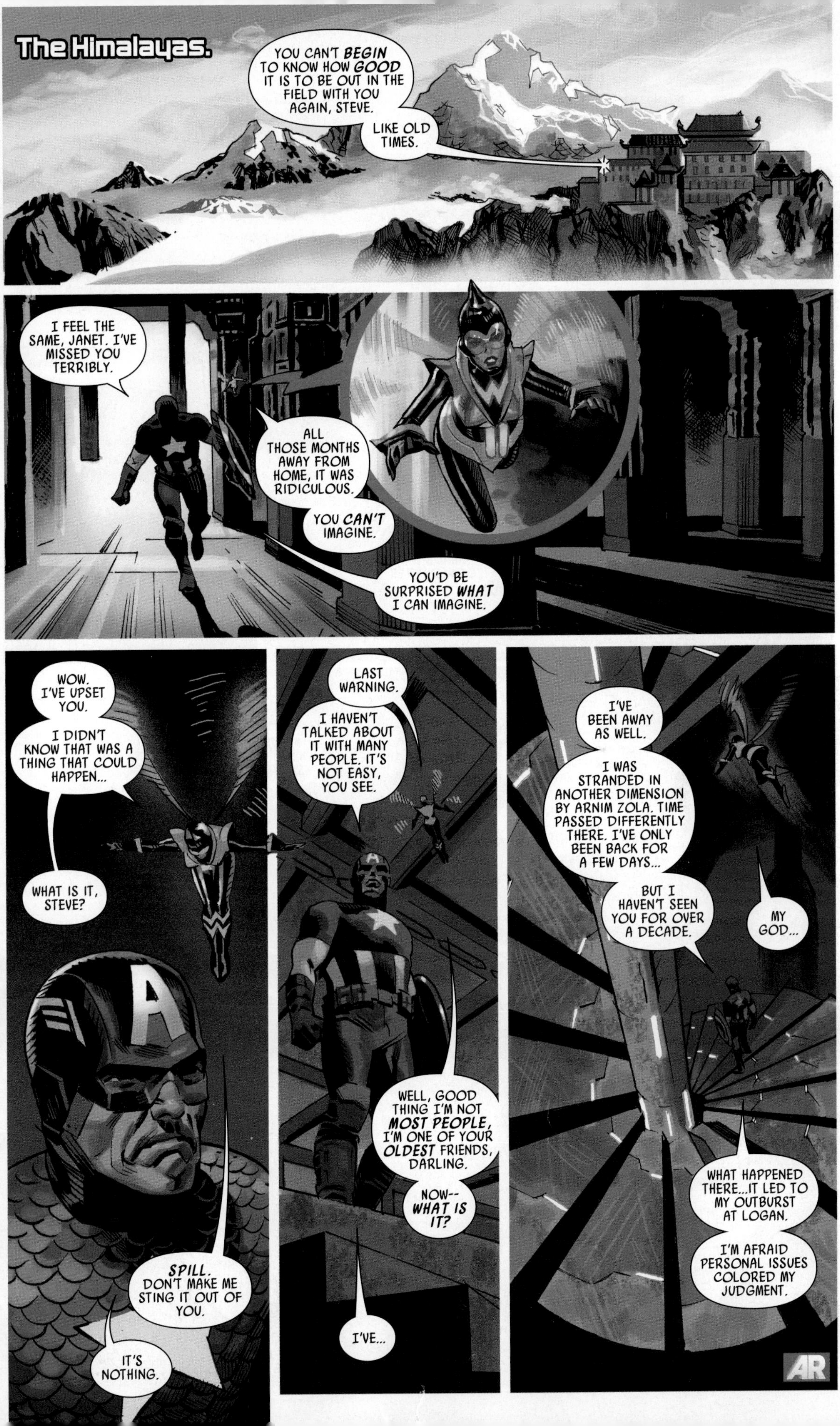
The Himalayas.
YOU CAN'T BEGIN TO KNOW HOW GOOD IT IS TO BE OUT IN THE FIELD WITH YOU AGAIN, STEVE.
LIKE OLD TIMES.
I FEEL THE SAME, JANET. I'VE MISSED YOU TERRIBLY.
ALL THOSE MONTHS AWAY FROM HOME, IT WAS RIDICULOUS.
YOU CAN'T IMAGINE.
YOU'D BE SURPRISED WHAT I CAN IMAGINE.
WOW. I'VE UPSET YOU.
I DIDN'T KNOW THAT WAS A THING THAT COULD HAPPEN...
WHAT IS IT, STEVE?
SPILL. DON'T MAKE ME STING IT OUT OF YOU.
IT'S NOTHING.
LAST WARNING.
I HAVEN'T TALKED ABOUT IT WITH MANY PEOPLE. IT'S NOT EASY, YOU SEE.
WELL, GOOD THING I'M NOT MOST PEOPLE, I'M ONE OF YOUR OLDEST FRIENDS, DARLING.
NOW-- WHAT IS IT?
I'VE...
I'VE BEEN AWAY AS WELL.
I WAS STRANDED IN ANOTHER DIMENSION BY ARNIM ZOLA. TIME PASSED DIFFERENTLY THERE. I'VE ONLY BEEN BACK FOR A FEW DAYS...
BUT I HAVEN'T SEEN YOU FOR OVER A DECADE.
MY GOD...
WHAT HAPPENED THERE...IT LED TO MY OUTBURST AT LOGAN.
I'M AFRAID PERSONAL ISSUES COLORED MY JUDGMENT.
AR

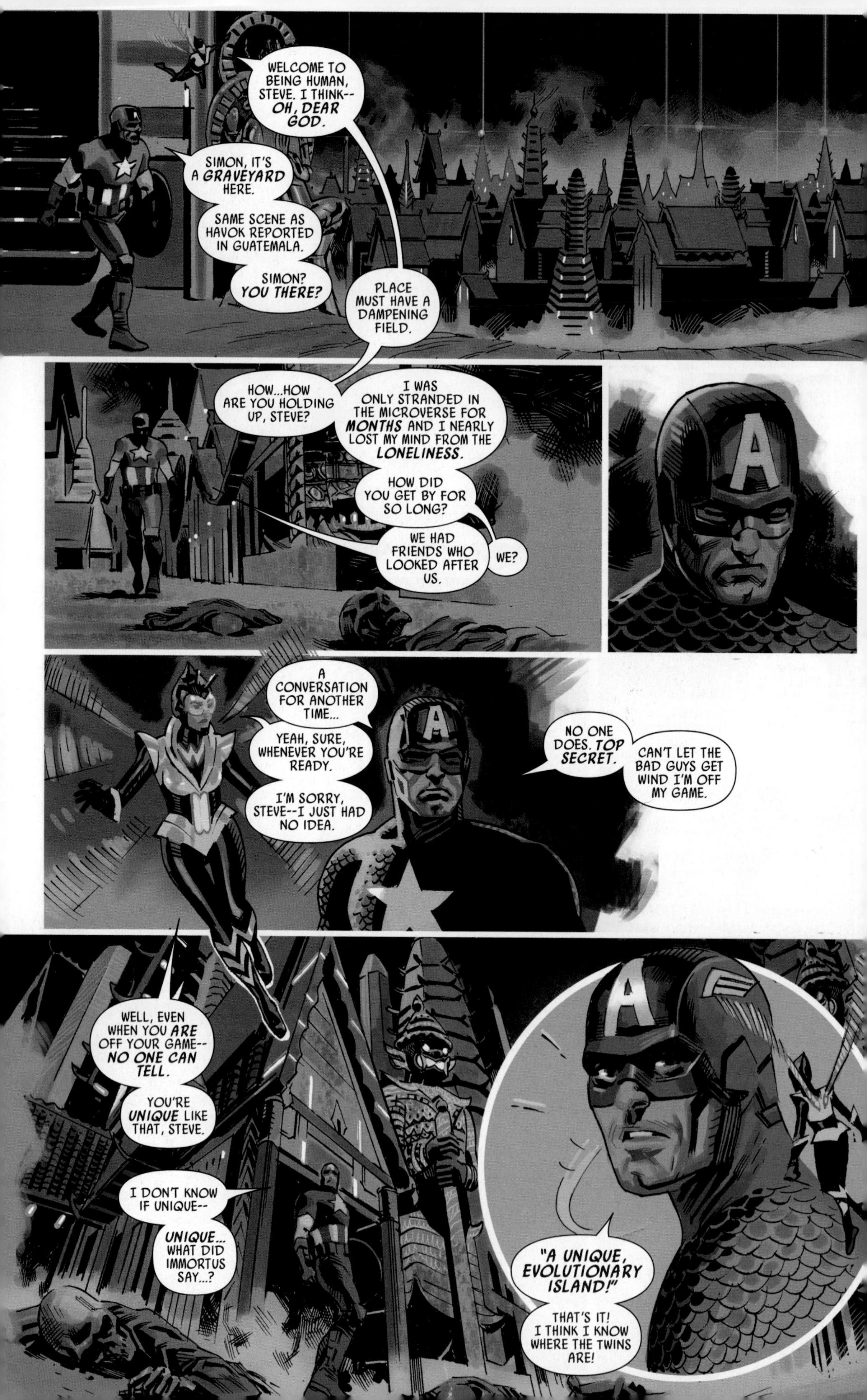

WELCOME TO BEING HUMAN, STEVE. I THINK-- OH, DEAR GOD.
SIMON, IT'S A GRAVEYARD HERE.
SAME SCENE AS HAVOK REPORTED IN GUATEMALA.
SIMON? YOU THERE?
PLACE MUST HAVE A DAMPENING FIELD.
HOW...HOW ARE YOU HOLDING UP, STEVE?
I WAS ONLY STRANDED IN THE MICROVERSE FOR MONTHS AND I NEARLY LOST MY MIND FROM THE LONELINESS.
HOW DID YOU GET BY FOR SO LONG?
WE HAD FRIENDS WHO LOOKED AFTER US.
WE?
A CONVERSATION FOR ANOTHER TIME...
YEAH, SURE, WHENEVER YOU'RE READY.
I'M SORRY, STEVE--I JUST HAD NO IDEA.
NO ONE DOES. TOP SECRET.
CAN'T LET THE BAD GUYS GET WIND I'M OFF MY GAME.
WELL, EVEN WHEN YOU ARE OFF YOUR GAME-- NO ONE CAN TELL.
YOU'RE UNIQUE LIKE THAT, STEVE.
I DON'T KNOW IF UNIQUE--
UNIQUE... WHAT DID IMMORTUS SAY...?
"A UNIQUE, EVOLUTIONARY ISLAND!"
THAT'S IT! I THINK I KNOW WHERE THE TWINS ARE!

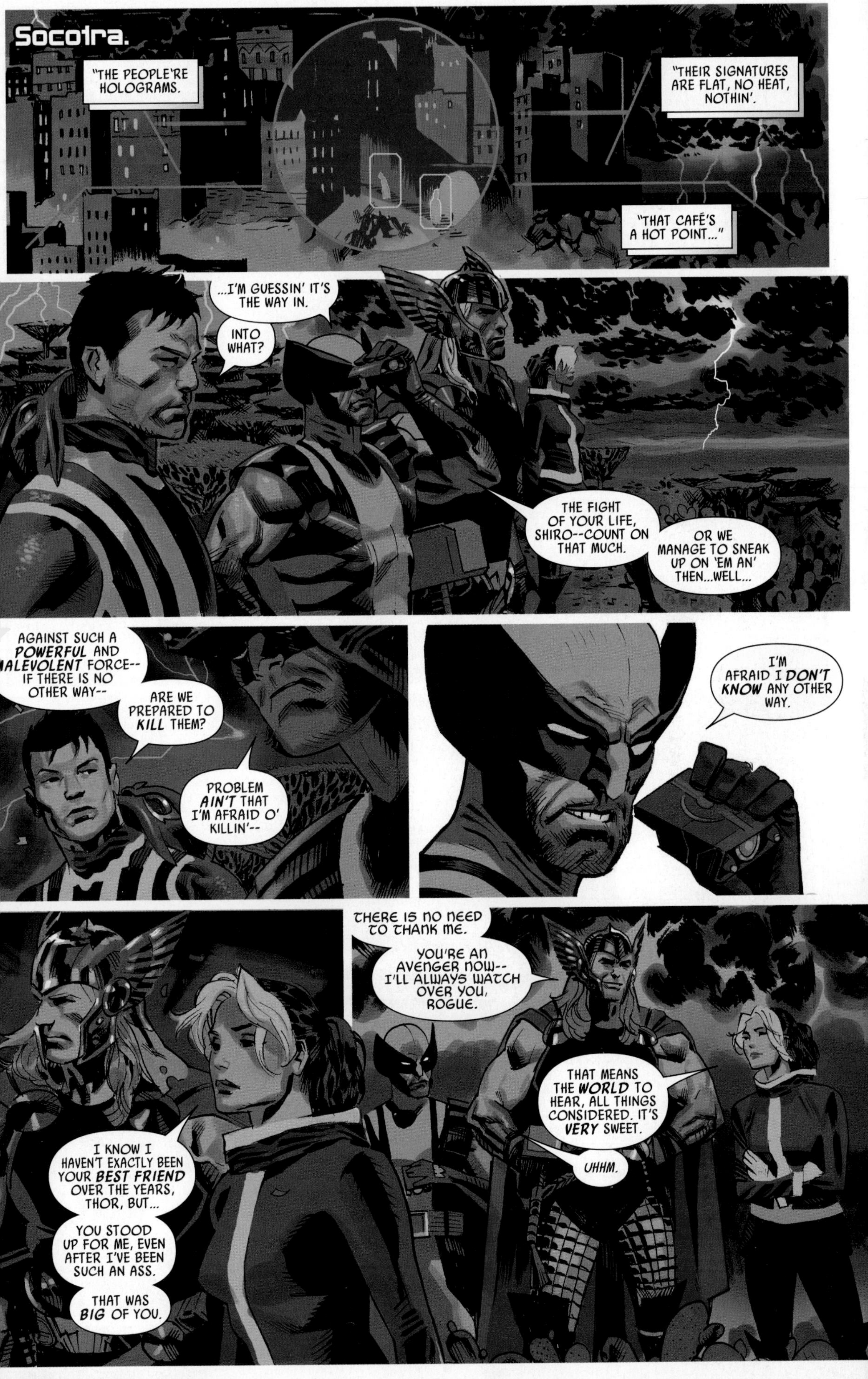
Socotra.
"THE PEOPLE'RE HOLOGRAMS.
"THEIR SIGNATURES ARE FLAT, NO HEAT, NOTHIN'.
"THAT CAFÉ'S A HOT POINT..."
...I'M GUESSIN' IT'S THE WAY IN.
INTO WHAT?
THE FIGHT OF YOUR LIFE, SHIRO--COUNT ON THAT MUCH.
OR WE MANAGE TO SNEAK UP ON 'EM AN' THEN...WELL...
AGAINST SUCH A POWERFUL AND MALEVOLENT FORCE--IF THERE IS NO OTHER WAY--
ARE WE PREPARED TO KILL THEM?
PROBLEM AIN'T THAT I'M AFRAID O' KILLIN'--
I'M AFRAID I DON'T KNOW ANY OTHER WAY.
I KNOW I HAVEN'T EXACTLY BEEN YOUR BEST FRIEND OVER THE YEARS, THOR, BUT...
YOU STOOD UP FOR ME, EVEN AFTER I'VE BEEN SUCH AN ASS.
THAT WAS BIG OF YOU.
THERE IS NO NEED TO THANK ME.
YOU'RE AN AVENGER NOW--I'LL ALWAYS WATCH OVER YOU, ROGUE.
THAT MEANS THE WORLD TO HEAR, ALL THINGS CONSIDERED. IT'S VERY SWEET.
UHHM.

IF YOU TWO ARE DONE ASS GRABBIN', WE'RE READY--*TIME TO GO IN.*

IS IT TOO MUCH TO HOPE WE CAN JUST SIMPLY TAKE THEM DOWN AND BE DONE?

PUT THE MONSTERS ON TRIAL, SHOW THE WORLD WHO BROUGHT DOWN PEAK STATION AND DEFUSE THIS SITUATION?

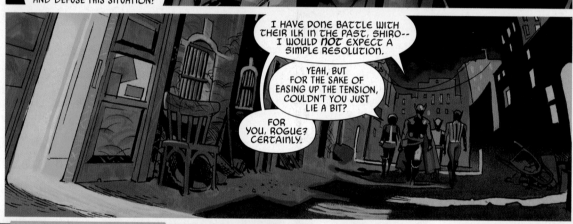

I HAVE DONE BATTLE WITH THEIR ILK IN THE PAST, SHIRO-- I WOULD *NOT* EXPECT A SIMPLE RESOLUTION.

YEAH, BUT FOR THE SAKE OF EASING UP THE TENSION, COULDN'T YOU JUST LIE A BIT?

FOR YOU, ROGUE? CERTAINLY.

WE WILL HAVE *NO* DIFFICULTY.

WE WILL *SOUNDLY* DEFEAT OUR OPPONENTS IN TIME FOR AN EARLY SUPPER.

YOU PAINT A PRETTY PICTURE, FABIO...

...THIS *DOESN'T* HELP SELL IT ANY.

READOUT SAYS THE PLACE IS *FILTHY* WITH ADVANCED PYM PARTICLES.

IMPOSSIBLE! THEY COULDN'T HAVE SHRUNK DOWN AN *ENTIRE* GALAXY...

THEY MANAGED TO OBTAIN *JARNBJORN*-- WHO CAN SAY WHAT OTHER TREASURES THESE MONSTERS MAY HAVE ACQUIRED.

YOU HEAR THAT...?

WOLVERINE'S HEIGHTENED HEARING PICKS UP A SONIC BOOM HUNDREDS OF MILES AWAY--

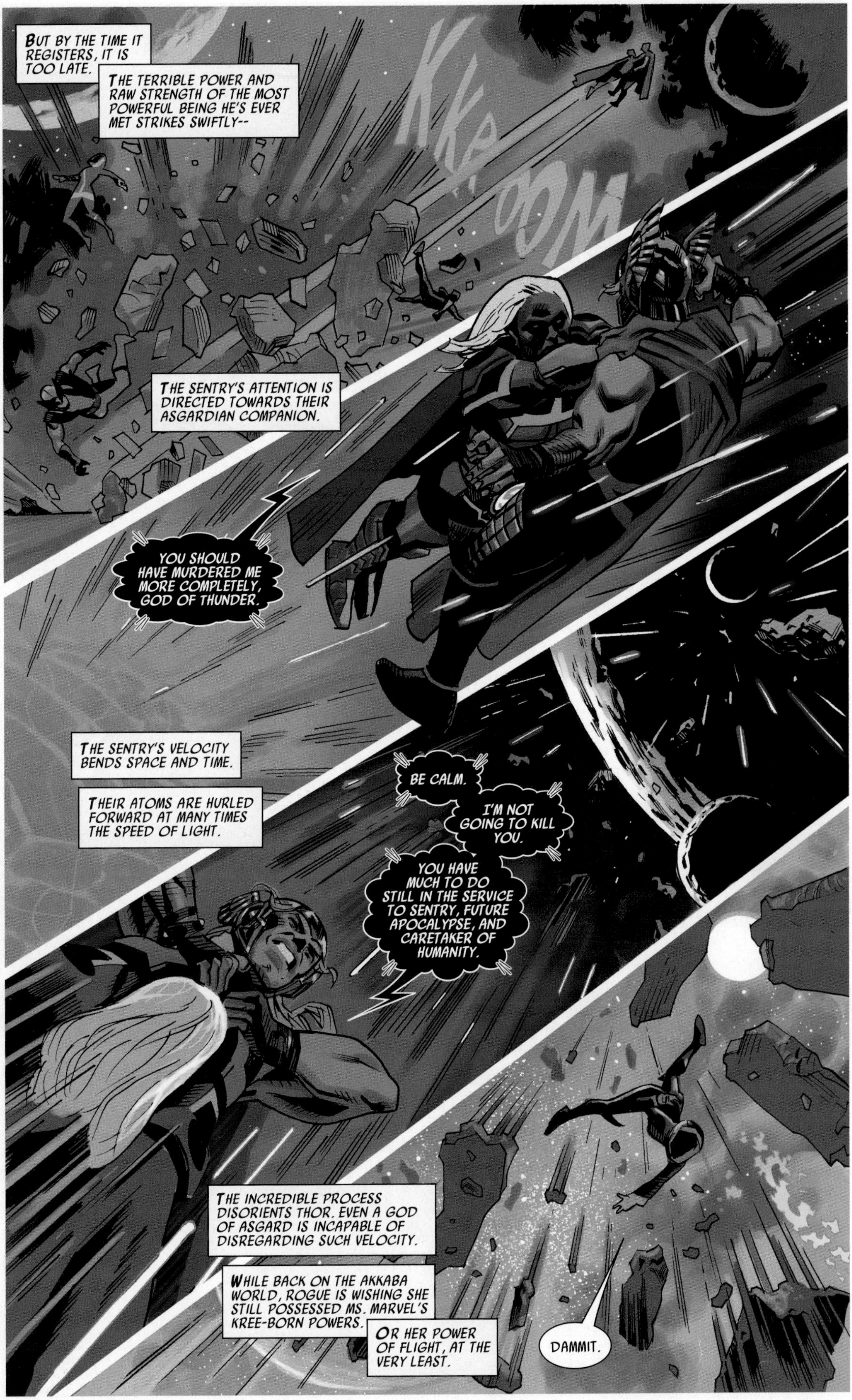
BUT BY THE TIME IT REGISTERS, IT IS TOO LATE.
THE TERRIBLE POWER AND RAW STRENGTH OF THE MOST POWERFUL BEING HE'S EVER MET STRIKES SWIFTLY--
KKRROOM
THE SENTRY'S ATTENTION IS DIRECTED TOWARDS THEIR ASGARDIAN COMPANION.
YOU SHOULD HAVE MURDERED ME MORE COMPLETELY, GOD OF THUNDER.
THE SENTRY'S VELOCITY BENDS SPACE AND TIME.
THEIR ATOMS ARE HURLED FORWARD AT MANY TIMES THE SPEED OF LIGHT.
BE CALM.
I'M NOT GOING TO KILL YOU.
YOU HAVE MUCH TO DO STILL IN THE SERVICE TO SENTRY, FUTURE APOCALYPSE, AND CARETAKER OF HUMANITY.
THE INCREDIBLE PROCESS DISORIENTS THOR. EVEN A GOD OF ASGARD IS INCAPABLE OF DISREGARDING SUCH VELOCITY.
WHILE BACK ON THE AKKABA WORLD, ROGUE IS WISHING SHE STILL POSSESSED MS. MARVEL'S KREE-BORN POWERS.
OR HER POWER OF FLIGHT, AT THE VERY LEAST.
DAMMIT.

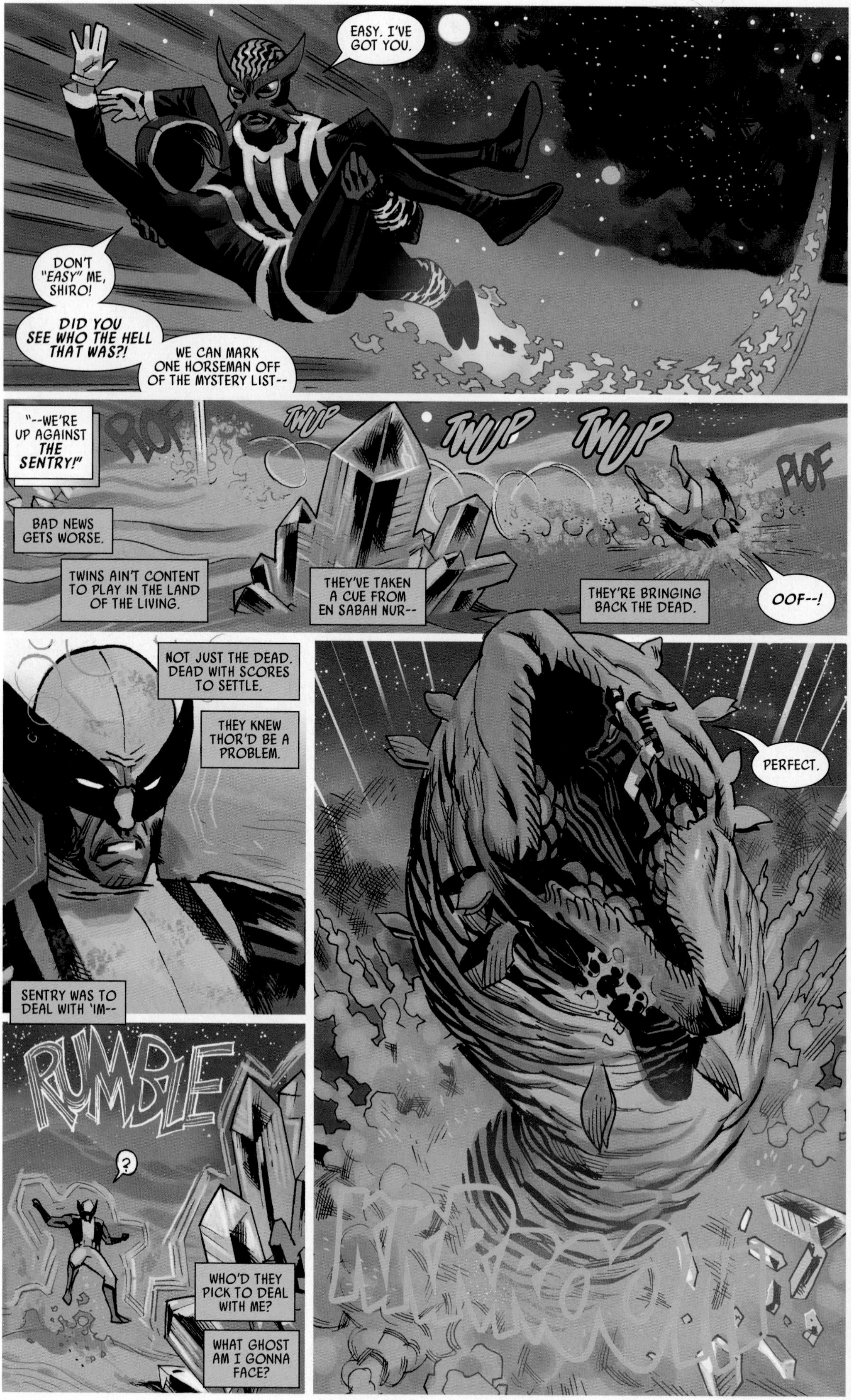
EASY. I'VE GOT YOU.
DON'T "EASY" ME, SHIRO!
DID YOU SEE WHO THE HELL THAT WAS?!
WE CAN MARK ONE HORSEMAN OFF OF THE MYSTERY LIST--
"--WE'RE UP AGAINST THE SENTRY!"
PLOF
TWUP
TWUP
TWUP
PLOF
BAD NEWS GETS WORSE.
TWINS AIN'T CONTENT TO PLAY IN THE LAND OF THE LIVING.
THEY'VE TAKEN A CUE FROM EN SABAH NUR--
THEY'RE BRINGING BACK THE DEAD.
OOF--!
NOT JUST THE DEAD. DEAD WITH SCORES TO SETTLE.
THEY KNEW THOR'D BE A PROBLEM.
SENTRY WAS TO DEAL WITH 'IM--
RUMBLE
?
WHO'D THEY PICK TO DEAL WITH ME?
WHAT GHOST AM I GONNA FACE?
PERFECT.

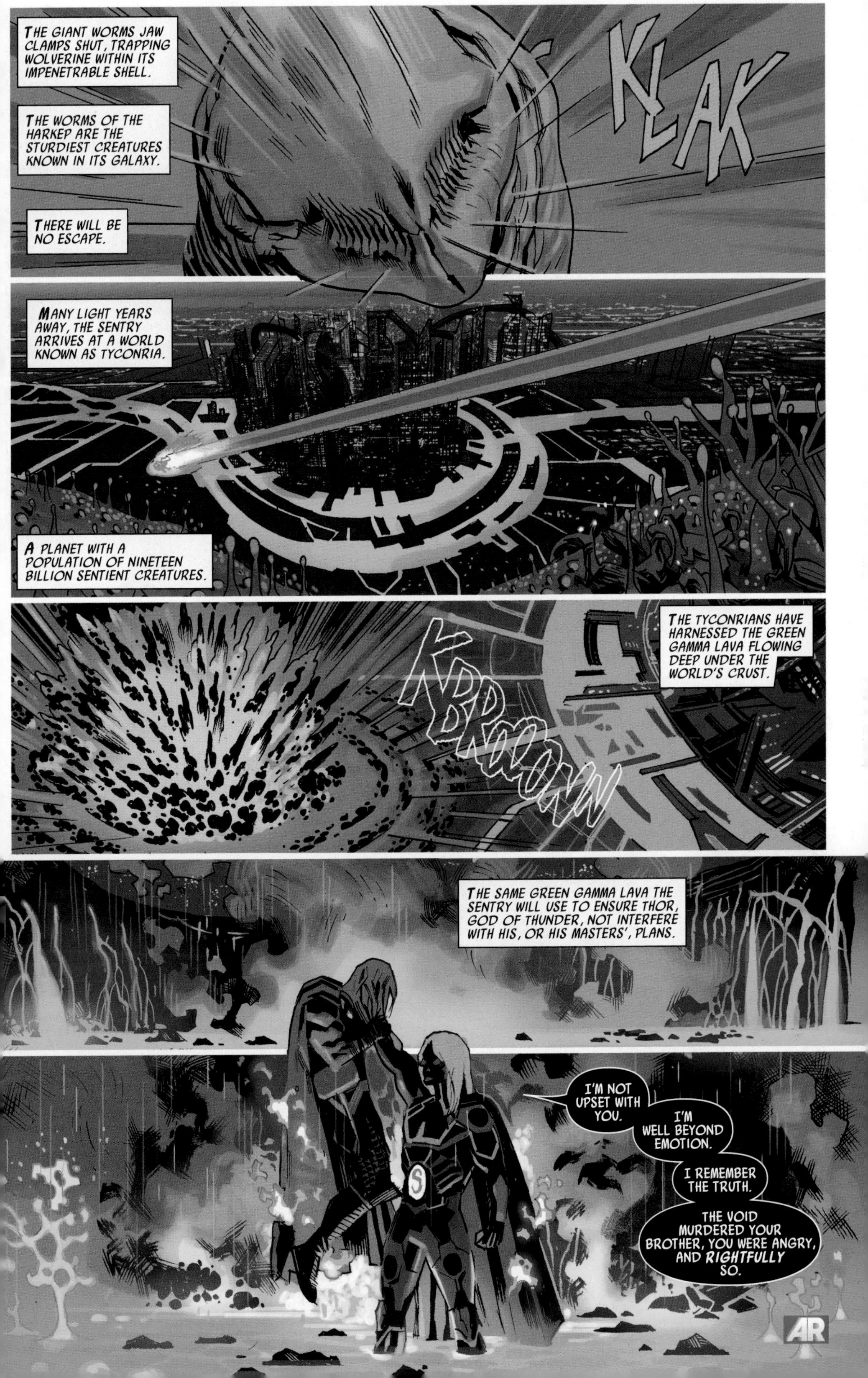
THE GIANT WORMS JAW CLAMPS SHUT, TRAPPING WOLVERINE WITHIN ITS IMPENETRABLE SHELL.
KLAK
THE WORMS OF THE HARKEP ARE THE STURDIEST CREATURES KNOWN IN ITS GALAXY.
THERE WILL BE NO ESCAPE.
MANY LIGHT YEARS AWAY, THE SENTRY ARRIVES AT A WORLD KNOWN AS TYCONRIA.
A PLANET WITH A POPULATION OF NINETEEN BILLION SENTIENT CREATURES.
KBROOOOWN
THE TYCONRIANS HAVE HARNESSED THE GREEN GAMMA LAVA FLOWING DEEP UNDER THE WORLD'S CRUST.
THE SAME GREEN GAMMA LAVA THE SENTRY WILL USE TO ENSURE THOR, GOD OF THUNDER, NOT INTERFERE WITH HIS, OR HIS MASTERS', PLANS.
I'M NOT UPSET WITH YOU.
I'M WELL BEYOND EMOTION.
I REMEMBER THE TRUTH.
THE VOID MURDERED YOUR BROTHER, YOU WERE ANGRY, AND RIGHTFULLY SO.

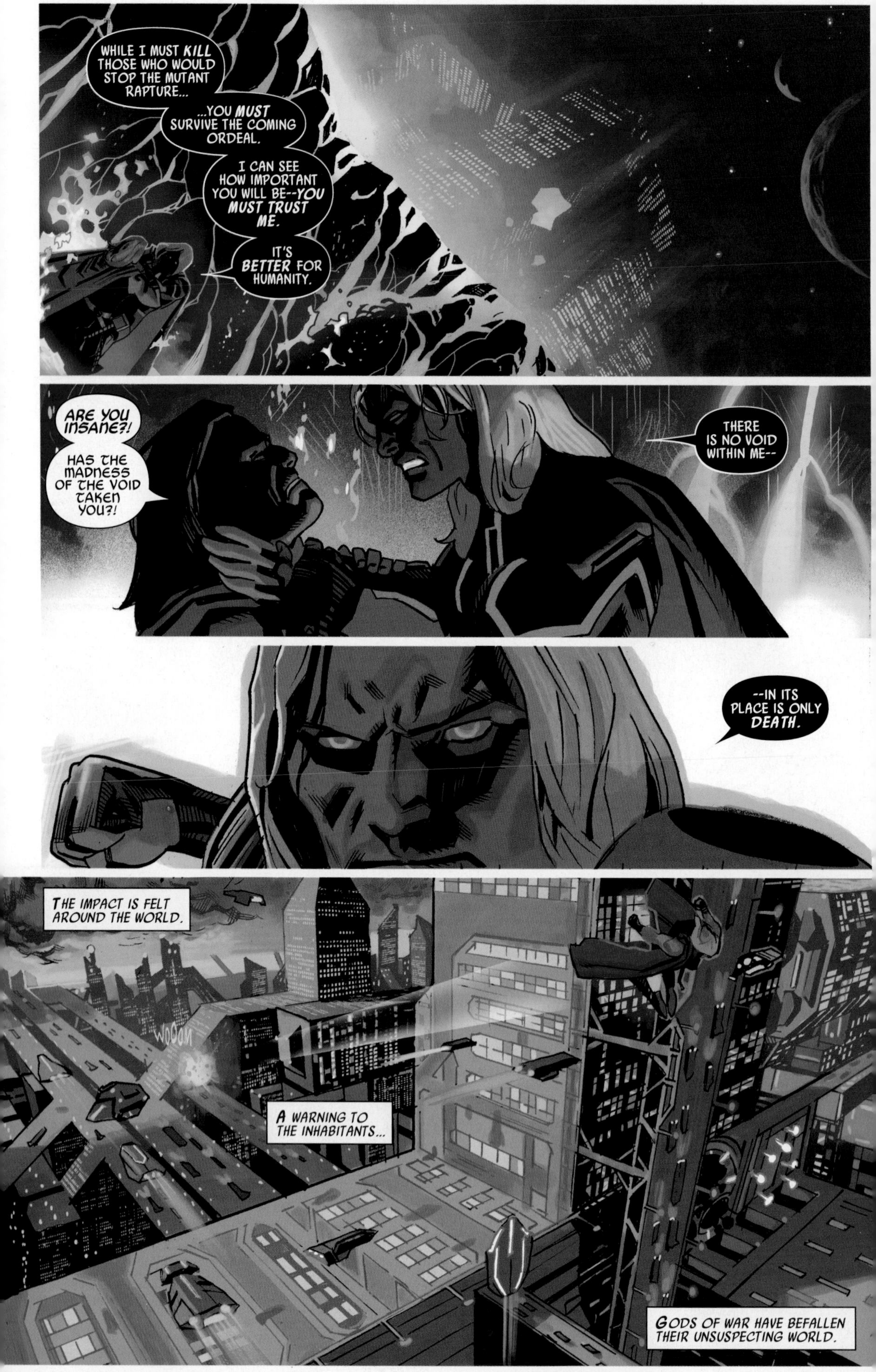
WHILE I MUST KILL THOSE WHO WOULD STOP THE MUTANT RAPTURE...
...YOU MUST SURVIVE THE COMING ORDEAL.
I CAN SEE HOW IMPORTANT YOU WILL BE--YOU MUST TRUST ME.
IT'S BETTER FOR HUMANITY.
ARE YOU INSANE?!
HAS THE MADNESS OF THE VOID TAKEN YOU?!
THERE IS NO VOID WITHIN ME--
--IN ITS PLACE IS ONLY DEATH.
THE IMPACT IS FELT AROUND THE WORLD.
WOOOM
A WARNING TO THE INHABITANTS...
GODS OF WAR HAVE BEFALLEN THEIR UNSUSPECTING WORLD.

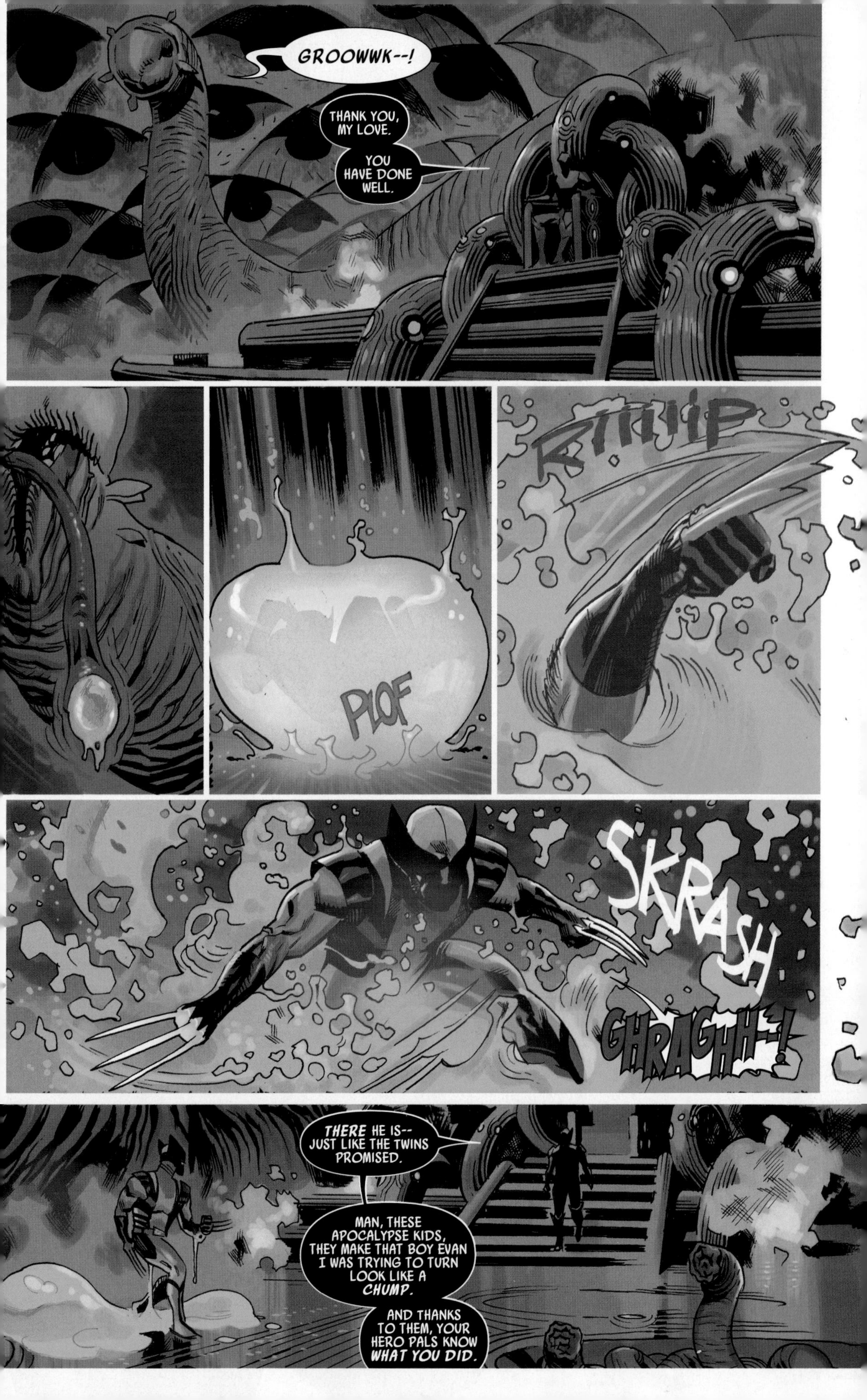
GROOWWK--!
THANK YOU, MY LOVE.
YOU HAVE DONE WELL.
PLOF
RIIIIIIP
SKRASH
GHRAGHH--!
THERE HE IS-- JUST LIKE THE TWINS PROMISED.
MAN, THESE APOCALYPSE KIDS, THEY MAKE THAT BOY EVAN I WAS TRYING TO TURN LOOK LIKE A CHUMP.
AND THANKS TO THEM, YOUR HERO PALS KNOW WHAT YOU DID.

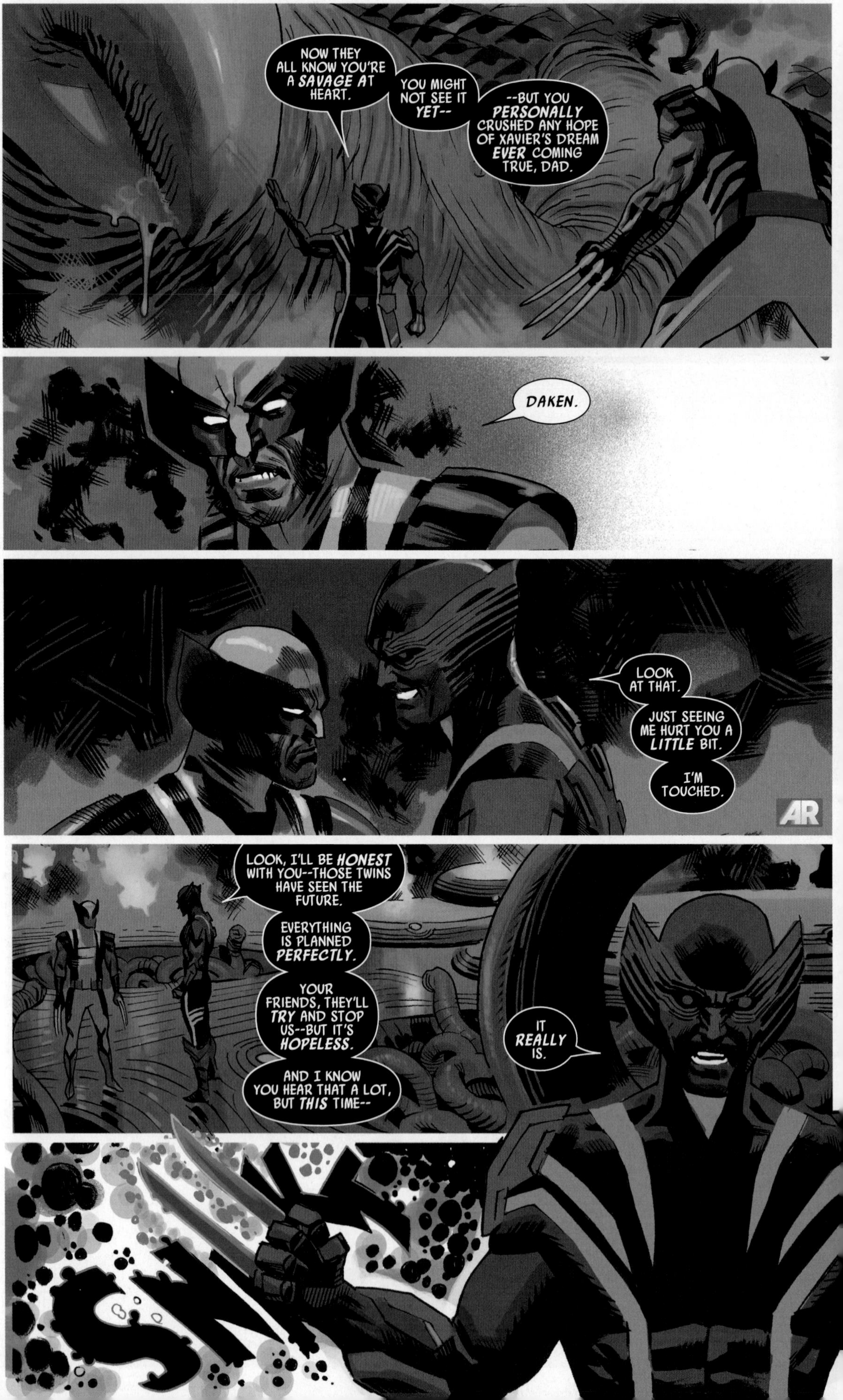
NOW THEY ALL KNOW YOU'RE A SAVAGE AT HEART.
YOU MIGHT NOT SEE IT YET--
--BUT YOU PERSONALLY CRUSHED ANY HOPE OF XAVIER'S DREAM EVER COMING TRUE, DAD.
DAKEN.
LOOK AT THAT.
JUST SEEING ME HURT YOU A LITTLE BIT.
I'M TOUCHED.
LOOK, I'LL BE HONEST WITH YOU--THOSE TWINS HAVE SEEN THE FUTURE.
EVERYTHING IS PLANNED PERFECTLY.
YOUR FRIENDS, THEY'LL TRY AND STOP US--BUT IT'S HOPELESS.
AND I KNOW YOU HEAR THAT A LOT, BUT THIS TIME--
IT REALLY IS.

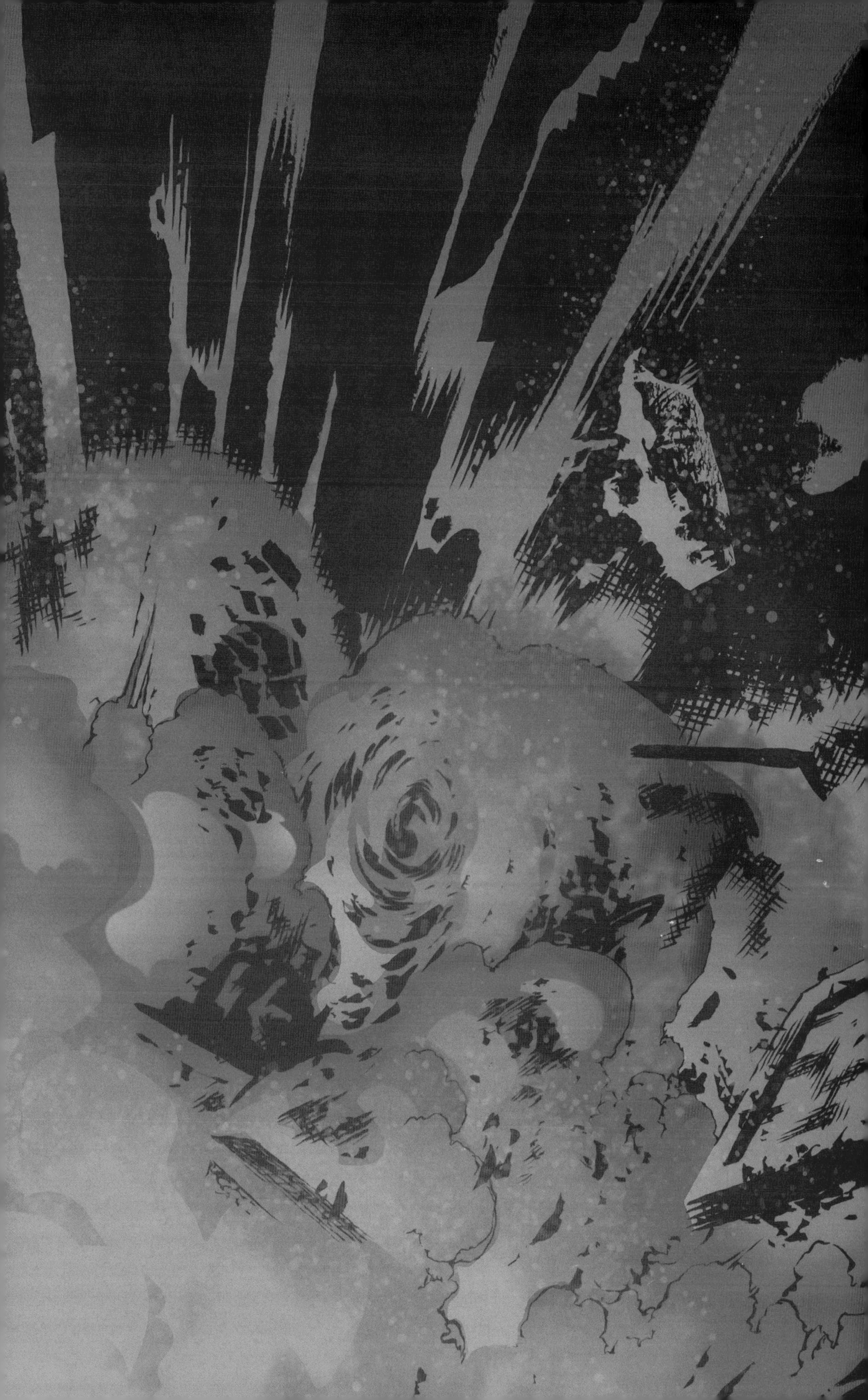

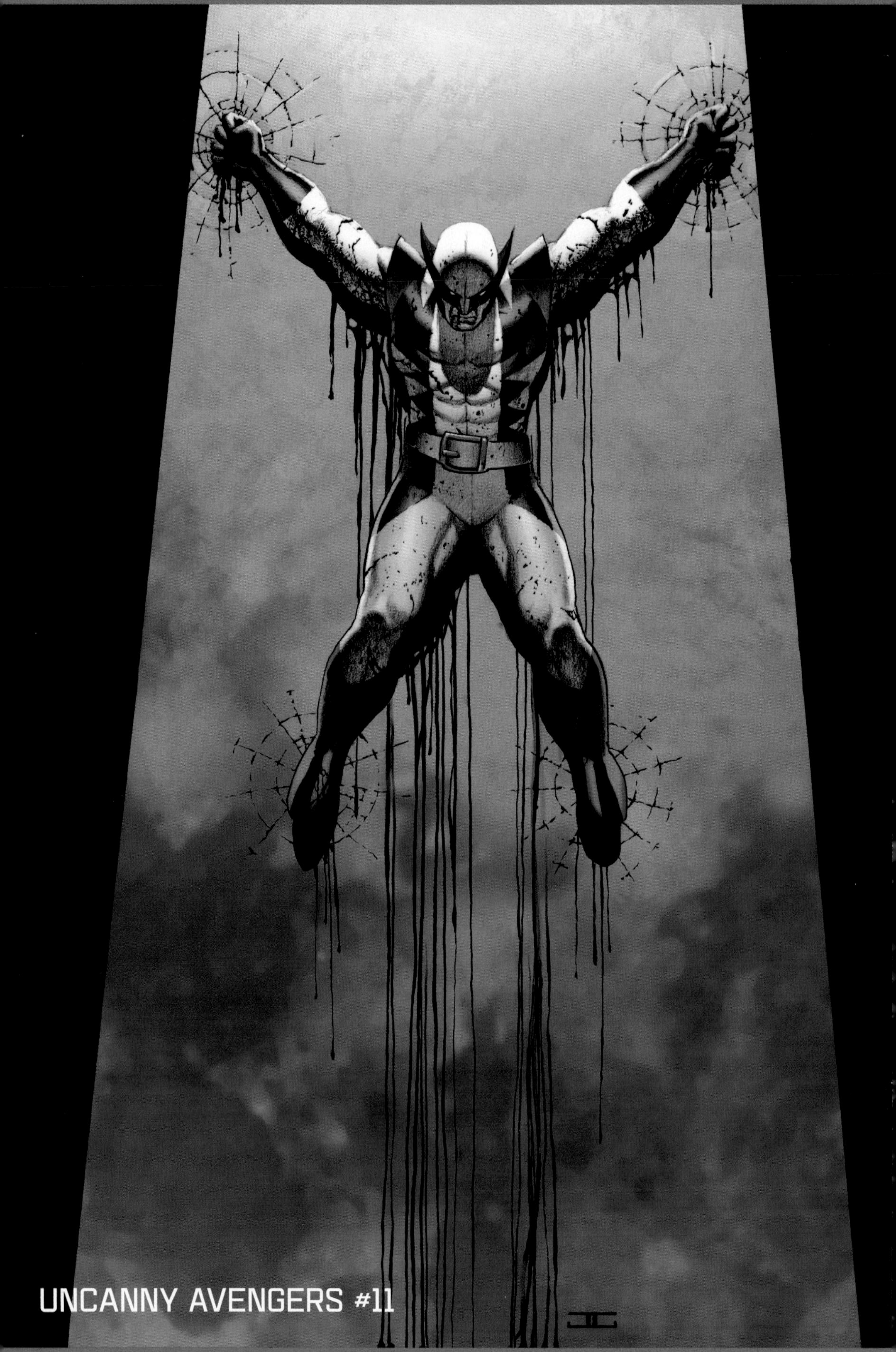

UNCANNY AVENGERS #11

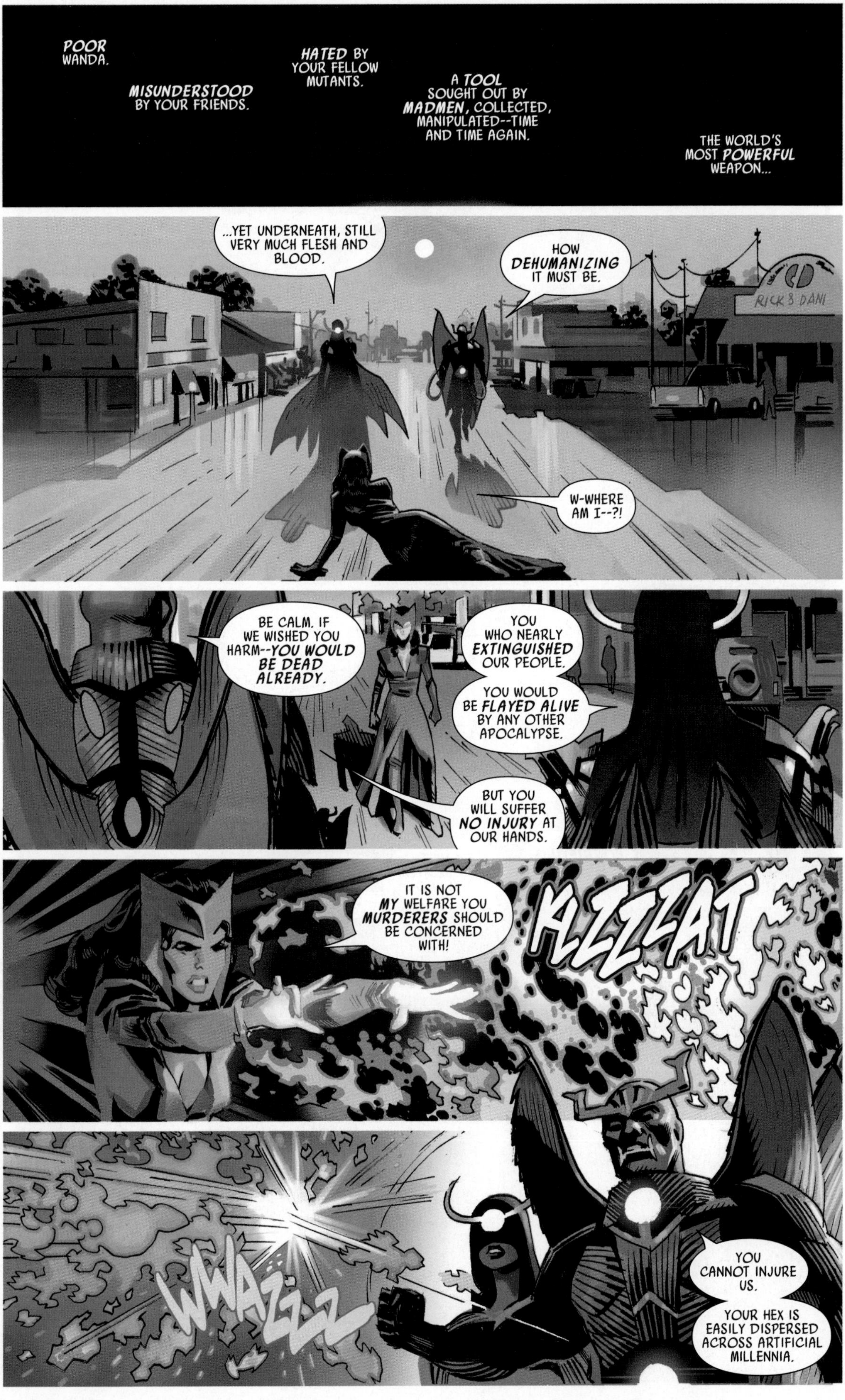
POOR WANDA.
MISUNDERSTOOD BY YOUR FRIENDS.
HATED BY YOUR FELLOW MUTANTS.
A TOOL SOUGHT OUT BY MADMEN, COLLECTED, MANIPULATED--TIME AND TIME AGAIN.
THE WORLD'S MOST POWERFUL WEAPON...
...YET UNDERNEATH, STILL VERY MUCH FLESH AND BLOOD.
HOW DEHUMANIZING IT MUST BE.
RICK & DANI
W-WHERE AM I--?!
BE CALM. IF WE WISHED YOU HARM--YOU WOULD BE DEAD ALREADY.
YOU WHO NEARLY EXTINGUISHED OUR PEOPLE.
YOU WOULD BE FLAYED ALIVE BY ANY OTHER APOCALYPSE.
BUT YOU WILL SUFFER NO INJURY AT OUR HANDS.
IT IS NOT MY WELFARE YOU MURDERERS SHOULD BE CONCERNED WITH!
KZZZZAT
WWAZZZZ
YOU CANNOT INJURE US.
YOUR HEX IS EASILY DISPERSED ACROSS ARTIFICIAL MILLENNIA.

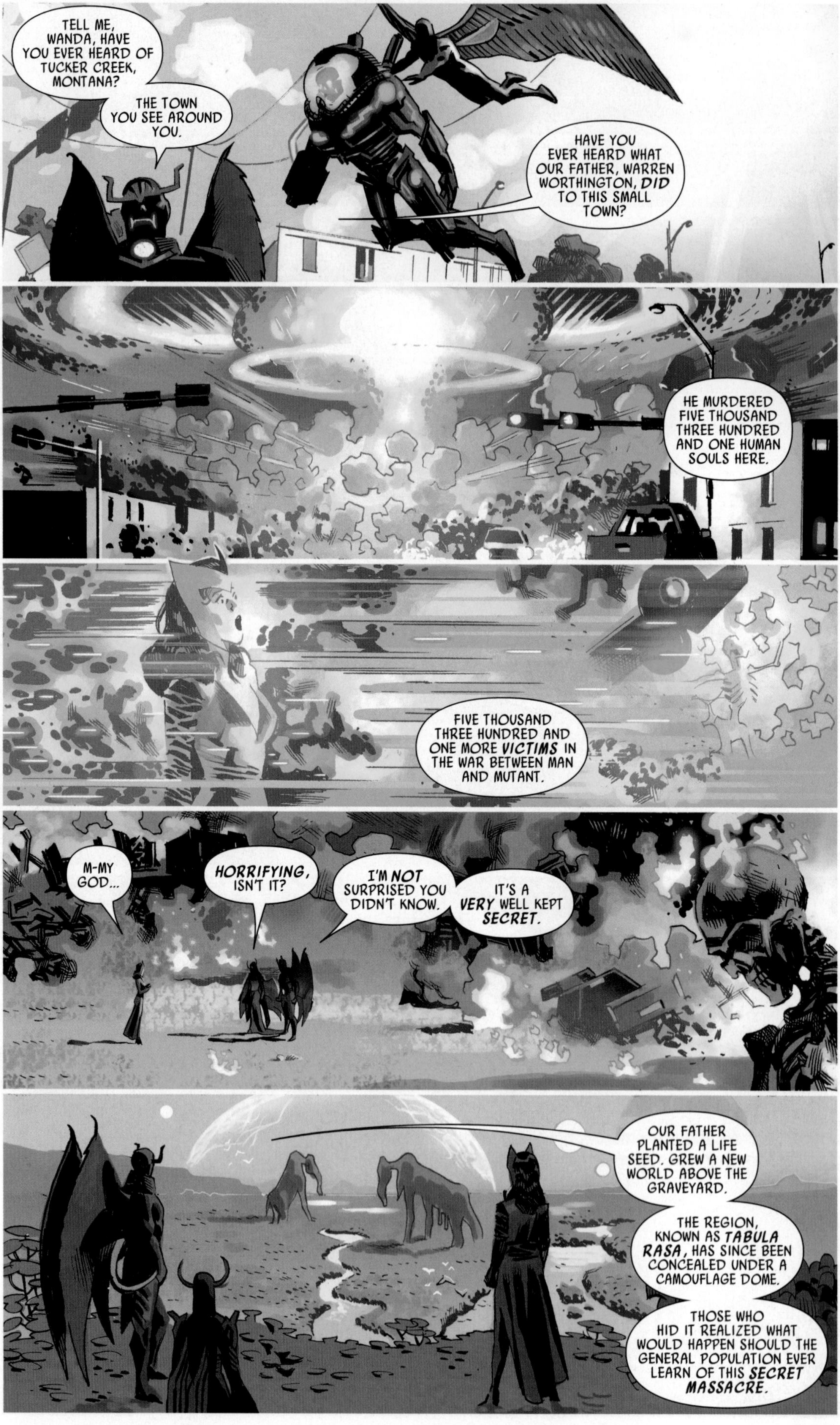
TELL ME, WANDA, HAVE YOU EVER HEARD OF TUCKER CREEK, MONTANA?
THE TOWN YOU SEE AROUND YOU.
HAVE YOU EVER HEARD WHAT OUR FATHER, WARREN WORTHINGTON, DID TO THIS SMALL TOWN?
HE MURDERED FIVE THOUSAND THREE HUNDRED AND ONE HUMAN SOULS HERE.
FIVE THOUSAND THREE HUNDRED AND ONE MORE VICTIMS IN THE WAR BETWEEN MAN AND MUTANT.
M-MY GOD...
HORRIFYING, ISN'T IT?
I'M NOT SURPRISED YOU DIDN'T KNOW.
IT'S A VERY WELL KEPT SECRET.
OUR FATHER PLANTED A LIFE SEED. GREW A NEW WORLD ABOVE THE GRAVEYARD.
THE REGION, KNOWN AS TABULA RASA, HAS SINCE BEEN CONCEALED UNDER A CAMOUFLAGE DOME.
THOSE WHO HID IT REALIZED WHAT WOULD HAPPEN SHOULD THE GENERAL POPULATION EVER LEARN OF THIS SECRET MASSACRE.

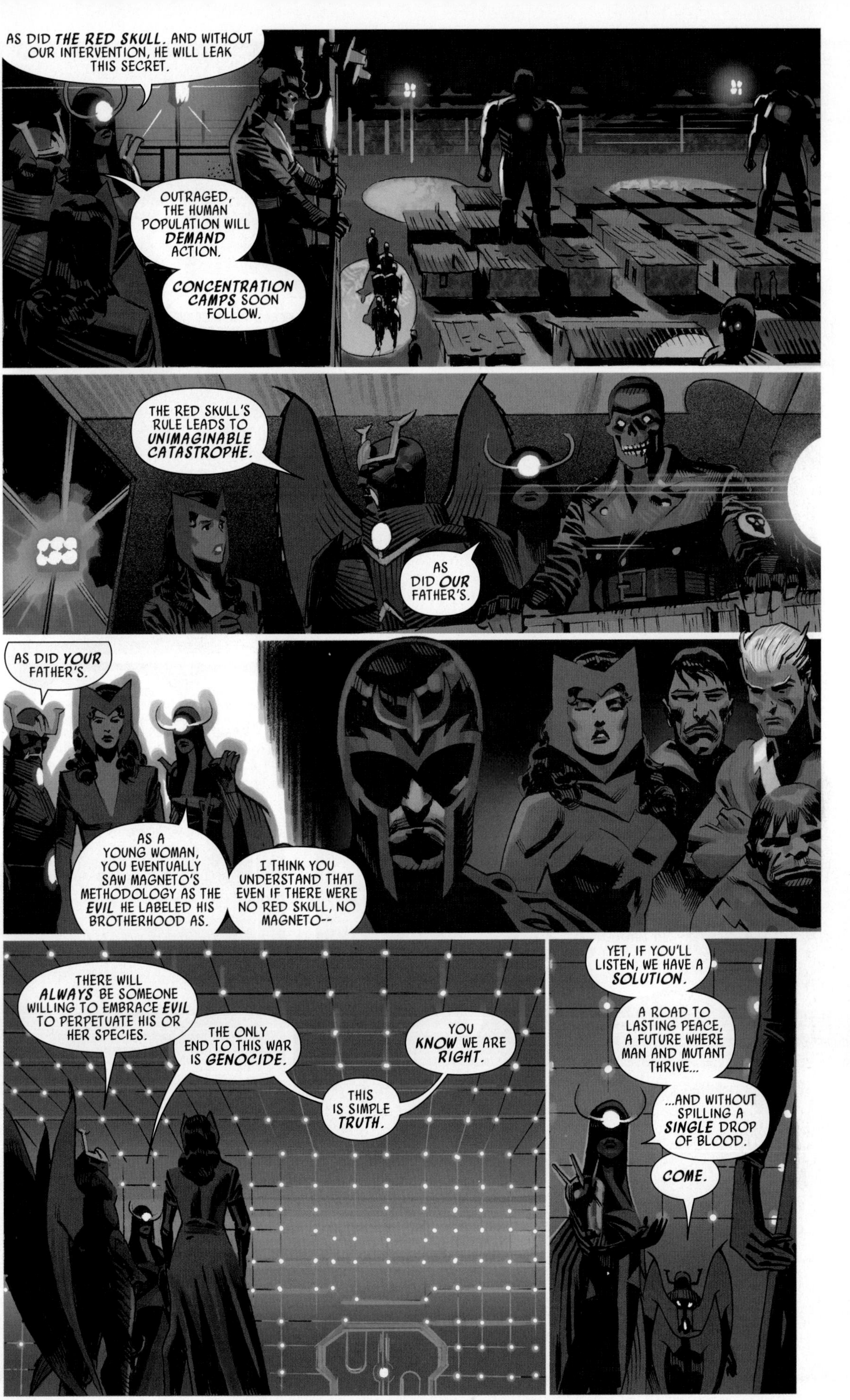

AS DID THE RED SKULL. AND WITHOUT OUR INTERVENTION, HE WILL LEAK THIS SECRET.
OUTRAGED, THE HUMAN POPULATION WILL DEMAND ACTION.
CONCENTRATION CAMPS SOON FOLLOW.
THE RED SKULL'S RULE LEADS TO UNIMAGINABLE CATASTROPHE.
AS DID OUR FATHER'S.
AS DID YOUR FATHER'S.
AS A YOUNG WOMAN, YOU EVENTUALLY SAW MAGNETO'S METHODOLOGY AS THE EVIL HE LABELED HIS BROTHERHOOD AS.
I THINK YOU UNDERSTAND THAT EVEN IF THERE WERE NO RED SKULL, NO MAGNETO--
THERE WILL ALWAYS BE SOMEONE WILLING TO EMBRACE EVIL TO PERPETUATE HIS OR HER SPECIES.
THE ONLY END TO THIS WAR IS GENOCIDE.
THIS IS SIMPLE TRUTH.
YOU KNOW WE ARE RIGHT.
YET, IF YOU'LL LISTEN, WE HAVE A SOLUTION.
A ROAD TO LASTING PEACE, A FUTURE WHERE MAN AND MUTANT THRIVE...
...AND WITHOUT SPILLING A SINGLE DROP OF BLOOD.
COME.

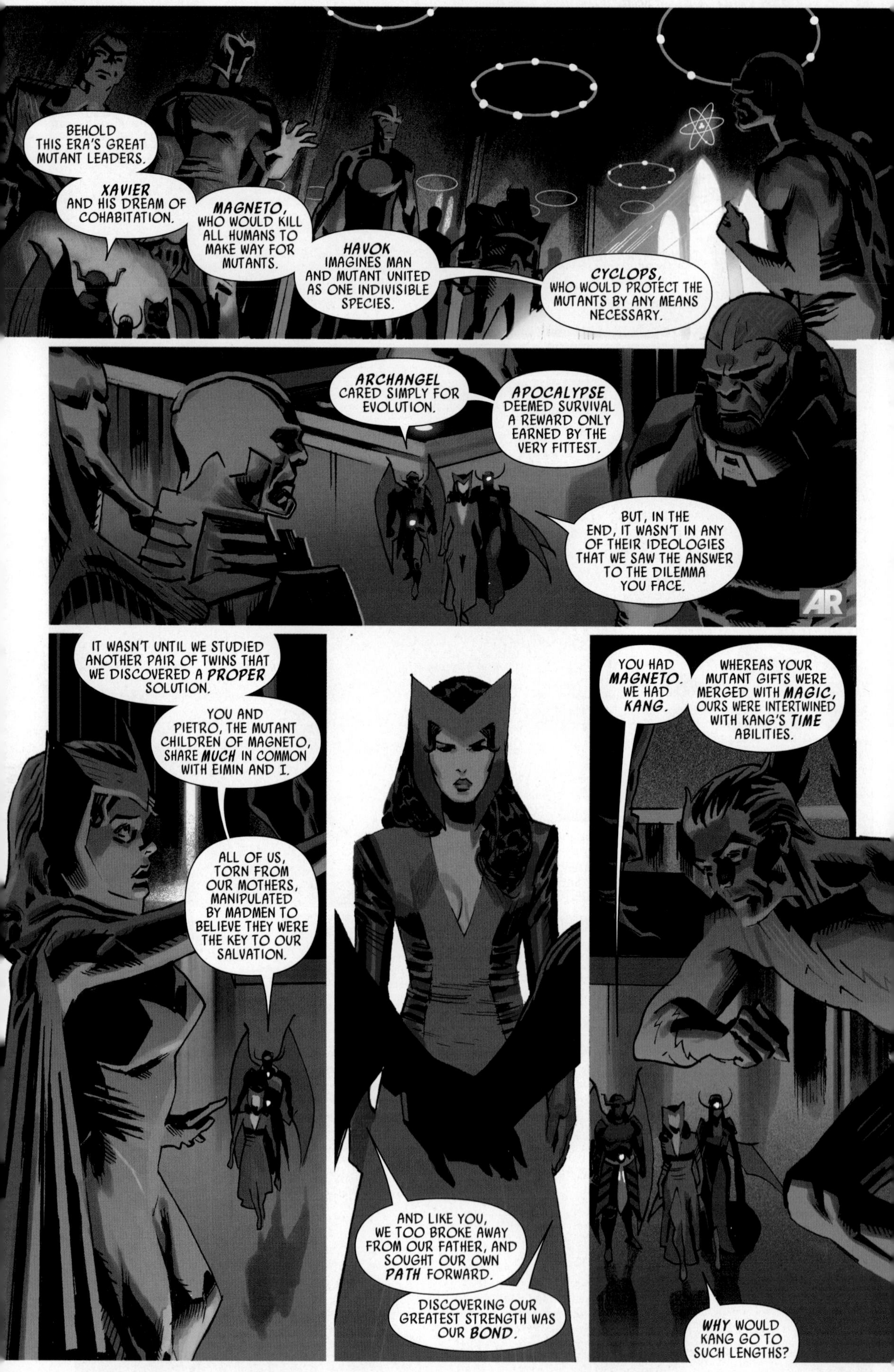
BEHOLD THIS ERA'S GREAT MUTANT LEADERS.
XAVIER AND HIS DREAM OF COHABITATION.
MAGNETO, WHO WOULD KILL ALL HUMANS TO MAKE WAY FOR MUTANTS.
HAVOK IMAGINES MAN AND MUTANT UNITED AS ONE INDIVISIBLE SPECIES.
CYCLOPS, WHO WOULD PROTECT THE MUTANTS BY ANY MEANS NECESSARY.
ARCHANGEL CARED SIMPLY FOR EVOLUTION.
APOCALYPSE DEEMED SURVIVAL A REWARD ONLY EARNED BY THE VERY FITTEST.
BUT, IN THE END, IT WASN'T IN ANY OF THEIR IDEOLOGIES THAT WE SAW THE ANSWER TO THE DILEMMA YOU FACE.
IT WASN'T UNTIL WE STUDIED ANOTHER PAIR OF TWINS THAT WE DISCOVERED A PROPER SOLUTION.
YOU AND PIETRO, THE MUTANT CHILDREN OF MAGNETO, SHARE MUCH IN COMMON WITH EIMIN AND I.
ALL OF US, TORN FROM OUR MOTHERS, MANIPULATED BY MADMEN TO BELIEVE THEY WERE THE KEY TO OUR SALVATION.
AND LIKE YOU, WE TOO BROKE AWAY FROM OUR FATHER, AND SOUGHT OUR OWN PATH FORWARD.
DISCOVERING OUR GREATEST STRENGTH WAS OUR BOND.
YOU HAD MAGNETO. WE HAD KANG.
WHEREAS YOUR MUTANT GIFTS WERE MERGED WITH MAGIC, OURS WERE INTERTWINED WITH KANG'S TIME ABILITIES.
WHY WOULD KANG GO TO SUCH LENGTHS?

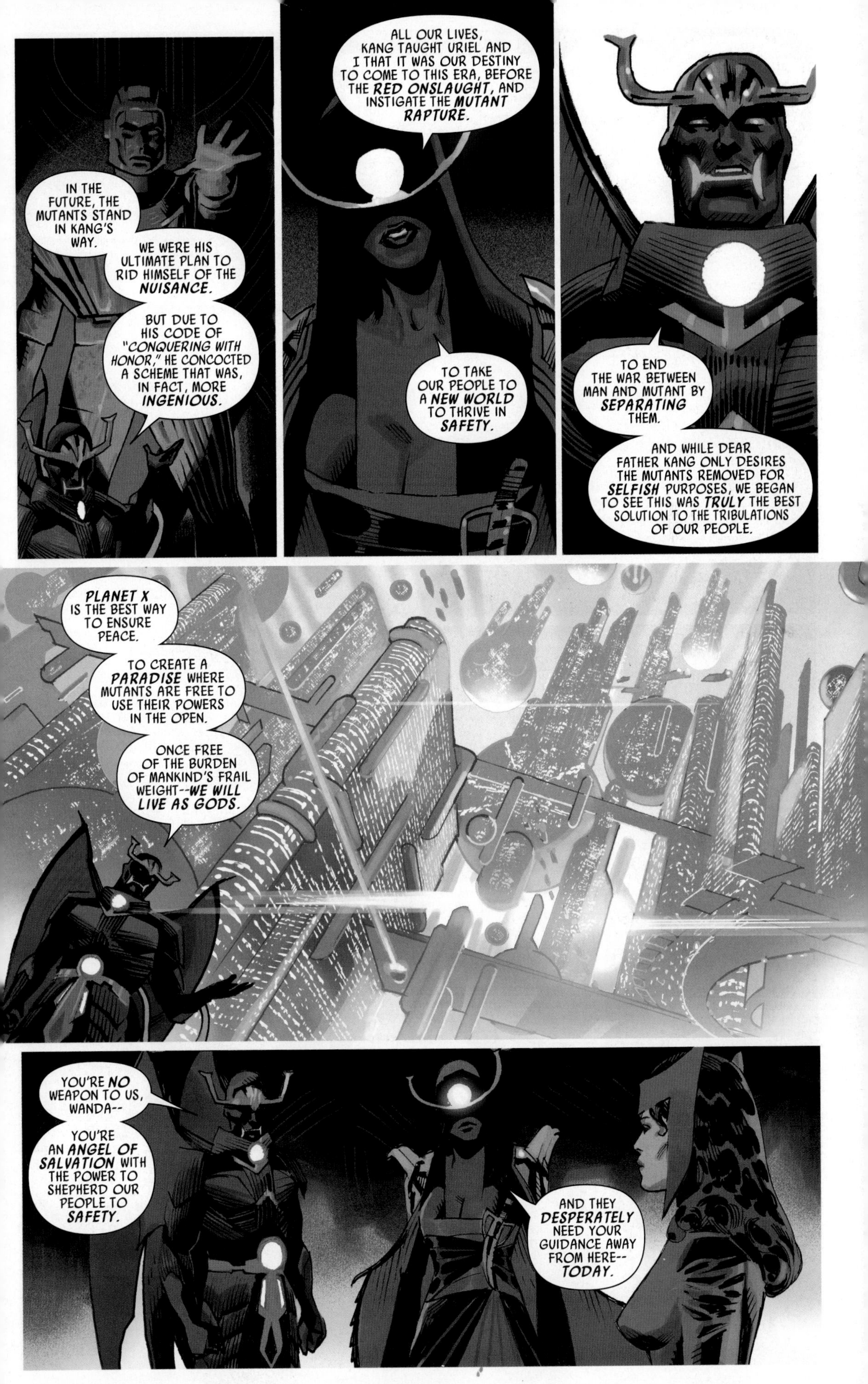

IN THE FUTURE, THE MUTANTS STAND IN KANG'S WAY.
WE WERE HIS ULTIMATE PLAN TO RID HIMSELF OF THE NUISANCE.
BUT DUE TO HIS CODE OF "CONQUERING WITH HONOR," HE CONCOCTED A SCHEME THAT WAS, IN FACT, MORE INGENIOUS.
ALL OUR LIVES, KANG TAUGHT URIEL AND I THAT IT WAS OUR DESTINY TO COME TO THIS ERA, BEFORE THE RED ONSLAUGHT, AND INSTIGATE THE MUTANT RAPTURE.
TO TAKE OUR PEOPLE TO A NEW WORLD TO THRIVE IN SAFETY.
TO END THE WAR BETWEEN MAN AND MUTANT BY SEPARATING THEM.
AND WHILE DEAR FATHER KANG ONLY DESIRES THE MUTANTS REMOVED FOR SELFISH PURPOSES, WE BEGAN TO SEE THIS WAS TRULY THE BEST SOLUTION TO THE TRIBULATIONS OF OUR PEOPLE.
PLANET X IS THE BEST WAY TO ENSURE PEACE.
TO CREATE A PARADISE WHERE MUTANTS ARE FREE TO USE THEIR POWERS IN THE OPEN.
ONCE FREE OF THE BURDEN OF MANKIND'S FRAIL WEIGHT--WE WILL LIVE AS GODS.
YOU'RE NO WEAPON TO US, WANDA--
YOU'RE AN ANGEL OF SALVATION WITH THE POWER TO SHEPHERD OUR PEOPLE TO SAFETY.
AND THEY DESPERATELY NEED YOUR GUIDANCE AWAY FROM HERE-- TODAY.

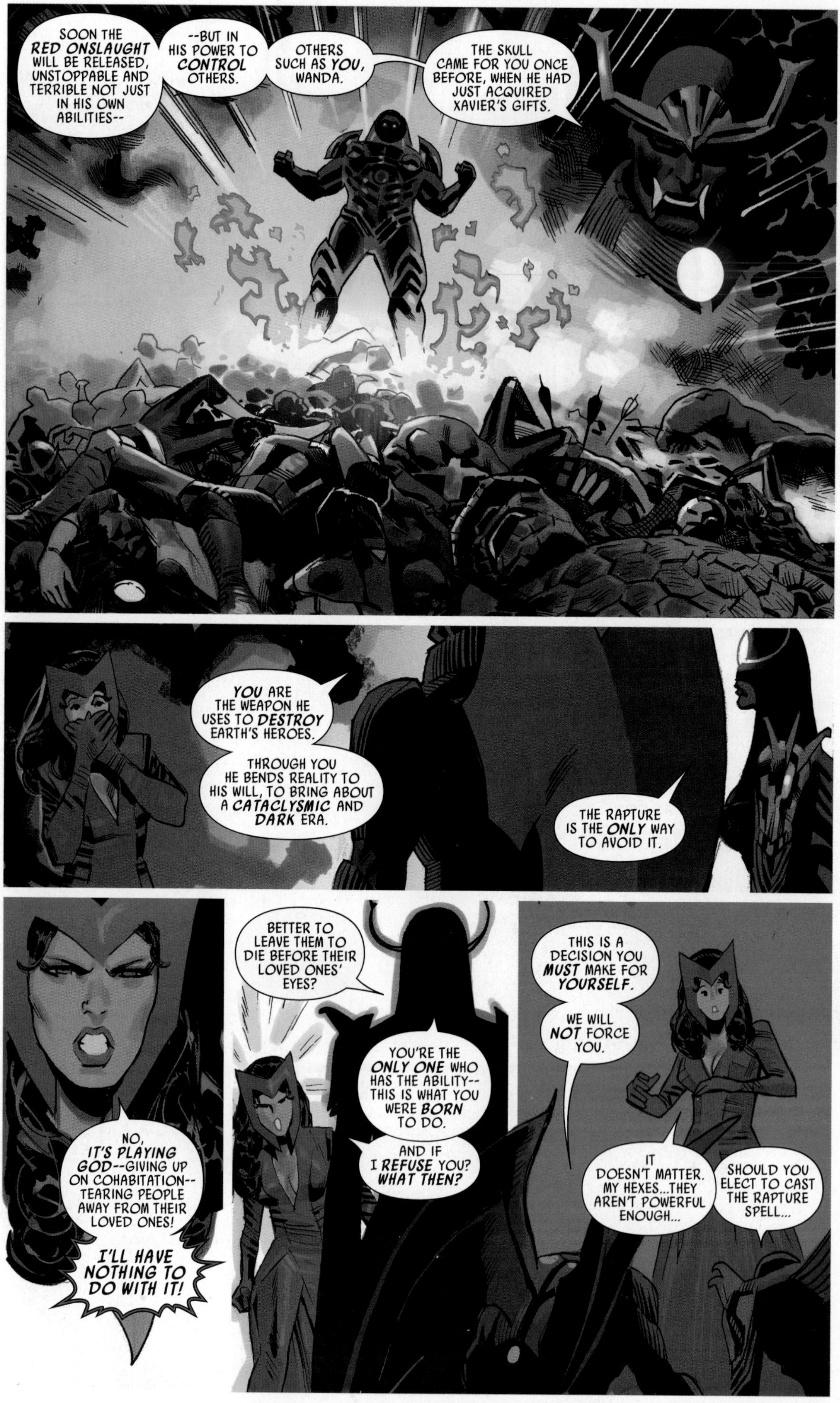
SOON THE RED ONSLAUGHT WILL BE RELEASED, UNSTOPPABLE AND TERRIBLE NOT JUST IN HIS OWN ABILITIES--
--BUT IN HIS POWER TO CONTROL OTHERS.
OTHERS SUCH AS YOU, WANDA.
THE SKULL CAME FOR YOU ONCE BEFORE, WHEN HE HAD JUST ACQUIRED XAVIER'S GIFTS.
YOU ARE THE WEAPON HE USES TO DESTROY EARTH'S HEROES.
THROUGH YOU HE BENDS REALITY TO HIS WILL, TO BRING ABOUT A CATACLYSMIC AND DARK ERA.
THE RAPTURE IS THE ONLY WAY TO AVOID IT.
NO, IT'S PLAYING GOD--GIVING UP ON COHABITATION--TEARING PEOPLE AWAY FROM THEIR LOVED ONES!
I'LL HAVE NOTHING TO DO WITH IT!
BETTER TO LEAVE THEM TO DIE BEFORE THEIR LOVED ONES' EYES?
YOU'RE THE ONLY ONE WHO HAS THE ABILITY-- THIS IS WHAT YOU WERE BORN TO DO.
AND IF I REFUSE YOU? WHAT THEN?
THIS IS A DECISION YOU MUST MAKE FOR YOURSELF.
WE WILL NOT FORCE YOU.
IT DOESN'T MATTER. MY HEXES...THEY AREN'T POWERFUL ENOUGH...
SHOULD YOU ELECT TO CAST THE RAPTURE SPELL...

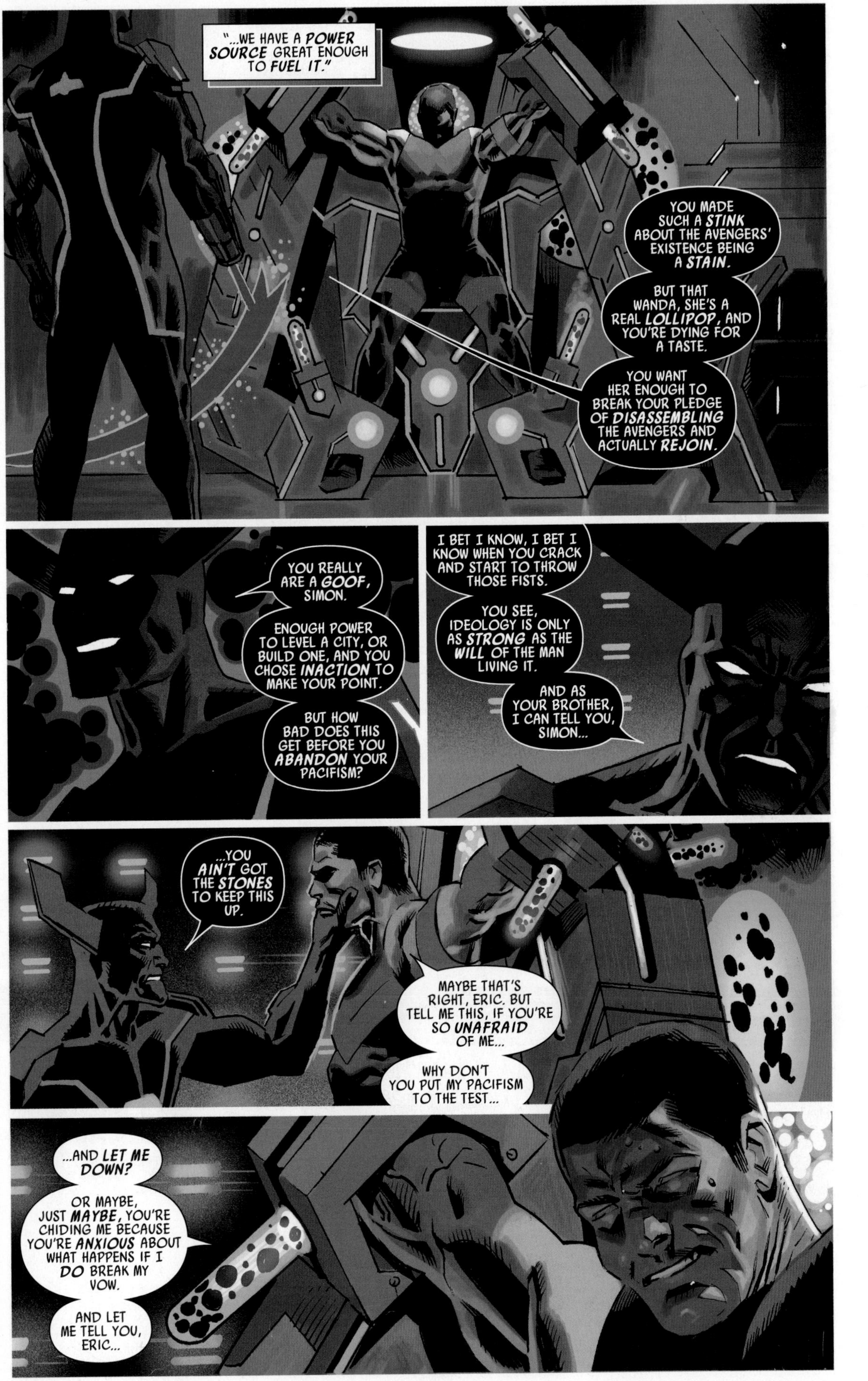
"...WE HAVE A POWER SOURCE GREAT ENOUGH TO FUEL IT."
YOU MADE SUCH A STINK ABOUT THE AVENGERS' EXISTENCE BEING A STAIN.
BUT THAT WANDA, SHE'S A REAL LOLLIPOP, AND YOU'RE DYING FOR A TASTE.
YOU WANT HER ENOUGH TO BREAK YOUR PLEDGE OF DISASSEMBLING THE AVENGERS AND ACTUALLY REJOIN.
YOU REALLY ARE A GOOF, SIMON.
ENOUGH POWER TO LEVEL A CITY, OR BUILD ONE, AND YOU CHOSE INACTION TO MAKE YOUR POINT.
BUT HOW BAD DOES THIS GET BEFORE YOU ABANDON YOUR PACIFISM?
I BET I KNOW, I BET I KNOW WHEN YOU CRACK AND START TO THROW THOSE FISTS.
YOU SEE, IDEOLOGY IS ONLY AS STRONG AS THE WILL OF THE MAN LIVING IT.
AND AS YOUR BROTHER, I CAN TELL YOU, SIMON...
...YOU AIN'T GOT THE STONES TO KEEP THIS UP.
MAYBE THAT'S RIGHT, ERIC. BUT TELL ME THIS, IF YOU'RE SO UNAFRAID OF ME...
WHY DON'T YOU PUT MY PACIFISM TO THE TEST...
...AND LET ME DOWN?
OR MAYBE, JUST MAYBE, YOU'RE CHIDING ME BECAUSE YOU'RE ANXIOUS ABOUT WHAT HAPPENS IF I DO BREAK MY VOW.
AND LET ME TELL YOU, ERIC...

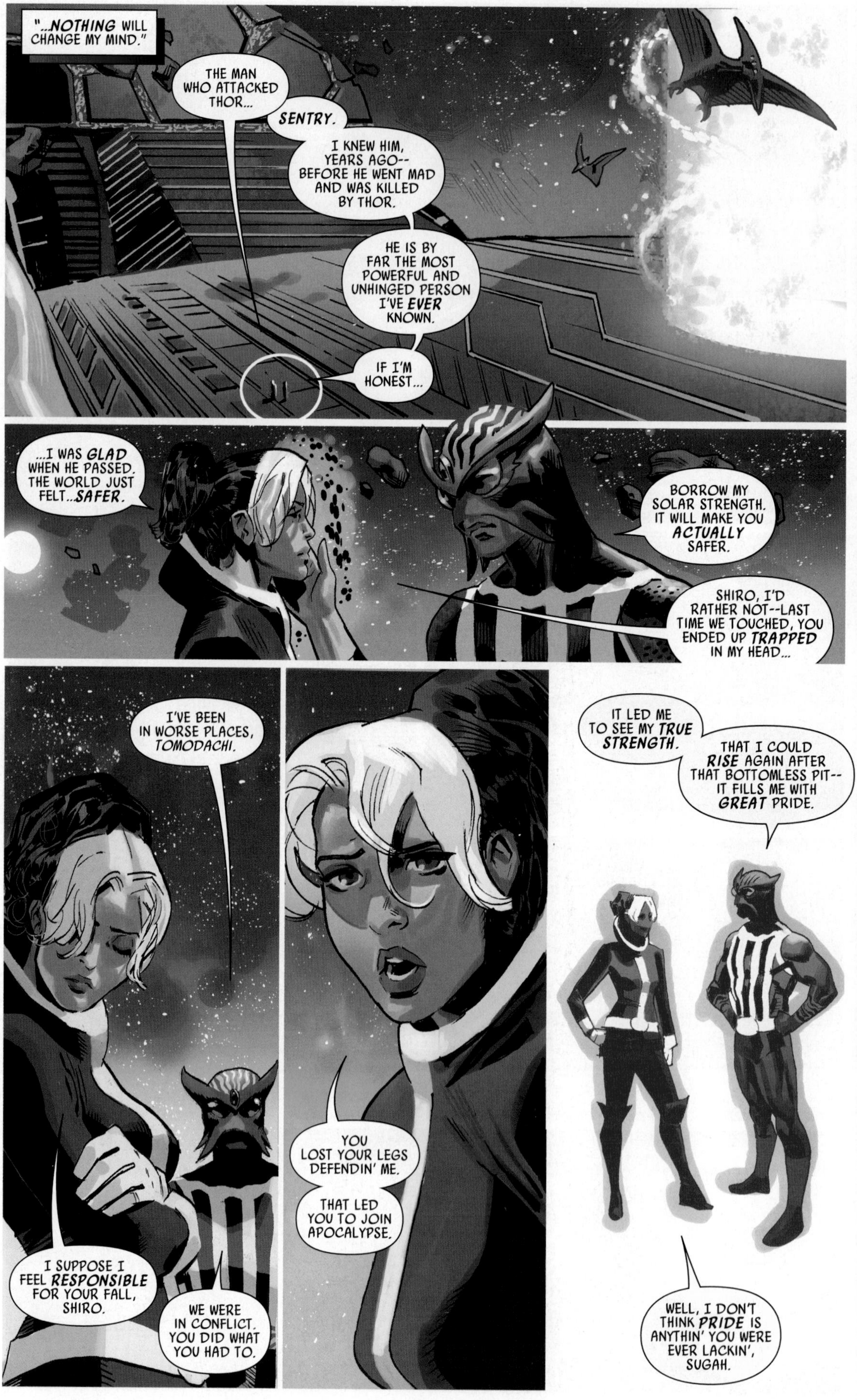
"...NOTHING WILL CHANGE MY MIND."
THE MAN WHO ATTACKED THOR...
SENTRY.
I KNEW HIM, YEARS AGO-- BEFORE HE WENT MAD AND WAS KILLED BY THOR.
HE IS BY FAR THE MOST POWERFUL AND UNHINGED PERSON I'VE EVER KNOWN.
IF I'M HONEST...
...I WAS GLAD WHEN HE PASSED. THE WORLD JUST FELT...SAFER.
BORROW MY SOLAR STRENGTH. IT WILL MAKE YOU ACTUALLY SAFER.
SHIRO, I'D RATHER NOT--LAST TIME WE TOUCHED, YOU ENDED UP TRAPPED IN MY HEAD...
I'VE BEEN IN WORSE PLACES, TOMODACHI.
I SUPPOSE I FEEL RESPONSIBLE FOR YOUR FALL, SHIRO.
WE WERE IN CONFLICT. YOU DID WHAT YOU HAD TO.
YOU LOST YOUR LEGS DEFENDIN' ME.
THAT LED YOU TO JOIN APOCALYPSE.
IT LED ME TO SEE MY TRUE STRENGTH.
THAT I COULD RISE AGAIN AFTER THAT BOTTOMLESS PIT-- IT FILLS ME WITH GREAT PRIDE.
WELL, I DON'T THINK PRIDE IS ANYTHIN' YOU WERE EVER LACKIN', SUGAH.

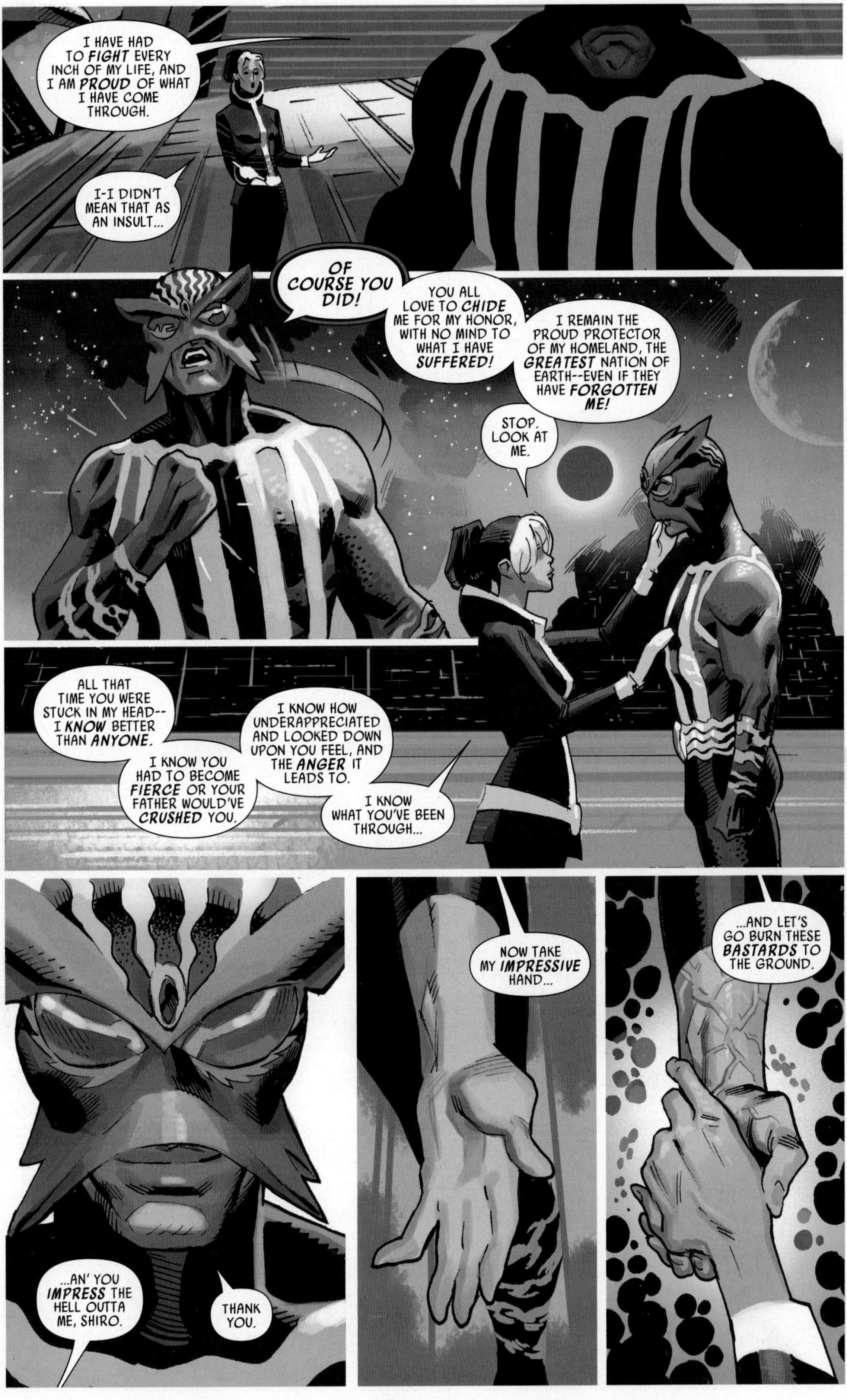
I HAVE HAD TO FIGHT EVERY INCH OF MY LIFE, AND I AM PROUD OF WHAT I HAVE COME THROUGH.
I-I DIDN'T MEAN THAT AS AN INSULT...
OF COURSE YOU DID!
YOU ALL LOVE TO CHIDE ME FOR MY HONOR, WITH NO MIND TO WHAT I HAVE SUFFERED!
I REMAIN THE PROUD PROTECTOR OF MY HOMELAND, THE GREATEST NATION OF EARTH--EVEN IF THEY HAVE FORGOTTEN ME!
STOP. LOOK AT ME.
ALL THAT TIME YOU WERE STUCK IN MY HEAD--I KNOW BETTER THAN ANYONE.
I KNOW YOU HAD TO BECOME FIERCE OR YOUR FATHER WOULD'VE CRUSHED YOU.
I KNOW HOW UNDERAPPRECIATED AND LOOKED DOWN UPON YOU FEEL, AND THE ANGER IT LEADS TO.
I KNOW WHAT YOU'VE BEEN THROUGH...
...AN' YOU IMPRESS THE HELL OUTTA ME, SHIRO.
THANK YOU.
NOW TAKE MY IMPRESSIVE HAND...
...AND LET'S GO BURN THESE BASTARDS TO THE GROUND.

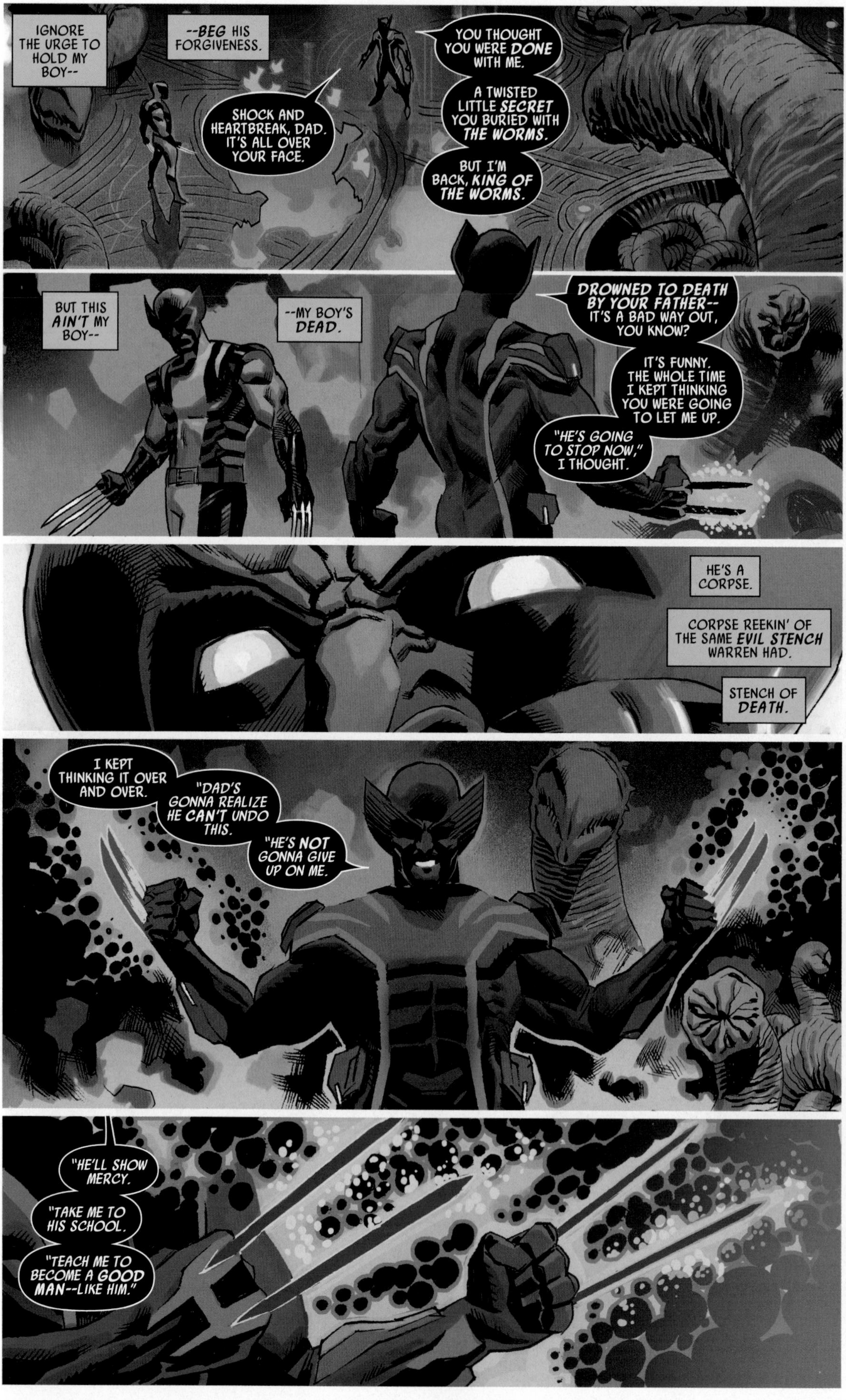
IGNORE THE URGE TO HOLD MY BOY--
--BEG HIS FORGIVENESS.
SHOCK AND HEARTBREAK, DAD. IT'S ALL OVER YOUR FACE.
YOU THOUGHT YOU WERE DONE WITH ME.
A TWISTED LITTLE SECRET YOU BURIED WITH THE WORMS.
BUT I'M BACK, KING OF THE WORMS.
BUT THIS AIN'T MY BOY--
--MY BOY'S DEAD.
DROWNED TO DEATH BY YOUR FATHER-- IT'S A BAD WAY OUT, YOU KNOW?
IT'S FUNNY. THE WHOLE TIME I KEPT THINKING YOU WERE GOING TO LET ME UP.
"HE'S GOING TO STOP NOW," I THOUGHT.
HE'S A CORPSE.
CORPSE REEKIN' OF THE SAME EVIL STENCH WARREN HAD.
STENCH OF DEATH.
I KEPT THINKING IT OVER AND OVER.
"DAD'S GONNA REALIZE HE CAN'T UNDO THIS.
"HE'S NOT GONNA GIVE UP ON ME.
"HE'LL SHOW MERCY.
"TAKE ME TO HIS SCHOOL.
"TEACH ME TO BECOME A GOOD MAN--LIKE HIM."

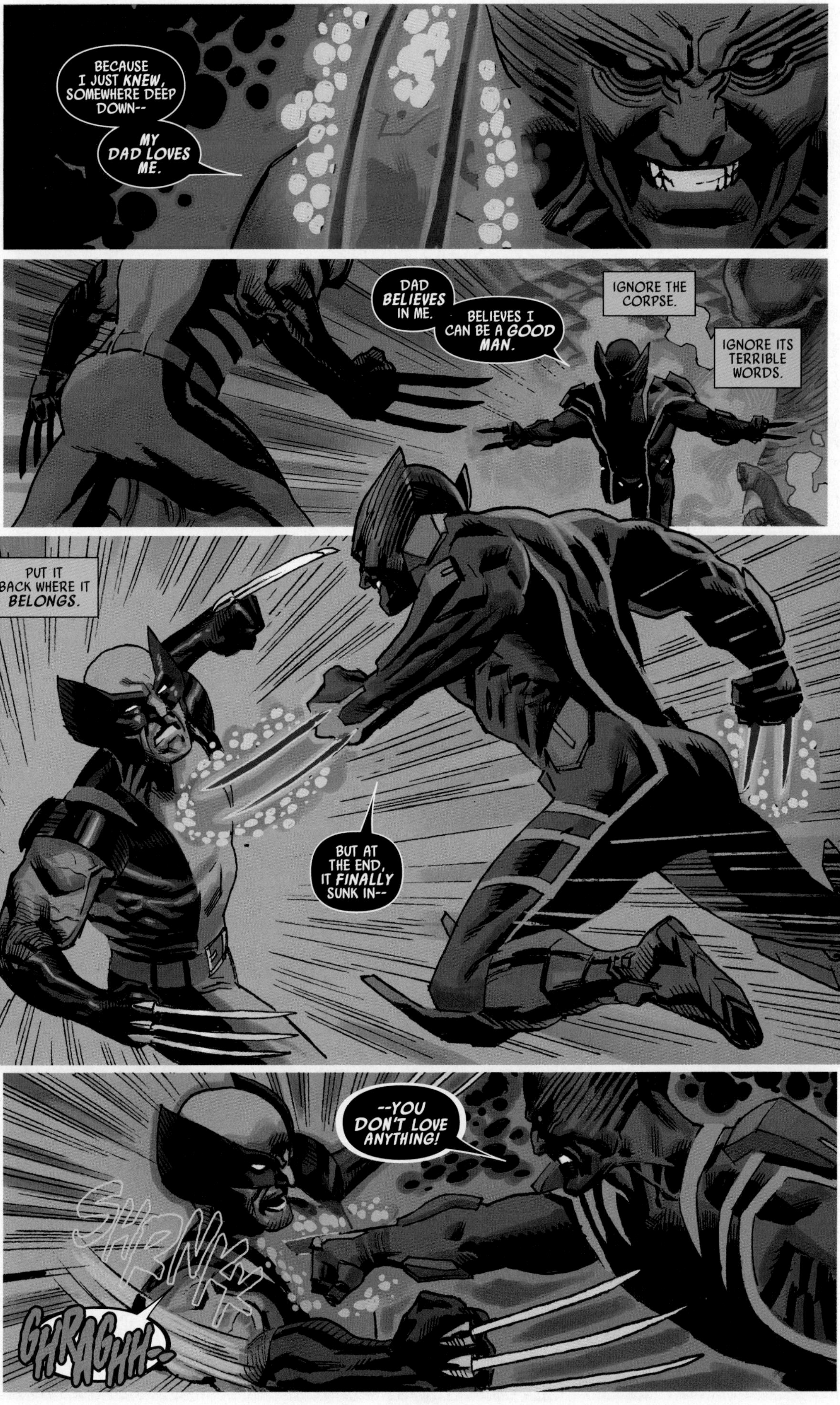
BECAUSE I JUST KNEW, SOMEWHERE DEEP DOWN--
MY DAD LOVES ME.
DAD BELIEVES IN ME.
BELIEVES I CAN BE A GOOD MAN.
IGNORE THE CORPSE.
IGNORE ITS TERRIBLE WORDS.
PUT IT BACK WHERE IT BELONGS.
BUT AT THE END, IT FINALLY SUNK IN--
--YOU DON'T LOVE ANYTHING!
SHRNK
GHRAGHH--

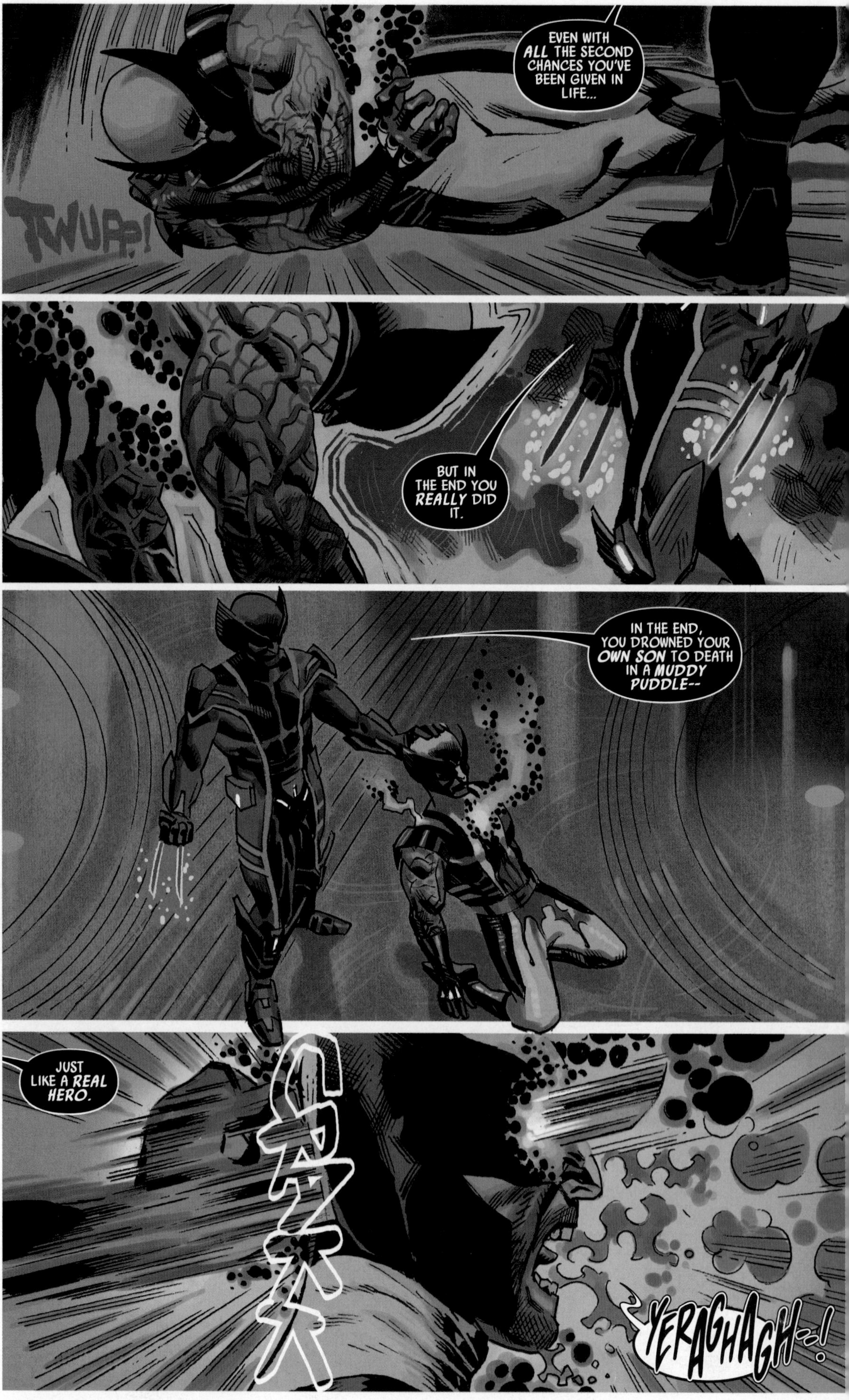
EVEN WITH ALL THE SECOND CHANCES YOU'VE BEEN GIVEN IN LIFE...
TWUPP!
BUT IN THE END YOU REALLY DID IT.
IN THE END, YOU DROWNED YOUR OWN SON TO DEATH IN A MUDDY PUDDLE--
JUST LIKE A REAL HERO.
YERAGHAGH--!

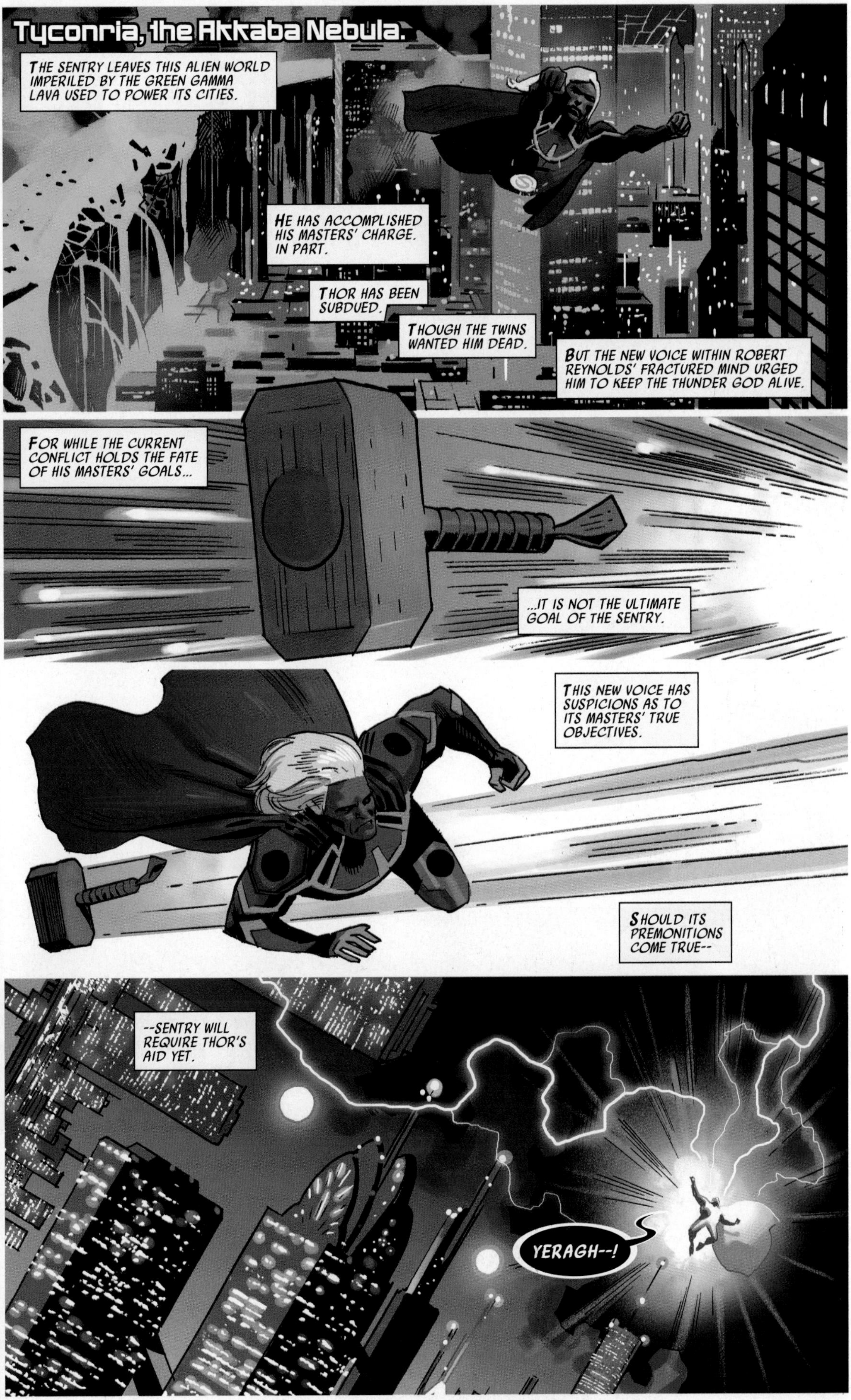
Tyconria, the Akkaba Nebula.
THE SENTRY LEAVES THIS ALIEN WORLD IMPERILED BY THE GREEN GAMMA LAVA USED TO POWER ITS CITIES.
HE HAS ACCOMPLISHED HIS MASTERS' CHARGE. IN PART.
THOR HAS BEEN SUBDUED.
THOUGH THE TWINS WANTED HIM DEAD.
BUT THE NEW VOICE WITHIN ROBERT REYNOLDS' FRACTURED MIND URGED HIM TO KEEP THE THUNDER GOD ALIVE.
FOR WHILE THE CURRENT CONFLICT HOLDS THE FATE OF HIS MASTERS' GOALS...
...IT IS NOT THE ULTIMATE GOAL OF THE SENTRY.
THIS NEW VOICE HAS SUSPICIONS AS TO ITS MASTERS' TRUE OBJECTIVES.
SHOULD ITS PREMONITIONS COME TRUE--
--SENTRY WILL REQUIRE THOR'S AID YET.
YERAGH--!

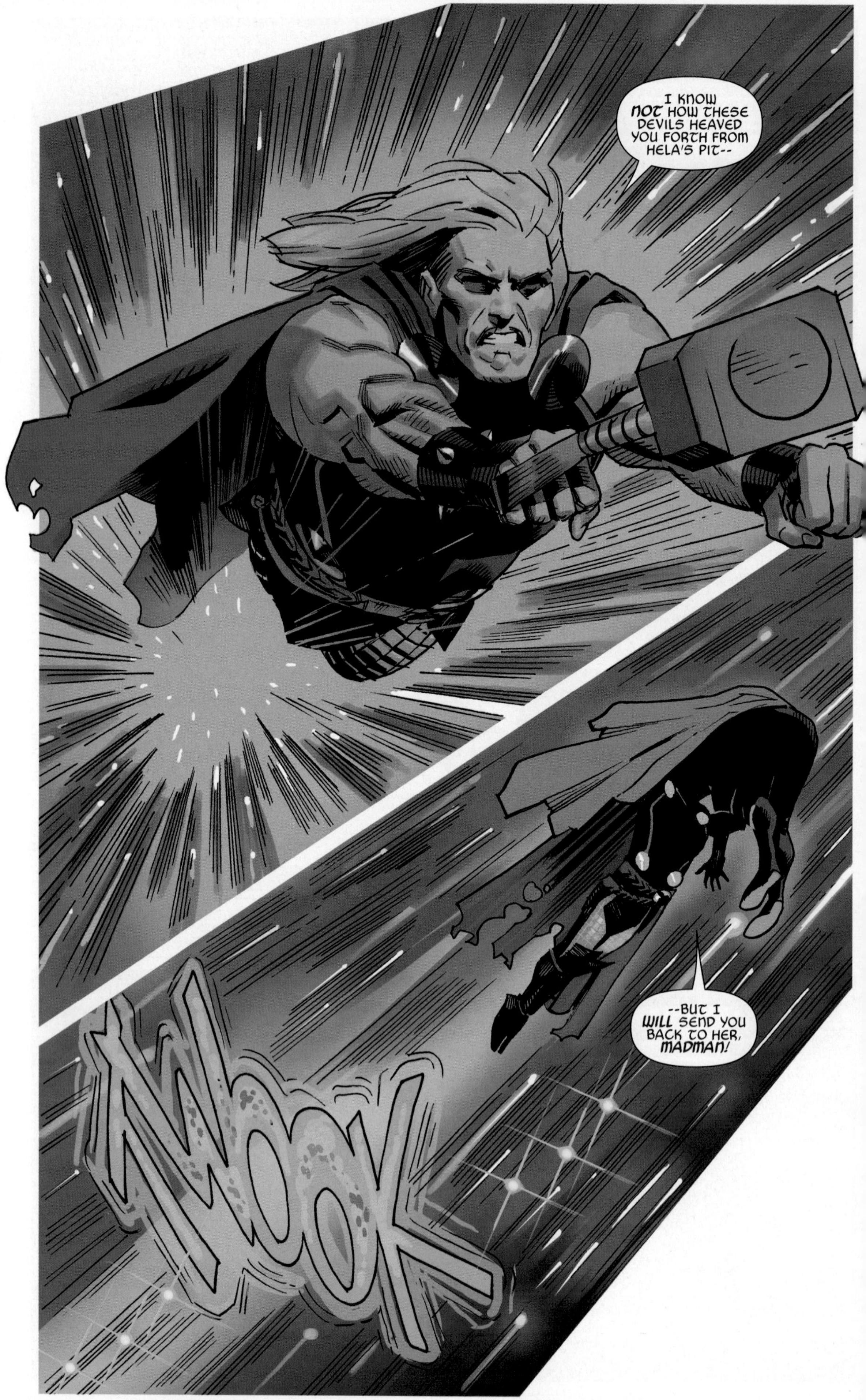

I KNOW NOT HOW THESE DEVILS HEAVED YOU FORTH FROM HELA'S PIT--
--BUT I WILL SEND YOU BACK TO HER, MADMAN!
WOOK

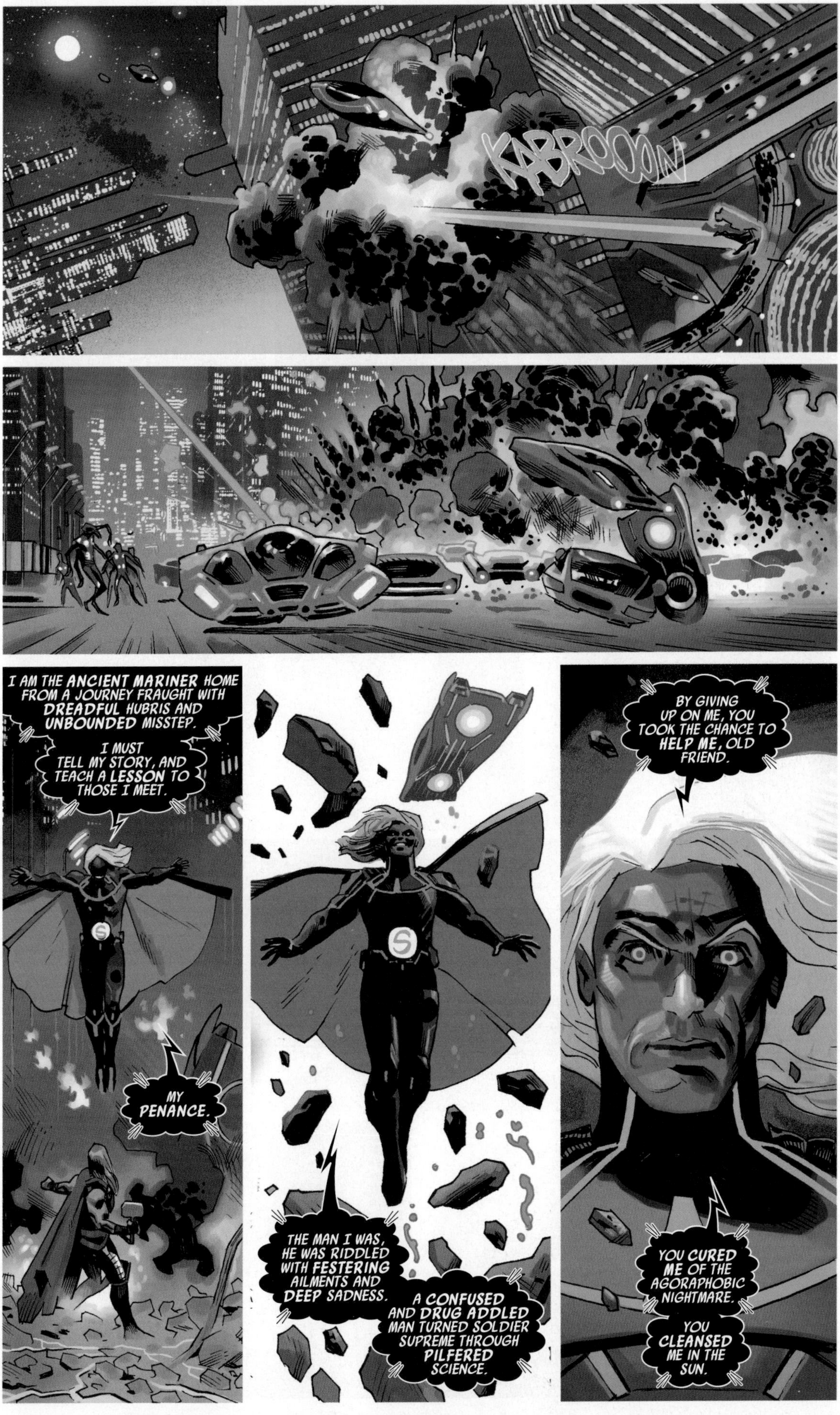
KABROOOON
I AM THE ANCIENT MARINER HOME FROM A JOURNEY FRAUGHT WITH DREADFUL HUBRIS AND UNBOUNDED MISSTEP.
I MUST TELL MY STORY, AND TEACH A LESSON TO THOSE I MEET.
MY PENANCE.
THE MAN I WAS, HE WAS RIDDLED WITH FESTERING AILMENTS AND DEEP SADNESS.
A CONFUSED AND DRUG ADDLED MAN TURNED SOLDIER SUPREME THROUGH PILFERED SCIENCE.
BY GIVING UP ON ME, YOU TOOK THE CHANCE TO HELP ME, OLD FRIEND.
YOU CURED ME OF THE AGORAPHOBIC NIGHTMARE.
YOU CLEANSED ME IN THE SUN.

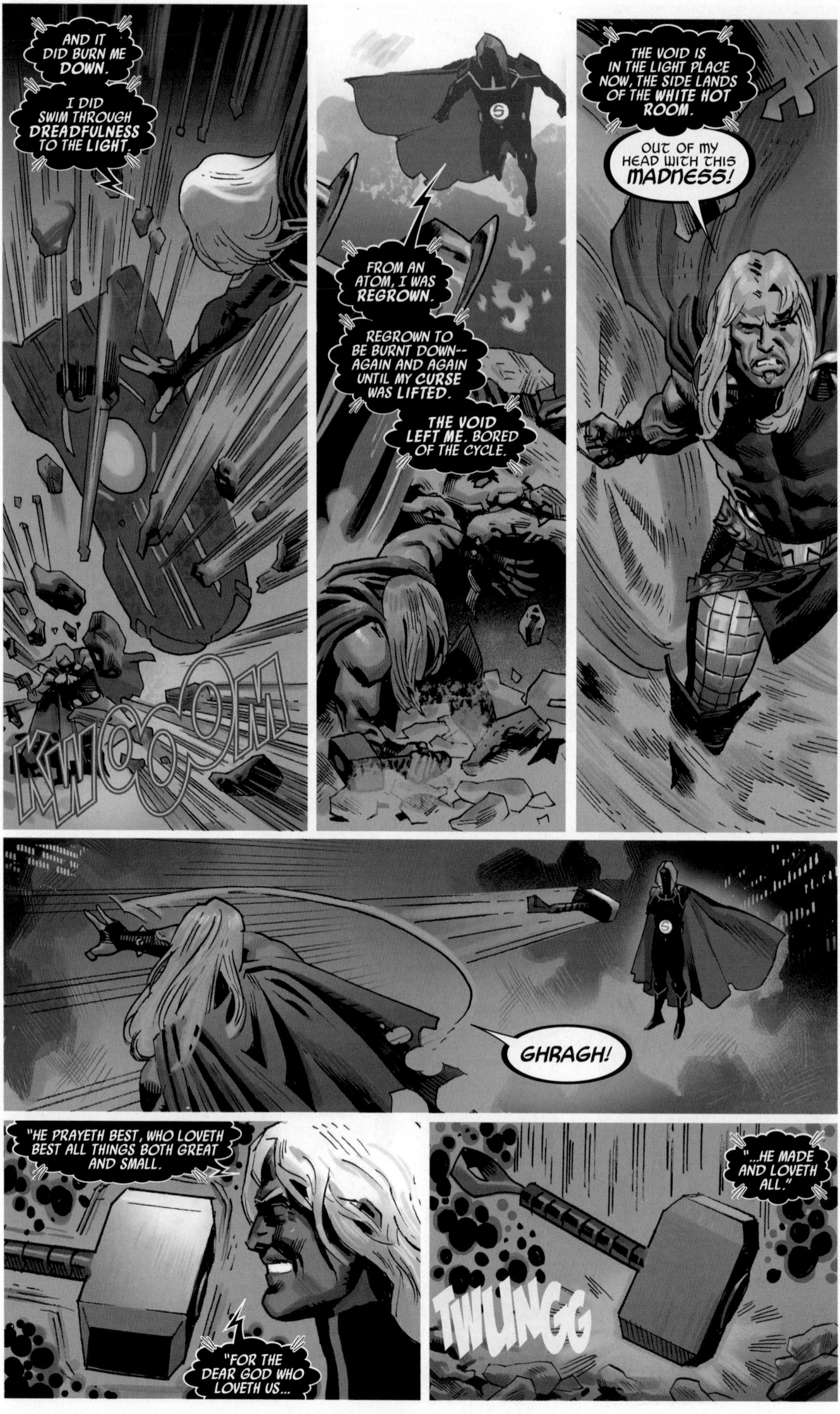
AND IT DID BURN ME DOWN.
I DID SWIM THROUGH DREADFULNESS TO THE LIGHT.
KWOOOOM
FROM AN ATOM, I WAS REGROWN.
REGROWN TO BE BURNT DOWN-- AGAIN AND AGAIN UNTIL MY CURSE WAS LIFTED.
THE VOID LEFT ME. BORED OF THE CYCLE.
THE VOID IS IN THE LIGHT PLACE NOW, THE SIDE LANDS OF THE WHITE HOT ROOM.
OUT OF MY HEAD WITH THIS MADNESS!
GHRAGH!
"HE PRAYETH BEST, WHO LOVETH BEST ALL THINGS BOTH GREAT AND SMALL.
"FOR THE DEAR GOD WHO LOVETH US...
TWUNGG
"...HE MADE AND LOVETH ALL."

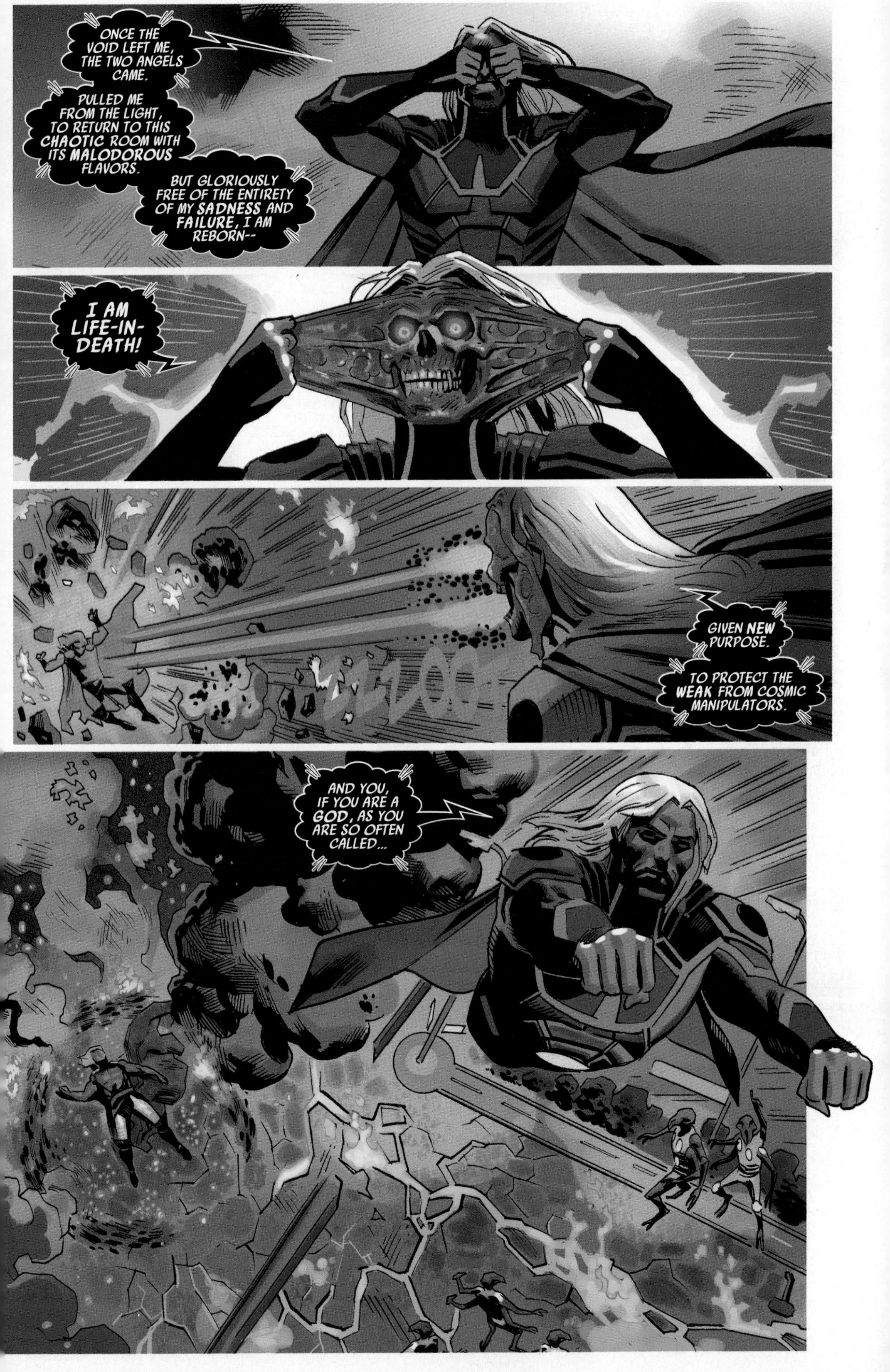
ONCE THE VOID LEFT ME, THE TWO ANGELS CAME.
PULLED ME FROM THE LIGHT, TO RETURN TO THIS CHAOTIC ROOM WITH ITS MALODOROUS FLAVORS.
BUT GLORIOUSLY FREE OF THE ENTIRETY OF MY SADNESS AND FAILURE, I AM REBORN--
I AM LIFE-IN-DEATH!
GIVEN NEW PURPOSE.
TO PROTECT THE WEAK FROM COSMIC MANIPULATORS.
AND YOU, IF YOU ARE A GOD, AS YOU ARE SO OFTEN CALLED...

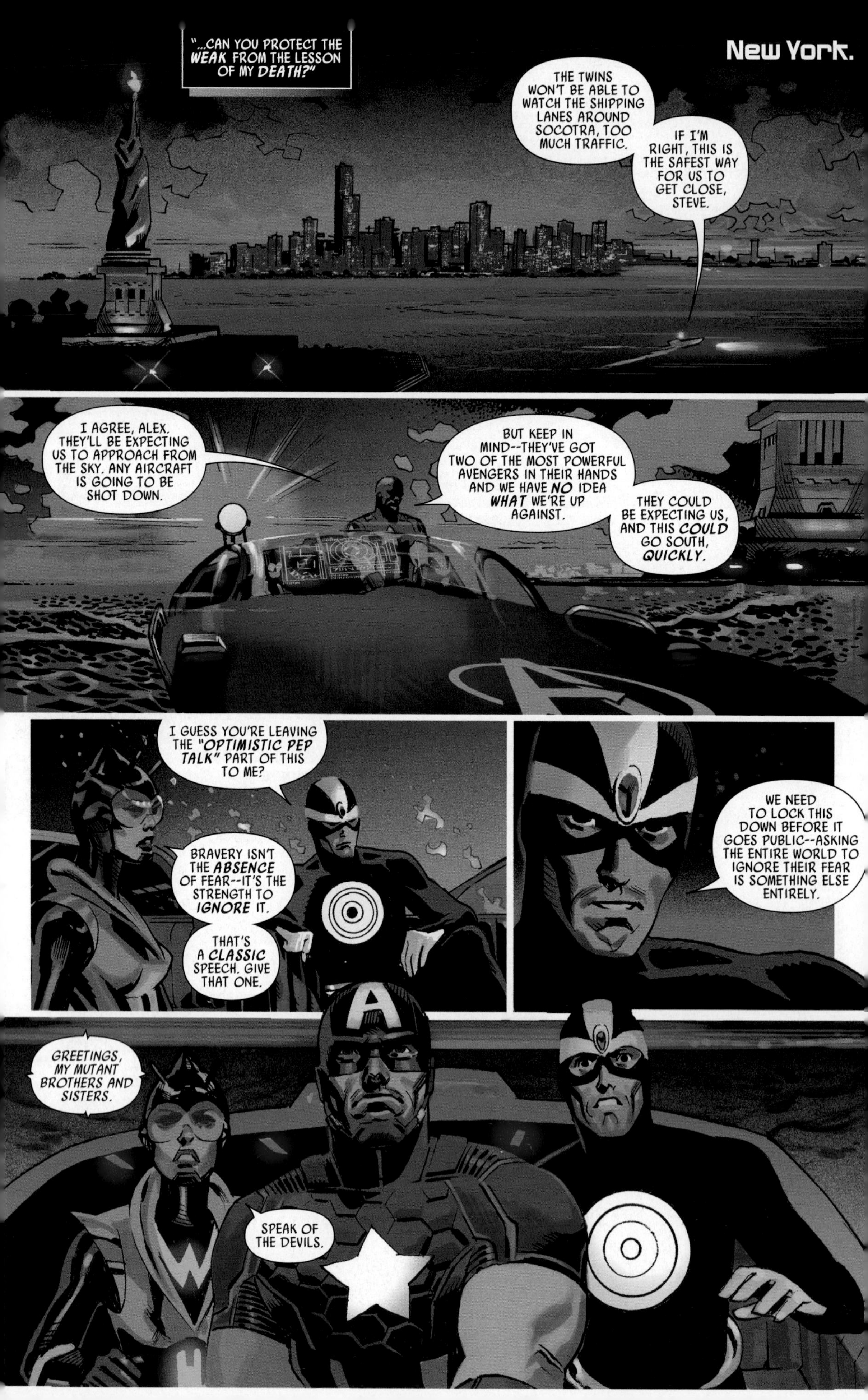
"...CAN YOU PROTECT THE WEAK FROM THE LESSON OF MY DEATH?"
New York.
THE TWINS WON'T BE ABLE TO WATCH THE SHIPPING LANES AROUND SOCOTRA, TOO MUCH TRAFFIC.
IF I'M RIGHT, THIS IS THE SAFEST WAY FOR US TO GET CLOSE, STEVE.
I AGREE, ALEX. THEY'LL BE EXPECTING US TO APPROACH FROM THE SKY. ANY AIRCRAFT IS GOING TO BE SHOT DOWN.
BUT KEEP IN MIND--THEY'VE GOT TWO OF THE MOST POWERFUL AVENGERS IN THEIR HANDS AND WE HAVE NO IDEA WHAT WE'RE UP AGAINST.
THEY COULD BE EXPECTING US, AND THIS COULD GO SOUTH, QUICKLY.
I GUESS YOU'RE LEAVING THE "OPTIMISTIC PEP TALK" PART OF THIS TO ME?
BRAVERY ISN'T THE ABSENCE OF FEAR--IT'S THE STRENGTH TO IGNORE IT.
THAT'S A CLASSIC SPEECH. GIVE THAT ONE.
WE NEED TO LOCK THIS DOWN BEFORE IT GOES PUBLIC--ASKING THE ENTIRE WORLD TO IGNORE THEIR FEAR IS SOMETHING ELSE ENTIRELY.
GREETINGS, MY MUTANT BROTHERS AND SISTERS.
SPEAK OF THE DEVILS.

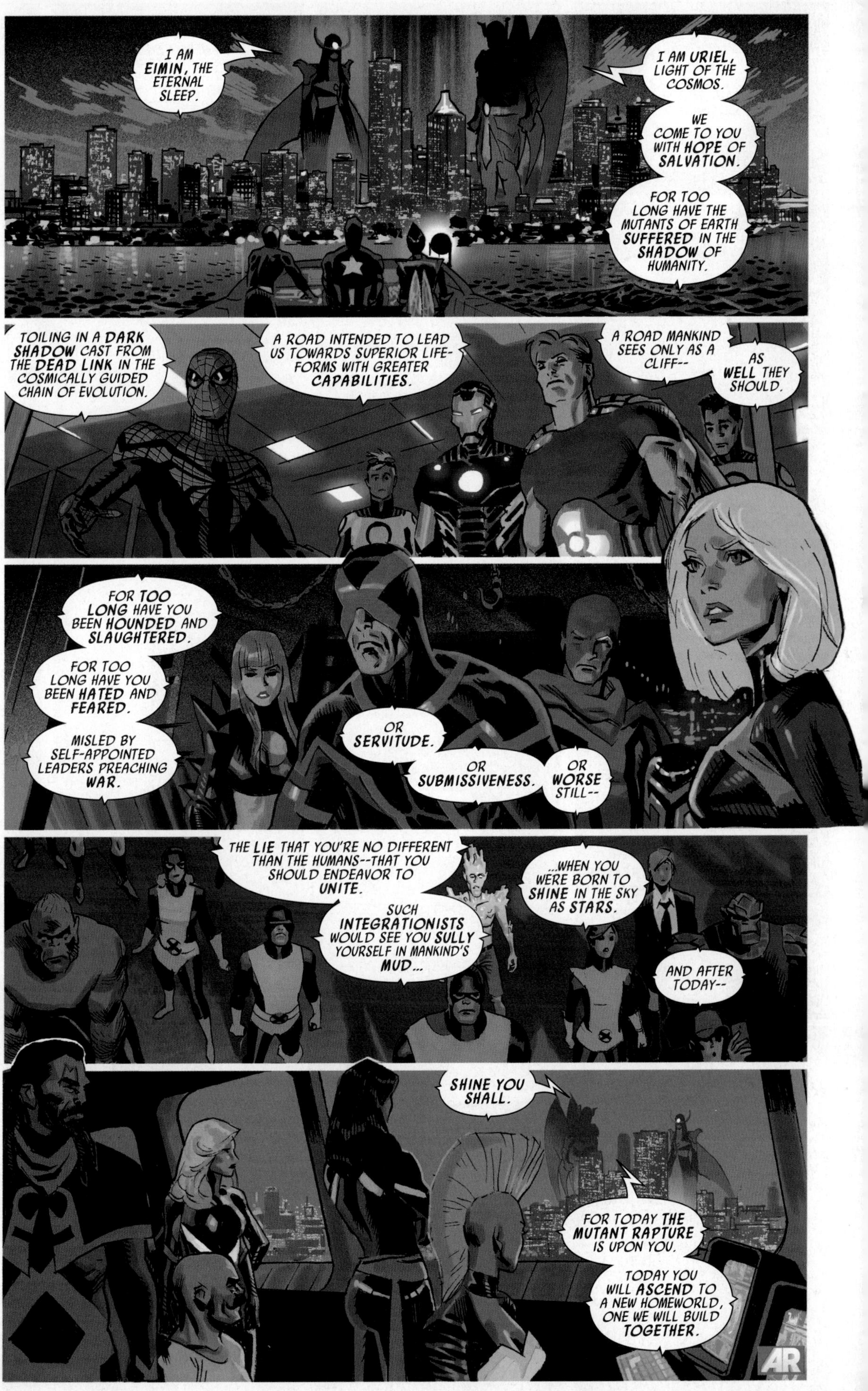
I AM EIMIN, THE ETERNAL SLEEP.
I AM URIEL, LIGHT OF THE COSMOS.
WE COME TO YOU WITH HOPE OF SALVATION.
FOR TOO LONG HAVE THE MUTANTS OF EARTH SUFFERED IN THE SHADOW OF HUMANITY.
TOILING IN A DARK SHADOW CAST FROM THE DEAD LINK IN THE COSMICALLY GUIDED CHAIN OF EVOLUTION.
A ROAD INTENDED TO LEAD US TOWARDS SUPERIOR LIFE-FORMS WITH GREATER CAPABILITIES.
A ROAD MANKIND SEES ONLY AS A CLIFF--
AS WELL THEY SHOULD.
FOR TOO LONG HAVE YOU BEEN HOUNDED AND SLAUGHTERED.
FOR TOO LONG HAVE YOU BEEN HATED AND FEARED.
MISLED BY SELF-APPOINTED LEADERS PREACHING WAR.
OR SERVITUDE.
OR SUBMISSIVENESS.
OR WORSE STILL--
THE LIE THAT YOU'RE NO DIFFERENT THAN THE HUMANS--THAT YOU SHOULD ENDEAVOR TO UNITE.
SUCH INTEGRATIONISTS WOULD SEE YOU SULLY YOURSELF IN MANKIND'S MUD...
...WHEN YOU WERE BORN TO SHINE IN THE SKY AS STARS.
AND AFTER TODAY--
SHINE YOU SHALL.
FOR TODAY THE MUTANT RAPTURE IS UPON YOU.
TODAY YOU WILL ASCEND TO A NEW HOMEWORLD, ONE WE WILL BUILD TOGETHER.
AR

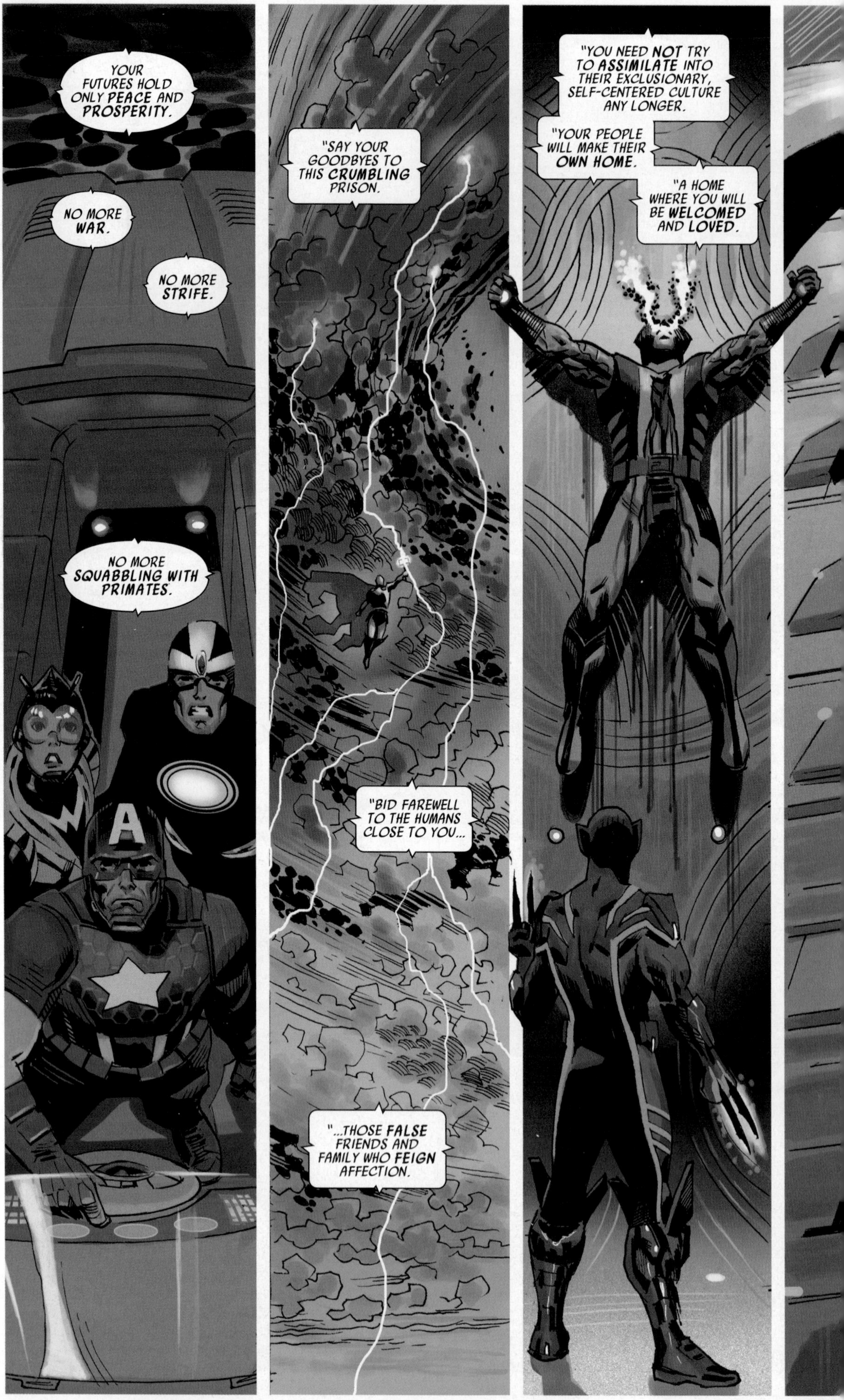
YOUR FUTURES HOLD ONLY PEACE AND PROSPERITY.
NO MORE WAR.
NO MORE STRIFE.
NO MORE SQUABBLING WITH PRIMATES.
"SAY YOUR GOODBYES TO THIS CRUMBLING PRISON.
"BID FAREWELL TO THE HUMANS CLOSE TO YOU...
"...THOSE FALSE FRIENDS AND FAMILY WHO FEIGN AFFECTION.
"YOU NEED NOT TRY TO ASSIMILATE INTO THEIR EXCLUSIONARY, SELF-CENTERED CULTURE ANY LONGER.
"YOUR PEOPLE WILL MAKE THEIR OWN HOME.
"A HOME WHERE YOU WILL BE WELCOMED AND LOVED.

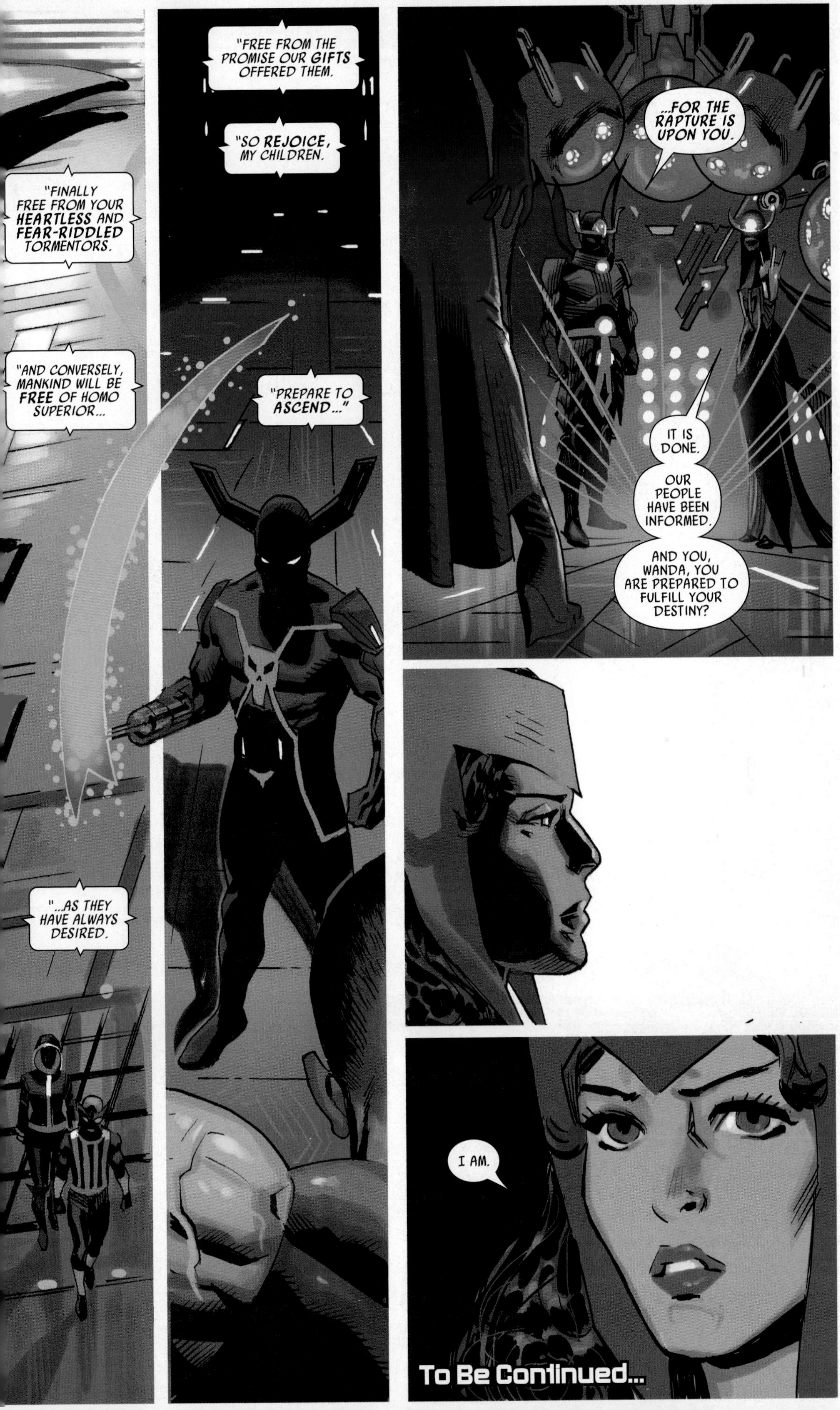
"FINALLY FREE FROM YOUR HEARTLESS AND FEAR-RIDDLED TORMENTORS.
"AND CONVERSELY, MANKIND WILL BE FREE OF HOMO SUPERIOR...
"...AS THEY HAVE ALWAYS DESIRED.
"FREE FROM THE PROMISE OUR GIFTS OFFERED THEM.
"SO REJOICE, MY CHILDREN.
"PREPARE TO ASCEND..."
...FOR THE RAPTURE IS UPON YOU.
IT IS DONE.
OUR PEOPLE HAVE BEEN INFORMED.
AND YOU, WANDA, YOU ARE PREPARED TO FULFILL YOUR DESTINY?
I AM.
To Be Continued...

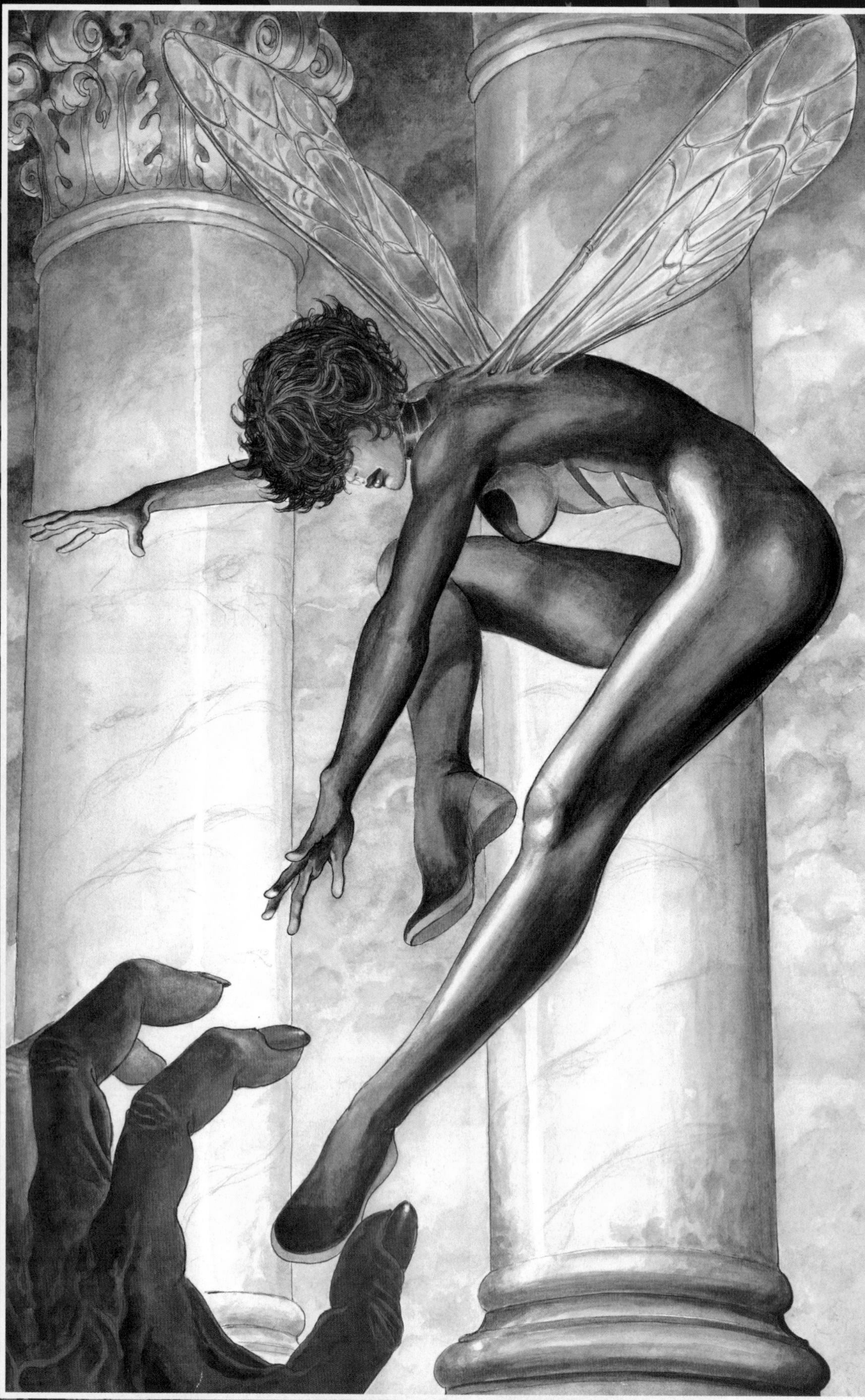

TO ACCESS THE FREE *MARVEL AUGMENTED REALITY APP* THAT ENHANCES AND CHANGES THE WAY YOU EXPERIENCE COMICS

1. Download the app for free via
marvel.com/ARapp
2. Launch the app on your camera-enabled Apple iOS® or Android™ device*

3. Hold your mobile device's camera over any cover or panel with the graphic
4. Sit back and see the future of comics in action!

*Available on most camera-enabled Apple iOS® and Android™ devices. Content subject to change and availability.

AR INDEX

TO REDEEM YOUR CODE FOR A FREE DIGITAL COPY:

1. GO TO MARVEL.COM/REDEEM.
OFFER EXPIRES ON 10/23/15.
2. FOLLOW THE ON-SCREEN INSTRUCTIONS TO REDEEM YOUR DIGITAL COPY.
3. LAUNCH THE MARVEL COMICS APP TO READ YOUR COMIC NOW!
4. YOUR DIGITAL COPY WILL BE FOUND UNDER THE *MY COMICS* TAB.
5. READ & ENJOY!

YOUR FREE DIGITAL COPY WILL BE AVAILABLE ON:

TMAGQ46Q7WI3

MARVEL COMICS APP
FOR APPLE® iOS DEVICES

MARVEL COMICS APP
FOR ANDROID™ DEVICES